*Thomas Fuller's*
THE HOLY STATE AND
THE PROFANE STATE
*IN TWO VOLUMES*

NUMBER 136 OF THE
COLUMBIA UNIVERSITY STUDIES IN ENGLISH
AND COMPARATIVE LITERATURE

*Thomas Fuller's*

# THE HOLY STATE
# AND THE
# PROFANE STATE

EDITED BY

MAXIMILIAN GRAFF WALTEN

*VOLUME II*
*A FACSIMILE OF THE FIRST EDITION, 1642*
*REDUCED IN SIZE*

NEW YORK: MORNINGSIDE HEIGHTS
COLUMBIA UNIVERSITY PRESS
1938

COPYRIGHT 1938
COLUMBIA UNIVERSITY PRESS, NEW YORK

Foreign agents: OXFORD UNIVERSITY PRESS, Humphrey Milford, Amen House, London, E.C. 4, England, AND B. I. Building, Nicol Road, Bombay, India; KWANG HSUEH PUBLISHING HOUSE, 140 Peking Road, Shanghai, China; MARUZEN COMPANY, LTD., 6 Nihonbashi, Tori-Nichome, Tokyo, Japan

MANUFACTURED IN THE UNITED STATES OF AMERICA

# Contents of Volume II

The Emblematic Title Page

The Crown and Feathers Design

Printed Title Page for *The Holy State*

To the Reader

An Index of the severall Chapters

Book I
    The good Wife . . . . . . . . . . . . . . 1
    The life of Monica . . . . . . . . . . . . 4
    The good Husband . . . . . . . . . . . . 8
    The life of Abraham . . . . . . . . . . . 10
    The good Parent . . . . . . . . . . . . 12
    The good Child . . . . . . . . . . . . . 14
    The good Master . . . . . . . . . . . . 17
    The good Servant . . . . . . . . . . . . 19
    The life of Eliezer . . . . . . . . . . . . 22
    The good Widow . . . . . . . . . . . . 24
    The life of the Lady Paula . . . . . . . . 27
    The constant Virgin . . . . . . . . . . . 34
    The life of Hildegardis . . . . . . . . . . 40
    The Elder Brother . . . . . . . . . . . . 44
    The Younger Brother . . . . . . . . . . 47

Book II
    The good Advocate . . . . . . . . . . . 51
    The good Physician . . . . . . . . . . . 53

The life of Paracelsus . . . . . . . . . . . . . . . 56
The Controversiall Divine . . . . . . . . . . . . . 60
The life of Dr. Whitaker . . . . . . . . . . . . . . 65
The true Church Antiquary . . . . . . . . . . . . 69
The generall Artist . . . . . . . . . . . . . . . . 72
The life of Julius Scaliger . . . . . . . . . . . . . 76
The faithfull Minister . . . . . . . . . . . . . . . 80
The life of Mr. Perkins . . . . . . . . . . . . . . 88
The good Parishioner . . . . . . . . . . . . . . . 93
The good Patron . . . . . . . . . . . . . . . . . 95
The good Landlord . . . . . . . . . . . . . . . . 99
The good Master of a Colledge . . . . . . . . . . 102
The life of Dr. Metcalf . . . . . . . . . . . . . . 105
The good Schoolmaster . . . . . . . . . . . . . . 109
The good Merchant . . . . . . . . . . . . . . . . 113
The good Yeoman . . . . . . . . . . . . . . . . . 116
The Handicrafts-man . . . . . . . . . . . . . . . 119
The good Souldier . . . . . . . . . . . . . . . . 119
The good Sea-Captain . . . . . . . . . . . . . . 128
The life of Sir Francis Drake . . . . . . . . . . . 132
The good Herald . . . . . . . . . . . . . . . . . 141
The life of Mr. W. Cambden . . . . . . . . . . . 145
The true Gentleman . . . . . . . . . . . . . . . 149

Book III
Of Hospitality . . . . . . . . . . . . . . . . . . 153
Of Jesting . . . . . . . . . . . . . . . . . . . . 155
Of Self-praysing . . . . . . . . . . . . . . . . . 157
Of Travelling . . . . . . . . . . . . . . . . . . . 158
Of Company . . . . . . . . . . . . . . . . . . . 161
Of Apparell . . . . . . . . . . . . . . . . . .194 [164]
Of Building . . . . . . . . . . . . . . . . . . . 166

| | |
|---|---|
| Of Anger | 169 |
| Of Expecting Preferment | 171 |
| Of Memory | 174 |
| Of Phancie | 177 |
| Of Naturall Fools | 180 |
| Of Recreations | 183 |
| Of Tombes | 187 |
| Of Deformitie | 190 |
| Of Plantations | 193 |
| Of Contentment | 195 |
| Of Books | 199 |
| Of Time-serving | 202 |
| Of Moderation | 205 |
| Of Gravity | 209 |
| Of Marriage | 212 |
| Of Fame | 215 |
| Of the Antiquity of Churches and Necessity of them | 219 |
| Of Ministers maintenance | 228 |

Book IV

| | |
|---|---|
| The Favourite | 237 |
| The life of Haman | 245 |
| The life of Card. Wolsey | 249 |
| The life of Charles Brandon, Duke of Suffolk | 254 |
| The wise Statesman | 257 |
| The life of William Cecil Lord Burleigh | 265 |
| The good Judge | 270 |
| The life of Sr. John Markham | 274 |
| The good Bishop | 277 |
| The life of S. Augustine | 284 |
| The life of Bishop Ridley | 289 |
| The true Nobleman | 296 |

| | |
|---|---:|
| The Court-Lady | 300 |
| The life of Ladie Jane Grey | 307 |
| The life of Queen Elizabeth | 312 |
| The Embassadour | 319 |
| The good Generall | 326 |
| The life of Gustavus Adolphus King of Sweden | 330 |
| The Prince or Heir apparent to the Crown | 336 |
| The life of Edward the Black Prince | 342 |
| The King | 349 |
| Printed Title Page for *The Profane State* | 355 |

Book V

| | |
|---|---:|
| The Harlot | 357 |
| The life of Joan Queen of Naples | 361 |
| The Witch | 365 |
| The Witch of Endor | 369 |
| The life of Joan of Arc | 372 |
| The Atheist | 378 |
| The life of Cesar Borgia | 383 |
| The Hypocrite | 388 |
| The life of Jehu | 390 |
| The Heretick | 393 |
| The rigid Donatists | 396 |
| The Lyer | 406 |
| The common Barreter | 408 |
| The Degenerous Gentleman | 410 |
| The Traytour | 418 |
| The Pazzians conspiracie | 421 |
| The Tyrant | 425 |
| The life of Andronicus | 429 |
| The life of Duke D'Alva | 435 |

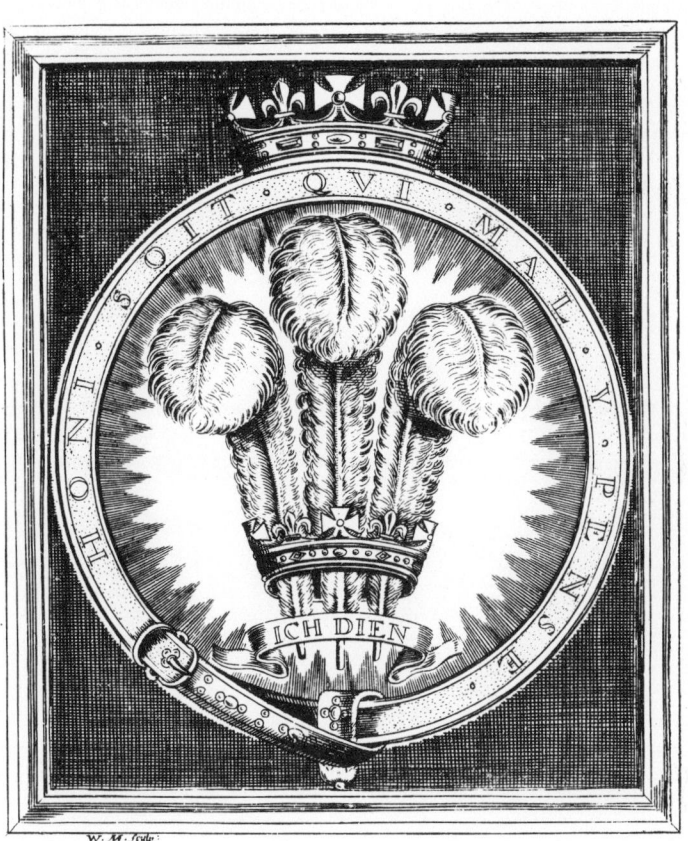

# THE
# HOLY
## STATE.

BY
THOMAS FULLER, B. D.
and Prebendarie of
Sarum.

---

ZECHARIAH 14. 20.

*In that day shall there be upon the bells of the horses,* HOLINESSE UNTO THE LORD.

---

CAMBRIDGE:
¶ Printed by ROGER DANIEL for
*John Williams*, and are to be sold at the signe
of the Crown in S. Pauls
Churchyard. 1642.

# To the Reader.

**W**Ho is not sensible with sorrow of the distractions of this age? To write books therefore may seem unseasonable, especially in a time wherein the *Presse*, like an unruly horse, hath cast off his bridle of being *Licensed*, and some serious books, which dare flie abroad, are hooted at by a flock of Pamphlets.

But be pleased to know that when I left my home, it was fair weather, and my journey was half past, before I discovered the tempest, and had gone so farre in this Work, that I could neither go backward with credit, nor forward with comfort.

As for the matter of this Book, therein I am resident on my Profession; Holinesse in the latitude thereof falling under the cognizanse of a Divine. For curious method, expect none, Essays for the most part not being placed as at a *Feast*, but placing themselves as at an *Ordinary*.

The characters I have conformed to the then

A 2          standing

## To the Reader.

standing Laws of the Realm, (a twelvemoneth agoe were they sent to the presse) since which time the wisdome of the King and State hath thought fitting to alter many things, and I expect the discretion of the Reader should make his alterations accordingly. And I conjure thee by all Christian ingenuity, that if lighting here on some passages, rather harsh-sounding then ill-intended, to construe the same by the generall drift and main scope which is aimed at.

Nor let it render the modestie of this Book suspected, because it presumes to appear in company unmann'd by any Patron: If right, it will defend it self; if wrong, none can defend it: Truth needs not, falshood deserves not a Supporter. And indeed the matter of this Work is too high for a subjects, the workmanship thereof too low for a Princes patronage.

And now I will turn my pen into prayer, That God would be pleased to discloud these gloomy dayes with the beams of his mercie: which if I may be so happy as to see, it will then encourage me to count it freedome to serve two apprentiships (God spinning out the thick thred of my life so long) in writing the Ecclesiasticall History from Christs time to our dayes, if I shall from remoter parts be so planted, as to enjoy the benefit of walking, and standing Libraries, without which advantages

tages the best vigilancie doth but vainly dream to undertake such a task.

Mean time I will stop the leakage of my soul, and what heretofore hath run out in writing, shall hereafter (God willing) be improved in constant preaching, in what place soever Gods providence, and friends good will shall fix

*Thine in all Christian offices*

THOMAS FULLER.

# An Index of the severall Chapters contained in this Book; the first figure shewing the book, the second the chapter, the third the page.

| B. | Ch. | | Page | B. | Ch. | | Page |
|---|---|---|---|---|---|---|---|
| 1 | 4 | Abrahams life. | 10 | 4 | 20 | Edward the black Prince his life. | 342 |
| 2 | 1 | The Advocate. | 51 | 1 | 9 | Eliezers life. | 22 |
| 5 | 19 | Duke D'Alva's life. | 435 | 4 | 15 | Queen Elizabeth her life. | 312 |
| 5 | 18 | Andronicus his life. | 429 | 4 | 16 | The Embassadour. | 319 |
| 3 | 8 | Anger. | 169 | 5 | 4 | Endor Witch, her life. | 369 |
| 2 | 6 | Antiquary. | 69 | 3 | 9 | Expecting Preferment. | 171 |
| 3 | 6 | Apparell. | 164 | 3 | 23 | Fame. | 215 |
| 2 | 7 | Artist. | 72 | 4 | 1 | Favourite. | 237 |
| 5 | 6 | Atheist. | 378 | 3 | 12 | Fools. | 180 |
| 4 | 11 | S. Augustines life. | 284 | 4 | 17 | The Generall. | 326 |
| 5 | 13 | Barrettour. | 408 | 2 | 24 | The Gentleman. | 149 |
| 4 | 9 | The Bishop. | 277 | 3 | 21 | Gravity. | 209 |
| 3 | 18 | Books. | 199 | 4 | 2 | Hamans life. | 245 |
| 5 | 7 | Borgia his life. | 383 | 2 | 19 | Handicrafts-man. | 119 |
| 4 | 4 | Brandon his life. | 254 | 5 | 1 | Harlot. | 357 |
| 1 | 14 | Elder } Brother. | 44 | 2 | 22 | Herald. | 141 |
| 1 | 15 | Younger } Brother. | 47 | 5 | 10 | Heretick. | 393 |
| 3 | 7 | Building. | 166 | 1 | 13 | Hildegardis her life. | 40 |
| 4 | 6 | Lord Burleigh his life. | 265 | 3 | 1 | Hospitality. | 153 |
| 2 | 23 | Cambdens life. | 145 | 1 | 3 | Husband. | 8 |
| 1 | 6 | Child. | 14 | 5 | 8 | Hypocrite. | 388 |
| 3 | 24 | Churches. | 219 | 4 | 14 | Lady Jane her life. | 307 |
| 3 | 5 | Company. | 161 | 5 | 9 | Jehu his life. | 390 |
| 3 | 17 | Contentment. | 195 | 3 | 2 | Jesting. | 155 |
| 2 | 4 | The Controversiall Divine. | 60 | 5 | 5 | Joan of Arc her life. | 372 |
| 3 | 15 | Deformity. | 190 | 5 | 2 | Joan Queen of Naples her life. | 361 |
| 5 | 14 | The Degenerous Gentleman | 410 | 4 | 7 | Judge. | 270 |
| 5 | 11 | The Donatists. | 396 | 4 | 21 | The King. | 349 |
| 2 | 21 | Sr. Francis Drakes life. | 132 | | | | The |

| B. | Ch. |  | Page | B. | Ch. |  | Page |
|---|---|---|---|---|---|---|---|
| 4 | 13 | Lady. | 301 | 3 | 16 | Plantations. | 193 |
| 2 | 13 | Landlord. | 99 | 4 | 19 | The Prince. | 336 |
| 5 | 12 | The Lyer. | 406 | 3 | 13 | Recreations. | 183 |
| 3 | 22 | Marriage. | 212 | 4 | 11 | Bishop Ridleys life. | 289 |
| 4 | 8 | Markham his life. | 274 | 2 | 8 | Scaliger his life. | 76 |
| 1 | 7 | Master. | 17 | 2 | 16 | Schoolmaster. | 109 |
| 2 | 14 | Master of a Colledge. | 102 | 2 | 20 | Sea-Captain. | 128 |
| 3 | 10 | Memory. | 174 | 3 | 3 | Self-praising. | 157 |
| 2 | 17 | Merchant. | 113 | 1 | 8 | Servant. | 19 |
| 2 | 15 | Metcalfe his life. | 105 | 2 | 19 | Souldier. | 119 |
| 2 | 9 | The Minister. | 80 | 4 | 5 | Statesman. | 257 |
| 3 | 25 | Ministers maintenance. | 228 | 4 | 18 | Swedens King. | 330 |
| 3 | 20 | Moderation. | 205 | 3 | 19 | Time-serving. | 202 |
| 1 | 2 | Monica her life. | 4 | 3 | 14 | Tombes. | 187 |
| 4 | 12 | The Nobleman. | 296 | 5 | 15 | Traitour. | 418 |
| 2 | 3 | Paracelsus his life. | 56 | 3 | 4 | Travell. | 158 |
| 1 | 5 | Parent. | 12 | 5 | 17 | Tyrant. | 425 |
| 2 | 11 | Parishioner. | 93 | 1 | 12 | The Virgin. | 34 |
| 2 | 12 | Patron. | 95 | 2 | 5 | Whitakers his life. | 65 |
| 1 | 11 | Lady Paula her life. | 27 | 1 | 10 | Widow. | 24 |
| 5 | 16 | Pazzians conspiracie. | 421 | 1 | 1 | Wife. | 1 |
| 2 | 10 | Perkins his life. | 88 | 5 | 3 | Witch. | 365 |
| 3 | 11 | Phancy. | 177 | 4 | 3 | Cardinall Wolsey his life. | 249 |
| 2 | 2 | Physician. | 53 | 2 | 18 | The Yeoman. | 116 |

### ERRATA.

Page 70 line 29 after superstition adde, How the Fathers. 121. 9. r. wear. 152. 8. r. ( Yea Mercury was a greater speaker then Jupiter himself ) 202. 5. r. affectation.

# The Holy State.

## THE FIRST BOOK.

### CHAP. I.
### *The good Wife*

PAUL to the Colossians chap. 3. verf. 18. first adviseth women to submit themselves to their husbands, and then counselleth men to love their wives. And sure it was fitting that women should first have their lesson given them, because it is hardest to be learned, and therefore they need have the more time to conne it. For the same reason we first begin with the character of a good Wife.

She commandeth her husband in any equall matter, by constant obeying him. It was alwayes observed, that what the English gained of the French in battel by valour, the French regained of the English by cunning in *Treaties: So if the husband should chance by his power in his pasion to prejudice his wives right, she wisely knoweth by compounding and complying to recover and rectifie it again.

She never crosseth her husband in the spring-tide of his anger, but stayes till it be ebbing-water. And then mildly she argues the matter, not so much to condemn him, as to acquit her self. Surely men, contrary to iron, are worst

*Maxime* 1

*\* Comineus lib. 4. cap. 8. & Bodinus De Repub. lib. 5. p. 782.*

2

B to

to be wrought upon when they are hot; and are farre more tractable in cold bloud. It is an observation of Seamen,* That if a single meteor or fireball falls on their mast, it portends ill luck; but if two come together(which they count Castor and Pollux) they presage good successe: But sure in a family it bodeth most bad, when two firebals (husbands and wives anger) come both together.

*Erasmus Dial. in naufragio.*

3. She keeps home if she hath not her husbands company, or leave for her patent to go abroad: For the house is the womans centre. It is written, Psalm 104. 2. *The sunne ariseth,---man goeth forth unto his work, and to his labour untill the evening*: but it is said of the good woman, Prov. 31. 15. *She riseth whiles it is yet night*: For man in the race of his work starts from the rising of the sunne, because his businesse is without doores, and not to be done without the light of heaven: but the woman hath her work within the house, and therefore can make the sunne rise by lighting of a candle.

4. Her clothes are rather comely then costly, and she makes plain cloth to be velvet by her handsome wearing it. She is none of our dainty dames, who love to appear in variety of sutes every day new, as if a good gown, like a stratageme in warre, were to be used but once: But our good wife sets up a sail according to the keel of her husbands estate; and if of high parentage, she doth not so remember what she was by birth, that she forgets what she is by match.

5. *Arcana imperii* (her husbands secrets) she will not divulge. Especially she is carefull to conceal his infirmities. If he be none of the wisest, she so orders it that he appears on the publick stage but seldome; and then he hath conn'd his part so well, that he comes off with great applause. If his *Forma informans* be but bad, she provides him better *formas assistentes*, gets him wise servants and secretaries.

6. In her husbands absence she is wife and deputy husband,
which

which makes her double the files of her diligence. At his return he finds all things so well, that he wonders to see himself at home when he was abroad.

*Her carriage is so modest, that she dis-heartens wantons not onely to take but even to besiege her chastity.* I confesse some desperate men will hope any thing; yea, their shamelesse boldnesse will fasten on impossibilities, measuring other folks badnesse by their own: yet seldome such Salamanders, which live in the fire of lust, dare approch, without seeing the smoke of wantonnesse in looks, words, apparell, or behaviour. And though charity commands me to beleeve, that some women which hang out signes, notwithstanding will not lodge strangers; yet these mock-guests are guilty in tempting others to tempt them.

*In her husbands sicknesse she feels more grief then she shews.* Partly that she may not dis-hearten him; and partly because she is not at leisure to seem so sorrowfull, that she may be the more serviceable.

*Her children, though many in number, are none in noyse, steering them with a look whither she listeth.* When they grow up, she teacheth them not pride but painfulnesse, making their hands to clothe their backs, and them to wear the livery of their own industry. She makes not her daughters Gentlewomen before they be women, rather teaching them what they should pay to others, then receive from them.

*The heaviest work of her servants she maketh light, by orderly and seasonable enjoyning it:* Wherefore her service is counted a preferment, and her teaching better then her wages. Her maids follow the president of their mistresse, live modestly at home. One askt a grave Gentlewoman, How her maids came by so good husbands, and yet seldome went abroad; *Oh,* said she, *good husbands come home to them.* So much for this subject: and what is defective in this description shall be supplied by the pattern ensuing.

B 2          CHAP. 2.

MONICA wife of Patricius, and Mother to
S.t Augustine. She Died at Ostia in Italye. A.º Do
389. aged 56 yeares.    W. Marshall sculp:

## Chap. 2.

### The life of Monica.

**M**ONICA is better known by the branch of her issue, then root of her parentage, and was born in or nigh Tagasta in Africk. * Her parents, whose names we find not, were Christians, and carefull of her education, committing her to the breeding of an old maid in the house, who, though herself crooked with age, was excellent to straighten the manners of youth. She instructed her with holy severity, never allowing

*August. confess. lib. 9. c. 8.*

allowing her to drink wine, or between meals. Having out-grown her tuition, she began by degrees to sip, and drink wine, lesser draughts like wedges widening her throat for greater, till at last (ill customes being not knockt, but insensibly scru'd into our souls) she could fetch off her whole ones. Now it happened that a young maid (formerly her partner in potting) fell at variance with her, and (as malice when she shoots draws her arrow to the head) called her Tos-pot, and drunkard; whereupon Monica reformed her self, and turned temperate. Thus bitter taunts sometime make wholesome Physick, when God sanctifies unto us the malice of our enemies to perform the office of good will.

After this was she married to Patricius, one of more honour then wealth, and as yet a pagan; wherein she brake S. Pauls precept, *To marry onely in the Lord.* Perchance then there was a dearth of husbands, or she did it by her parents importunity, or out of promise of his conversion: and the history herein being but lamely delivered us, it is charity to support it with the most favourable construction. He was of a stern nature, none more lamb when pleased, or lion when angry; and which is worse, his wild *affections did prey abroad, till she lured them home by her loving behaviour. Not like those wives who by their hideous outcries drive their wandring husbands farther out of the way.

Her own house was to her a house of correction, wherein her husbands mother was bitter unto her, having a quarrell not so much to her person as relation, because a daughter in law. Her servants, to climbe into the favour of their old mistresse, trampled on their young, they bringing tales, and the old woman belief; though the teeth of their malice did but file her innocency the brighter. Yea at last her mother in law, turning her compurgatour, caused her sonne to punish

* *August. confess. lib.9, c.9.*

those

those maids which causelesly had wronged their mistresse.

When her neighbours, which had husbands of far milder dispositions, would shew her their husbands cruelty legible in their faces, all her pitying was reproving them: and whereas they expected to be praysed for their patience, she condemned them for deserving such punishment. She never had blow from, or jarre with her husband, she so suppled his hard nature with her obedience, and to her great comfort saw him converted to Christianity before his death. Also she saw Augustine her sonne, formerly vitious in life, and erroneous in doctrine (whose soul she bathd in her Tears) become a worthy Christian, who coming to have his eares tickled, had his heart touched, and got Religion in to boot with the eloquence of S. Ambrose. She survived not long after her sonnes conversion ( God sends his servants to bed when they have done their work ) and her candle was put out, as soon as the day did dawn in S. Augustine.

Take an instance or two of her signall piety. There was a custome in * Africk to bring pulse bread and wine to the monuments of dead Saints, wherein Monica was as forward as any. But being better instructed that this custome was of heathenish parentage, and that Religion was not so poore as to borrow rites from Pagans, she instantly left off that ceremony: and as for pietie's sake she had done it thus long, so for pietie's sake she would do it no longer. How many old folks now adayes, whose best argument is use, would have flown in their faces, who should stop them in the full career of an ancient custome.

There was one Licentius a novice-convert, who had got these words by the end, *Turn us again, O Lord God of hosts: show us the light of thy countenance and we shall be whole.* And ( as it is the fashion of many mens tongues to echo forth the last sentence they learnt ) he said it

* *August. confess. lib. 6. c. 2.*

in

in all places he went to. But Monica, over-hearing him to sing it in the house of office, was * highly offended at him: because holy things are to be suted to holy places; and the harmonie could not be sweet where the song did jarre with the place. And although some may say, that a gracious heart consecrateth every place into a Chapell; yet sure though pious things are no where unfitting to be thought on, they may somewhere be improper to be uttered.

* *August.lib.1. De ordine, c.8.*

Drawing near her death, she sent most pious thoughts as harbingers to heaven, and her soul saw a glimpse of happinesse through the chincks of her sicknesse-broken body. She was so inflamed with zeal, that she turned all objects into fewell to feed it. One day standing with S. Augustine at an East-window, * she raised her self to consider the light of Gods presence, in respect whereof all corporall light is so farre from being match'd, it deserves not to be mentioned. Thus mounted on heavenly meditations, and from that high pitch surveying earthly things, the great distance made them appear unto her like a little point, scarce to be seen, and lesse to be respected.

* *August. confess. lib.9.c.10.*

She died at Ostia in Italy in the fiftie sixth yeare of her age, Augustine closing her eyes, when through grief he had scarce any himself.

CHAP. 3.

## Chap. 3.

### The good Husband.

Having formerly described a good Wife, she will make a good Husband, whose character we are now to present.

*Maxime 1*  *His love to his wife weakeneth not his ruling her, and his ruling lesseneth not his loving her.* Wherefore he avoideth all fondnesse, (a sick love, to be praised in none, and pardoned onely in the newly married) whereby more have wilfully betrayed their command, then ever lost it by their wives rebellion. Methinks the he-viper is right enough served, which (as *Pliny reports) puts his head into the she-vipers mouth, and she bites it off. And what wonder is it if women take the rule to themselves, which their uxorious husbands first surrender unto them?

*Plin. Nat. hist. lib. 10. cap. 62.*

2   *He is constant to his wife, and confident of her.* And sure where jealousie is the Jailour, many break the prison, it opening more wayes to wickednesse then it stoppeth; so that where it findeth one, it maketh ten dishonest.

3   *He alloweth her meet maintenance, but measures it by his own estate:* nor will he give lesse, nor can she ask more. Which allowance, if shorter then her deserts and his desire, he lengtheneth it out with his courteous carriage unto her; chiefly in her sicknesse, then not so much word-pitying her, as providing necessaries for her.

4   *That she may not intrench on his prerogative, he maintains her propriety in feminine affairs:* yea, therein he follows her advice: For the soul of a man is planted so high, that he overshoots such low matter as lie levell to a womans eye, and therefore her counsell therein may better hit the mark. Causes that are properly of feminine cognizance he suffers her finally to decide, not so much as per-

permitting an appeal to himself, that their jurisdictions may not interfere. He will not countenance a stubborn servant against her, but in her maintains his own Authority. Such husbands as bait the mistris with her maids, and clap their hands at the sport, will have cause to wring them afterwards.

*Knowing she is the weaker vessell he bears with her infirmities.* All hard using of her he detests, desiring therein to do not what may be lawfull, but fitting. And grant her to be of a servile nature, such as may be bettered by beating; yet he remembers he hath enfranchised her by marrying her. On her wedding-day she was like S. Paul free born, and priviledged from any servile punishment.

*He is carefull that the wounds betwixt them take not ayre, and be publickly known.* Jarres conceald are half reconciled; which if generally known, 'tis a double task to stop the breach at home, and mens mouths abroad. To this end he never publickly reproves her. An open reproof puts her to do penance before all that are present, after which many rather study revenge then reformation.

*He keeps her in the wholsome ignorance of unnecessary secrets.* They will not be starved with the ignorance, who perchance may surfet with the knowledge of weighty Counsels, too heavy for the weaker sex to bear. He knows little, who will tell his wife all he knows.

*He beats not his wife after his death.* One having a shrewd wife, yet loth to use her hardly in his life time, awed her with telling her that he would beat her when he was dead, meaning that he would leave her no maintenance. This humour is unworthy a worthy man, who will endeavour to provide her a competent estate: yet he that impoverisheth his children to enrich his widow, destroyes a quick hedge to make a dead one.

## Chap. 4.
### *The life of* ABRAHAM.

I Intend not to range over all his life as he stands threesquare in relation, Husband, Father, Master. We will onely survey and measure his conjugall side, which respecteth his wife.

We reade not that ever he upbraided her for her barrennesse, as knowing that naturall defects are not the creatures fault, but the Creatours pleasure: all which time his love was loyall to her alone. As for his going in to Hagar, it was done not onely with the consent but by the advice of Sarah, who was so ambitious of children she would be made a mother by a proxie. He was not jealous of her (though a grand beauty) in what company soever he came. Indeed he feared the Egyptians, because the Egyptians feared not God; suspecting rather them of force, then her of falsenesse, and beleeving that sooner they might kill him, then corrupt her.

Yet (as well as he loved her) he expected she should do work fit for her calling. *Make ready quickly three measures of meal and knead it.* Well may Sarah be cook, where Abraham was caterer, yea where God was guest. The print of her fingers still remain in the meal, and of crumbling dow she hath made a lasting monument of her good houswifry.

Being falsely indited by his wife, he never travers'd the bill, but compounded with her on her own terms. The case this. Hagar being with child by Abraham, her pride sweld with her belly, and despiseth her mistresse: Sarah, laying her action wrong, sues Abraham for her maids fault, and appeals to God. I see the Plaintiff hath not alwayes the best cause; nor are they most guilty which are most blamed. However Abraham passes by her peevishnesse, and remits his maid to

stand

stand or fall to her own mistresse. Though he had a great part in Hagar, he would have none in Hagars rebellion. Masters which protect their faulty servants hinder the proceeding of justice in a family.

He did denie himself to grant his wives will in a matter of great consequence. Sarah desired, *Cast out this bondwoman and her sonne.* Oh hard word! She might as well have said, Cast out of thy self nature and naturall affection. See how Abraham struggles with Abraham, the Father in him striving with the Husband in him, till God moderated with his casting-voyce, and Abraham was contented to hearken to the counsel of his wife.

Being to sacrifice Isaac, we find not that he made Sarah privie to his project. To tell her, had been to torture her, fearing her affections might be too strong for her faith. Some secrets are to be kept from the weaker sex; not alwayes out of a distrust, lest they hurt the counsel by telling it, but lest the counsel hurt them by keeping it.

The dearest Husband cannot bail his wife when death arrests her. Sarah dies, and Abraham weeps. Tears are a tribute due to the dead. Tis fitting that the body when it's sown in corruption should be watered by those that plant it in the earth. The Hittites make him a fair offer, *In the chiefest of our sepulchres bury thy dead*: But he thinks the best of them too bad for his Sarah. Her chast ashes did love to lie alone; he provides her a virgin tombe in the cave of Machpelah, where her corps sweetly sleep till he himself came to bed to her, and was buried in the same grave.

## Chap. 5.
### The good Parent.

HE beginneth his care for his children not at their birth but conception, giving them to God to be, if not ( as *Hannah did ) his Chaplains, at least his Servants. This care he continueth till the day of his death, in their Infancy, Youth, and Mans estate. In all which,

*1.Sam.1.11.*

**Maxime 1** *He sheweth them in his own practice what to follow and imitate; and in others, what to shun and avoid.* For though *The words of the wise be as* nayles fastened by the masters of the Assemblies, yet sure their examples are the hammer to drive them in to take the deeper hold. A father that whipt his sonne for swearing, and swore himself whilest he whipt him, did more harm by his example then good by his correction.

*Eccles 12.11.*

**2** *He doth not welcome and imbrace the first essayes of sinne in his children.* Weeds are counted herbs in the beginning of the spring: nettles are put in pottage, and sallads are made of eldern-buds. Thus fond fathers like the oathes and wanton talk of their little children, and please themselves to heare them displease God. But our wise Parent both instructs his children in Piety, and with correction blasts the first buds of profanenesse in them. He that will not use the rod on his child, his child shall be used as a rod on him.

**3** *He observeth* Gavel-kind in dividing his affections, though not his estate. He loves them (though leaves them not) all alike. Indeed his main land he settles on the eldest: for where man takes away the birth-right, God commonly takes away the blessing from a family. But as for his love, therein, like a well-drawn picture, he eyes all his children alike ( if there be a parity of deserts ) not parching one to drown another. Did not that mother shew little wit in her great partiality, to whom

*Gives each child a part, Versteg. Of decayed intell. cap 3.*

# Chap. 5.   *The good Parent.*   13

whom when her neglected sonne complained that his brother (her darling) had hit and hurt him with a stone, whipt him onely for standing in the way where the stone went which his brother cast? This partiality is tyrannie, when Parents despise those that are deformed, enough to break them whom God had bowed before.

*He allows his children maintenance according to their quality:* 4
Otherwise it will make them base, acquaint them with bad company and sharking tricks; and it makes them surfet the sooner when they come to their estates. It is observed of camels, that having travelled long without water through sandy deserts, * *Implentur cum bibendi est occasio & in præteritum & in futurum* : and so these thirsty heirs soak it when they come to their means, who whilest their fathers were living might not touch the top of his money, and think they shall never feel the bottom of it when they are dead.

\* *Plin. Nat. Hist. lib.8.c. 18.*

*In choosing a profession he is directed by his childs disposition:* 5
whose inclination is the strongest indenture to bind him to a trade. But when they set Abel to till the ground, and send Cain to keep sheep; Jacob to hunt, and Esau to live in tents; drive some to school, and others from it; they commit a rape on nature, and it will thrive accordingly. Yet he humours not his child when he makes an unworthy choice beneath himself, or rather for ease then use, pleasure then profit.

*If his sonne prove wild he doth not cast him off so farre, but* 6
*he marks the place where he lights.* With the mother of Moses, he doth not suffer his sonne so to sink or swim, but he leaves one to * stand afarre off to watch what will become of him. He is carefull whilest he quencheth his luxury, not withall to put out his life. The rather, because their souls, who have broken and run out in their youth, have proved the more healthfull for it afterwards.

\* *Exod.2.4.*

*He moves him to marriage rather by arguments drawn from* 7
*his*

*his good, then his own authority.* It is a style too Princely for a Parent herein, To will and command, but sure he may will and desire. Affections like the conscience are rather to be led then drawn; and 'tis to be feared, They that marry where they do not love, will love where they do not marry.

8. *He doth not give away his loaf to his children, and then come to them for a piece of bread.* He holds the reins (though loosely) in his own hands, and keeps to reward duty, and punish undutifulnesse; yet on good occasion for his childrens advancement he will depart from part of his means. Base is their nature who will not have their branches lopt, till their bodie be fell'd; and will let go none of their goods, as if it presaged their speedy death: whereas it doth not follow that he that puts off his cloke must presently go to bed.

9. *On his death-bed he bequeaths his blessing to all his children:* Nor rejoyceth he so much to leave them great portions, as honestly obtained. Onely money well and lawfully gotten is good and lawfull money. And if he leaves his children young, he principally nominates God to be their Guardian, and next him is carefull to appoint provident overseers.

## Chap. 6.
### The good Child.

Maxime 1

HE reverenceth the person of his Parent though old, poore, and froward. As his Parent bare with him when a child, he bears with his Parent if twice a child: nor doth his dignity above him, cancell his duty unto him. When *S<sup>r</sup>. Thomas More was Lord Chancellour of England, and S<sup>r</sup>. John his father one of the Judges of the Kings-Bench, he would in Westminster-Hall beg his blessing of him on his knees.

* Stapleton. in vita Tho. Mori, cap. 1.

*He*

| | |
|---|---|
| *He observes his lawfull commands, and practiseth his precepts with all obedience.* I cannot therefore excuse S. Barbara from undutifulnesse, and occasioning her own death. The matter this. Her father being a pagan commanded his workmen building his house, to make two windows in a room: Barbara, knowing her fathers pleasure, in his absence injoyned them to make *three, that seeing them she might the better contemplate the mystery of the holy Trinity. (Methinks two windows might as well have raised her meditations, and the light arising from both, would as properly have minded her of the Holy Spirit proceding from the Father and the Sonne.) Her father enraged at his return, thus came to the knowledge of her religion, and accused her to the magistrate, which cost her her life. | 2  *Alphonſ. Villeg. in the life of Barbara on the 4. of Decemb.* |
| *Having practised them himself, he entayls his Parents precepts on his posterity.* Therefore such instructions are by Solomon, Proverbs 1. 9. compared to frontlets and chains (not to a sute of clothes, which serves but one, and quickly weares out, or out of fashion) which have in them a reall lasting worth, and are bequeathed as legacies to another age. The same counsels observed are chains to grace, which neglected prove halters to strangle undutifull children. | 3 |
| *He is patient under correction, and thankfull after it.* When Mr West, formerly Tutour (such I count *in loco parentis*) to Dr. Whitaker, was by him, then *Regius Professor*, created Doctour, Whitaker solemnly gave him thanks before the University for giving him correction when his young scholar. | 4 |
| *In marriage he first and last consults with his father*: when propounded, when concluded. He best bowls at the mark of his own contentment, who besides the aim of his own eye, is directed by his father, who is to give him the ground. | 5 |
| *He is a stork to his parent, and feeds him in his old age.* Not onely if his father hath been a pelican, but though he | 6 |

he hath been an estridge unto him, and neglected him in his youth. He confines him not a long way off to a short pension, forfeited if he comes in his presence; but shews piety at home, and learns (as S. Paul saith the 1. Timothy. 5. 4.) to requite his Parent. And yet the debt (I mean onely the principall, not counting the interest) cannot fully be paid, and therefore he compounds with his father to accept in good worth the utmost of his endeavour.

7 *Such a child God commonly rewards with long life in this world.* If he chance to die young, yet he lives long that lives well; and time misspent is not lived but lost. Besides, God is better then his promise, if he takes from him a long lease, and gives him a free-hold of better value. As for disobedient children,

8 *If preserved from the gallows, they are reserved for the rack, to be tortured by their own posterity.* One complained, that never father had so undutifull a child as he had. Yes, said his sonne, with lesse grace then truth, my grandfather had.

I conclude this subject with the example of a Pagans sonne, which will shame most Christians. Pomponius * Atticus, making the funerall oration at the death of his mother, did protest that living with her threescore and seven years, he was never reconciled unto her, *Se nunquam cum matre in gratiam rediisse;* because (take the comment with the text) there never happened betwixt them the least jarre which needed reconciliation.

* *In vita Attici in fine Epist. ad Attic.*

CHAP. 7.

## Chap. 7.

### The good Master.

HE is the heart in the midst of his houshold, *primum vivens et ultimum moriens*, first up and last a-bed, if not in his person yet in his providence. In his carriage he aimeth at his own and his servants good, and to advance both.

*He oversees the works of his servants.* One said that the dust that fell from the masters shooes was the best compost to manure ground. The lion * out of state will not run whilst any one looks upon him, but some servants out of slothfulnesse will not run except some do look upon them, spurr'd on with their Masters eye. Chiefly he is carefull exactly to take his servants reckonings. If their Master takes no account of them, they will make small account of him, and care not what they spend who are never brought to an audit.

*He provides them victualls, wholsome, sufficient and seasonable.* He doth not so allay his servants bread to debase it so much as to make that servants meat which is not mans meat. He alloweth them also convenient rest and recreation, whereas some Masters, like a bad conscience, will not suffer them to sleep that have them. He remembers the old law of the Saxon King Ina, * *If a villain work on Sunday by his lords command, he shall be free.*

*The wages he contracts for he duly and truly payes to his servants.* The same word in the Greek ἰὸ signifies *rust* and *poyson*: and some strong poyson is made of the rust of mettalls, but none more venemous then the rust of money in the rich mans purse unjustly detained from the labourer, which will poyson and infect his whole estate.

*He never threatens* * *his servant but rather presently corrects him.* Indeed conditionall threatnings with promise of pardon on amendment are good and usefull. Absolute threat-

Maxime 1

* *Plin. nat. Hist. lib. 8. cap 16.*

2

* *S. H. Spilman in conciliis, An. ch. 692. pag. 188.*

3

4
* *Ephes. 6. 9.*

threatnings torment more, reform lesse, making servants keep their faults, and forsake their Masters: wherefore herein he never passeth his word, but makes present paiment, left the creditour runne away from the debtour.

5. *In correcting his servant, he becomes not a slave to his own passion.* Not cruelly making new indentures of the flesh of his apprentice. To this end he never beats him in the height of his passion. Moses being to fetch water out of the rock, and commanded by God onely to speak to it with his rod in his hand, being transported with anger smote it thrice. Thus some Masters, which might fetch penitent tears from their servants with a chiding word (onely shaking the rod withall for terrour) in their fury strike many blows which might better be spared. If he perceives his servant incorrigible, so that he cannot wash the black-moore, he washeth his hands of him, and fairly puts him away.

6. *He is tender of his servant in his sicknesse and age.* If crippled in his service, his house is his hospitall: yet how many throw away those dry bones out of the which themselves have suckt the marrow? It is as usuall to see a young serving-man an old beggar, as to see a light-horse first frõ the great saddle of a Nobleman to come to the hackney-coach, and at last die in drawing a carre. But the good Master is not like the cruell hunter in the fable, who beat his old dogge because his toothlesse mouth let go the game; he rather imitates the noble nature of our Prince Henrie, who took order for the keeping of an* old English mastiffe which had made a Lion runne away. Good reason good service in age should be rewarded. Who can without pity and pleasure behold that trusty vessell which carried S$^r$. Francis Drake about the world.

Hitherto our discourse hath proceeded of the carriage of Masters towards free covenant servants, not intermedling with their behaviour towards slaves & vassals, whereof

*Hows continuat. of Stows Chron. pag. 836.*

Chap. 8.   *The good Servant.*

whereof we onely report this passage: When Charles the fifth Emperour returning with his fleet from Algier was extremely beaten with a tempest, and their ships overloaden, he caused them to cast their best horses into the sea to save the life of many *slaves, which according to the market price was not so much worth. Are there not many that in such a case had rather save Jack the horse then Jocky the keeper. And yet those who first called England *the Purgatory of servants*, sure did us much wrong: Purgatory it self being as false in the application to us, as in the doctrine thereof; servants with us living generally on as good conditions as in any other countrey. And well may masters consider how easie a transposition it had been for God, to have made him to mount into the saddle that holds the stirrop; and him to sit down at the table, who stands by with a trencher.

* *Pantaleon part. 3. De illust. Germ. & alii autores.*

---

## Chap. 8.
### *The good Servant.*

HE is one that out of conscience serves God in his Master, and so hath the principle of obedience in himself. As for those servants who found their obedience on some externall thing, with engines, they will go no longer then they are wound, or weighed up.

*He doth not dispute his Masters lawfull will, but doeth it.*   Maxime 1
Hence it is that simple servants ( understand such whose capacity is bare measure, without surplusage equall to the busines he is used in ) are more usefull, because more manageable, then abler men, especially in matters wherein not their brains but hands are required. Yet if his Master out of want of experience injoyns him to do what is hurtfull, and prejudiciall

to his own estate, duty herein makes him undutifull (if not to deny, to demurre in his performance) and chusing rather to displease then hurt his master, he humbly represents his reasons to the contrary.

2. *He loves to go about his busines with cheerfulnesse.* One said, *He loved to heare his carter though not his cart to sing.* God loveth a cheerfull giver; and Christ reproved the Pharisees for disfiguring their faces with a sad countenance. Fools! who to perswade men that Angels lodged in their hearts, hung out a devil for a signe in their faces. Sure cheerfulnesse in doing renders a deed more acceptable. Not like those servants, who doing their work unwillingly, their looks do enter a protestation against what their hands are doing.

3. *He dispatcheth his busines with quicknes and expedition.* Hence the same English word *Speed* signifies celerity, and successe; the former in businesse of execution causing the latter. Indeed haste and rashnesse are storms and tempests, breaking and wrecking businesse; but nimblenesse is a fair full wind, blowing it with speed to the haven. As he is good at hand, so is he good at length, continually and constantly carefull in his service. Many servants, as if they had learnd the nature of the besoms they use, are good for a few dayes, and afterwards grow unserviceable.

4. *He disposeth not of his masters goods without his privity or consent:* no not in the smallest matters. Open this wicket, and it will be in vain for masters to shut the doore. If servants presume to dispose small things without their masters allowance (besides that many little leaks may sink a ship) this will widen their consciences to give away greater. But though he hath not alwayes a particular leave, he hath a generall grant, and a warrant dormant from his master to give an almes to the poore in his absence, if in absolute necessity.

5. *His answers to his master are true, direct, and dutifull.* If a dumbe devil possesseth a servant, a winding cane is the fittest

fittest circle, and the master the exorcist to drive it out. Some servants are so talkative, one may as well command the echo as them not to speak last; and then they count themselves conquerours, because last they leave the field. Others, though they seem to yield and go away, yet with the flying Parthians shoot backward over their shoulders, and dart bitter taunts at their masters; yea, though with the clock they have given the last stroke, yet they keep a jarring, muttering to themselves a good while after.

*Just correction he bears patiently, and unjust he takes cheerfully*; knowing that stripes unjustly given more hurt the master then the man: and the Logick maxime is verified, *Agens agendo repatitur*, the smart most lights on the striker. Chiefly he disdains the basenesse of running away.

*Because charity is so cold, his industry is the hotter to provide something for himself, whereby he may be maintained in his old age.* If under his master he trades for himself (as an apprentice may do if he hath *covenanted so before-hand) he provides good bounds and sufficient fences betwixt his own and his masters estate (*Jacob* Gen. 30. 36. *set his flock three dayes journey from Labans*) that no quarrell may arise about their proprietie, nor suspicion that his remnant hath eaten up his masters whole cloth.

*Bracton. lib. 5. tract. 2. cap. 3. num. 7.*

## Chap. 9.
### The life of Eliezer.

Eliezer was Steward of Abrahams houshold, Lieutenant generall over the army of his servants, ruler over all his Master had: the confidence in his loyalty, causing the largenesse of his commission.

But as for those who make him the founder of Damascus, on no other evidence but because he is called *Eliezer of Damascus*, they build a great city on too narrow a foundation. It argues his goodnesse that Abraham, if dying without a sonne, intended him his heir ( a kinsman in grace is nearest by the surest side ) till Isaac stepping in stopt out Eliezer, and reverst those resolutions.

The Scripture presents us with a remarkable president of * his piety, in a matter of great moment: Abraham, being to send him into Mesopotamia, caused him to swear that he would faithfully fetch Isaac a wife from his own kinred. Eliezer demurr'd awhile before he would swear, carefully surveying the latitude of the oath, lest some unseen ambushes therein should surprise his conscience. The most scrupulous to take an oath will be the most carefull to perform it, whereas those that swear it blindly will do it lamely. He objects, *Peradventure the woman will not be willing to follow me*. At last being satisfied in this quære, he takes the oath: as no honest man which means to pay, will refuse to give his bond if lawfully required.

He takes ten camells ( then the coaches of the Eastcountrey ) with servants and all things in good equipage, to shew a sample of his Masters greatnesse ; and being a stranger in the countrey asked direction of him who best knew the way, God himself. If any object that his craving of a signe was a signe of infidelity, and unmannerly boldnesse to confine God to particulars ; yet

* *That the namelesse servant, Gen. 24. was this Eliezer Abrahams steward, is the opinion of Luther in his comment on that chapter, Rivet on the same,* Exercit. 111. *with many others.*

yet perchance Gods spirit prompted him to make the request, who sometimes moves men to ask what he is minded to give, and his petition seemeth just because granted.

Rebecca meets him at the well. The lines drawn from every part of the signe required centre themselves in her. *Drink my Lord,* said she, *and I will draw water for thy camells.* Her words Prophesie that she will be a good housewife, and a good housekeeper. Eliezers eyes are dazeled with the beams of Gods providence: Her drawing of water drew more wonder from him; and the more he drinks of her pitcher, the more he is athirst to know the issue of the matter. He questions her of her parentage, and finds all his mysticall expectation historically expounded in her. Then he bowed down his head, and did homage to Gods providence, blessing him for his protection. Many favours which God giveth us ravell out for want of hemming, through our own unthankfulnesse: for though prayer purchaseth blessings, giving praise doth keep the quiet possession of them.

Being come into the house, his first care is for his cattell, whose dumbenesse is oratory to a conscientious man; and he that will not be mercifull to his beast, is a beast himself. Then preferring his message before his meat, he empties his mind before he fills his body. No dainties could be digested, whilst his errand like a crudity lay on his stomach.

In delivering his message, first he reads his commission, I am Abrahams servant; then he reports the fulnesse of his Masters wealth without any hyperboles. How many, employed in such a matter, would have made mountains of gold of molehills of silver? not so Eliezer, reporting the bare truth; and a good estate if told, commends it self. As plain also is his narration of the passages of Gods providence, the artificialnesse whereof best appeard in his naturall relation. Then
concludes

concludes he, with desiring a direct answer to his motion.

The matter was soon transacted betwixt them; for seeing that heaven did ask the banes, why should earth forbid them? onely her friends desire Rebecca should stay ten dayes with them, which Eliezer would not yield to. He would speedily finish that bargain whereof God had given the happy earnest; and because blest hitherto, make more haste hereafter. If in a dark businesse we perceive God to guide us by the lantern of his providence, it is good to follow the light close, lest we lose it by our lagging behind. He will not truant it now in the afternoon, but with convenient speed returns to Abraham, who onely was worthy of such a Servant, who onely was worthy of such a Master.

## Chap. 10.
### The good Widow.

SHe is a woman whose head hath been quite cut off, and yet she liveth, and hath the second part of virginity. Conceive her to have buried her Husband decently according to his quality and condition, and let us see how she behaves her self afterwards.

*Maxime* 1. *Her grief for her Husband though reall, is moderate.* Excessive was the sorrow of King Richard the second beseeming him neither as king, man, or Christian, who so fervently loved Anna of Bohemia his Queen, that when she dyed at Shean in Surrey, he both cursed the place, and also out of madnesse * overthrew the whole house.

\* *Weaver fun. monum. p. 473. out of Stows Annals.*

2. *But our Widows sorrow is no storm but a still rain.* Indeed some foolishly discharge the surplusage of their passions on themselves, tearing their hair, so that their friends

Chap. 10.  *The good Widow.*  25

friends coming to the funerall, know not which most to bemoan the dead husband, or the dying widow. Yet commonly it comes to passe, that such widows grief is quickly emptyed, which streameth out at so large a vent; whilest their tears that but drop, will hold running a long time.

3

*She continues a competent time in her widows estate.* Anciently they were, at least, to live out their *annum luctus*, their yeare of sorrow. But as some * erroneously compute the long lives of the Patriarks before the flood not by solary, but lunary years, making a moneth a yeare: so many overhasty widows cut their yeare of mourning very short, and within few weeks make post speed to a second marriage.

* *vid. August. de c vitat Dei lib. 15. cap. 12.*

4

*She doth not onely live sole and single, but chaste and honest.* We know pesthouses always stand alone, and yet are full of infectious diseases. Solitarinesse is not an infallible argument of sanctity: and it is not enough to be unmarried, but to be undefiled.

5

*Though going abroad sometimes about her businesse, she never makes it her businesse to go abroad.* Indeed *man goeth forth to his labour,* and a widow in civill affairs is often forced to act a double part of man and woman, and must go abroad to solicite her businesse in person, what she cannot do by the proxie of her friends. Yet even then she is most carefull of her credit, and tender of her modesty, not impudently thrusting into the society of men. Oh 'tis improper for tinder to strike fire, and for their sexe which are to be sued to, first to intrude, and offer their companie.

6

*She loves to look on her husbands picture, in the children he hath left her*: not foolishly fond over them for their fathers sake (this were to kill them in honour of the dead) but giveth them carefull education. Her husbands friends are ever her welcomest guests, whom she entertaineth with her best cheer, and with honourable mention of their friends, and her husbands memorie.                     E                     If

7      *If she can speak little good of him, she speaks but little of him.* So handsomely folding up her discourse, that his virtues are shown outwards, and his vices wrapped up in silence, as counting it Barbarisme to throw dirt on his memorie who hath moulds cast on his body. She is a champion for his credit if any speak against him. Foolish is their project who by raking up bad savour against their former husbands think thereby to perfume their bed for a second marriage.

8      *She putteth her especiall confidence in Gods providence.* Surely if he be *a father to the fatherlesse,* it must needs follow that he is an husband to the widow. And therefore she seeks to gain and keep his love unto her, by her constant prayer and religious life.

9      *She will not morgage her first husbands pawns, thereby to purchase the good will of a second.* If she marrieth (for which she hath the Apostles licence, not to say mandate, *I will that the younger widows marry*) she will not abridge her children of that which justly belongs unto them. Surely a broken faith to the former is but a weak foundation to build thereon a loyall affection to a latter love. Yet if she becomes a mother in law, there is no difference betwixt her carriage to her own and her second husbands children, save that she is severest to her own, over whom she hath the sole jurisdiction. And if her second husbands children by a former wife commit a fault, she had rather bind them over to answer for it before their own father, then to correct them her self, to avoid all suspicion of hard using of them.

CHAP. 11.

PAVLA *Widdow of* Toxotius, *and Mother to* Evstochium. *She Died at Bethlehem, An° dom̄* 404 *Aged* 56 *yeares* 8 *moneths* 21 *dayes*
W. M. *sculp.*

## Chap. II.

### *The life of the Lady* Paula.

WHat? (will some say) having a wood of widows of upright conversation, must you needs gather one crooked with superstition to be pattern to all the rest? must Paula be their president? whose life was a very masse-book, so that if every point of popery were lost, they might be found in her practice.

Nothing lesse. Indeed Paula lived in an age which was, as I may say, in the knuckle and bending betwixt

the

the primitive times and superstition, popery being then a hatching, but farre from being fledg'd. Yea no Papist (though picking out here and there some passages which make to his purpose) will make her practice in grosse the square of his own: for where she embraces some superstitions with her left hand, she thrusts away more with her right. I have therefore principally made choice to write her life, that I may acquaint both my self and the reader with the garb of that age in Church-matters, wherein were many remarkable passages, otherwise I might and would have taken a farre fitter example.

I know two trades together are too much for one man to thrive upon, and too much it is for me to be an Historian and a Critick, to relate and to judge: yet since Paula, though a gratious woman, was guilty of some great errours, give me leave to hold a pencil in one hand, and a spunge in the other, both to draw her life and dash it where it is faultie. And let us that live in purer times be thankfull to God for our light, and use our quicker sight to guide our feet in Gods paths, left we reel from one extremitie to another.

To come to the Lady Paula's birth: the Noblest blood in the world by a confluence ran in her veins. I must confesse the most Ancient Nobilitie is junior to no Nobilitie, when all men were equall. Yet give others leave to see Moses his face to shine, when he knew it not himself; and seeing Paula was pleased not to know, but to neglect and trample on her high birth, we are bound to take notice thereof. She was descended from * Agamemnon, Scipio, and the Gracchi's, and her husband Toxotius from * Æneas, and the Julian familie; so that in their marriage the warres of the Grecians and Trojanes were reconciled.

Some years they lived together in the Citie of Rome, in holy and happy wedlock, and to her husband she bare foure daughters, Blesilla, Paulina, Eustochium, and Ruffina.

*Hieron. Epist. ad Eustoch. pag. 185.
* Idem in eadem epist. p. 172.

Ruffina. Yet still her husband long'd for posteritie, like those who are so covetous of a male heir, they count none children but sonnes: and at last God, who keeps the best for the close, bestowed Toxotius, a young sonne upon her.

But commonly after a great blessing comes a great crosse: scarce was she made a mother to a sonne, when she was made a widow, which to her was a great and grievous affliction. But as a rubbe to an overthrown bowl proves an help by hindering it; so afflictions bring the souls of Gods Saints to the mark, which otherwise would be gone and transported with too much earthly happinesse. However Paula grieved little lesse then excessively hereat, she being a woman that in all her actions (to be sure to do enough) made always measure with advantage.

Yet in time she overcame her sorrow, herein being assisted by the counsel and comfort of S. Hierome, whose constant frequenting of her, commented upon by his enemies malice (which will pry narrowly and talk broadly) gave occasion to the report, that he accompanied with her for dishonest intents. Surely if the accusations of slanderous tongues be proofs, the primitive times had no Churches but stews. It is to be suspected that * Ruffin his sworn enemie raised the report; and if the Lady Paula's memorie wanted a compurgatour, I would be one my self, it being improbable that those her eyes would burn with lust which were constantly drownd with tears. But the reader may find S. Hierome purging * himself; and he who had his tongue and an innocent heart needed no body else to speak for him.

It happened that the Bishops of the East and West were summoned by the * Emperours letters to appear at Rome for the according of some differences in the Church. (It seemes by this that the Pope did not so command in chief at Rome, but that the power of congregating

* *Erasmus in scholia in epitaphium Paulæ p. 193.*

* *In epistola quæ incipit, Si tibi putem, tom. 2. fol. 368.*

* *Hieronym. Epist. prædict. pag. 172.*

congregating Synods still resided in the Emperour.) Hither came Paulinus Bishop of Antioch, and Epiphanius Bishop of Salamine in Cyprus, who lodged at the Lady Paula's, and his virtues so wrought upon her, that she determined to leave her native countrey, and to travel into the East, and in Judea to spend the remainder of her life. The reasons that moved her to remove, was because Rome was a place of riot and luxury, her soul being almost stifled with the frequencie of Ladyes visits; and she feared courtesie in her would justle out piety, she being fain to crowd up her devotions to make room for civill entertainments. Besides, of her own nature she ever loved privacie and a sequestred life, being of the Pelicans nature, which use not to flie in flocks. Lastly, she conceived that the sight of those holy places would be the best comment on the History of the Bible, and fasten the passages thereof in her mind. Wherefore she intended to survey all Palestine, and at last to go to Bethlehem, making Christs inne her home, and to die there where he was born, leaving three of her daughters, and her poore infant Toxotius behind her.

For mine own part, I think she had done as acceptable a deed to God, in staying behind to rock her child in the cradle, as to visit Christs manger, seeing Grace doth not cut of the affections of nature but ripen them: the rather, because Christianity is not naild to Christs crosse and mount Calvary, nor Piety fastned (as we may say) to the freehold of the land of Palestine. But if any Papist make her a pattern for pilgrimages, let them remember that she went from Rome: and was it not an unnaturall motion in her to move from that centre of Sanctitie?

She with her daughter Eustochium began her journie, and taking Cyprus in her way, where she visited Epiphanius, she came at last to Judea. She measured
that

Chap. II.    *The life of* Paula.    31

that countrey with her travelling, and drew the truest mappe thereof with her own feet, so accurately that she left out no particular place of importance. At last she was fixed at Bethlehem, where she built one monasterie for men, and three for women. It will be worth our pains to take notice of some principall of the orders she made in those feminine Academies; because Paula's practice herein was a leading case, though those that came after her went beyond her. For in the rules of monasticall life, Paula stood at the head game, and the Papists in after ages, desirous to better her hand, drew themselves quite out.

Each monasterie had a chief matrone, whilst Paula was Principall over all. These societies were severd at their meat and work, but met together at their prayers: they were carefully kept apart from men, not like those Epicœne monasteries not long since invented by Joan Queen of Sweden, wherein men and women lived under one roof, not to speak of worse libertines. Well were Nunnes called *Recluses*, which according to the true meaning of the word signifie those which are set wide open, or left at libertie, though that Barbarous age mistook the sense of the word, for such as were shut up, and might not stirre out of their * Cloyster.

* *Littleton fol. 92.*

They used to sing Halelujah, which serv'd them both for a psalm, and a bell to call them all together. In the * morning, at nine a clock, at noon, at three a clock in the afternoon, and at night they had prayers, and sang the psalmes in order. This I believe gave originall to canonicall houres. The Apostles precept is the plain song, *Pray continually*; and thus mens inventions ran their descants upon it, and confin'd it to certain houres. A practice in it self not so bad for those who have leisure to observe it, save that when devotion is thus artificially plaited into houres it may take up mens minds in formalities to neglect the substance.                                They

*Mane, horâ tertiâ, sextâ, nonâ, vesperi. Hieron. in præfat. Epist. p. 180. surely living in Palestine he meaneth the Jewish computation of houres.*

They rose also at midnight to sing psalmes. A custome begun before in the time of persecution, when the Christians were forced to be Antipodes to other men, so that when it was night with others, it was day with them, and they then began their devotions. These night-prayers, begun in necessitie, were continued in Paula's time in gratefull remembrance, and since corrupted with superstition: the best is, their rising at midnight breaks none of our sleep.

These virgins did every day learn some part of the holy Scriptures; whereas those Nunnes which pretend to succeed them learn onely with post-horses to run over the stage of their beads ( so many Ave Maries, and Pater nosters ) and are ignorant in all the Scripture besides. Such as were faultie, she caused to take their meat apart from others at the entrance of the dining-room; with which mild severitie she reclaimed many: shame in ingenuous natures making a deeper impression then pain. Mean time I find amongst them no vow of virginitie, no tyrannicall Penance, no whipping themselves; as if not content to interre their sinnes in Christs grave, they had rather bury them in furrows digg'd in their own backs. They wrought hard to get their living, and on the Lords day alone went out of their monasterie to hear Gods word.

Yet was she more rigid and severe towards her self, then to any of them, macerating her body with fasting, and refusing to drink any wine, when advised thereto by Physicians for her health. So that ( as an * holy man complained of himself, whilest he went about to subdue an enemie he kild a subject ) she overturned the state of her bodie, and whilest she thought to snuff the candle put it quite out. Yea S. Hierome himself, what his Eloquence herein doth commend in her, his Charity doth excuse, and his Judgement doth * condemne. But we must Charitably believe that these her fastings proceeded out of true humiliation and sorrow

for

* Bernard. devot. devotis

* Hæc refero, non quòd inconsideranter & ultra vires sumta onera probem, p. 181.

for her sinnes; otherwise where opinion of merit is annexed to them, they are good onely to fill the body with wind, and the soul with pride. Certainly prodigious Popish self-penance is will-worship, and the purest Epicurisme, wherein pain is pleasant: for as long as people impose it on themselves, they do not deny their own will, but fulfill it; and whilst they beat down the body they may puff up the flesh.

Nor can her immoderate bounty be excused, who gave all and more then all away, taking up money at interest to give to the poore, and leaving Eustochium her daughter deep in debt, a great charge, and nothing to maintain it. Sure none need be more bountifull in giving then the Sunne is in shining, which though freely bestowing his beams on the world keeps notwithstanding the body of light to himself. Yea it is necessary that Liberality should as well have banks as a stream.

She was an excellent text-woman, yea could say the holy Scriptures by heart, and attained to understand and speak the Hebrew tongue, a language which Hierome himself got with great difficultie, and kept with constant use (skill in Hebrew will quickly go out, and burn no longer then 'tis blown) yet she in her old age did speedily learn it. She diligently heard Hierome expounding the old and new Testament, asking him many doubts, and Quæres in difficult places (such constant scouring makes our knowledge brighter) and would not suffer his judgement to stand neuter in hard points, but made him expresse the probable opinion.

Most naturally flie from death; Gods Saints stand still till death comes to them; Paula went out to meet it, not to say, call'd death unto her by consuming her self in fasting: she died in the fiftie sixth yeare of her age, and was solemnly buried in Bethlehem. People of all countreys flockt to her funerall: Bishops carried her

F  corps

corps to the grave: others carried torches and lamps before it, which though some may condemne to be but burning of day was no more then needed, she being buried in a cave or grot as an * eyewitnesse doth testifie. Psalmes were sung at her buriall in the Hebrew, Greek, Latine, and Syriack tongue, it being fit there should be a key for every lock, and languages to be understood by all the miscelany company there present.

<small>* G. Sandys Travells, pag. 179.</small>

Eustochium her daughter had little comfort to be Executrix or Administratrix unto her, leaving her not a pennie of monie, great debts, and many brothers and sisters to provide for, *quos sustentare arduum, abjicere impium.* I like not this charitie reversed, when it begins farre off & neglects those at home.

To conclude, I can do her memorie no better right, then to confesse she was wrong in somethings. Yet surely Gods Glory was the mark she shot at, though herein the hand of her practice did sometimes shake, and oftener the eye of her judgement did take wrong aim.

### Chap. 12.

## *The constant Virgin*

IS one who hath made a resolution with herself to live chaste, and unmarryed. Now there is a grand difference betwixt a Resolution and a Vow. The former is a covenant drawn up betwixt the party and herself; and commonly runs with this clause, *durante nostro beneplacito*, as long as we shall think fitting; and therefore on just occasion she may give a release to herself. But in a vow God is interested as the Creditour, so that except he be pleased to give up the band, none can give an acquittance to themselves. Being now to describe the Virgin, let the reader know that virginity belongs to both sexes; and though in Courtesie

# Chap. 12. *The constant Virgin.*

tesie we make our Maid a female, let not my pen be chalenged of improprietie, if casually sometimes it light on the Masculine Gender.

*She chooseth not a single life solely for its self, but in reference to the better serving of God.* I know none but beggars that desire the Church-Porch to lye in, which others onely use as a passage into the Church. Virginity is none of those things to be desired in and for it self, but because it leads a more convenient way to the worshipping of God, especially in time of persecution. For then if Christians be forced to run races for their lives, the unmarryed have the advantage, lighter by many ounces, and freed from much encumbrance, which the married are subject to; who, though private Persons, herein are like Princes, they must have their train follow them.

*She improveth her single life therewith to serve God the more constantly.* Housekeepers cannot so exactly mark all their family-affairs, but that sometimes their ranks will be broken; which disorder by necessary consequence will disturb their duties of pietie, to make them contracted, omitted, or unseasonably performed. The Apostle saith, *Such shall have troubles in the flesh*; and grant them sanctified troubles, yet even Holy-thistle and Sweet-brier have their prickles. But the Virgin is freed from these encumbrances. No lording Husband shall at the same time command her presence and distance, to be alwayes near in constant attendance, and alwayes to stand aloof off in an awfull observance; so that providing his break-fast hazards her soul to fast a meal of morning prayer: No crying Children shall drown her singing of psalmes, and put her devotion out of tune: No unfaithfull Servants shall force her to divide her eyes betwixt lifting them up to God and casting them down to oversee their work; but making her Closet her Chappell, she freely enjoyeth God and good thoughts at what time she pleaseth.

*Maxime* 1

2

*Yet*

3     *Yet in all her discourse she maketh an honourable mention of marriage.* And good reason that virginity should pay a chief rent of honour unto it, as acknowledging her selfe to be a *colonia deducta* from it. Unworthy is the practice of those who in their discourse plant all their arguments point-blank to batter down the married estate, bitterly inveighing against it; yea base is the behaviour of some young men, who can speak nothing but Satyres against Gods ordinance of Matrimony, and the whole sex of women. This they do either out of deep dissimulation, to divert supicion, that they may prey the farthest from their holes; or else they do it out of revenge: having themselves formerly lighted on bad women (yet no worse then they deserved) they curse all adventures because of their own shipwrack; or lastly they do it out of mere spight to nature and God himself: and pity it is but that their fathers had been of the same opinion. Yet it may be tolerable if onely in harmlesse mirth they chance to bestow a jest upon the follyes of married people. Thus when a Gentlewoman told an ancient Batchelour who lookd very young, that she thought he had eaten a snake; *No mistris* (said he) *it is because I never meddled with any snakes which maketh me look so young.*

4     *She counts her self better lost in a modest silence then found in a bold discourse.* Divinity permits not women to speak in the Church; morality forbids maids to talk in the House, where their betters are present. She is farre from the humours of those, who (more bridling in their chinnes then their tongues) love in their constant prating to make sweet musick to their own ears, and harsh jarring to all the rest of the company: yea as some report of sheep, that when they runne they are afraid of the noise of their own feet; so our Virgin is afraid to heare her own tongue runne in the presence of graver persons. She conceives the bold maintaining of any argument concludes against her own civil behaviour;

behaviour; and yet she will give a good account of any thing whereof she is questioned, sufficient to shew her silence is her choice, not her refuge. In speaking she studiously avoids all suspicious expressions, which wanton apprehensions may colourably comment into obscenity.

*She blusheth at the wanton discourse of others in her company.* 5
As fearing that being in the presence where treason against modesty is spoken, all in the place will be arraigned for principalls: yea if silent, she is afraid to be taken to consent; if offering to confute it, she fears lest by stirring a dunghill, the savour may be more noysome. Wherefore that she may not suffer in her title to modesty, to preserve her right she enters a silent caveat by a blush in her cheeks, and embraceth the next opportunity to get a gaole-delivery out of that company where she was detained in durance. Now because we have mentioned Blushing, which is so frequent with virgins that it is called *a maidens blush*, (as if they alone had a patent to die this colour) give us leave a little to enlarge our selves on this subject.

1 *Blushing oftentimes proceeds from guiltines*; when the offender being pursued after seeks as it were to hide himself under the visard of a new face.

2 *Blushing is othertimes rather a compurgatour then an accuser*; not arising from guiltinesse in our Virgin, but from one of these reasons: First because she is surprised with a sudden accusation, and though armed with innocency, that she cannot be pierced, yet may she be amazed with so unexpected a charge. Secondly from sensiblenesse of disgrace, ashamed, though innocent, to be within the suspicion of such faults, and that she hath carried her self so that any tongue durst be so impudent as to lay it to her charge. Thirdly from a disability to acquit her self at the instant (her integrity wanting rather clearing then clearnesse) and perchance

F 3

chance she wants boldnesse to traverse the action, and so non-suiting her self, she fears her cause will suffer in the judgements of all that be present: and although accused but in jest, she is jealous the accusation will be believed in earnest; and edg'd tools thrown in merriment may wound reputations. Fourthly out of mere anger: for as in fear the blood makes not an orderly retreat but a confused flight to the heart; so in blushing the blood sallies out into our Virgins cheeks, and seems as a champion to challenge the accuser for wronging her.

3 *Where small faults are committed blushing obtaines a pardon of course with ingenuous beholders.* As if she be guilty of casuall incivilities, or solœcismes in manners occasioned by invincible ignorance, and unavoidable mistakes, in such a case blushing is a sufficient penance to restore her to her state of innocencie.

6 *She imprisons not her self with a solemn vow never to marry.* For first, none know their own strength herein. Who hath sailed about the world of his own heart, sounded each creek, surveied each corner, but that still there remains therein much *terra incognita* to himself? Junius, at the first little better then a * Misogynist, was afterwards so altered from himself, that he successively married foure wives. Secondly, fleshly corruption being pent will swell the more, and Shemei being confin'd to Jerusalem will have the greater mind to gad to Gath. Thirdly, the devil will have a fairer set mark to shoot at, and will be most busie to make people break their vow. Fourthly, God may justly desert people for snatching that to themselves, which is most proper for him to give, I mean, Continency. Object not, that thou wilt pray to him to take from thee all desire of marriage, it being madnesse to vow that one will not eat, and then pray to God that he may not

* *Junius in his life writ by himself.*

not be hungry. Neither say that now thou may'st presume on thy self, because thou art well stricken in years, for there may happen an autume-spring in thy soul; and lust is an unmannerly guest, we know not how late in the evening of our lives it may intrude into us for a lodging.

*She counts it virginitie to be unspotted, not unmarried.* Or else even in old age, when nature hath given an inhibition, they may be strong in desiring who are weak in acting of wickednesse; yea they may keep stews in their hearts, and be so pregnant and ingravidated with lustfull thoughts, that they may as it were die in travail because they cannot be delivered. And though there be no fire seen outwardly, as in the English chymnies, it may be hotter within, as in the Dutch stoves; and as well the devils as the Angels in heaven, *neither marry nor are given in marriage.*

*As she lives with lesse care, so she dies with more cheerfulnesse.* Indeed she was rather a sojourner, then an inhabitant in this world, and therefore forsakes it with the lesse grief. In a word, the way to heaven is alike narrow to all estates, but farre smoother to the Virgin then to the married. Now the great advantage Virgins have to serve God above others, & high favours he hath bestowed on some of them, shall appear in this Virgin prophetesse, whose life we come to present.

CHAP. 13.

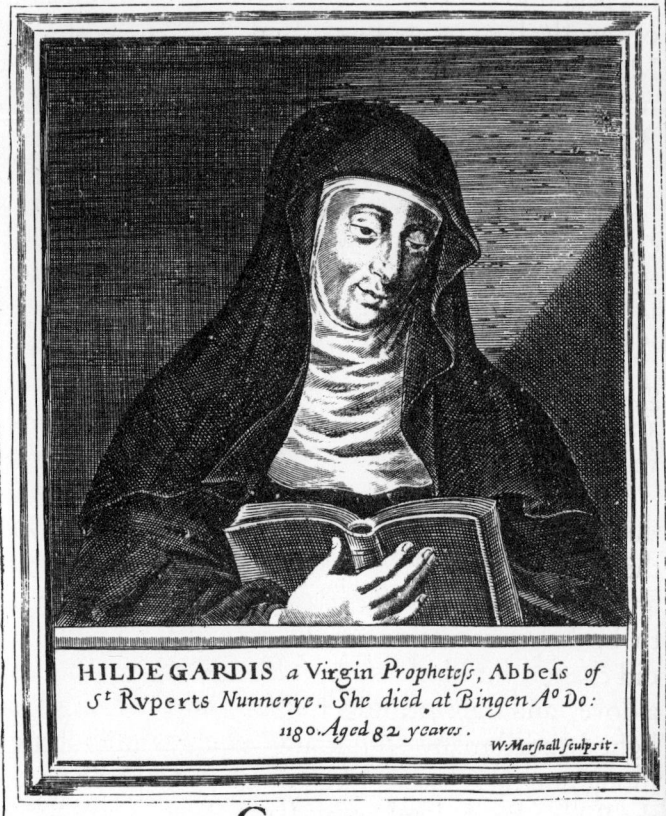

HILDEGARDIS a Virgin Prophetess, Abbess of S.t Ruperts Nunnerye. She died at Bingen A.o Do: 1180. Aged 82 yeares.   W. Marshall sculpsit.

## Chap. 13.

### *The life of* HILDEGARDIS.

Hildegardis was born in Germany, in the County of Spanheim, in the yeare 1098. So that she lived in an age which we may call the first cock-crowing after the midnight of Ignorance and Superstition. Her parents (Hidebert, and Mechtilda) dedicated her to God from her infancie: And surely those whose Childhood, with Hildegardis, hath had the advantage of pious education may be said to have been

Chap. 13.  *The life of* Hildegardis.                    41

been good time out of mind, as not able to remember the beginning of their own goodnesse. At eight years of age she became a Nunne under S. Jutta sister to Megenhard, Earl of Spanheim, and afterwards she was made Abbesse of S. Ruperts Nunnery in Bingen on Rhene in the Palatinate.

Men commonly do beat and bruise their links before they light them, to make them burn the brighter: God first humbles and afflicts whom he intends to illuminate with more then ordinary grace. Poore Hildegardis was constantly and continually sick, and so * weak that she very seldome was strong enough to go. But God who denied her legs, gave her wings, and raised her high-mounted soul in Visions and Revelations.

I know a generall scandall is cast on Revelations in this ignorant age: first, because many therein intitled the Meteors of their own brain to be Starres at least, and afterwards their Revelations have been revealed to be forgeries: secondly, because that night-raven did change his black feathers into the silver wings of a dove, and transforming himself into an Angel of light deluded many with strange raptures and visions, though in their nature farre different from those in the Bible. For S. Paul in his Revelations was caught up into the third heaven ; whereas most Monks with a contrary motion were carried into hell and purgatorie, and there saw apparitions of strange torments. Also S. Johns Revelation forbids all additions to the Bible, under heavie penalties ; their visions are commonly on purpose to piece out the Scripture, and to establish such superstitions as have no footing in Gods word.

However all held Hildegardis for a Prophet, being induced thereunto by the piety of her life: no breck was ever found in her veil, so spotlesse was her conversation ; by the sanctity of her writings, and by the

* Fuerunt ei ab ipsa penè infantia crebri ac ferè continui languorum dolores, ità ut pedum incessu perraro uteretur, *Theod. Abbas in vita Hildegardis, lib.* 1. *cap.* 2.

G                              generall

generall approbation the Church gave unto her. For Pope Eugenius the third, after exact examination of the matter, did in the Councell of Trevers (wherein S. Bernard was present) allow and priviledge her Revelations for authenticall. She was of the Popes Conclave, and Emperours Counsel, to whom they had recourse in difficulties: yea the greatest torches of the Church lighted themselves at her candle. The Patriarch of Jerusalem, the Bishops of Mentz, Colen, Breme, Trevers sent such knots as posed their own fingers to our Hildegardis to untie.

She never learn'd word of Latine; and yet *therein would she fluently expresse her Revelations to those notaries that took them from her mouth; so that throwing words at randome she never brake Priscian's head: as if the Latine had learn'd to make it self true without the speakers care. And no doubt, he that brought the single parties to her married them also in her mouth, so that the same Spirit which furnished her with Latine words, made also the true Syntaxis. Let none object that her very writing of fifty eight Homilies on the Gospel is false construction, where the feminine Gender assumes an employment proper to men: for though S. Paul silenceth women for speaking in the Church, I know no Scripture forbids them from writing on Scripture.

*Trithemius de Scriptor. Eccles. fol. 92.

Such infused skill she had also of Musick, whereof she was naturally ignorant, and wrote a whole book of verses very good according to those times. Indeed in that age the trumpet of the warlike Heroick, and the sweet harp of the Lyrick verse, were all turned into the gingling of Cymballs, tinckling with rhythmes, and like-sounding cadencies.

But let us heare a few lines of her Prophecies, and thence guesse the rest. *In those dayes there shall rise up a people without understanding, proud, covetous, and deceitfull, the which shall eat the sins of the people, holding a certain order of foolish devotion*

# Chap. 13.   *The life of* Hildegardis.   43

votion under the feigned cloke of beggery. Also they shall instantly preach without devotion or example of the holy Martyrs, and shall detract from the secular Princes, taking away the Sacraments of the Church from the true pastours, receiving almes of the poore, having familiarity with women, instructing them how they shall deceive their husbands, and rob their husbands to give it unto them, * &c. What could be said more plain to draw out to the life those Mendicant friers (rogues by Gods statutes) which afterwards swarm'd in the world.

Heare also how she foretold the low water of Tiber, whilest as yet it was full tide there. *The Kings and other Rulers of the world, being stirred up by the just judgement of God, shall set themselves against them, and run upon them, saying, We will not have these men to reigne over us with their rich houses, and great possessions, and other worldly riches, over the which we are ordained to be Lords and Rulers : and how is it meet or comely that those shavelings with their stoles and chesils should have more souldiers or richer armour and artillery then we ? wherefore let us take away from them what they do not justly but wrongfully possesse.*

It is well the Index expurgatorius was not up in those dayes, nor the Inquisition on foot, otherwise dame Hildegardis must have been call'd to an after account. I will onely ask a Romanist this question, This Prophesie of Hildegardis, was it from heaven or from men ? If from heaven, why did ye not believe it ? If from men, why did the Pope allow it, & canonize her?

As for miracles, which she wrought in her life time, their number is as admirable as their nature. I must confesse at my first reading * of them, my belief digested some but surfeted on the rest : for she made no more to cast out a devil, then a barber to draw a tooth, and with lesse pain to the patient. I never heard of a great feast made all of Cordialls : and it seems improbable that miracles (which in Scripture are used sparingly, and chiefly for conversion of unbelievers)

*should*

\* *See much more to this purpose in Catalog. Testium veritatis in Hildegarde : Also in Foxes Acts and monuments, p. 461.*

\* *In Lipoman. in vitis Sanct. Tom. 5 fol. 91. & sequen.*

should be heaped so many together, made every dayes work, and by her commonly, constantly, and ordinarily, wrought. And I pray why is the Popish Church so barren of true works nowadayes here wrought at home amongst us? For as for those reported to be done farre of, it were ill for some if the gold from the Indies would abide the touch no better then the miracles.

However Hildegardis was a gratious Virgin, and God might perform some great wonders by her hand; but these *piæ fraudes* with their painting have spoyled the naturall complexion of many a good face, and have made Truth it self suspected. She dyed in the 82. yeare of her age, was afterwards Sainted by the Pope, and the 17 day of September assign'd to her memory.

I cannot forget how Udalrick Abbat of Kempten in Germany made a most * courteous law for the weaker sexe, That no woman, guilty of what crime soever, should ever be put to death in his dominions, because two women condemn'd to die were miraculously delivered out of the prison by praying to S. Hildegardis.

* *Bruschius Demonaster.& Centuriatores, Centur. 11. Col. 350.*

## Chap. 14.

### The Elder Brother

IS one who made hast to come into the world to bring his Parents the first news of male-posterity, and is well rewarded for his tidings. His composition is then accounted most pretious when made of the losse of a double Virginitie.

*Maxime* I

* *Quæstionibus ex utroque mixtim Tom. 40 Col. 874.*

He is thankfull for the advantage God gave him at the starting in the race into this world. When twinnes have been even match'd, one hath gained the gole but by his length. S. * Augustine saith, *That it is every mans bounden*

*bounden duty solemnly to celebrate his birth-day.* If so, Elder Brothers may best afford good cheer on the festivall.

2. *He counts not his inheritance a* Writ *of ease to free him from industry*: As if onely the Younger Brothers came into the world to work, the Elder to complement. These are the Toppes of their houses indeed, like cotlofts, highest and emptiest. Rather he laboureth to furnish himself with all gentile accomplishment, being best able to go to the cost of learning. He need not fear to be served as Ulrick Fugger was (chief of the noble family of the Fuggers in Auspurg) who was disinherited of a great patrimony onely for his *studiousnesse, and expensivenesse in buying costly Manuscripts.

\* *Thuan. de obit. vir. doct. in Ann.* 1584.

3. *He doth not so remember he is an Heire, that he forgets he is a Sonne.* Wherefore his carriage to his Parents is alwayes respectfull. It may chance that his father may be kept in a charitable Prison, whereof his Sonne hath the keyes; the old man being onely Tenant for life, and the lands entaild on our young Gentleman. In such a case when it is in his power, if necesfity requires, he enlargeth his father to such a reasonable proportion of liberty as may not be injurious to himself.

4. *He rather desires his fathers Life then his Living.* This was one of the principall reasons (but God knows how true) why Philip the second, King of Spain, caused in the yeare 1568. Charles his Eldest Sonne to be executed for plotting his fathers death, as was pretended. And a \* Wit in such difficult toyes accommodated the numerall letters in Ovids verse to the yeare wherein the Prince suffered.

\* *Opmerus was the Authour thereof: Famianus Strada de bello Belgico lib.* 7.*pag.* 432.

FILIV*s ante* DI*e*M *patr*I*os* I*nq*V*l*rI*t In annos.*
1568.
*Before the-t*IM*e, the o*V*er-hasty sonne*
*Seeks forth ho*VV *near the fathers* LI*fe* I*s Done.*
1568.

But if they had no better evidence againſt him but this poeticall Synchroniſme, we might well count him a martyr.

5. *His fathers deeds and grants he ratifies and confirms.* If a ſtitch be fallen in a leaſe, he will not widen it into an hole by cavilling, till the whole ſtrength of the grant run out thereat; or take advantage of the default of the Clark in writing where the deed appears really done, and on a valuable conſideration: He counts himſelf bound in honour to perform what by marks and ſignes he plainly underſtands his father meant, though he ſpake it not out.

6. *He reflecteth his luſtre to grace and credit his younger brethren.* Thus Scipio Africanus, after his great victories againſt the Carthaginians and conquering of Hannibal, was content to ſerve as a * Lieutenant in the warres of Aſia, under Lucius Scipio his younger Brother.

* *Plutar. in the life of Scipio.*

7. *He relieveth his diſtreſſed kinred, yet ſo as he continues them in their calling.* Otherwiſe they would all make his houſe their hoſpitall, his kinred their calling. When one being an Husbandman challenged kinred of Robert Groſthead Biſhop of Lincoln, and thereupon requeſted favour of him to beſtow an office on him, *Couſen* (quoth the Biſhop) *if your cart be broken, I'le mend it; if your plough old, I'le give you a new one, and ſeed to ſow your land: but an Husbandman I found you, and an Husbandman I'le leave you.* It is better to eaſe poore kinred in their Profeſſion, then to eaſe them from their Profeſſion.

8. *He is carefull to ſupport the credit and dignity of his family:* neither waſting his paternall eſtate by his unthriftineſſe, nor marring it by parcelling his ancient mannours and demeſnes amongſt his younger children, whom he provides for by annuities, penſions, moneys, leaſes, and purchaſed lands. He remembers how when our King Alfred divided the river of Lee (which parts Hartfordſhire and Eſſex) into three ſtreams,

streams, it became so shallow that boats could not row, where formerly ships did ride. Thus the ancient family of the Woodfords (which had long continued in Leicestershire and elsewhere in England in great account, estate and livelihood) is at this day quite extinct. For when S.r Thomas Woodford in the reigne of King Henrie the sixth made almost an even partition of his means betwixt his five Grandchildren, the House in short space utterly decay'd; not any part of his lands now in the *tenure or name of any of his male line, some whereof lived to be brought to a low ebbe of fortune. Yet on the other side to leave all to the eldest, and make no provision for the rest of their children, is against all rules of religion, forgetting their Christian-name to remember their Sir-name.

* *Burton in his descrip. of Leicestershire, p. 264.*

## Chap. 15.

### The Younger Brother.

SOme account him the better Gentleman of the two, because sonne to the more ancient Gentleman. Wherein his Elder Brother can give him the hearing, and a smile into the bargain. He shares equally with his Elder Brother in the education, but differs from him in his portion, and though he giveth also his Fathers Armes, yet to use the Herauld's language, he may say,

*This to my Elder Brother I must yield,*
*I have the Charge but he hath all the Field.*

Like herein to a young nephew of Tarquines in Rome, who was called *Egereus*, from wanting of maintenance, because his Grandfather left him nothing. It was therefore a mannerly answer which a young Gentleman gave to King James, when he asked him what kinne he was to such a Lord of his name: *Please your Majestie* (said he) *my Elder Brother is his Cousen german.*

* *Livi. lib. 1.*

He

**Maxime 1**   *He repines not at the Providence of God in ordering his birth.* Heirs are made, even where matches are, both in heaven. Even in twinnes God will have one next the doore to come first into the world.

**2**   *He labours by his endeavours to date himself an Elder Brother.* Nature makes but one; Industry doth make all the sonnes of the same man Heirs. The fourth Brother gives a Martilet for the difference of his Armes: a bird * observed to build either in Castles, Steeples, or Ships; shewing that the bearer hereof, being debarr'd from all hopes of his fathers inheritance, must seek by warre, learning, or merchandize to advance his estate.

*\* Gerard Leigh in his 9. differences of Brothers Armes.*

**3**   *In warre he cuts out his fortunes with his own sword.* William the Conquerour, when he first landed his forces in England, burnt all his ships; that despair to return might make his men the more valiant. Younger Brothers, being cut off at home frō all hopes, are more zealous to purchase an honourable support abroad. Their small Arteries with great Spirits have wrought miracles, & their resolution hath driven successe before it. Many of them have adventured to cheapen dear enterprises, & were onely able to pay the earnest, yet fortune hath accepted them for chapmen, and hath freely forgiven thē the rest of the payment for their boldnes.

**4**   *Nor are they lesse happy if applying themselves to their book.* Nature generally giving them good wits, which because they want room to burnish may the better afford to soar high.

**5**   *But he gaineth more wealth if betaking himself to merchandize.* Whence often he riseth to the greatest annuall honour in the kingdome. Many families in England though not first raised frō the City, yet thence have been so restored and enriched that it may seem to amount to an originall raising. Neither doth an apprentiship extinguish native, nor disinable to acquisitive Gentry; and they are much mistaken who hold it to be in the nature of bondage. For first, his indenture is a civill contract,

contract, whereof a bondman is uncapable: secondly, no work can be base prescribed in reference to a noble end, as theirs is that learn an honest mystery to inable them for the service of God and the Countrey: thirdly, they give round summes of money to be bound. Now if apprentiship be a servitude, it is either a pleasing bondage, or strange madnesse to purchase it at so dear a rate. Gentry therefore may be suspended perchance, & asleep during the apprentiship, but it awakens afterwards.

*Sometimes he raiseth his estate by applying himself to the Court.* A pasture wherein Elder Brothers are observed to grow lean, and Younger Brothers fat. The reasons whereof may be these.

1 Younger Brothers, being but slender in estate, are easier bowed to a Court-complyance then Elder Brothers, who stand more stiff on their means, and think scorn to crave what may be a Princes pleasure to grant, and their profit to receive.

2 They make the Court their calling, and studie the mysterie thereof, whilest Elder Brothers, divided betwixt the Court and the Countrey, can have their endeavours deep in neither, which run in a double channel.

3 Elder Brothers spend highly in proportion to their estates, expecting afterwards a return with increase, which notwithstanding never payes the principall: and whilest they thus build so stately a stair-case to their preferment, the Younger Brothers get up by the back stairs in a private silent way, little expence being expected from them that have little.

*Sometimes he lighteth on a wealthy match to advance him.* If meeting with one that is Pilot of her own affections, to steer them without guidance of her friends, and such as disdaineth her marriage should be contracted in an exchange, where joynture must weigh every grain even to the portion. Rather she counts it an act both of love and charity to affect one rich in deserts, who commonly hath the advantage of birth, as she hath of means, and so it's made levell betwixt them. And thus many a young Gentleman hath gotten honourable maintenance by an Heiresse, especially when the crying of the child hath caused the laughing of the father.

8. *His means the more hardly gotten are the more carefully kept.* Heat gotten by degrees, with motion and exercise, is more naturall and stayes longer by one, then what is gotten all at once by coming to the fire. Goods acquired by industry prove commonly more lasting then lands by descent.

9. *He ever owneth his Elder Brother with dutifull respect*: yea though God should so blesse his endeavours as to go beyond him in wealth and honour. The pride of the Jesuites is generally taxed, who being the youngest of all other Orders, and therefore by canon to go last, will never go in * Procession with other Orders, because they will not come behind them.

\* *Vid. Preface to the Jesuites Catechism.*

10. *Sometimes the Paternall inheritance falls to them who never hoped to rise to it.* Thus John, sirnamed Sans-terre, or, Without land, having five Elder Brothers came to the kingdome of England, death levelling those which stood betwixt him and the Crown. It is observ'd of the * Coringtons, an ancient familie in Cornwall, that for eight lineall descents never any one that was born heir had the land, but it ever fell to Younger Brothers.

\* *Carew Survey of Cornwall, fol. 117.*

To conclude, there is a hill in Voitland (a small countrey in Germany) called *Feitchtelberg*, out of which arise foure rivers running foure severall wayes, viz. 1. Eger, East, 2. Menus, West, 3. Sala, North, & 4. Nabus, South: so that he that sees their fountains so near together would admire at their falls so farre asunder. Thus the younger sons issuing out of the same mothers wombe and fathers loyns, and afterwards embracing different courses to trie their fortunes abroad in the world, chance often to die farre off, at great distance, which were all born in the same place.

# The Holy State.

## THE SECOND BOOK.

### CHAP. I.
### *The good * Advocate.*

<small>* we take it promiscuously for Civil or Common Lawyer.</small>

HE is one that will not plead that cause, wherein his tongue must be confuted by his conscience. It is the praise of the Spanish souldier, that (whilest all other Nations are mercenary, and for money will serve on any side) he will never fight against his own King: nor will our Advocate against the Sovereigne Truth, plainly appearing to his conscience.

*He not onely hears but examines his Client, and pincheth the cause, where he fears it is foundred.* For many Clients in telling their case rather plead then relate it, so that the Advocate hears not the true state of it, till opened by the adverse party. Surely the Lawyer that fills himself with instructions will travell longest in the cause without tiring. Others that are so quick in searching, seldome search to the quick; and those miraculous apprehensions who understand more then all, before the Client hath told half, runne without their errand, and will return without their answer.

*If the matter be doubtfull, he will onely warrant his own diligence.* Yet some keep an Assurance-office in their chamber,

<small>Maxime 1</small>

<small>2</small>

chamber, and will warrant any cause brought unto them, as knowing that if they fail they lose nothing but what long since was lost, their credit.

3   He makes not a Trojan-siege of a suit, but seeks to bring it to a set battell in a speedy triall. Yet sometimes suits are continued by their difficulty, the potencie and stomach of the parties, without any default in the Lawyer. Thus have there depended suits in * Glocester-shire, betwixt the Heirs of the Lord Barkley, and S[r]. Thomas Talbot Viscount Lisle, ever since the reigne of King Edward the fourth untill now lately they were finally compounded.

*Cambdens Brit. in Glocest.*

4   He is faithfull to the side that first retains him. Not like * Demosthenes, who secretly wrote one oration for Phormio, and another in the same matter for Apolidorus his adversary.

*Plutarch. in vita Demosth.*

5   In pleading he shoots fairly at the head of the cause, and having fastened, no frowns nor favours shall make him let go his hold. Not snatching aside here and there, to no purpose, speaking little in much, as it was said of Anaximenes, *That he had a flood of words, and a drop of reason.* His boldnesse riseth or falleth as he apprehends the goodnesse or badnesse of his cause.

6   He joyes not to be retain'd in such a suit, where all the right in question, is but a drop blown up with malice to be a bubble. Wherefore in such triviall matters he perswades his Client to sound a retreat, and make a composition.

7   *When his name is up, his industry is not down, thinking to plead not by his study but his credit.* Commonly Physicians like beer are best when they are old, & Lawyers like bread when they are young and new. But our Advocate grows not lazie. And if a leading case be out of the road of his practice, he will take pains to trace it thorow his books, and prick the footsteps thereof wheresoever he finds it.

8   He is more carefull to deserve, then greedy to take fees. He accounts the very pleading of a poore widows honest cause

cause sufficient fees, as conceiving himself then the King of Heavens Advocate, bound *ex officio* to prosecute it. And although some may say that such a Lawyer may even go live in Cornwall, where it is * observed that few of that profession hitherto have grown to any great livelihood, yet shall he (besides those two felicities of * common Lawyers, that they seldome die either without heirs or making a will) find Gods blessing on his provisions and posterity.

* *Carew Sur. of Cornwall, fol.* 60.

* *Coke in his Preface to Littletons Tenures.*

We will respit him a while till he comes to be a Judge, and then we will give an example of both together.

## Chap. 2.
## The good Physician.

*HE trusteth not the single witnesse of the water if better testimony may be had.* For reasons drawn from the urine alone are as brittle as the urinall. Sometimes the water runneth in such post-haft through the sick mans body, it can give no account of any thing memorable in the passage, though the most judicious eye examine it. Yea the sick man may be in the state of death, and yet life appear in his state.

Maxime 1

*Coming to his patient he perswades him to put his trust in God the fountain of health.* The neglect hereof hath caused the bad successe of the best Physicians: for God will manifest that though skill comes mediately from him to be gotten by mans pains, successe comes from him immediately to be disposed at his pleasure.

2

*He hansells not his new experiments on the bodies of his patients;* letting loose mad receipts into the sick mans body, to try how well Nature in him will fight against them, whilest himself stands by and sees the battel, except it be in desperate cases when death must be expell'd by death.

3

*To poore people he prescribes cheap but wholesome medicines:*

4

H 3                not

not removing the confumption out of their bodies into their purfes; nor fending them to the Eaft Indies for drugs, when they can reach better out of their gardens.

5

*Stephens Apology for Herodotus, lib. 1. cap. 16.*

Left his Apothecary fhould overfee, he overfees his Apothecary. For though many of that profefsion be both able and honeft, yet fome out of ignorance or hafte may miftake: witneffe one of Bloys, * who being to ferve a Doctours bill, in ftead of *Optimi* (fhort written) read *Opii*, and had fent the patient afleep to his grave, if the Doctours watchfulneffe had not prevented him; worfe are thofe who make wilfull errours, giving one thing for another. A prodigall who had fpent his eftate was pleafed to jeer himfelf, boafting that he had cofened thofe who had bought his means; They gave me (faid he) good new money, and I fold them my Great-great-grandfathers old land. But this cofenage is too too true in many Apothecaries, felling to fick folk for new money antiquated drugs, and making dying mens Phyfick of dead ingredients.

6

He brings not news with a falfe fpie that the coaft is clear till death furprifes the fick man. I know Phyficians love to make the beft of their patients eftate. Firft 'tis improper that *Adjutores vitæ* fhould be *Nuncii mortis*. Secondly, none, with their good will, will tell bad news. Thirdly, their fee may be the worfe for't. Fourthly, 'tis a confefsing that their art is conquer'd. Fifthly, it will poyfon their patients heart with grief, and make it break before the time. However they may fo order it, that the party may be inform'd of his dangerous condition, that he be not outed of this world before he be provided for another.

7

When he can keep life no longer in, he makes a fair & eafie paffage for it to go out. He giveth his attendance for the facilitating and affwaging of the pains and agonies of death. Yet generally 'tis death to a Phyfician to be with a dying man.

*Vnworthy*

*Vnworthy pretenders to Physick are rather foils then stains to the Profession.* Such a one was that counterfeit, who called himself *The Baron of* *Blackamore*, and feigned he was sent from the Emperour to our young King Henry the sixth, to be his principall Physician: but his forgery being discovered, he was apprehended, and executed in the Tower of London, *Anno* 1426. and such the world daily swarms with. Well did the Poets feigne Æsculapius and Circe, brother and sister, and both children of the Sunne: for in all times in the opinion of the multitude, witches, old women, and impostours have had a competition with Physicians. And commonly the most ignorant are the most confident in their undertakings, and will not stick to tell you what disease the gall of a dove is good to cure. He took himself to be no mean Doctour, who being guilty of no Greek, and being demanded why it was called an *Hectick fever*; *because* ( saith he ) *of an hecking cough which ever attendeth that disease.* And here it will not be amisse to describe the life of the famous Quacksalver Paracelsus, both because it is not ordinarily to be met with, and that men may see what a monster many make a miracle of learning, and propound him their pattern in their practice.

8

* *Stowes Survey of London.* pag. 55.

CHAP. 3.

Physick Proffessor at Basil.
Philip Theophrastus PARACELSUS *He died at Saltzburge* Anº. Dom: 1540. *aged 47 yeares*.
W. Marshall *sculpsit.*

## CHAP. 3.

### *The life of* PARACELSUS.

PHilip Theophrastus Bombastus of Hoenhaim, or Paracelsus, born as he saith himself in the wildernesse of Helvetia, *Anno* 1493. of the noble and ancient family of the Hoenhaims. But Thomas Erastus making strict enquiry after his pedigree found none of his name or kinred in that place. Yet it is fit so great a Chymist should make himself to be of noble extraction: And let us believe him to be of high descent,

scent, as perchance born on some mountain in Switzerland.

As for his Education, he himself * boasts that he lived in most Universities of Europe; surely rather as a traveller then a student, and a vagrant then a traveller. Yea some will not allow him so much, and * one who hath exactly measured the length of his life, though crowding his pretended travells very close, finds not room enough for them. But 'tis too ridiculous what a * Scholar of his relates, that he lived ten years in Arabia to get learning, and conversed in Greece with the Athenian Philosophers. Whereas in that age Arabia the Happy was accursed with Barbarisme, and Athens grown a stranger to her self; both which places being then subjected to the Turks, the very ruines of all learning were ruin'd there. Thus we see how he better knew to act his part, then to lay his Scene, and had not Chronologie enough to tell the clock of time, when and where to place his lies to make them like truth.

The first five & twenty years of his age he lived very civilly; being thirty years old he came to Basill, just at the alteration of Religion, when many Papists were expell'd the University, and places rather wanted Professours, then Professours places. Here by the favour of Oecolampadius he was admitted to reade Physick, & for two years behaved himself fairly, till this accident caused his departure. A rich * Canon of Basill being sick promised Paracelsus an hundred florens to recover him, which being restored to his health he denied to pay. Paracelsus sues him, is cast in his suit, the Magistrate adjudging him onely an ordinary fee, because the cure was done presently with a few pills. The Physician enraged hereat talked treason against the State in all his discourses, till the nimblenesse of his tongue forc'd the nimblenesse of his feet, and he was fain to fly into Alsatia. Here keeping company with the

* *In præfatione Chirurgiæ magnæ.*

* *Sennertus de Chymicorum consensu, cap. 4. pag. 35.*

* *Bickerus in Hermete redivivo.*

* *Bezoldus consideratione vitæ & mort. p. 76. ex Andreæ Jocisio.*

the Gentry of the countrey, he gave himself over to all licentiousnesse: His body was the sea wherein the tide of drunkennesse was ever ebbing and flowing; for by putting his finger in his throat he used to spew out his drink and drunkennesse together, and from that instant date himself sober to return to his cups again. Every moneth he had a new sute, not for pride but necessity; his apparel serving both for wearing and bedding: and having given his clothes many vomits, he gave them to the poore. Being Codrus over night, he would be Crœsus in the morning, flush of money as if he carried the invisible Indies in his pocket: some suspected the devil was his pursebearer, and that he carried a spirit in the pomel of his sword his constant companion, whilest others maintain that by the heat of the furnace he could ripen any metall into gold.

All the diet he prescribed his patients was this, to eat what, and how often, they thought fitting themselves, and yet he did most strange cures. Like the quicksilver (he so much dealt with) he would never be fixt in one place, or live any where longer then a twelvemoneth: for some observe that by that time the maladies reverted again, which he formerly cured. He gave so strong physick as summoned Nature with all her force to expell the present disease, but the remnant dregs thereof afterwards reinforcing themselves did assault Nature tired out with the violence of her former task, and easily subdued it.

His Scholars brag that the fragments of his learning would feast all the Philosophers in the world, boasting that the gout, the disgrace of Physick, was the honour of Paracelsus, who by curing it removed that scandall from his profession: whereas others say he had little Learning, and lesse Latine. When any asked him the name of an herb he knew not, he would tell them there was no * use thereof in Physick; and

\* *Beroldus ut prius pag.*77.

Chap. 3.   *The life of* Paracelsus.

and yet this man would undertake not onely to cure men, but to cure the Art of curing men, and reform Physick it self.

As for his religion, it would as well pose himself as others to tell what it was. He boasted that shortly he would order Luther and the Pope, as well as he had done Galen and Hippocrates. He was never seen to pray, and seldome came to Church. He was not onely skilled in naturall Magick (the utmost bounds whereof border on the suburbs of hell) but is charged to converse constantly with familiars. Guilty he was of all vices but wantonnesse; and I find an * honest man his Compurgatour, that he was not given to women; perchance he drank himself into wantonnesse and past it, quenching the fire of his lust by piling fuell too hard and fast upon it.

\* *Oporinus in Epist. de Paracelso.*

Boasting that he could make a man immortall, he himself died at fourty seven years in the City of Saltzburg. His Scholars say he was poysoned through the envy (that dark shadow ever waiting on a shining merit) and malice of his adversaries. However his body should have been so fenced with antidotes, that the battery of no poyson might make a breach therein; except we impute it more to his neglect then want of skill, and that rather his own security then his enemies malice brought him to his grave. But it may be he was willing to die, counting a twelvemoneths time enough to stay in one place, and fourty seven years long enough to live in one world. We may more admire that so beastly a drunkard lived so long, then that so skilfull a man died so soon. In a word, He boasted of more then he could do, did more cures seemingly then really, more cures really then lawfully; of more parts then learning, of more fame then parts; a better Physician then a man, and a better Chirurgeon then Physician.

I 2    CHAP. 4.

## Chap. 4.

### The Controversiall Divine.

HE is Truths Champion to defend her against all adversaries, Atheists, Hereticks, Schismaticks, and Erroneous persons whatsoever. His sufficiency appears in Opposing, Answering, Moderating, and Writing.

*Maxime 1*    *He engageth both his judgement, and affections in opposing of falsehood.* Not like countrey Fencers, who play onely to make sport, but like Duellers indeed, at it for life and limbe; chiefly if the question be of large prospect, and great concernings, he is zealous in the quarrell. Yet some, though their judgement weigh down on one side, the beam of their affections stands so even, they care not which part prevails.

2    *In opposing a truth, he dissembles himself her foe, to be her better friend.* Wherefore he counts himself the greatest conquerour when Truth hath taken him captive. With Joseph having sufficiently sifted the matter in a disguise, he discovereth himself, * *I am Joseph your brother*, and then throws away his visard. Dishonest they, who though the debt be satisfied will never give up the bond, but continue wrangling, when the objection is answered.

\* Gen. 45. 4.

3    *He abstains from all foul and railing language.* What? make the Muses, yea the Graces scolds? Such purulent spittle argues exulcerated lungs. Why should there be so much railing about the body of Christ? when there was none about the body of Moses in the Act kept betwixt the devil and Michael the Archangel.

4    *He tyrannizeth not over a weak and undermatch'd Adversary*; but seeks rather to cover his weaknesse if he be a modest man. When a Professour pressed an Answerer

er ( a better Christian then a Clerk ) with an hard argument, *Reverende Professor* ( said he ), *ingenuè confiteor me non posse respondere huic argumento.* To whom the Professour, *Recte respondes.*

In *answering he states the question, and expoundeth the terms thereof.* Otherwise the disputants shall end, where they ought to have begun, in differences about words, and be Barbarians each to other, speaking in a Language neither understand. If the Question also be of Historicall cognizanse, he shews the pedigree thereof, who first brew'd it, who first broch'd it, and sends the wandring Errour with a pasport home to the place of its birth.

In *taking away an objection he not onely puts by the thrust, but breaks the weapon.* Some rather escape then defeat an argument, and though by such an evasion they may shut the mouth of the Opponent, yet may they open the difficulty wider in the hearts of the hearers. But our Answerer either fairly resolves the doubt; or else shews the falseness of the argument, by beggering the Opponent to maintain such a fruitfull generation of absurdities, as his argument hath begotten; or lastly returns and retorts it back upon him again. The first way unties the knot; the second cuts it asunder; the third whips the Opponent with the knot himself tyed. Sure 'tis more honour to be a clear Answerer, then a cunning Opposer, because the latter takes advantage of mans ignorance, which is ten times more then his knowledge.

*What his answers want in suddennesse they have in solidity.* Indeed the speedy answer addes lustre to the disputation, and honour to the disputant; yet he makes good payment, who though he cannot presently throw the money out of his pocket, yet will pay it, if but going home to unlock his chest. Some that are not for speedy may be for sounder performance. When Melanchthon at the disputation of Ratisbon was

I 3 pressed

*The Holy State.* Book II.

pressed with a shrewd argument by Ecchius, I will answer thee, said he, to morrow. Nay, said Ecchius, do it now or it's nothing worth. Yea, said Melanchthon, I seek the Truth, and not mine own Credit, and therefore it will be as good if I answer thee to * morrow by Gods assistance.

<small>* Melchior Adam. in vitis Germ.Theolog. p. 339.</small>

8. *In moderating he sides with the Answerer, if the Answerer sides with the truth.* But if he be conceited, & opinioned of his own sufficiency, he lets him swound before he gives him any hot water. If a Paradox-monger, loving to hold strange yea dangerous Opinions, he counts it charity to suffer such a one to be beaten without mercy, that he may be weaned from his wilfulnesse. For the main, he is so a staff to the Answerer, that he makes him stand on his own legs.

9. *In writing, his Latine is pure, so farre as the subject will allow.* For those who are to climbe the Alpes are not to expect a smooth and even way. True it is that Schoolmen, perceiving that fallacy had too much covert under the nap of flourishing Language, used thredbare Latine on purpose, and cared not to trespasse on Grammar, and tread down the fences thereof to avoid the circuit of words, and to go the nearest way to expresse their conceits. But our Divine though he useth barbarous School-terms, which like standers are fixt to the controversie, yet in his moveable Latine, passages, and digressions his style is pure and elegant.

10. *He affects clearnesse and plainnesse in all his writings.* Some mens heads are like the world before God said unto it, *Fiat lux.* These dark-lanterns may shine to themselves, and understand their own conceits, but no body else can have light from them. Thus Matthias Farinator Professour at Vienna, assisted with some other learned men, as the Times then went, was thirty years making a book of applying Plato's, Aristotle's, and Galen's rules in Philosophy, to Christ and his Prophets, and 'tis call'd * *Lumen animæ ; quo tamen nihil est caliginosius,*

<small>* Mercator Atlas in the descrip. of Austria.</small>

*caliginosius, labore magno, sed ridiculo, & inani.* But this obscurity is worst when affected, when they do as Persius, of whom * one saith, *Legi voluit quæ scripsit, intelligi noluit quæ legerentur.* Some affect this darknesse, that they may be accounted profound, whereas one is not bound to believe that all the water is deep that is muddy.

* Scalig. de Arte poet. lib. 6. c. 6.

11

*He is not curious in searching matters of no moment.* Captain Martin * Forbisher fetcht from the farthest northern Countries a ships lading of minerall stones (as he thought) which afterwards were cast out to mend the high wayes. Thus are they served, and misse their hopes, who long seeking to extract hidden mysteries out of nice questions, leave them off, as uselesse at last. Antoninus Pius, for his desire to search to the least differences, was called *Cumini sector,* the Carver of cumine seed. One need not be so accurate: for as soon shall one scowr the spots out of the moon, as all ignorance out of man. When Eunomius the Heretick vaunted that he knew God and his divinity, S. * Basil gravells him in 21 questions about the body of an ant or pismire: so dark is mans understanding. I wonder therefore at the boldnesse of some, who as if they were Lord Mashalls of the Angels place them in ranks and files. Let us not believe them here, but rather go to heaven to confute them.

* Cambdens Elisab. anno. 1576.

* Epist. 168. quæ est ad Eunomium.

12

*He neither multiplies needlesse, nor compounds necessary Controversies.* Sure they light on a labour in vain, who seek to make a bridge of reconciliation over the μέγα χάσμα betwixt Papists and Protestants; for though we go 99 steps, they (I mean their Church) will not come one to give us a meeting. And as for the offers of Clara's and private men (besides that they seem to be more of the nature of baits then gifts) they may make large profers, without any Commission to treat, and so the Romish Church not bound to pay their promises. In * Merionethshire in Wales there are high mountains,

* Giraldus Camb. in descr. of Wales.

mountains, whose hanging tops come so close together that shepherds on the tops of severall hills may audibly talk together, yet will it be a dayes journey for their bodies to meet, so vast is the hallownesse of the vallies betwixt them. Thus upon sound search shall we find a grand distance and remotenesse betwixt Popish and Protestant tenents to reconcile them, which at the first view may seem near, and tending to an accomodation.

*He is resolute and stable in fundamentall points of Religion.* These are his fixed poles, and axletree about which he moves, whilest they stand unmoveable. Some sail so long on the Sea of controversies, toss'd up and down, to and fro, *Pro* and *Con*, that the very ground to them seems to move, and their judgements grow scepticall and unstable in the most settled points of Divinity. When he cometh to Preach, especially if to a plain Auditory, with the Paracelsians he extracts an oyl out of the driest and hardest bodies, and knowing that knotty timber is unfit to build with, he edifies people with easie and profitable matter.

CHAP. 5.

WILLIAM WHITACRES D<sup>r</sup>. of D: Kinges Professor and Master of S<sup>nt</sup> Iohns Coll in Cambridge. where He died An° 1595. Aged 47 yeares.

*W. Marshall sculp:*

## Chap. 5.

### The life of D<sup>r</sup>. Whitaker.

William Whitaker born at Holm in the County of Lancaster of good parentage, especially by his mothers side, allied to two worshipfull families. His reverend unckle, Alexander Nowell, Dean of S. Pauls ( the first fruits of the English Confessours in the dayes of Queen Marie, who after her death first return'd into England from beyond the Seas ) took him young from his parents, sent him first to Pauls School,

School, thence to Trinity Colledge in Cambridge; where he so profited in his studies, that he gave great promises of his future perfection.

I passe by his youthfull exercises, never striving for the garland, but he wonne and wore it away. His prime appearing to the world, was when he stood for the Professours place against two Competitours, in age farre his superiours. But the seven Electours in the Universitie who were to choose the Emperour of the Schools, preferring a golden head before silver hairs, conferr'd the place on Whitaker; and the strict form of their Election hath no room for corruption. He so well acquitted himself in the place that he answered expectation, the strongest opponent in all disputes and lectures, and by degrees taught envie to admire him.

By this time the Papists began to assault him, and the Truth. First Campian, one fitter for a Trumpeter then a Souldier, whose best ability was that he could boast in good Latine, being excellent at the flat hand of Rhetorick (which rather gives pats then blows) but he could not bend his fist to dispute. Whitaker both in writing and disputing did teach him, that it was easier to make then maintain a challenge against our Church; and in like manner he handled both Duræus, and Sanders, who successively undertook the same cause, solidly confuting their arguments.

But these Teazers, rather to rouze then pinch the Game, onely made Whitaker find his spirits. The fiercest dog is behind even Bellarmine himself, a great scholar, and who wanted nothing but a good cause to defend, and generally writing ingeniously, using sometimes slenting, seldome down-right railing. Whitaker gave him all fair quarter, stating the question betwixt them, yielding all which the other in reason could ask, and agreeing on terms to fall out with him, plaid fairly but fiercely on him, till the other forsook the field.

Bellarmine

# Chap. 5. *The life of D<sup>r</sup>. Whitaker.*

Bellarmine had no mind to reinforce his routed arguments, but rather consigned over that service to a new Generall, Stapleton an English man: He was born the same * yeare and moneth wherein S<sup>r</sup>. Thomas More was beheaded, an observation little lesse then mysticall with the Papists, as if God had substituted him to grow up in the room of the other for the support of the Catholick cause. If Whitaker in answering him put more gall then usuall into his ink, Stapleton (whose mouth was as foul as his cause) first infected him with bitternesse: and none will blame a man for arming his hands with hard and rough gloves, who is to meddle with bryers and brambles.

* *Pitzeus, De illust. Angl. scrip. Ætat. 16. pag. 796.*

Thus they baited him constantly with fresh dogs: None that ran at him once desired a second course at him; and as * one observes, *Cum nullo hoste unquam conflixit, quem non fudit & fugavit.*

* *Davenant. in Præfat. De Judice & Norma fidei.*

He filled the Chair with a gracefull presence, so that one needed not to do with him as * Luther did with Melanchthon when he first heard him reade, abstract the opinion and sight of his stature and person, lest the meannesse thereof should cause an undervaluing of him: for our Whitakers person carried with it an excellent port. His style was manly for the strength, maidenly for the modesty, and elegant for the phrase thereof; shewing his skill in spinning a fine thred out of course wool, for such is controversiall matter. He had by his second wife, a modest woman, eight children. It being true of him also, what is said of the famous Lawyer * Andreas Tiraquillus, *singulis annis singulos libros & liberos Reipublicæ dedit.*

* *In epist. ad Spalatinum.*

* *Thuanus, obit. doct. vir. anno 1558.*

My Father hath told me, that he often wished that he might lose so much Learning as he had gotten in after-supper studies, on condition he might gain so much strength as he had lost thereby. Indeed his body was strongly built for the naturall temper, and well repair'd repair'd by his temperate diet and recreations; but first he foundred the foundation of this house by immoderate study, and at last the roof was set on fire by a hot disease.

The unhappy controversie was then started, Whether justifying faith may be lost. And this thorny question would not suffer our Nightingale to sleep. He was sent for up by Arch-bishop Whitgift to the conference at Lambeth, after which returning home, unseasonable riding, late studying, and night-watching brought him to a burning-fever, to which his body was naturally disposed; as appeared by the mastery of rednesse in his complexion. Thus lost he the health of his body, in maintaining, That the health of the soul could not be lost. All agreed that he should be let bloud; which might then easily have been done, but was deferred by the fault of some about him, till it was too late. Thus, when God intends to cut a mans life off, his dearest friends by dangerous involuntarie mistakes shall bring the knife. He died in the 47. yeare of his age, *Anno Dom.* 1595. and in S. Johns Colledge ( whereof he was Master ) was solemnly interred, with the grief of the University, and whole Church of God.

CHAP. 6.

## Chap. 6.

### The true Church Antiquary.

HE is a traveller into former times, whence he hath learnt their language and fashions. If he meets with an old manuscript, which hath the mark worn out of its mouth, and hath lost the date, yet he can tell the age thereof either by the phrase or character.

*He baits at middle Antiquity, but lodges not till he comes at that which is ancient indeed.* Some scoure off the rust of old inscriptions into their own souls, cankering themselves with superstition, having read so often *Orate pro anima*, that at last they fall a praying for the departed; and they more lament the ruine of Monasteryes, then the decay and ruine of Monks lives, degenerating from their ancient piety and painfulnesse. Indeed a little skill in Antiquity inclines a man to Popery; but depth in that study brings him about again to our religion. A Nobleman who had heard of the extreme age of one dwelling not farre off, made a journey to visit him, and finding an aged person sitting in the chimney-corner, addressed himself unto him with admiration of his age, till his mistake was rectified: for, *Oh Sʳ*, (said the young-old man) *I am not he whom you seek for, but his sonne; my father is farther off in the field.* The same errour is daily comitted by the Romish Church, adoring the reverend brow and gray hairs of some ancient Ceremonyes, perchance but of some seven or eight hundred years standing in the Church, and mistake these for their fathers, of farre greater age in the Primitive times.

*He desires to imitate the ancient Fathers, as well in their Piety, as in their Postures.* Not onely conforming his hands and knees, but chiefly his heart to their

Maxime 1.

2

pattern. O the holinesse of their living and painfulnesse of their preaching! how full were they of mortified thoughts, and heavenly meditations! Let us not make the ceremoniall part of their lives onely Canonicall, and the morall part thereof altogether Apocrypha, imitating their devotion not in the finenesse of the stuff, but onely in the fashion of the making.

3. *He carefully marks the declination of the Church from the Primitive purity.* Observing how sometimes humble devotion was contented to lie down, whilest proud superstition got on her back. Yea not onely Frederick the Emperour, but many a godly Father some hundreds of years before held the Popes stirrop, and by their well-meaning simplicity gave occasion to his future greatnesse. He takes notice how their Rhetoricall hyperboles were afterwards accounted the just measure of dogmaticall truths; How plain people took them at their word in their funerall apostrophes to the dead; How praying for the departed brought the fuell, under which after-ages kindled the fire of Purgatory; How one Ceremony begat another, there being no bounds in will-worship, wherewith one may sooner be wearied then satisfied; the inventours of new Ceremonyes endeavouring to supply in number, what their conceits want in solidity; How mens souls being in the full speed and career of the Historicall use of Pictures could not stop short, but must lash out into superstition, vailing their bonnets to Rome in civill courtesie, when making honourable mention thereof, are interpreted by modern Papists to have done it in adoration of the idole of the Popes infallibility. All these things he ponders in his heart, observing both the times and places, when and where they happened.

4. *He is not zealous for the introducing of old uselesse Ceremonies.* The mischief is, some that are most violent to bring

Chap. 6.   *The true Church Antiquary.*   71

bring such in, are most negligent to preach the cautions in using them; and simple people, like Children in eating of fish, swallow bones and all to their danger of choking. Besides, what is observed of horse-hairs, that lying nine dayes in water they turn to snakes; so some Ceremonies though dead at first, in continuance of time quicken, get stings, and may do much mischief, especially if in such an age wherein the meddling of some have justly awaked the jealousie of all. When many Popish tricks are abroad in the countrey; if then men meet with a Ceremony which is a stranger, especially if it can give but a bad account of it self, no wonder if the watch take it up for one on suspicion.

5. *He is not peremptory but conjecturall in doubtfull matters.* Not forcing others to his own opinion; but leaving them to their own libertie; not filling up all with his own conjectures to leave no room for other men: nor tramples he on their credits, if in them he finds slips and mistakes. For here our souls have but one eye (the Apostle saith, *we know in part*) be not proud if that chance to come athwart thy seeing side, which meets with the blind side of another.

6. *He thankfully acknowledgeth those by whom he hath profited.* Base natured they, who when they have quenched their own thirst, stop up, at least muddy, the fountain. But our Antiquary, if he be not the first Founder of a commendable conceit, contents himself to be a Benefactour to it in clearing and adorning it.

7. *He affects not phancy-full singularity in his behaviour*: Nor cares he to have a proper mark in writing of words, to disguise some peculiar letter from the ordinary character. Others, for fear travellers should take no notice that skill in Antiquity dwells in such an head, hang out an antique hat for the signe, or use some
obsolete

obsolete garb in their garments, gestures, or discourse.

**8** He doth not *so adore the Ancients as to despise the Modern.* Grant them but dwarfs, yet stand they on giants shoulders, and may see the further. Sure, as stout champions of Truth follow in the rere, as ever march'd in the front. Besides, as * one excellently observes, *Antiquitas seculi juventus mundi.* These times are the ancient times, when the world is ancient; and not those which we count ancient *ordine retrogrado,* by a computation backwards from our selves.

* *Sr. Fran. Ba on Advance.of learn. p. 46.*

## Chap. 7.

### *The generall Artist.*

I Know the generall cavill against generall learning is this, that *aliquis in omnibus est nullus in singulis.* He that sips of many arts, drinks of none. However we must know, that all learning, which is but one grand Science, hath so homogeneall a body, that the parts thereof do with a mutuall service relate to, and communicate strength and lustre each to other. Our Artist knowing language to be the key of learning, thus begins.

Maxime 1. *His tongue being but one by nature he gets cloven by art and industry.* Before the confusion of Babel, all the world was one continent in language; since divided into severall tongues, as severall ilands. Grammer is the ship, by benefit whereof we passe from one to another, in the learned languages generally spoken in no countrey. His mother-tongue was like the dull musick of a monochord, which by study he turns into the harmony of severall instruments.

2. *He first gaineth skill in the Latine and Greek tongues.* On the

the credit of the former alone, he may trade in discourse over all *Christendome*: But the Greek, though not so generally spoken, is known with no lesse profit, and more pleasure. The joynts of her compounded words are so naturally oyled, that they run nimbly on the tongue; which makes them though long never tedious, because significant. Besides, it is full and stately in sound: onely it pities our Artist to see the vowels therein rackt in pronouncing them, hanging oftentimes one way by their native force, and haled another by their accents which countermand them.

*Hence he proceeds to the Hebrew, the mother-tongue of the world.* More pains then quicknesse of wit is required to get it, and with daily exercise he continues it. Apostacy herein is usuall to fall totally from the language by a little neglect. As for the Arabick, and other Orientall languages, he rather makes sallies and incursions into them, then any solemn sitting down before them.

*Then he applies his study to Logick, and Ethicks.* The latter makes a mans soul mannerly & wise; but as for Logick, that is the armory of reason, furnished with all offensive and defensive weapons. There are Syllogismes, long swords; Enthymems, short daggers; Dilemma's, two-edged swords that cut on both sides; Sorites, chain-shot: And for the defensive, Distinctions, which are shields; Retortions, which are targets with a pike in the midst of them, both to defend and oppose. From hence he raiseth his studies to the knowledge of Physicks, the great hall of Nature, and Metaphysicks the closet thereof; and is carefull not to wade therein so farre, till by subtle distinguishing of notions he confounds himself.

*He is skilfull in Rhetorick, which gives a speech colour, as Logick doth favour, and both together beauty.* Though some condemne Rhetorick as the mother of lies, speaking more then the truth in Hyperboles, lesse in her Miosis,

L     other-

otherwise in her metaphors, contrary in her ironies; yet is there excellent use of all these, when disposed of with judgement. Nor is he a stranger to Poetry, which is musick in words; nor to Musick, which is poetry in sound: both excellent sauce, but they have liv'd and died poore, that made them their meat.

6. *Mathematicks he moderately studieth to his great contentment.* Using it as ballast for his soul, yet to fix it not to stall it; nor suffers he it to be so unmannerly as to justle out other arts. As for judiciall Astrology (which hath the least judgement in it) this vagrant hath been whipt out of all learned corporations. If our Artist lodgeth her in the out-rooms of his soul for a night or two, it is rather to heare then believe her relations.

7. *Hence he makes his progresse into the study of History.* Nestor, who lived three ages, was accounted the wisest man in the world. But the Historian may make himself wise by living as many ages as have past since the beginning of the world. His books enable him to maintain discourse, who besides the stock of his own experience may spend on the common purse of his reading. This directs him in his life, so that he makes the shipwracks of others sea-marks to himself; yea accidents which others start from for their strangenes, he welcomes as his wonted acquaintance, having found presidents for them formerly. Without History a mans soul is purblind, seeing onely the things which almost touch his eyes.

8. *He is well seen in Chronology, without which History is but an heap of tales.* If by the Laws of the land he is counted a Naturall, who hath not wit enough to tell twenty, or to tell his \* age; he shall not passe with me for wise in learning, who cannot tell the age of the world, and count hundreds of years: I mean not so critically, as to solve all doubts arising thence; but that he may be able to give some tolerable account thereof. He is also acquainted

*Fits Herbert de nat. brev. de Idiota inquiren.*

quainted with Cosmography, treating of the world in whole joynts; with Chorography, shredding it into countries; and with Topography, mincing it into particular places.

Thus taking these Sciences in their generall latitude, he hath finished the round circle or golden ring of the arts; onely he keeps a place for the diamond to be set in, I mean for that predominant profession of Law, Physick, Divinity, or State-policie, which he intends for his principall Calling hereafter.

CHAP. 8.

Iulius Cæsar SCALIGER, a great Restorer of Learninge. He died at Agen in France. Anº. Dñi. 1558. aged 75 yeares. *W.M. sculp:*

## Chap. 8.

### The life of Julius Scaliger.

I Know my choice herein is liable to much exception. Some will make me the pattern of ignorance, for making this Scaliger the pattern of the generall Artist, whose own sonne Joseph might have been his father in many arts. But all things considered, the choice will appear well advised, even in such variety of examples. Yet let him know that undertakes to pick out the best ear amongst an acre of wheat, that
he

he shall leave as good if not a better behind him, then that which he chooseth.

He was born *Anno* 1484. in Italie, at the Castle of Ripa upon lacus Benacus, now called *Lago di Garda*, of the illustrious and noble family of the Scaligers, Princes, for many hundreds of years, of Verona, till at last the Venetians outed them of their ancient inheritance. Being about eleven years old, he was brought to the Court of Maximilian Emperour of Germany, where for seventeen years together he was taught learning, and military discipline. I passe by his valiant performances atchieved by him, save that this one action of his is so great and strong, it cannot be kept in silence, but will be recorded.

In the cruel battel at Ravenna betwixt the Emperour and the French, he not onely bravely fetch'd off the dead bodies of Benedictus and Titus his father and brother, but also with his own hands rescued the Eagle (the standard Imperiall) which was taken by the enemies. For which his prowesse Maximilian knighted him, and with his own hands put on him the golden spurres, and chain, the badges of knight-hood.

Amidst these his Martiall employments he made many a clandestine match with the Muses, and whilest he expected the tides and returns of businesse, he fill'd up the empty places of leisure with his studies. Well did the Poets feigne Pallas Patronesse of arts and armes, there being ever good intelligence betwixt the two Professions, and as it were but a narrow cut to ferry over out of one into the other. At last Scaliger sounded a retreat to himself from the warres, and wholly applyed himself to his book, especially after his wandring life was fixed by marriage unto the beautifull Andietta Lobeiaca, with whom he lived at Agin, near Montpeliar in France.

His Latine was twice refined, and most criticall, as appears by his own writings, and notes on other Authours.

thours. He was an accurate Grecian, yet began to study it, when well nigh fourty years old, when a mans tongue is too stiff to bow to words. What a torture was it to him who flowed with streams of matter then to learn words, yea letters, drop by drop? But nothing was unconquerable to his pains, who had a golden wit in an iron body. Let his book of Subtilties witnesse his profound skill in Logick, and Naturall Philosophy.

His skill in Physick was as great, as his practice therein was happy; in so much that he did many strange and admirable cures. Heare how a * noble and learned pen doth commend him:

*Stephanus Boetius Regius Senator Burdigolæ ad Vidum Brassacum Præsidem.*

> Non hunc fefellit ulla vis recondita
> Salubris herbæ, saltibus si quam aviis
> Celat nivosus Caucasus, seu quam procul
> Riphæa duro contigit rupes gelu.
> Hic jamq; spectantes ad orcum non semel
> Animas repressit victor, & membris suis
> Hærere succis compulit felicibus,
> Nigriq; avaras Ditis elusit manus.

> On snowy Caucasus there grew no root
> Of secret power, but he was privy to't;
> On cold Riphean hills no simple grew,
> But he the force thereof and virtue knew.
> Wherewith (apply'd by his successefull art)
> Such sullen souls as would this world depart,
> He forc'd still in their bodies to remain,
> And from deaths doore fetch'd others back again.

As for his skill in Physiognomy, it was wonderfull. I know some will say, that cannot be read in mens faces which was never wrote there, and that he that seeks to find the disposition of mens souls in the figures of their bodies, looks for letters on the backside of

Chap. 8.   *The life of* Julius Scaliger.   79

of the book. Yet is it credibly *averred that he never look'd on his infant-sonne Audectus but with grief, as sorrow struck with some sad signe of ill successe he saw in his face: which child at last was found stifled in bed with the embraces of his nurce being fast asleep.

*In vita Jul. Scalig. p. 54.

In Mathematicks he was no Archimedes, though he shewed his skill therein with the best advantage, and stood therein on his tiptoes, that his learning might seem the taller.

But in Poetry his over-measure of skill might make up this defect, as is attested by his book *de Arte Poetica*. Yet his own Poems are harsh, and unsmooth, (as if he rather snorted then slept on Parnassus) and they sound better to the brain then the eare. Indeed his censure in Poetry was incomparable; but he was more happy in repairing of Poems then in building them from the ground, which speaks his judgement to be better then his invention.

What shall I speak of his skill in History? whose own actions were a sufficient History. He was excellently vers'd in the passages of the world, both modern and ancient. Many modern languages, which departed from Babel in a confusion, met in his mouth in a method, being skilfull in the Sclavonick tongue, the Hungarian, Dutch, Italian, Spanish, and French.

But these his excellent parts were attended with prodigious pride; and he had much of the humour of the Ottomans in him, to kill all his brethren, and cry down all his equalls, which were corrivalls with him in the honour of arts, which was his principall quarrell with Cardan. Great was his spight at Erasmus, the morning-starre of learning, and one by whom Julius himself had profited, though afterwards he sought to put out that candle whereat he had lighted his own. In the bickering betwixt them, Erasmus pluckt Scaliger

ger by the long locks of his immoderate boasting, and touched him to the quick (a proud man lies pat for a jeering mans hand to hit) yea Erasmus was a badger in his jeeres, where he did bite he would make his teeth meet. Nor came Scaliger behind him in railing. However afterward Scaliger repented of his bitternesse, and before his death was * reconciled unto him.

<small>* Thuan. obit. Illustr. Anno. 1558.</small>

Thus his learning, being in the circuit of arts, spread so wide, no wonder if it lay thinne in some places. His parts were nimble, that starting so late he overtook, yea overran his equalls: so that we may safely conclude that making abatement for his military avocations, and late applying himself to study, scarce any one is to be preferred before him for generality of humane learning. He died *Anno* 1558. in the 75. yeare of his age.

### Chap. 9.
### *The faithfull Minister.*

WE suppose him not brought up by hand onely in his own countrey studies, but that he hath suckt of his Mother University, and throughly learnt the arts: Not as S. * Rumball, who is said to have spoken as soon as he was born, doth he preach as soon as he is Matriculated. Conceive him now a Graduate in arts, and entred into orders, according to the solemn form of the Church of England, and presented by some Patrone to a pastorall charge, or place equivalent, and then let us see how well he dischargeth his office.

<small>* Camb. Brit. in Northamptonshire.</small>

<small>Maxime 1</small>

*He endeavours to get the generall love and good will of his parish.* This he doth not so much to make a benefit of them, as a benefit for them, that his ministry may be more effectuall; otherwise he may preach his own heart out, before he preacheth any thing into theirs.

The

The good conceit of the Physician is half a cure, and his practice will scarce be happy where his person is hated; yet he humours them not in his Doctrine to get their love: for such a spanniel is worse then a dumbe dog. He shall sooner get their good will by walking uprightly, then by crouching and creeping. If pious living and painfull labouring in his calling will not win their affections, he counts it gain to lose them. As for those which causelessely hate him, he pities and prayes for them: and such there will be, I should suspect his preaching had no salt in it, if no gald horse did winse

*He is strict in ordering his conversation.* As for those who clense blurres with blotted fingers, they make it the worse. It was said of one who preach'd very well, & liv'd very ill, *That when he was out of the Pulpit, it was pity he should ever go into it, & when he was in the Pulpit, it was pity he should ever come out of it*: But our Minister lives Sermons. And yet I deny not but dissolute men, like unskilfull horsemen which open a gate on the wrong side, may by the virtue of their office open heaven for others, and shut themselves out.

*His behaviour towards his people is grave and courteous.* Not too austere and retired; which is laid to the charge of good Mr * Hooper the martyr, that his rigidnesse frighted people from consulting with him. *Let your light* (saith Christ) *shine before men*; whereas over reservednesse makes the brightest virtue burn dimme. Especially he detesteth affected gravity (which is rather on men then in them) whereby some belie their register-book, antedate their age to seem farre older then they are, and plait and set their brows in an affected sadnesse. Whereas S * Anthony the Monk might have been known among hundreds of his order by his cheerfull face, he having ever (though a most mortified man) a merry countenance.

*He doth not clash Gods ordinances together about precedency.* Not making odious comparisons betwixt Prayer and Preaching,

2

3

* *Fox, Acts and Mon. in his life.*

* *Athanasius in ejus vita.*

4

M

Preaching, Preaching and Catechising, Publick prayer and Private, Premeditate prayer and *Ex tempore*. When at the taking of new Carthage in Spain two Souldiers contended about the Murall crown (due to him who first climbed the walls) so that the whole army was thereupon in danger of division, * Scipio the Generall said, He knew that they both got up the wall together, and so gave the Scaling crown to them both. Thus our Minister compounds all controversies betwixt Gods ordinances, by praysing them all, practising them all, and thanking God for them all. He counts the reading of Common-prayers to prepare him the better for preaching; and as one said, if he did first toll the bell on one side, it made it afterwards ring out the better in his Sermons.

* *Plutarch in Scipio's life, pag. 1807.*

5 *He carefully Catechiseth his people in the elements of religion.* Except he hath (a rare thing) a flock without lambs, all of old sheep; and yet even Luther did not scorn to professe himself *Discipulum Catechismi*, a scholar of the Catechisme. By this Catechising the Gospel first got ground of Popery; and let not our Religion now grown rich be ashamed of that which first gave it credit and set it up, lest the Jesuites beat us at our own weapon. Through the want of this Catechising many which are well skilled in some dark out-corners of Divinity have lost themselves in the beaten road thereof.

6 *He will not offer to God of that which costs him nothing;* but takes pains aforehand for his Sermons. * Demosthenes never made any oration on the sudden; yea being called upon he never rose up to speak, except he had well studied the matter: and he was wont to say, *That he shewed how he honoured and reverenced the people of Athens because he was carefull what he spake unto them.* Indeed if our Minister be surprised with a sudden occasion, he counts himself rather to be excused then commended, if premeditating onely the bones of his Sermon he clothes

* *Plutarch in the life of Demosth.*

clothes it with flesh *ex tempore*. As for those, whose long custome hath made preaching their nature, that they can discourse Sermons without study, he accounts their examples rather to be admired then imitated.

*Having brought his Sermon into his head, he labours to bring it into his heart, before he preaches it to his people.* Surely that preaching which comes from the soul most works on the soul. Some have questioned ventriloquie, when men strangely speak out of their bellies, whether it can be done lawfully or no: might I coin the word *cordiloquie*, when men draw the doctrines out of their hearts, sure all would count this lawfull and commendable.

*He chiefly reproves the raigning sins of the time, and place he lives in.* We may observe that our Saviour never inveighed against Idolatry, Usury, Sabbath-breaking amongst the Jews; not that these were not sins, but they were not practised so much in that age, wherein wickednesse was spun with a finer thred: and therefore Christ principally bent the drift of his preaching against spirituall Pride, Hypocrisie, and Traditions then predominant amongst the people. Also our Minister confuteth no old Heresies which time hath confuted; nor troubles his Auditory with such strange, hideous cases of Conscience, that it is more hard to find the case then the resolution. In publick reproving of sinne, he ever whips the vice, and spares the person.

*He doth not onely move the bread of life, and tosse it up and down in generalities, but also breaks it into particular directions*: drawing it down to cases of Conscience, that a man may be warranted in his particular actions, whether they be lawfull or not. And he teacheth people their lawfull liberty as well as their restraints and prohibitions; for amongst men it is as ill taken to turn back favours, as to disobey commands.

*The places of Scripture he quotes are pregnant and pertinent.*

As for heaping up of many quotations, it smacks of a vain ostentation of memory. Besides, it is as impossible that the hearer should profitably retain them all, as that the preacher hath seriously perused them all: yea, whilest the auditours stop their attention, and stoop down to gather an impertinent quotation, the Sermon runs on, and they lose more substantiall matter.

11 *His similes and illustrations are alwayes familiar, never contemptible.* Indeed reasons are the pillars of the fabrick of a Sermon, but similitudes are the windows which give the best light. He avoids such stories whose mention may suggest bad thoughts to the auditours, and will not use a light comparison to make thereof a grave application, for fear lest his poyson go farther then his antidote.

12 *He provideth not onely wholsome but plentifull food for his people.* Almost incredible was the painfulnesse of Baronius, the compiler of the voluminous Annals of the Church, who for thirty years together preached * three or foure times aweek to the people. As for our Minister, he preferreth rather to entertain his people with wholsome cold meat which was on the table before, then with that which is hot from the spit, raw and half roasted. Yet in repetition of the same Sermon, every edition hath a new addition, if not of new matter of new affections. *Of whom*, saith S. Paul, *we have told you often, and now we tell you weeping.*

* The words being somwhat ambiguous are thus, In audiendis confessionibus, & sermonibus ad populum ter in hebdomada quatérve habendis per triginta & ampliùs annos diligentissimâ assiduitate laboravit, Spondanus in vita Baronii, pag.2. part.7.

13 *He makes not that wearisome, which should ever be welcome.* Wherefore his Sermons are of an ordinary length except on an extraordinary occasion. What a gift had John * Haselbach, Professour at Vienna, in tediousnesse? who being to expound the Prophet Esay to his auditours read twenty one years on the first Chapter, and yet finished it not.

* Mercator Atlas in the descrip. of Austria.

14 *He counts the successe of his Ministry the greatest preferment.* Yet herein God hath humbled many painfull pastours,
in

in making them to be clouds to rain, not over Arabia the happy, but over the stonie or desert: so that they may complain with the Herdsman in the Poet,

> *Heu mihi, quam pingui macer est mihi taurus in arvo?*
>   My starveling bull,
>   Ah woe is me,
>   In pasture full,
>   How lean is he?

Yet such Pastours may comfort themselves that great is their reward with God in heaven, who measures it not by their successe but endeavours. Besides, though they see not, their people may feel benefit by their Ministry. Yea the preaching of the Word in some places is like the planting of woods, where though no profit is received for twenty years together, it comes afterwards. And grant, that God honours thee not to build his temple in thy parish, yet thou maist with David provide metall and materialls for Solomon thy successour to build it with.

15. *To sick folks he comes sometimes before he is sent for,* as counting his vocation a sufficient calling. None of his flock shall want the extreme unction of Prayer and Counsell. Against the Communion especially he endeavours that Janus his temple be shut in the whole parish, and that all be made friends.

16. *He is never plaintiff in any suit but to be rights defendant.* If his dues be detained from him, he grieves more for his parishioners bad conscience then his own damage. He had rather suffer ten times in his profit, then once in his title, where not onely his person, but posterity is wronged: And then he proceeds fairly and speedily to a tryall, that he may not vex and weary others, but right himself. During his suit he neither breaks off nor slacks offices of courtesie to his adversary; yea though he loseth his suit, he will not also lose his charity. Chiefly he is respectfull to his Patrone, that as

he presented him freely to his living, so he constantly presents his Patrone in his prayers to God.

17. *He is moderate in his tenets and opinions.* Not that he gilds over lukewarmnesse in matters of moment with the title of discretion, but withall he is carefull not to entitle violence in indifferent and in concerning matters to be zeal. Indeed men of extraordinary tallnesse, (though otherwise little deserving) are made porters to lords, & those of unusuall littlenesse are made ladies dwarfs, whilest men of moderate stature may want masters. Thus many notorious for extremities may find favourers to preferre them, whilest moderate men in the middle truth may want any to advance them. But what saith the Apostle? *If in this life onely we had hope we are of all men the most miserable.*

18. *He is sociable and willing to do any courtesie for his neighbour Ministers.* He willingly communicates his knowledge unto them. Surely the gifts and graces of Christians lay in common, till base envy made the first enclosure. He neither slighteth his inferiours, nor repineth at those who in parts and credit are above him. He loveth the company of his neighbour Ministers. Sure as ambergreece is nothing so sweet in it self, as when it is compounded with other things; so both godly and learned men are gainers by communicating themselves to their neighbours.

19. *He is carefull in the discreet ordering of his own family.* A good Minister and a good father may well agree together. When a certain Frenchman came to visit * Melanchthon, he found him in his stove with one hand dandling his child in the swadling-clouts, and in the other hand holding a book and reading it. Our Minister also is as hospitable as his estate will permit, and makes every almes two by his cheerfull giving it. He loveth also to live in a well-repaired house, that he may serve God therein more cheerfully. A Clergieman who built his house from the ground,

* Pantaleon de Illustr. Germ. in vita Melanch.

ground wrote in it this counsell to his successour,
*If thou dost find an house built to thy mind*
     *Without thy cost,*
*Serve thou the more God and the poore;*
    *My labour is not lost.*

 Lying on his deathbed he bequeaths to each of his parishioners his *precepts* and *example* for a legacie: and they in requitall erect every one a monument for him in their hearts. He is so farre from that base jealousie that his memory should be outshined by a brighter successour, and from that wicked desire that his people may find his worth by the worthlesnesse of him that succeeds, that he doth heartily pray to God to provide them a better Pastour after his decease. As for outward estate, he commonly lives in too bare pasture to die fat: It is well if he hath gathered any flesh, being more in blessing then bulk.

20

CHAP. 10.

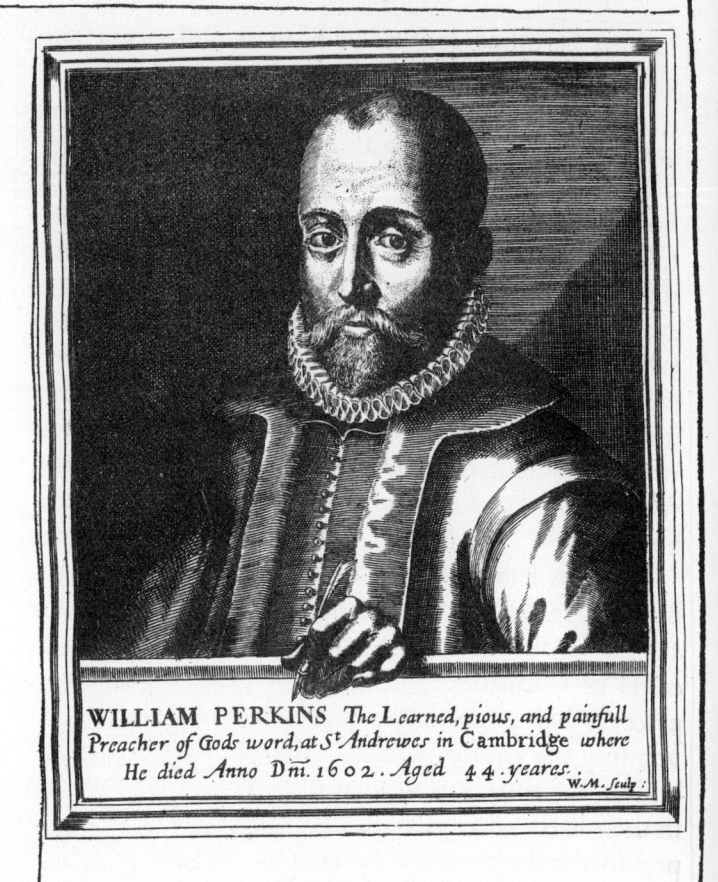

WILLIAM PERKINS The Learned, pious, and painfull Preacher of Gods word, at S.t Andrewes in Cambridge where He died Anno Dñi. 1602. Aged 44. yeares.
W.M. sculp:

CHAP. 10.

## The life of M.r PERKINS.

WIlliam Perkins, born at Marston nigh Coventry in Warwickshire, was afterwards brought up in Christ-Colledge in Cambridge, where he so well profited in his studies that he got the grounds of all liberall Arts, and in the 24. of Queen Elizabeth was chosen fellow of that Colledge, the same yeare wherein Doctour Andrew Willet (one of admirable industry ) and Doctour Richard Clark ( whose
learned

learned Sermons commend him to posterity ) were elected into the same Society.

There goeth an uncontroll'd tradition, that Perkins, when a young scholar, was a great studier of Magick, occasioned perchance by his skill in Mathematicks. For ignorant people count all circles above their own sphere to be conjuring, and presently cry out those things are done by black art for which their dimme eyes can see no colour in reason. And in such cases, when they cannot flie up to heaven to make it a Miracle, they fetch it from hell to make it Magick, though it may lawfully be done by naturall causes. True it is he was very wild in his youth till God ( the best Chymick who can fix quicksilver it self ) gratiously reclaim'd him.

After his entrance into the Ministry, the first beam he sent forth shined to those *which sat in darknesse and the shadow of death*, I mean the prisoners in the castle of Cambridge, people ( as generally in such places ) living in England out of Christendome, wanting the means of their salvation, bound in their bodies, but too loose in their lives, yea often branded in their flesh, and seared in their consciences. Perkins prevailed so farre with their jaylour, that the prisoners were brought (fetter'd) to the Shire-house hard by, where he preached unto them every Lords day. Thus was the prison his parish, his own Charity his Patron presenting him unto it, and his work was all his wages. Many an Onesimus here he begat, and as the instrument freed the prisoners from the captivity of sinne. When this began to be known, some of good quality of the neighbouring parishes became his auditours, and counted it their feast to feed out of the prisoners basket. Hence afterwards he became Preacher of S. Andrews parish in Cambridge, where he continued to the day of his death.

His Sermons were not so plain but that the piously learned

learned did admire them, nor so learned but that the plain did understand them. What was said of Socrates, That he first humbled the towring speculations of Philosophers into practice and morality; so our Perkins brought the schools into the Pulpit, and unshelling their controversies out of their hard school-terms, made thereof plain and wholsome meat for his people. For he had a capacious head with angles winding, and roomthy enough to lodge all controversiall intricasies; and, had not preaching diverted him from that way, he had no doubt attained to eminency therein. An excellent Chirurgeon he was at joynting of a broken soul, and at stating of a doubtfull conscience. And sure in Case-divinity Protestants are defective. For (save that a Smith or two of late have built them forges, and set up shop) we go down to our enemies to sharpen all our instruments, and are beholden to them for offensive and defensive weapons in Cases of Conscience.

He would pronounce the word *Damne* with such an emphasis as left a dolefull Echo in his auditours ears a good while after. And when Catechist of Christ-Colledge, in expounding the Commandments, applied them so home, able almost to make his hearers hearts fall down, and hairs to stand upright. But in his older age he altered his voice, and remitted much of his former rigidnesse, often professing that to preach mercie was that proper office of the Ministers of the Gospell.

Some object that his Doctrine, referring all to an absolute decree, hamstrings all industry, and cuts off the sinews of mens endeavours towards salvation. For ascribing all to the wind of Gods spirit, (which bloweth where it listeth) he leaveth nothing to the oars of mans diligence, either to help or hinder to the attaining of happinesse, but rather opens a wide doore to licentious security. Were this the hardest objection

*against*

*S. W. Mr. of S. C. C.*

against Perkins his doctrine, his own life was a sufficient answer thereunto, so pious, so spotlesse, that Malice was afraid to bite at his credit, into which she knew her teeth could not enter.

He had a rare felicity in speedy reading of books, and as it were but turning them over would give an exact account of all considerables therein. So that as it were riding post thorow an Authour, he took strict notice of all passages, as if he had dwelt on them particularly, perusing books so speedily, one would think he read nothing; so accurately, one would think he read all.

He was of a cheerfull nature and pleasant disposition: Indeed to mere strangers he was reserved and close, suffering them to knock a good while before he would open himself unto them; but on the least acquaintance he was merry and very familiar.

Besides his assiduity in preaching he wrote many books, extant at this day. And pity it was, that he set not forth more of them himself; for though some of his Orphan works lighted on good Guardians, yet all were not so happy; and indeed no nurse for a child to the own mother.

He dyed in the 44. yeare of his age of a violent fit of the stone. It hath been reported that he dyed in the conflict of a troubled conscience; which admit were so, had been no wonder. For God sometimes seemingly leaves his Saints when they leave the world, plunging them on their death-beds in deep temptations, and casting their souls down to hell, to rebound the higher to heaven. Besides, the devil is most busie on the last day of his Term; and a Tenant to be outed cares not what mischief he doth. But here was no such matter. Indeed he alwayes cryed out *Mercy Mercy:* which some standers by misinterpreted for despair, as if he felt not Gods favour, because he call'd for it: whereas Mercy is a Grace which they hold the fastest,

*S. W. ut priús.*

that most catch after it. 'Tis true that many on lesse reason have expressed more confidence of their future happinesse, and have delivered themselves in larger speeches concerning the same. But who could expect a long oration from him, where every word was accented with pain in so sharp a disease.

His funeralls were solemnly and sumtuously perform'd of the sole charges of Christ-Colledge, which challenged, as she gave him his breeding, to pay for his buriall; the University and Town lovingly contending which should expresse more sorrow thereat. Doctour Mountague, afterwards Bishop of Winchester, preached his Funerall-Sermon, and excellently discharg'd the place, taking for his Text, *Moses my servant is dead.*

He was of a ruddy complexion, very fat and corpulent, lame of his right hand; and yet this Ehud with a lefthanded pen did stab the Romish Cause, and * as one saith,

<small>* Hugh Holland in his Icones.</small>

*Dextera quantumvis fuerat tibi manca, docendi*
   *Pollebas mira dexteritate tamen.*

Though nature thee of thy right hand bereft,
Rightwell thou writest with thy hand that's left.

He was born the first, and dyed the last yeare of Queen Elisabeth, so that his life streamed in equall length with her reigne, and they both had their fountains, and falls together.

I must not forget, how his books after his death were translated into most modern Christian languages. For though he excellently improved his talent in the English tongue, yet forreiners thought it but wrapt up in a napkin, whilest folded in an unknown language. Wherefore some translated the main body of his works into French, Dutch, and Italian; and his books speak more tongues, then the Maker ever understood. His *Reformed Catholick* was done into Spanish, and no Spaniard ever since durst take up that
                                            gantlet

gantlet of defiance our Champion cast down: yea their Inquisition rather chose to answer it with tortures, then arguments.

## Chap. II.

### *The good Parishioner.*

WE will onely describe his Church-reference; his Civill part hath and shall be met with under other Heads. Conceive him to live under such a faithfull Minister as before was character'd, as, either judging charitably that all Pastours are such, or wishing heartily that they were.

*Though near to the Church he is not farre from God.* Like unto Justus, Acts 18.8. *One that worshipped God, and his house joyned hard to the Synagogue.* Otherwise if his distance from the church be great, his diligence is the greater to come thither in season.   *Maxime* 1

*He is timely at the beginning of Common prayer.* Yet as *Tullie Charged some dissolute people for being such sluggards that they never saw the sunne rising or setting, as being alwayes up after the one, and abed before the other; so some negligent people never heare prayers begun, or sermon ended: the Confession being past before they come, and the Blessing not come before they are passed away.   2  *De finibus boni & mali, lib. 2.*

*In sermon he sets himself to heare God in the Minister.* Therefore divesteth he himself of all prejudice, the jaundise in the eyes of the soul presenting colours false unto it. He hearkens very attentively: 'Tis a shame when the Church it self is *Cœmeterium*, wherein the living sleep above ground as the dead do beneath.   3

*At every Point that concerns himself, he turns down a leaf in his heart;* and rejoyceth that Gods word hath peirc'd him, as hoping that whilest his soul smarts it heals. And as it is no manners for him that hath good ve-   4 nison before him, to ask whence it came, but rather fairly to fall to it; so hearing an excellent Sermon, he never enquires whence the Preacher had it, or whether it was not before in print, but falls aboard to practise it.

5. *He accuseth not his Minister of spight for particularizing him.* It does not follow that the archer aimed, because the arrow hit. Rather our Parishioner reasoneth thus; If my sinne be notorious, how could the Minister misse it? if secret, how could he hit it without Gods direction? But foolish hearers make even the bells of Aarons garments *to clink as they think.* And a guilty conscience is like a whirlpool, drawing in all to it self which otherwise would passe by. One, causelessely disaffected to his Minister, complained that he in his last Sermon had personally inveighed against him, and accused him thereof to a grave religious Gentleman in the parish: *Truly,* said the Gentleman, *I had thought in his Sermon he had meant me, for it touched my heart.* This rebated the edge of the others anger.

6. *His Tithes he payes willingly with cheerfulnesse.* How many part with Gods portions grudgingly, or else pinch it in the paying.* *Decimum,* the Tenth, amongst the Romanes was ever taken for what was best or biggest. It falls out otherwise in paying of Tithes, where the least and leanest are shifted off to make that number.

\* *Fluctus Decimus,* pro *maximo.* Ovidio & Lucano.

7. *He hides not himself from any Parish-office which seeks for him.* If chosen Churchwarden, he is not busily-idle, rather to trouble then reform, presenting all things but those which he should. If Overseer of the poore, he is carefull the rates be made indifferent (whose inequality oftentimes is more burthensome then the summe) and well disposed of. He measures not peoples wants by their clamorous complaining, and dispenseth more to those that deserve then to them that onely need relief.

*He*

*He is bountifull in contributing to the repair of Gods house.* For though he be not of their opinion, who would have the Churches under the Gospell conform'd to the magnificence of Solomons Temple ( whose porch would serve us for a Church ) and adorn them so gaudily, that devotion is more distracted then raised, and mens souls rather dazeled, then lightened; yet he conceives it fitting that such sacred places should be handsomly and decently maintained : The rather because the climactericall yeare of many Churches from their first foundation, may seem to happen in our dayes; so old, that their ruine is threatned if not speedily repaired.

*He is respectfull to his Ministers widow and posterity for his sake.* When the onely daughter of Peter Martyr was, through the riot and prodigality of her debauched husband, brought to extreme poverty, the *State of Zurick, out of gratefull remembrance of her Father, supported her with bountifull maintenance. My prayers shall be, that Ministers widows, and children may never stand in need of such relief, and may never want such relief when they stand in need.

8

9

* *Thuan obit. vir. doct. Anno. 1562.*

## Chap. 12.

## *The good Patron.*

THat in the Primitive times ( though I dare not say generally in all Churches ) if not the sole choyce, at least the consent of the people was required in appointing of Ministers, may partly appear out of * Scripture, more plainly out of *Cyprian, and is confessed by reverend *Dr. Whitgift. These popular elections were well discharged in those purer times, when men being scoured with constant persecution had little leasure to rust with factions, and when there were no baits for Corruption; the places of Ministers being then of great pains and perill, and

* Acts 14.23.
χειροτονήσαντες
* *Lib.1.epist.4*
* *Defence of the Answer to the Admonition. pag.*164.

& small profit. But dissension creeping in, in after-ages (the eyes of common people at the best but dimme through ignorance being wholly blinded with partiality) it may seem their right of election was either devolved to, or assumed of the Bishop of the Dioces, who * onely was to appoint Curates in every parish. Afterwards to invite lay-men to build and endow Churches, the Bishops departed with their right to the lay Patrons according to the verse,

*Concil. Toletan. Anno 589. Can. 9. Synod. Antiochen. Can. 24. and 2. Contil. Gangrense Can. 7. and 8.*

*Patronum faciunt Dos, Aedificatio, Fundus.*
A Patron's he that did endow with lands,
Or built the Church, or on whose ground it stands.

It being conceived reasonable that he who payed the Churches portion, should have the main stroke in providing her an husband. Then came Patronages to be annexed to Mannours, and by sale or descent to passe along with them; nor could any justly complain thereof, if all Patrons were like him we describe.

**Maxime 1** *He counts the Living his to dispose, not to make profit of.* He fears more to lapse his conscience, then his Living, fears more the committing then the discovery of Simony.

**2** *A Benefice he sometimes giveth speedily, never rashly.* Some are long in bestowing them out of state, because they love to have many suiters; others out of covetousnesse will not open their wares till all their chapmen are come together, pretending to take the more deliberation.

**3** *He is deaf to opportunity, if wanting desert.* Yet is he not of the mind of Tamberlane the Scythian King, who never gave Office to any that sought for it: for desiring proceeds not alwayes from want of deserving; yea God himself likes well that his favours should be sued for. Our Patron chiefly respects piety, sufficiency, and promise of painfulnesse, whereby he makes his election. If he can by the same deed provide for Gods house and

Chap. 12.   *The good Patron.*   97

and his own familie, he counts it lawfull, but on no terms will preferre his dearest and nearest sonne or kinsman if unworthy

*He hates not onely direct simony, or rather Gehazisme, by the string, but also that which goes about by the bow.* Ancient Councels present us with severall forms hereof. I find how the Patrons sonnes and nephews were wont to feed upon the Incumbent, and eat out the presentation in great banquets and dinners, till at last the Palentine Councel brought a voyder to such feasts, and made a canon against them. But the former ages were bunglers to the cunning contrivance of the simony-engineers of our times. *O my soul come thou not into their secrets.* As if they cared not to go to hell, so be it were not the nearest way, but that they might fetch a farre compasse round about. And yet father * Campian must not carry it so clearly, who taxeth the Protestants for maintaining of simony. We confesse it a personall vice amongst us, but not to be charged as a Church-sinne, which by penall Laws it doth both prohibit and punish. Did Rome herein look upon the dust behind her own doores, she would have but little cause to call her neighbour slut. What saith the Epigram?

*An Petrus fuerat Romæ sub judice lis est;*
*Simonem Romæ nemo fuisse negat.*

That Peter was at Rome, there's strife about it;
That Simon was there, none did ever doubt it.

*He hates corruption not onely in himself, but his servants.* Otherwise it will do no good for the Master to throw bribes away, if the Men catch them up at the first rebound, yea before ever they come to the ground. * Cambden can tell you what Lord-Keeper it was in the dayes of Queen Elizabeth, who though himself an upright man was hardly spoken of for the basenesse of his servants in the sale of Ecclesiasticall preferments.

*margin:*
4
*Concil. Palent.*
*Anno 1322.*
*Constit. 14.*

* *Vid. Videl.*
*Comment. in*
*Epist. Ignatii*
*ad Trallenses.*

5

* *In the life of*
*Queen Elizab.*
*Anno Dom.*
*1596.*

O   *When*

6 *When he hath freely bestowed a Living, he makes no boasts of it.* To do this were a kind of spirituall simony, to ask and receive applause of others; as if the commonnesse of faulting herein made a right, and the rarity of giving things freely merited *ex condigno* a generall commendation. He expects nothing from the Clerk he presented but his prayers to God for him, respectfull carriage towards him, and painfulnesse in his Calling, who having gotten his place freely may discharge it the more faithfully: whereas those will scarce afford to feed their sheep fat, who rent the pasture at too high a rate.

To conclude, let Patrons imitate this particular example of King William Rufus, who (though sacrilegious in other acts) herein discharged a good conscience. Two Monks came to him to buy an Abbots place of him, seeking to outvie each other in offering great summes of money, whilest a third Monk stood by, and said nothing. To whom said the King, What wilt thou give for the place. Not a penny, answered he, for it is against my conscience; but here I stay to wait home on him whom your Royall pleasure shall designe Abbot. Then quoth the King, Thou of the three best deservest the place, and shalt have it, and so bestowed it on him.

CHAP. 13.

## Chap. 13.
### The good Landlord.

IS one that lets his land on a reasonable rate, so that the Tenant by employing his stock, and using his industry, may make an honest livelihood thereby, to maintain himself and his children.

*His rent doth quicken his Tenant but not gall him.* Indeed 'tis observed, that where Landlords are very easy, the Tenants ( but this is *per Accidens*, out of their own lazinesse ) seldome thrive, contenting themselves to make up the just measure of their rent, and not labouring for any surplusage of estate. But our Landlord puts some metall into his Tenants industry, yet not grating him too much, lest the Tenant revenge the Landlords cruelty to him upon his land.

*Yet he raiseth his rents ( or fines equivalent ) in some proportion to the present price of other commodities.* The plenty of money makes a seeming scarcity of all other things, and wares of all sorts do daily grow dear. If therefore our Landlord should let his rents stand still as his Grandfather left them, whilest other wares dayly go on in price, he must needs be cast farre behind in his estate.

*What he sells or sets to his Tenant, he suffers him quietly to enjoy according to his covenants.* This is a great joy to a Tenant, though he buyes dear to possesse without disturbance. A strange example there was of Gods punishing a covetous Landlord at * Rye in Sussex, *Anno* 1570. He having a certain marish, wherein men on poles did dry their fishnets, received yearly of them a sufficient summe of money, till not content therewith he caused his servant to pluck up the poles, not suffering the fishermen to use them any longer, except they would compound at a greater rate. But it came to passe the same night that the sea breaking in covered

*Maxime* 1

2

3

* *Holinshed p.* 1224.

covered the same marish with water, and so it still continueth.

**4**

*He detests and abhorres all inclosure with depopulation.* And because this may seem a matter of importance, we will break it into severall propositions.

1. *Inclosure may be made without depopulating.* Infinites of examples shew this to be true. But depopulation hath cast a slander on inclosure, which because often done with it, people suspect it cannot be done without it.

2. *Inclosure made without depopulating is injurious to none.* I mean if proportionable allotments be made to the poore for their commonage, and free & lease-holders have a considerable share with the lord of the mannour.

3. *Inclosure without depopulating is beneficiall to private persons.* Then have they most power and comfort to improve their own parts, and for the time, and manner thereof may mould it to their own conveniencie. The Monarch of one acre will make more profit thereof then he that hath his share in fourty in common.

4. *Inclosure without depopulating is profitable to the Commonwealth.* If injurious to no private person, and profitable to them all, it must needs be beneficiall to the Commonwealth, which is but the *Summa totalis* of sundry persons, as severall figures. Besides, if a Mathematician should count the wood in the hedges, to what a mighty forrest would it amount? This underwood serves for supplies to save timber from burning, otherwise our wooden walls in the water must have been sent to the fire. Adde to this the strength of an inclosed Countrey against a forrein invasion. Hedges and counter-hedges (having in number what they want in height and depth) serve for barracadoes, and will stick as birdlime in the wings of the horse, and

and scotch the wheeling about of the foot. Small resistance will make the enemy to earn every mile of ground as he marches. Object not, That inclosure destroyes tillage, the staff of a countrey, for it need not all be converted to pasturage. Cain and Abel may very well agree in the Commonwealth, the Plowman and Shepherd part the inclosures betwixt them.

5 *Inclosure with depopulation is a canker to the Commonwealth.* It needs no proof: wofull experience shews how it unhouses thousands of people, till desperate need thrusts them on the gallows. Long since had this land been sick of a plurisie of people, if not let blood in their Western Plantations.

6 *Inclosure with depopulation endammageth the parties themselves.* 'Tis a paradox and yet a truth, that reason shews such inclosures to be gainfull, and experience proves them to be losse to the makers. It may be, because God being φιλάνθρωπος, a Lover of man, mankind, and mens society, and having said to them, *Multiply and increase*, counts it an affront unto him, that men depopulate, and whereas bees daily swarm, men make the hives fewer. The margin shall direct you to the * Authour that counts eleven mannours in Northhamptonshire thus inclosed: which towns have vomited out (to use his own expression) and unburthened themselves of their former desolating and depopulating owners, and I think of their posterity.

* M<sup>r</sup> Benthams *Christian Conflict*, pag. 322.

*He rejoyceth to see his Tenants thrive.* Yea he counts it a great honour to himself, when he perceiveth that God blesseth their endeavours, and that they come forward in the world. I close up all with this pleasant story. A Farmer rented a Grange generally reported to be haunted by Faries, and paid a shrewd rent for the same at each

each half years end. Now a Gentleman asked him how he durst be so hardy as to live in the house, and whether no Spirits did trouble him. Truth (said the Farmer) *there be two Saints in heaven vex me more then all the devils in hell, namely the Virgin Mary, and Michael the Archangel*; on which dayes he paid his rent

## Chap. 14.

### The good Master of a Colledge.

THe Jews *Anno* 1348. were banished out of most countreys of Christendome, principally for poysoning of springs and *fountains. Grievous therefore is their offense, who infect Colledges, the fountains of learning and religion; and it concerneth the Church and State, that the Heads of such houses be rightly qualified, such men as we come to character.

* *Munster de German. lib. 3. pag. 457.*

**Maxime 1** *His learning if beneath eminency is farre above contempt.* Sometimes ordinary scholars make extraordinary good Masters. every one who can play well on Apollo's harp cannot skilfully drive his chariot, there being a peculiar mystery of Government. Yea as a little allay makes gold to work the better, so (perchance) some dulnesse in a man makes him fitter to manage secular affairs; and those who have climbed up Parnassus but half way better behold worldly businesse (as lying low and nearer to their sight) then such as have climbed up to the top of the mount.

**2** *He not onely keeps the Statutes (in his Study) but observes them*: for the maintaining of them will maintain him, if he be questioned. He gives them their true dimensions, not racking them for one, and shrinking them for another, but making his conscience his daily Visitour. He that breaks the Statutes, and thinks to rule better by his own discretion, makes many gaps in the hedge, and then stands to stop one of them with a stake

### Chap. 14. *The good Master of a Colledge.* 103

stake in his hand. Besides, thus to confound the will of the dead Founders, is the ready way to make living mens charitie ( like Sr Hugh Willoughby in discovering the Northern passage ) to be frozen to death, and will dishearten all future Benefactours.

*He is principall Porter, and chief Chappell-monitour.* For where the Master keeps his chamber alwayes, the scholars will keep theirs seldome, yea perchance may make all the walls of the Colledge to be gate. He seeks to avoid the inconvenience when the gates do rather divide then confine the scholars, when the Colledge is distinguished ( as France into *Cis & Transalpina*) into the part on this, and on the otherside of the walls. As for out-lodgings ( like galleries, necessary evils in populous Churches ) he rather tolerates then approves them.

3

*In his Elections he respecteth merit, not onely as the condition but as the cause thereof.* Not like Leofricus Abbot of S. Albans, who would scarce admit any into his Covent though well deserving, except he was a* Gentleman born. He more respects literature in a scholar, then great mens letters for him. A learned Master of a Colledge in Cambridge ( since made a reverend Bishop, and, to the great grief of good men and great losse of Gods Church, lately deceased ) refused a Mandate for choosing of a worthlesse man fellow. And when it was expected, that at the least he should have been outed of his Mastership for this his contempt, King James highly commended him, and encouraged him ever after to follow his own conscience, when the like occasion should be given him.

4

*Math. Parif. in 23. Abbat. S. Alban. pag. 42.*

*He winds up the Tenants to make good musick, but not to break them.* Sure Colledge-lands were never given to fat the Tenants and sterve the scholars, but that both might comfortably subsist. Yea generally I heare the Muses commended for the best Landladies, and a Colledge-lease is accounted but as the worst kind of freehold.

5

He

6    *He is observant to do all due right to Benefactours.* If not piety, policy would dictate this unto him. And though he respects not Benefactours kinsmen, when at their first admission they count themselves born heirs apparent to all preferment which the house can heap on them, and therefore grow lazy & idle; yet he counts their alliance, seconded with mediocrity of desert, a strong title to Colledge-advancement.

7    *He counts it lawfull to enrich himself, but in subordination to the Colledge good.* Not like Varus, Governour of Syria, who came poore into the countrey, and found it rich, but departed thence rich, and left the countrey poore. Methinks 'tis an excellent commendation which Trinity Colledge in Cambridge in her records bestows on Doctour Still once Master thereof. *Se ferebat Patremfamilias providum,* ἀγαθὸν κυρότροφον, *nec Collegio gravis fuit aut onerosus.*

8    *He disdains to nourish dissension amongst the members of his house.* Let Machiavills Maxime, *Divide & regnabis,* if offering to enter into a Colledge-gate, sink thorow the grate, and fall down with the durt. For besides that the fomenting of such discords agrees not with a good conscience, each party will watch advantages, and Pupils will often be made to suffer for their Tutours quarrells: *Studium partium* will be *magna pars studiorum,* and the Colledge have more rents then revenues.

9    *He scorneth the plot, to make onely dunces Fellows, to the end he may himself command in chief.* As thinking that they who know nothing, will do any thing, and so he shall be a figure amongst cyphers, a bee amongst drones. Yet oftentimes such Masters are justly met with, and they find by experience, that the dullest horses are not easiest to be reined. But our Master endeavours so to order his elections, that every Scholar may be fit to make a Fellow, and every Fellow a Master.

CHAP. 15.

## Chap. 14.
### The life of Dr. Metcalf.

Nicholas Metcalf Doctour of Divinity, extracted out of an ancient and numerous family of Gentry in Yorkshire, was Archdeacon of Rochester, & Chaplain to John Fisher the Bishop thereof; by whom this our Doctour was employed to issue forth the monies for the building of S. Johns Colledge in Cambridge. For Margaret Countesse of Richmond and Derby intending to graft S. Johns Colledge into the old stock of S. Johns Hospitall, referr'd all to the Bishop of Rochester, and he used Metcalf as an agent in all proceedings which did concern that Foundation: which will inferre him to be both a wise and an honest man.

Some make him to be but meanly *learned; and* one telleth us a long storie how a Sophister put a fallacie upon him, *a sensu diviso ad sensum compositum*, and yet the Doctours dimme eyes could not discern it. But such trifles were beneath him; and what wonder is it if a Generall long used in governing an armie, hath forgotten his school-play, and Fencers rules, to put by every thrust?

Doubtlesse, had not his learning been sufficient, Bishop Fisher, a great clerk himself, would not have placed him to govern the Colledge. But we know that some count all others but dry scholars, whose learning runneth in a different channell from their own: and it is possible, that the great distance betwixt men in matter of Religion might hinder the new learning in one to see the old learning in the other.

But grant that Metcalf, with Themistocles, could not fiddle, yet he could make a little city a great one: though dull in himself, he could whet others by his encouragement. He found the Colledge spending

* *Ascham: Schoolmaster, 2. Book, fol. 47.*
* *Lively in his Chron. of Persian Monarch. p. 196.*

P          scarce

scarce two hundred marks by the yeare, he left it spending a *thousand marks and more. For he not onely procured and settled many donations, and by-foundations (as we term them) of Fellowships, and Scholarships, founded by other; but was a Benefactour himself, *Pro certis ornamentis & structuris in Capella, & pro ædificatione sex Camerarum a tergo Coquinæ*, &c. as it is evidenced in the Colledge books. He counted the Colledge his own home, and therefore cared not what cost he bestowed on it: not like those Masters, who making their Colledges as steps to higher advancement will trample on them to raise up themselves, and using their wings to flie up to their own honour, cannot afford to spread them to brood their Colledge. But the thriving of the nourcery, is the best argument to prove the skill and care of the nource. See what store of worthy men the house in his time did yield:

*\* Ascham. in loco priùs citato.*

William Cecill, *Lord Burly,*  
S.<sup>r</sup> John Cheek, } *Statesmen.*  
Walter Haddon.

Ralph Bain, } { Coventrie and Lichfield  
John Christopherson, | Chichester,  
Robert Horn, } Bishop of { Winton,  
James Pilkinton, | Duresme,  
John Tailour, | Lincoln,  
Thomas Watson. } { Lincoln.

Roger Ascham,  
George *Bullock,  
Roger *Hutchinson, } *Learned writers.*  
Alban Langdale,  
John Seaton.

*\* Pitzeus de Scriptor. Angli. pag. 773.*  
*\* Baleus de Scriptor. Anglicanis.*

Hugh Fitz-Herbert,  
William Jreland,  
Laurence Pilkinton, } *Learned Men.*  
----------Tomson,  
Henry Wright.

With

With very many more. For though I dare not say that all these were old enough to bear fruit in Metcalfs time, yet sure I am by him they were inoculated, and in his dayes admitted into the Colledge.

Yet for all these his deserts Metcalf in his old age was expell'd the Colledge, and driven out when he could scarce go. A new generation grew up (advanced by him) whose active spirits stumbled at his gravity (young seamen do count ballast needlesse yea burthensome in a ship) and endeavoured his removall. It appears not what particular fault they laid to his charge. Some think that the Bishop of Rochester his good lord being put to death, occasioned his ruine, Fishers misfortune being Metcalfs highest misdemeanour. He sunk with his Patron, and when his sunne was set it was presently night with him: for according to the Spanish proverb, * *where goes the bucket, there goes the rope*, where the principall miscarries, all the dependants fall with him.

* *Yrà la soga con el calderon.*

Others conceive it was for his partiality in preferring Northern men, as if in his compasse there were no points but such onely as looked to the North, advancing alone his own countrey-men, and more respecting their need then deserts. Indeed long * before, I find William Millington first Provost of Kings Colledge put out of his place, for his partiality in electing Yorkshire men.

* 1446. Manuscrip Hutcher. Coll. Regal.

But herein Metcalf is sufficiently justified: for he found Charity hottest in the cold countrey, *Northern men were most * partiall* (saith one) *in giving lands to the Colledge, for the furtherance of learning*. Good reason therefore Northern Scholars should be most watered there, where Northern Benefactours rained most.

* *Ascham. in loco citato.*

Well, good old Metcalf must forsake the House. Methinks the blushing bricks seem asham'd of their ingratitudes, and each doore, window, and casement

ment in the Colledge, was a mouth to plead for him.

But what shall we say? Mark generally the grand deservers in States, and you shall find them lose their lustre before they end their life. The world, out of covetousnesse to save charges to pay them their wages, quarrelling with them, as if an over-merit were an offence. And whereas some impute this to the malignant influence of the heavens, I ascribe it rather to a pestilent vapour out of the earth; I mean, That rather men then starres are to be blamed for it.

He was twenty years Master, and on the 4 day of June 1537. went out of his office, and it seems dyed soon after: his Epitaph is fastned on a piece of brasse on the wall, in the Colledge-Chappell. We must not forget that all who were great doers in his expulsion, were great sufferers afterwards, and dyed all in great * miserie. There is difference betwixt prying into Gods secrets, and being stark blind: Yea I question whether we are not bound to look where God points by so memorable a judgement, shewing that those branches most justly whithered which pluck'd up their own root.

\* Omnes qui Metcalfi excludendi autores exstiterunt, multis adversæ fortunæ procellis (sive divinâ ultione seu fato suo) jactati, de gradu dejecti & deturbati, ingloríi mortem obierunt exemplo memorabili, *Caius lib. 1. Hist. Cantabr. pag. 75, & 76.*

CHAP. 16.

## Chap. 16.
### The good Schoolmaster.

There is scarce any profession in the Commonwealth more necessary, which is so slightly performed. The reasons whereof I conceive to be these: first, young scholars make this calling their refuge, yea perchance before they have taken any degree in the University, commence Schoolmasters in the countrey, as if nothing else were required to set up this profession but onely a rod and a ferula. Secondly, others who are able use it onely as a passage to better preferment, to patch the rents in their present fortune, till they can provide a new one, and betake themselves to some more gainfull calling. Thirdly, they are disheartned from doing their best with the miserable reward which in some places they receive, being Masters to the children, and slaves to their parents. Fourthly, being grown rich, they grow negligent, and scorn to touch the school, but by the proxie of an Usher. But see how well our Schoolmaster behaves himself.

*His genius inclines him with delight to this profession.* **Maxime 1**
Some men had as lieve be schoolboyes as Schoolmasters, to be tyed to the school as Coopers Dictionary, and Scapula's Lexicon are chained to the desk therein; and though great scholars, and skilfull in other arts, are bunglers in this: But God of his goodnesse hath fitted severall men for severall callings, that the necessities of Church, and State, in all conditions may be provided for. So that he who beholds the fabrick thereof may say, God hewed out this stone, and appointed it to lie in this very place, for it would fit none other so well, and here it doth most excellent. And thus God mouldeth some for a Schoolmasters life, undertaking it with desire and delight, and discharging it with dexterity and happy successe.

2. *He studieth his scholars natures as carefully as they their books*; and ranks their dispositions into severall forms. And though it may seem difficult for him in a great school to descend to all particulars, yet experienced Schoolmasters may quickly make a Grammar of boyes natures, and reduce them all (saving some few exceptions) to these generall rules.

1 Those that are ingenious and industrious. The conjunction of two such Planets in a youth presage much good unto him. To such a lad a frown may be a whipping, and a whipping a death; yea where their Master whips them once, shame whips them all the week after. Such natures he useth with all gentlenesse.

2 Those that are ingenious and idle. These think with the hare in the fable, that running with snails (so they count the rest of their school-fellows) they shall come soon enough to the Post, though sleeping a good while before their starting. Oh, a good rod would finely take them napping.

3 Those that are dull and diligent. Wines the stronger they be the more lees they have when they are new. Many boyes are muddy-headed till they be clarified with age, and such afterwards prove the best. Bristoll diamonds are both bright, and squared and pointed by Nature, and yet are soft and worthlesse; whereas orient ones in India are rough and rugged naturally. Hard rugged and dull natures of youth acquit themselves afterwards the jewells of the countrey, and therefore their dulnesse at first is to be born with, if they be diligent. That Schoolmaster deserves to be beaten himself, who beats Nature in a boy for a fault. And I question whether all the whipping in the world can make their parts, which are naturally sluggish, rise one minute before the houre Nature hath appointed. Those

Chap. 16.   *The good Schoolmaster*.   111

4 Those that are invincibly dull and negligent also. Correction may reform the latter, not amend the former. All the whetting in the world can never set a rasours edge on that which hath no steel in it. Such boyes he consigneth over to other professions. Shipwrights and boatmakers will choose those crooked pieces of timber, which other carpenters refuse. Those may make excellent merchants and mechanicks which will not serve for Scholars.

*He is able, diligent, and methodicall in his teaching* ; not leading them rather in a circle then forwards. He minces his precepts for children to swallow, hanging clogs on the nimblenesse of his own soul, that his Scholars may go along with him.

*He is, and will be known to be an absolute Monarch in his school.* If cockering Mothers proffer him money to purchase their sonnes an exemption from his rod (to live as it were in a peculiar, out of their Masters jurisdiction) with disdain he refuseth it, and scorns the late custome in some places of commuting whipping into money, and ransoming boyes from the rod at a set price. If he hath a stubborn youth, correction-proof, he debaseth not his authority by contesting with him, but fairly if he can puts him away before his obstinacy hath infected others.

*He is moderate in inflicting deserv'd correction.* Many a Shoolmaster better answereth the name of παιδοτρίβης then παιδαγωγὸς, rather tearing his scholars flesh with whipping, then giving them good education. No wonder if his scholars hate the Muses, being presented unto them in the shapes of fiends and furies. Junius complains *de insolenti* carnificina* of his Schoolmaster, by whom *conscindebatur flagris septies aut octies in dies singulos.* Yea heare the lamentable verses of poore Tusser in his own life :

* In his life, of his own writing.

From

> From Pauls I went, to Eaton sent,
> To learn straightwayes the Latine phrase,
> Where fifty three stripes given to me
> >  At once I had.
> For fault but small, or none at all,
> It came to passe thus beat I was;
> See, *Udal, see the mercy of thee
> > To me poore lad.

*Nich. Udal Schoolmaster of Eaton in the Reigne of King Henry the eight.

Such an Orbilius marres more Scholars then he makes: Their Tyranny hath caused many tongues to stammer, which spake plain by nature, and whose stuttering at first was nothing else but fears quavering on their speech at their Masters presence. And whose mauling them about their heads hath dull'd those who in quicknesse exceeded their Master.

6. *He makes his school free to him, who sues to him* in forma pauperis. And surely Learning is the greatest alms that can be given. But he is a beast, who because the poore Scholar cannot pay him his wages, payes the Scholar in his whipping. Rather are diligent lads to be encouraged with all excitements to Learning. This minds me of what I have heard concerning Mr. Bust, that worthy late Schoolmaster of Eaton, who would never suffer any wandring begging Scholar (such as justly the Statute hath ranked in the forefront of Rogues) to come into his school, but would thrust him out with earnestnesse (however privately charitable unto him) lest his school-boyes should be disheartned from their books, by seeing some Scholars after their studying in the University preferr'd to beggery.

7. *He spoyls not a good school to make thereof a bad Colledge*, therein to teach his Scholars Logick. For besides that Logick may have an action of trespasse against Grammar for encroaching on her liberties, Syllogismes are Solecismes taught in the school, and oftentimes they are forc'd afterwards in the University to unlearn the fumbling skill they had before.

*Out of his school he is no whit pedanticall in carriage or dis-*
*course*; contenting himself to be rich in Latine, though he doth not gingle with it in every company wherein he comes.

To conclude, Let this amongst other motives make Schoolmasters carefull in their place, that the eminencies of their Scholars have commended the memories of their Schoolmasters to posterity, who otherwise in obscurity had altogether been forgotten. Who had ever heard of R. * Bond in Lancashire but for the breeding of learned Ascham his Scholar? or of * Hartgrave in Brundly school, in the same County, but because he was the first did teach worthy Doctour Whitaker. Nor do I honour the memory of Mulcaster for any thing so much, as for his Scholar, that gulf of learning, Bishop Andrews. This made the Athenians, the day before the great feast of Theseus their founder, to sacrifice a ramme to the memory of * Conidas his Schoolmaster that first instructed him.

* *Grant. in vit. Ascham. pag. 629.*
* *Ashton in the life of Whitaker, pag. 29.*

* *Plutar. in vit. Thesei.*

## Chap. 17.
### The good Merchant

IS one who by his trading claspeth the iland to the continent, and one countrey to another. An excellent gardiner, who makes England bear wine, and oyl, and spices; yea herein goes beyond Nature in causing that *Omnis fert omnia tellus*. He wrongs neither himself, nor the Commonwealth, nor private chapmen which buy commodities of him. As for his behaviour towards the Commonwealth, it farre surpasses my skill to give any Rules thereof; onely this I know, that to export things of necesity, and to bring in forrein needlesse toyes, makes a rich Merchant, and a poore Kingdome: for the State loseth her radicall moysture, and gets little better then sweat in exchange, except

except the necessaries which are exported be exceeding plentifull, which then though necessary in their own nature become superfluous through their abundance. We will content our selves to give some generall advertisements concerning his behaviour towards his chapmen, whom he useth well in the quantity, quality, and price of the commodities he sells them.

*Maxime 1.*    *He wrongs not the buyer in Number, Weight, or Measure.* These are the Land-marks of all trading, which must not be removed: for such cosenage were worse then open felony. First, because they rob a man of his purse, & never bid him stand. Secondly, because highway-thieves defie, but these pretend justice. Thirdly, as much as lies in their power, they endeavour to make God accessary to their cosenage, deceiving by pretending his weights. For God is the principall clark of the market, *All the* * *weights of the bag are his work.*

\* Prov. 16.11.

2.    *He never warrants any ware for good but what is so indeed.* Otherwise he is a thief, and may be a murtherer, if selling such things as are apply'd inwardly. Besides, in such a case he counts himself guilty if he selleth such wares as are bad, though without his knowledge, if avouching them for good; because he may, professeth, & is bound to be Master in his own mystery, and therefore in conscience must recompence the buyers losse, except he gives him an Item to buy it at his own adventure.

3.    *He either tells the faults in his ware, or abates proportionably in the price he demands*: for then the low value shews the viciousnesse of it. Yet commonly when Merchants depart with their commodities, we heare (as in funerall orations) all the virtues but none of the faults thereof.

4.    *He never demands out of distance of the price he intends to take*: If not alwayes within the touch, yet within the reach of what he means to sell for. Now we must know there be foure severall prices of vendible things. First, the Price of the market, which ebbes and flows according

according to the plenty or scarcity of coyn, commodities, and chapmen. Secondly, the Price of friendship, which perchance is more giving then selling, and therefore not so proper at this time. Thirdly, the Price of fancie, as twenty pounds or more for a dog or hauk, when no such inherent worth can naturally be in them, but by the buyers and sellers fancie reflecting on them. Yet I believe the money may be lawfully taken. First, because the seller sometimes on those terms is as loth to forgo it, as the buyer is willing to have it. And I know no standard herein whereby mens affections may be measured. Secondly, it being a matter of pleasure, and men able and willing, let them pay for it, *Volenti non fit injuria*. Lastly, there is the Price of cosenage, which our Merchant from his heart detests and abhorres·

*He makes not advantage of his chapmans ignorance, chiefly if referring himself to his honesty*: where the sellers conscience is all the buyers skill, who makes him both seller and judge, so that he doth not so much ask as order what he must pay. When one told old Bishop Latimer that the Cutler had cosened him, in making him pay twopence for a knife not (in those dayes) worth a peny; *No*, quoth Latimer, *he cosen'd not me but his own conscience*. On the other side S.\*Augustine tells us of a seller, who out of ignorance asked for a book farre lesse then it was worth, and the buyer (conceive himself to be the man if you please) of his own accord gave him the full value thereof.

*He makes not the buyer pay the shot for his prodigality*; as when the Merchant through his own ignorance or ill husbandry hath bought dear, he will not bring in his unnecessary expences on the buyers score: and in such a case he is bound to sell cheaper then he bought.

*Selling by retail he may justifie the taking of greater gain*: because of his care, pains, and cost of fetching those wares

\* *Lib.* 13. *de Trinitat. c.* 3.

wares from the fountain, and in parcelling and dividing them. Yet because retailers trade commonly with those who have least skill what they buy, and commonly sell to the poorer sort of people, they must be carefull not to grate on their necessity.

But how long shall I be retailing out rules to this Merchant? It would employ a Casuist an apprentiship of years: take our Saviours whole-sale rule, *Whatsoever ye would have men do unto you, do you unto them; for this is the Low, and the Prophets.*

## Chap. 18.

### The good Yeoman

IS a Gentleman in Ore, whom the next age may see refined, and is the wax capable of a gentile impression, when the Prince shall stamp it. Wise Solon (who accounted *Tellus the Athenian the most happy man for living privately on his own lands) would surely have pronounced the English Yeomanry, a fortunate condition, living in the temperate Zone, betwixt greatnesse and want, an estate of people almost peculiar to England. France and Italy are like a die, which hath no points betwixt sink and ace, Nobility and Pesantry. Their walls though high, must needs be hollow, wanting filling-stones. Indeed Germany hath her Boores, like our Yeomen, but by a tyrannicall appropriation of Nobility to some few ancient families, their Yeomen are excluded from ever rising higher to clarifie their bloods. In England the Temple of Honour is bolted against none, who have passed through the Temple of Virtue: nor is a capacity to be gentile denyed to our Yeoman, who thus behaves himself.

*Maxime* 1. *He wears russet clothes, but makes golden payment,* having tinne in his buttons, and silver in his pocket. If he chance to appear in clothes above his rank, it is to grace

*Herodotus lib. 1. pag. 12*

grace some great man with his service, and then he blusheth at his own bravery. Otherwise he is the surest landmark, whence forreiners may take aim of the ancient English customes; the Gentry more floting after forrein fashions.

*In his house he is bountifull both to strangers, and poore people.* Some hold, when Hospitality dyed in England, she gave her last groan amongst the Yeomen of Kent. And still at our Yeomans table you shall have as many joints as dishes: No meat disguis'd with strange sauces; no straggling joynt of a sheep in the midst of a pasture of grasse, beset with sallads on every side, but solid substantiall food; no serviters (more nimble with their hands then the guests with their teeth) take away meat, before stomachs are taken away. Here you have that which in it self is good, made better by the store of it, and best by the welcome to it.

*He hath a great stroke in making a Knight of the shire.* Good reason, for he makes a whole line in the subsidie-book, where whatsoever he is rated he payes without any regret, not caring how much his purse is let blood, so it be done by the advise of the physicians of the State.

*He seldome goes farre abroad, and his credit stretcheth further then his travell.* He goes not to London, but *se defendendo*, to save himself of a fine, being returned of a Jurie, where seeing the King once, he prayes for him ever afterwards.

*In his own countrey he is a main man in Juries.* Where if the Judge please to open his eyes in matter of law, he needs not to be led by the nose in matters of fact. He is very observant of the Judges *item*, when it follows the truths *inprimis*; otherwise (though not mutinous in a Jurie) he cares not whom he displeaseth so he pleaseth his own conscience.

*He improveth his land to a double value by his good husbandry.* Some grounds that wept with water, or frown'd with thorns,

thorns, by draining the one, and clearing the other, he makes both to laugh and sing with corn. By marle and limestones burnt he bettereth his ground, and his industry worketh miracles, by turning stones into bread. Conquest and good husbandry both inlarge the Kings Dominions: The one by the sword, making the acres more in number; the other by the plough, making the same acres more in value. Solomon saith, *The King himself is maintained by husbandry.* Pythis * a King having discovered rich mines in his kingdome, employed all his people in digging of them, whence tilling was wholly neglected, insomuch as a great famine ensued. His Queen, sensible of the calamities of the countrey, invited the King her husband to dinner, as he came home hungry from overseeing his workmen in the mines. She so contrived it, that the bread and meat were most artificially made of gold; and the King was much delighted with the conceit thereof, till at last he called for reall meat to satisfie his hunger. *Nay,* said the Queen, *if you employ all your subjects in your mines, you must expect to feed upon gold, for nothing else can your kingdome afford.*

* Plutarch. de virtut. mulierum, exemplo ultimo.

7 *In time of famine he is the Joseph of the countrey, and keeps the poore from sterving.* Then he tameth his stacks of corn, which not his covetousnesse but providence hath reserv'd for time of need, and to his poore neighbours abateth somewhat of the high price of the market. The neighbour gentry court him for his acquaintance, which he either modestly waveth, or thankfully accepteth, but no way greedily desireth. He insults not on the ruines of a decayed Gentleman, but pities and relieves him: and as he is called *Goodman,* he desires to answer to the name, and to be so indeed.

8 *In warre, though he serveth on foot, he is ever mounted on an high spirit*: as being a slave to none, and a subject onely to his own Prince. Innocence and independance make a brave spirit: Whereas otherwise one must ask

Chap. 19.   *The Handicrafts-man.*

ask his leave to be valiant on whom he depends. Therefore if a State run up all to Noblemen and Gentlemen, so that the husbandmen be onely mere labourers, or cottagers, (which * one calls but hous'd beggers) it may have good Cavalry, but never good bands of foot; so that their armies will be like those birds call'd *Apodes*, without feet, alwayes onely flying on their wings of horse. Wherefore to make good Infantry, it requireth men bred, not in a servile or indigent fashion, but in some free and plentifull manner. Wisely therefore did that knowing Prince, King Henry the seventh, provide laws for the increase of his Yeomanry, that his kingdome should not be like to Coppice-woods, where the staddles being left too thick, all runs to bushes and briers, and there's little clean underwood. For enacting, that houses used to husbandry should be kept up with a competent proportion of land, he did secretly sow Hydra's teeth, whereupon (according to the Poets fiction) should rise up armed men for the service of this kingdome.

* *Bacons Henry. 7. pag. 74.*

## Chap. 19.

### *The Handicrafts-man.*

HE is a necessary member in a Common-wealth: For though Nature, which hath armed most other creatures, sent man naked into the world, yet in giving him hands and wit to use them, in effect she gave him Shells, Scales, Paws, Claws, Horns, Tusks, with all offensive and defensive weapons of Beasts, Fish and Fowl, which by the help of his hands in imitation he may provide for himself, and herein the skill of our Artisan doth consist.

*His trade is such whereby he provides things necessary for mankind.* What S. * Paul saith of the naturall, is also true

Maxime 1.
* *1. Cor. 12.*

of the politick body, those members of the body are much more necessary which seem most feeble. Mean trades for profit, are most necessary in the State; and a house may better want a gallery then a kitchin. The Philistins knew this when they massacred all the smiths in Israel (who might worse be spared then all the userers therein) and whose hammers nail the Commonwealth together, being necessary both in peace and warre.

2   *Or else his trade contributeth to mans lawfull pleasure.* God is not so hard a master, but that he alloweth his servants sauce (besides hunger) to eat with their meat.

3   *But in no case will he be of such a trade which is a mere Pander to mans lust*; and onely serves their wantonnesse (which is pleasure runne stark mad) and foolish curiosity. Yet are there too many extant of such professions, which, one would think, should stand in dayly fear left the world should turn wise, and so all their trades be cashierd, but that (be it spoken to their shame) 'tis as safe a tenure to hold a livelyhood by mens ryot, as by their necesfity.

4   *The wares he makes shew good to the eye, but prove better in the use.* For he knows if he sets his mark (the Towerstamp of his credit) on any bad wares, he sets a deeper brand on his own conscience. Nothing hath more debased the credit of our English cloth beyond the seas, then the deceitfulnesse in making them, since the Fox hath crept under the fliece of the Sheep.

5   *By his ingenuousnesse he leaves his art better then he found it.* Herein the Hollanders are excellent, where children get their living, when but newly they have gotten their life, by their industrie. Indeed Nature may seem to have made those Netherlanders the younger brethren of mankind, allowing them little land, and that also standing in dayly fear of a double deluge, of the sea and

and the Spaniard: but such is their painfulnesse and ingenuity, hating lazinesse as much as they love liberty, that what commodities grow not on their Countrey by nature they graft on it by art, and have wonderfully improved all making of Manufactures, Stuffes, Clocks, Watches: these latter at first were made so great and heavy, it was rather a burden then an ornament to wear them, though since watches have been made as light and little, as many that were them make of their time.

*He is willing to communicate his skill to posterity.* An invention though found is lost if not imparted. But as it is reported of some old toads, that before their death they suck up the gelly in their own heads (which otherwise would be hardned into a pretious stone) out of spight, that men should receive no benifit thereby; so some envious Artisans will have their cunning die with them, that none may be the better for it, and had rather all mankind should lose, then any man gain by them.

*He seldome attaineth to any very great estate:* except his trade hath some outlets and excursions into wholesale and merchandize; otherwise mere Artificers cannot heap up much wealth. It is difficult for gleaners, without stealing whole sheaves, to fill a barn. His chief wealth consisteth in enough, and that he can live comfortably, and leave his children the inheritance of their education.

*Yet he is a grand Benefactour to the Commonwealth.* England in former ages, like a dainty dame, partly out of state, but more out of lazinesse, would not suckle the fruit of her own body, to make the best to battle and improve her own commodities, but put them out to nurse to the Netherlanders, who were well paid for their pains. In those dayes the Sword and the Plough so took up all mens imployments that clothing was whollie neglected, and scarce any other webs to be found in houses, then what the spiders did make. But since she hath seen and mended her errour, making the best use of her own wooll; and indeed the riches of a kingdome doth consist in driving the home-commodities thereof as far as they will go, working them to their very perfection, imploying more handicrafts thereby. The sheep feeds more with his fleece then his flesh, doing the one but once, but the other once a yeare, many families subsisting by the working thereof. Let not meaner persons be displeased with reading those verses wherewith Queen Elizabeth her self was so highly affected, when in the one and twentieth yeare of her *reigne she came in progresse to Norwich, wherein a child, representing the state of the City, spake to her Highnesse as followeth,

* *Hollingshead. pag. 1290.*

> Most gratious Prince, undoubted Sovereigne Queen,
> Our onely joy, next God, and chief defence,
> In this small shew our whole estate is seen,
> The wealth we have, we find proceeds from hence:
>    The idle hand hath here no place to feed,
>    The painfull wight hath still to serve his need.
>
> Again, our seat denies us traffick here,
> The sea too near decides us from the rest:
> So weak we were within this dozen yeare,
> That care did quench the courage of the best:
>    But good advice hath taught these * little hands
>    To rend in twain the force of pining bands.
>
> From combed wooll we draw this slender thred,
> From thence the looms have dealing with the same,
> And thence again in order do proceed
> These severall works which skilfull art doth frame:
>    And all to drive dame Need into her cave
>    Our heads and hands together laboured have.

* *Sixteen little children were there presented to her Majestie, eight spinning worsted, and eight knitting yarne hose.*

*We bought before the things which now we sell:*
*These slender imps, their works do passe the waves:*
*Gods peace and thine we hold, and prosper well,*
*Of every mouth the hands the charges saves:*
   *Thus through thy help, and aid of power divine*
   *Doth Norwich live, whose hearts and goods are thine.*

We have cause to hope that as we have seen the cities Dornicks and Arras brought over into England, so posterity may see all Flaunders brought hither, I mean that their works shall be here imitated, and that either our land shall be taught to bear forrein commodities, or our people taught to forbear the using of them.

I should now come to give the description of the Day-Labourer (of whom we have onely a dearth in a plentifull harvest) but seeing his character is so co-incident with the hired servant, it may well be spared. And now wee'l rise from the hand to the arm, and come to describe the Souldier.

## Chap. 19.

### The good Souldier.

A Souldier is one of a lawfull, necessary, commendable, and honourable profession; yea God himself may seem to be one free of the company of Souldiers, in that he styleth himself, *A man of warre*. Now though many hate Souldiers as the twigs of the rod Warre, wherewith God scourgeth wanton countreys into repentance, yet is their calling so needfull, that were not some Souldiers we must be all Souldiers, dayly imployed to defend our own, the world would grow so licentious.

*He keepeth a clear and quiet conscience in his breast, which o-* | Maxime 1
*therwise will gnaw out the roots of all valour.* For vicious Souldiers

diers are compassed with enemies on all sides, their foes without them, and an ambush within them of fleshly lusts, which, as S. Peter saith, *fight against the soul*. None fitter to go to warre, then those who have made their peace with God in Christ; for such a mans soul is an impregnable fort: It cannot be scaled with ladders, for it reacheth up to heaven; nor be broken by batteries, for it is walled with brasse; nor undermined by pioners, for he is founded on a rock; nor betrayed by treason, for faith it self keeps it; nor be burnt by granadoes, for he can quench the fiery darts of the devil; nor be forced by famine, for *a good conscience is a continuall feast*.

2. *He chiefly avoids those sinnes, to which Souldiers are taxed as most subject.* Namely common swearing, which impayreth ones credit by degrees, and maketh all his promises not to be trusted; for he who for no profit will sinne against God, for small profit will trespasse against his neighbour; drinking, whoring. When valiant Zisca, near Pilsen in Bohemia, fought against his enemies, he commanded the women which followed his army, to cast their kerchiefs and partlets on the ground, wherein their enemies being entangled by their spurres (for though horsmen, they were forced to alight, and fight on foot, through the roughnesse of the place) were slain before they could * unloose their feet. A deep morall may be gathered hence, and women have often been the nets to catch and ensnare the souls of many Martiall men.

*\*Fox Acts and Monum pag. 646.*

3. *He counts his Princes lawfull command to be his sufficient warrant to fight.* In a defensive warre, when his countrey is * hostilely invaded, 'tis pity but his neck should hang in suspence with his conscience that doubts to fight; in offensive warre, though the case be harder, the common Souldier is not to dispute, but do * his Princes command. Otherwise

*\* In publicos hostes omnis homo miles, .. Tertull. Apol. cap. 2.*

*\* Amesius. Cas. Conscien. lib. 5. cap. 33.*

wise Princes, before they leavie an army of Souldiers, must first leavy an army of Casuists and Confessours to satisfie each scrupulous Souldier in point of right to the warre; and the most cowardly will be the most conscientious, to multiply doubts eternally. Besides, causes of warre are so complicated and perplex'd, so many things falling in the prosecution, as may alter the originall state thereof, and private Souldiers have neither calling nor ability to dive into such mysteries. But if the conscience of a Counsellour or Commander in chief remonstrates in himself the unlawfulnesse of this warre, he is bound humbly to represent to his Prince his reasons against it.

*He esteemeth all hardship easy through hopes of victory.* 4
Moneys are the sinews of war, yet if these sinews should chance to be shrunk, and pay casually fall short, he takes a fit of this convulsion patiently; he is contented though in cold weather his hands must be their own fire, and warm themselves with working; though he be better armed against their enemies then the weather, and his corslet wholler then his clothes; though he hath more Fasts and Vigills in his almanack then the Romish Church did ever enjoyn: he patiently endureth drought for desire of honour, and one thirst quencheth another. In a word, though much indebted to his own back and belly, and unable to pay them, yet he hath credit with himself, and confidently runnes on ticket with himself, hoping the next victory will discharge all scores with advantage.

*He looks at and also through his wages, at Gods glory, and* 5
*his countreys good.* He counts his pay an honourable addition, but no valuable compensation for his pains: for what proportion is there betwixt foure shillings a-week, and adventuring his life? I cannot see how their calling can be lawfull, who for greater wages will fight on any side against their own King and cause;

R yea

yea as false witnesses were hired against our blessed *Saviour (money will make the mouths of men plead against their Maker) so were the Giants now in the world, who, as the Poets feigned, made warre against God himself, and should they offer great pay, they would not want mercenary Souldiers to assist them.

*Mat. 28. 15.*

6 *He attends with all readinesse on the commands of his Generall*; rendring up his own judgement in obedience to the will and pleasure of his Leader, and by an implicite faith believing all is best which he enjoyneth; lest otherwise he be served as the French Souldier was in Scotland some eighty years since, who first mounted the bulwark of a fort besieged, whereupon ensued the gaining of the fort: but Marescal de *Thermes, the French Generall, first knighted him, and then hanged him within an houre after, because he had done it without commandment.

* Hollman in his book of the Embassadour.

7 *He will not in a bravery expose himself to needlesse perill.* 'Tis madnesse to holloe in the ears of sleeping temptation, to awaken it against ones self, or to go out of his calling to find a danger: But if a danger meets him (as he walks in his vocation) he neither stands still, starts aside, nor steps backward, but either goes over it with valour, or under it with patience. All single Duels he detesteth, as having first no command in Gods Word; yea this arbitrary deciding causes by the sword subverts the fundamentall Laws of the Scripture: Secondly, no example in Gods Word, that of David and Goliah moving in an higher Sphere, as extraordinary: Thirdly, it tempts God to work a Miracle for mans pleasure, and to invert the course of nature, whereby otherwise the stronger will beat the weaker: Fourthly, each Dueller challengeth his King as unable or unwilling legally to right him, and therefore he usurps the office himself: Fifthly, if slaying, he hazards his neck to the halter; if slain, in heat of malice,

without

without repentance, he adventures his soul to the devil.

*Object.* But there are some intricate cases ( as in Titles of land ) which cannot otherwise be decided. Seeing therefore that in such difficulties, the right in question cannot be delivered by the midwifery of any judiciall proceedings, then it must (with Julius Cæsar in his mothers belly ) be cut out and be determined by the sword.

*Answ.* Such a right may better be lost, then to light a candle from hell to find it out, if the Judges cannot find a middle way to part it betwixt them. Besides, in such a case Duells are no *medium proportionatum* to find out the truth, as never appointed by God to that purpose. Nor doth it follow that he hath the best in right, who hath the best in fight; for he that reads the lawfulnesse of actions by their events, holds the wrong end of the book upwards.

*Object.* But suppose an army of thirty thousand Infidells ready to fight against ten thousand Christians, yet so that at last the Infidells are contented to try the day upon the valour of a single Champion; whether in such a case may not a Christian undertake to combat with him, the rather because the treble oddes before is thereby reduced to terms of equalitie, and so the victory made more probable.

*Answ.* The victory was more probable before; because it is more likely God will blesse his own means, then means of mans appointing : and it is his prerogative to give victory, as well by few as by many. Probability of conquest is not to be measured by the eye of humane reason, contrary to the square of Gods Word. Besides, I question whether it be lawfull for a Christian army to derive their right of fighting Gods battels to any

R 2 single

single man. For the title every man hath to promote Gods glory, is so invested and inherent in his own particular person, that he cannot passe it over to another. None may appear in Gods service by an Atturney; and when Religion is at the stake, there must be no lookers on (except impotent people, who also help by their prayers) and every one is bound to lay his shoulders to the work. Lastly, would to God no Duels might be fought till this case came into question. But how many dayly fall out upon a more false, slight, and flitting ground, then the sands of Callis whereon they fight: especially, seeing there is an honourable Court appointed, or some other equivalent way, for taking up such quarrells, and allowing reparations to the party injured.

*Object.* But Reputation is so spirituall a thing it is inestimable, and Honour falls not under valuation: Besides, to complain to the civil Magistrate sheweth no manhood, but is like a childs crying to his father, when he is onely beaten by his equall; and my enemies forc'd acknowledgement of his fault (enjoyn'd him by the Court) shews rather his submission to the laws then to me. But if I can civilize his rudenesse by my sword, and chastize him into submission, then he sings his penitentiall song in the true tune, and it comes naturally indeed.

*Answ.* Honourable persons in that Court are the most competent Judges of Honour, and though Credit be as tender as the apple of the eye, yet such curious oculists can cure a blemish therein. And why, I pray, is it more disgrace to repair to the Magistrate for redresse in Reputation, then to have recourse to him in actions of trespasse? The pretence of a forced submission is nothing, all submissions having *aliquid violentum* in them; and even

even the Evangelicall repentance of Gods ser-vants hath a mixture of legall terrour frighting them thereto.

*Object.* But Gownmen speak out of an antipathy they bear to fighting: should we be rul'd by them, we must break all our swords into pen-knifes; and Lawyers, to inlarge their gains, send prohibitions to remove suits from the Camps to their Courts: Divines are not to be consulted with herein, as ignorant of the principles of Honour.

*Answ.* Indeed Honour is a word of course in the talk of roring boyes, and pure enough in it self, except their mouths soil it by often using of it: But indeed God is the fountain of Honour, Gods Word the Charter of Honour, and godly men the best Judges of it; nor is it any stain of cowardlinesse for one to fear hell and damnation.

We may therefore conclude that the laws of Duelling, as the laws of drinking, had their originall from the devil; and therefore the declining of needlesse quarrels in our Souldier, no abatement of Honour. I commend his discretion and valour, who walking in London-streetes met a gallant, who cryed to him a pretty distance beforehand, *I will have the wall?* Yea (answered he) *and take the house too, if you can but agree with the Landlord.* But when God, and his Prince, calls for him, our Souldier

*Had rather die ten times then once survive his credit.* 8
Though life be sweet, it shall not flatter the pallat of his soul, as with the sweetnesse of life to make him swallow down the bitternesse of an eternall disgrace: He begrutcheth not to get to his side a probability of victory by the certainty of his own death, and flieth from nothing so much as from the mention of flying. And though some say he is a mad-man that will pur-

chase Honour so dearly with his bloud, as that he cannot live to enjoy what he hath bought; our Souldier knows that he shall possesse the reward of his valour with God in heaven, and also making the world his executor, leave to it the rich inheritance of his memory.

9. *Yet in some cases he counts it no disgrace to yield, where it is impossible to conquer*; as when swarms of enemies crowd about him, so that he shall rather be stifled then wounded to death: In such a case if quarter be offered him, he may take it with more honour then the other can give it; and if he throws up his desperate game, he may happily winne the next, whereas if he playeth it out to the last, he shall certainly lose it and himself. But if he be to fall into the hand of a barbarous enemy, whose giving him quarter is but repriving him for a more ignominious death, he had rather disburse his life at the present, then to take day to fall into the hands of such remorslesse creditours.

10. *He makes none the object of his cruelty, which cannot be the object of his fear*. Lyons they say (except forc'd with hunger) will not prey on women and children, * though I would wish none to try the truth hereof: the truly valiant will not hurt women or infants, nor will they be cruell to old men. What conquest is it to strike him up, who stands but on one leg, and hath the other foot in the grave? But arrant cowards (such as would conquer victory it self, if it should stand in their way as they flie) count themselves never evenly match'd, except they have threefold oddes on their side, and esteem their enemie never disarmed till they be dead. Such love to shew a nature steep'd in gall of passion, and display the ignoble tyrany of prevailing dastards: these being thus valiant against no resistance, will make no resistance when they meet with true valour.

* *Plin. Nat. Hist. lib. 8. cap. 16.*

11. *He counts it murther to kill any in cold bloud*. Indeed in taking Cities by assault (especially when Souldiers have

have suffered long in an hard siege) it is pardonable what present passion doth with a sudden thrust; but a premeditated back-blow in cold bloud is base. Some excuse there is for bloud enraged, and no wonder if that scaldeth which boyleth: but when men shall call a consultation in their soul, and issue thence a deliberate act, the more advised the deed is, the lesse advised it is, when men raise their own passions, and are not raised by them; specially if fair quarter be first granted; an alms which he who gives to day may crave to morrow; yea, he that hath the hilt in his hand in the morning, may have the point at his throat ere night.

*He doth not barbarously abuse the bodies of his dead enemies.* 12
We find that Hercules was the * first (the most valiant are ever most mercifull) that ever suffered his enemies to carry away their dead bodies, after they had been put to the sword. Belike before his time they cruelly cut the corps in pieces, or cast them to the wild beasts.

\* Plutarch. in vita Thesei, Pagin. 15.

*In time of plenty he provides for want hereafter.* Yet generally Souldiers (as if they counted one Treasurer in an army were enough) so hate covetousnesse that they cannot affect providence for the future, and come home with more marks in their bodies then pence in their pockets. 13

*He is willing and joyfull to imbrace peace on good conditions.* 14
The procreation of peace, and not the satisfying of mens lusts and liberties, is the end of warre. Yet how many, having warre for their possession, desire a perpetuity thereof! Wiser men then King Henry the eights fool use to cry in fair weather, whose harvest being onely in storms, they themselves desire to raise them; wherefore fearing peace will starve, whom warre hath fatted, and to render themselves the more usefull they prolong discord to the utmost, and could wish when swords are once drawn that all scabbards might be cut asunder.

He

15 *He is as quiet and painfull in peace, as couragious in warre.* If he hath not gotten already enough whereon comfortably to subsist, he rebetakes himself to his former calling he had before the warre began: the weilding of his sword hath not made him unweildie to do any other work, and put his bones out of joynt to take pains. Hence comes it to passe, that some take by-courses on the high-wayes, and death, whom they honourably sought for in the field, meets them in a worse place.

But we leave our Souldier, seeking by his virtues to ascend from a private place, by the degrees of Sergeant, Lieutenant, Captain, Colonell, till he comes to be a Generall, and then in the next book, God willing, you shall have his example.

## Chap. 20.

### *The good Sea-Captain.*

His Military part is concurrent with that of the Souldier already described: He differs onely in some Sea-properties, which we will now set down. Conceive him now in a Man of warre, with his letters of mart, well arm'd victuall'd and appointed, and see how he acquits himself.

*Maxime* 1    *The more power he hath, the more carefull he is not to abuse it.* Indeed a Sea-captain is a King in the Iland of a ship, supreme Judge, above appeal, in causes civill and criminall, and is seldome brought to an account in Courts of Justice on land, for injuries done to his own men at sea.

2    *He is carefull in observing of the Lords day.* He hath a watch in his heart though no bells in a steeple to proclaim that day by ringing to prayers. S^r Francis Drake * in three years sailing about the world lost one whole day, which was scarce considerable in so long time. Tis to be feared some Captains at sea lose a day

\* *Manuscr. of Mr. Fortescu, who went with him.*

day every week, one in seven, neglecting the Sabbath.

*He is as pious and thankfull when a tempest is past, as devout when 'tis present*: not clamorous to receive mercies, and tongue-tied to return thanks. Many mariners are calm in a storm, and storm in a calm, blustring with oathes. In a tempest it comes to their turn to be religious, whose piety is but a fit of the wind, and when that's allayed, their devotion is ended.

*Escaping many dangers makes him not presumptuous to run into them.* Not like those Sea-men who ( as if their hearts were made of those rocks they have often sayled by ) are so alwayes in death they never think of it. These in their navigations observe that it is farre hotter under the Tropicks in the coming to the Line, then under the Line it self, & in like manner they conceive that the fear & phancy in preparing for death is more terrible then death it self, which makes them by degrees desperately to contemne it.

*In taking a prize he most prizeth the mens lives whom he takes*; though some of them may chance to be Negroes or Savages. 'Tis the custome of some to cast them overbord, and there's an end of them: for the dumbe fishes will tell no tales. But the murder is not so soon drown'd as the men. What, is a brother by the half bloud no kinne ? a Savage hath God to his father by creation, though not the Church to his mother, and God will revenge his innocent bloud. But our Captain counts the image of God neverthelesse his image cut in ebony as if done in ivory, and in the blackest Moores he sees the representation of the King of heaven.

*In dividing the gains he wrongs none who took pains to get them.* Not shifting off his poore mariners with nothing, or giving them onely the garbage of the prize, and keeping all the flesh to himself. In time of peace he quietly returns home, and turns not to the trade of

Pirates,

Pirates, who are the worst sea-vermine, and the devils water-rats.

7. *His voyages are not onely for profit, but some for honour and knowledge*; to make discoveries of new countreys, imitating the worthy Peter Columbus. Before his time the world was cut off at the middle; Hercules Pillars (which indeed are the navell) being made the feet, and utmost bounds of the continent, till his successefull industry inlarged it.

*Gen. 8. 11.

*Primus ab infusis quod terra emerserat undis*
*Nuncius adveniens ipsa* Columba fuit.*
*Occiduis primus qui terram invenit in undis*
*Nuncius adveniens ipse Columbus erat.*

Our Sea-captain is likewise ambitious to perfect what the other began. He counts it a disgrace, seeing all mankind is one familie, sundry countreys but severall rooms, that we who dwell in the parlour (so he counts Europe) should not know the out-lodgings of the same house, and the world be scarce acquainted with it self before it be dissolved from it self at the day of judgement.

8. *He daily sees, and duly considers Gods wonders in the deep.* Tell me, ye Naturalists, who sounded the first march and retreat to the Tide, *Hither shalt thou come, and no further?* why doth not the water recover his right over the earth, being higher in nature? whence came the salt, and who first boyled it, which made so much brine? when the winds are not onely wild in a storm, but even stark mad in an herricano, who is it that restores them again to their wits, and brings them asleep in a calm? who made the mighty whales, who swim in a sea of water, and have a sea of oyl swimming in them? who first taught the water to imitate the creatures on land? so that the sea is the stable of horse-fishes, the stall of kine-fishes, the stye of hog-fishes, the kennell of dog-fishes, and in all things the sea the ape of the land. Whence growes the amber-greece

in

in the Sea? which is not so hard to find where it is, as to know what it is. Was not God the first shipwright? and all vessels on the water descended from the loyns (or ribs rather) of Noahs ark; or else who durst be so bold with a few crooked boards nayled together, a stick standing upright, and a rag tied to it, to adventure into the ocean? what loadstone first touched the loadstone? or how first fell it in love with the North, rather affecting that cold climate, then the pleasant East, or fruitfull South, or West? how comes that stone to know more then men, and find the way to the land in a mist? In most of these men take sanctuary at *Occulta qualitas*, and complain that the room is dark, when their eyes are blind. Indeed they are Gods Wonders; and that Seaman the greatest Wonder of all for his blockishnesse, who seeing them dayly neither takes notice of them, admires at them, nor is thankfull for them.

S 2  CHAP. 21.

132　　　　　　*The Holy State.*　　　　Book II.

S^r FRANCIS DRAKE *one of the first of those w^ch in his Sea voyages put a Girdle about the World. He Died upon the Seas. Anno D̄m̄ 1595.* W.M. *sculp:*

CHAP. 21.

*The life of Sir* FRANCIS DRAKE.

*\* S^t. Francis Drake his nephew in the descript. of his third voyage, Epistle to the Reader.*

FRancis Drake was born nigh\* south Tavestock in Devonshire, and brought up in Kent; God dividing the honour betwixt two Counties, that the one might have his birth, and the other his education. His Father, being a Minister, fled into Kent for fear of the Six Articles, wherein the sting of Popery still remained in England, though the teeth thereof were knock'd out, and the Popes Supremacy abolish-

abolished. Coming into Kent, he bound his sonne Francis apprentice to the Master of a small bark, which traded into France, and Zealand, where he underwent a hard service; and pains with patience in his youth did knit the joynts of his soul, and made them more solid and compacted. His Master dying unmarried, in reward of his industry, bequeath'd his bark unto him for a Legacie.

For some time he continued his Masters profession: But the Narrow Seas were a prison for so large a spirit, born for greater undertakings. He soon grew weary of his bark, which would scarce go alone but as it crept along by the shore: wherefore selling it, he unfortunately ventured most of his estate with Captain John Hawkins into the West Indies, whose goods were taken by the Spaniards at S. John de Ulva, and he himself scarce escaped with life. The King of Spain being so tender in those parts, that the least touch doth wound him; and so jealous of the West Indies, his wife, that willingly he would have none look upon her, and therefore used them with the greater severity.

1567.

Drake was perswaded by the Minister of his ship that he might lawfully recover in value of the King of Spain, and repair his losses upon him any where else. The Case was clear in sea-divinity, and few are such Infidels, as not to believe doctrines which make for their own profit. Whereupon Drake, though a poore private man, hereafter undertook to revenge himself on so mighty a Monarch; who, as not contented that the Sun riseth and setteth in his dominions, may seem to desire to make all his own where he shineth. And now let us see how a dwarf, standing on the Mount of Gods providence, may prove an overmatch for a giant.

After two or three severall Voyages to gain intelligence in the West Indies, and some prizes taken, at last

last he effectually set forward from Plimouth with two ships, the one of seventy, the other twenty five tunnes, and seventy three men and boyes in both. He made with all speed and secrecy to Nombre de Dios, as loth to put the Town to too much charge (which he knew they would willingly bestow) in providing beforehand for his entertainment; which City was then the granary of the West Indies, wherein the golden harvest brought from Panama was hoarded up till it could be conveyed into Spain. They came hard aboard the shore, and lay quiet all night intending to attempt the Town in the dawning of the day.

But he was forced to alter his resolution, and assault it sooner; for he heard his men muttering amongst themselves of the strength and greatnesse of the Town: and when mens heads are once fly-blown with buzzes of suspicion, the vermine multiply instantly and one jealousie begets another. Wherefore he raised them from their nest before they had hatch'd their fears, and to put away those conceits, he perswaded them it was day-dawning when the Moon rose, and instantly set on the Town, and wonne it being unwalled. In the Market-place the Spaniards saluted them with a volley of shot; Drake returned their greeting with a flight of arrows, the best and ancient English complement, which drave their enemies away. Here Drake received a dangerous wound, though he valiantly conceal'd it a long time, knowing if his heart stooped, his mens would fall, and loth to leave off the action, wherein if so bright an opportunity once setteth, it seldome riseth again. But at length his men forced him to return to his ship, that his wound might be dressed, and this unhappy accident defeated the whole designe. Thus victory sometimes slips thorow their fingers, who have caught it in their hands.

But

But his valour would not let him give over the project as long as there was either life or warmth in it: And therefore having received intelligence from the Negroes, called Symerons, of many mules-lading of gold and silver, which was to be brought from Panama, he leaving competent numbers to man his ships went on land with the rest, and bestowed himself in the woods by the way as they were to passe, and so intercepted and carried away an infinite masse of gold. As for the silver which was not portable over the mountains, they digged holes in the ground and hid it therein.

There want not those who love to beat down the price of every honourable action, though they themselves never mean to be chapmen. These cry up Drakes fortune herein to cry down his valour; as if this his performance were nothing, wherein a golden opportunity ran his head with his long forelock into Drakes hands beyond expectation. But certainly his resolution and unconquerable patience deserved much praise, to adventure on such a designe, which had in it just no more probability then what was enough to keep it from being impossible: yet I admire not so much at all the treasure he took, as at the rich and deep mine of Gods providence.

Having now full fraughted himself with wealth, and burnt at the House of Crosses above two hundred thousand pounds worth of Spanish Merchandise, he returned with honour and safety into England, and some * years after undertook that his famous voyage about the world, most accurately described by our English Authours: and yet a word or two thereof will not be amisse.

* 1577. Decemb. 13.

Setting forward from Plimouth, he bore up for Caboverd, where near to the Iland of S. Jago he took prisoner Nuno-da-Silva, an experienc'd Spanish pilot, whose direction he used in the coasts of Brasil and
Magellan

Magellan straits, and afterwards safely landed him at Guatulco in New Spain. Hence they took their course to the iland of Brava, and hereabouts they met with those tempestuous winds, whose onely praise is, that they continue not above an houre, in which time they change *all the points of the compasse. Here they had great plenty of rain, poured ( not as in other places, as it were out of sives, but ) as out of spouts, so that a but of water falls down in a place: which notwithstanding is but a courteous injury in that hot climate farre from land, and where otherwise fresh water cannot be provided: then cutting the Line, they saw the face of that heaven which earth hideth from us, but therein onely three *starres of the first greatnesse, the rest few and small compared to our Hemisphere, as if God, on purpose, had set up the best and biggest candles in that room wherein his civilest guests are entertained.

Sayling the South of Brasile, he afterwards passed the *Magellan straits, and then entred *Mare pacificum*, came to the Southermost land at the height of 55 ½ latitude; thence directing his course Northward, he pillaged many Spanish Towns, and took rich prizes of high value in the kingdomes of Chily, Peru, and New Spain. Then bending Eastwards, he coasted China, and the Moluccoes, where by the King of Terrenate, a true Gentleman Pagan, he was most honourably entertain'd: The King told them, They and he were all of one religion in this respect, that they believed *not in Gods made of stocks and stones as did the Portugalls. He furnish'd them also with all necessaries that they wanted.

On the ninth of *January following, his ship, having a large wind and a smooth sea, ran a ground on a dangerous shole, and strook twice on it, knocking twice at the doore of death, which no doubt had opened the third time. Here they *stuck from eight a clock at night till

*Manusc. of Geor. Fortescue who went the voyage with Sr Fran. Drake.

*Cambd Eliza. Anno 1580. p. 323.

*August. 20. 1578.

*Manuscri. Geor. Fortescue

*1579.

*Hacluits voyage, p. 741. 3. vol.

Chap. 21.　*The life of Sir* Francis Drake.　137

till foure the next afternoon, having ground too much, and yet too little to land on, and water too much, and yet too little to sail in. Had God ( *who*, as the wiseman saith, Prov. 30. 4. *holdeth the winds in his fist* ) but opened his little finger, and let out the smallest blast, they had undoubtedly been cast away; but there blew not any wind all the while. Then they conceiving aright that the best way to lighten the ship, was first to ease it of the burthen of their sinnes by true repentance, humbled themselves by fasting under the hand of God : Afterwards they received the Communion, dining on Christ in the Sacrament, expecting no other then to sup with him in heaven : Then they cast out of their ship six great pieces of ordinance, threw over-board as much wealth as would break the heart of a Miser to think on't, with much suger, and packs of spices, making a caudle of the sea round about: Then they betook themselves to their prayers, the best lever at such a dead lift indeed, and it pleased God that the wind, formerly their mortall enemy, became their friend, which changing from the Starboard to the Larboard of the ship, and rising by degrees, cleared them off to the sea again, for which they returned unfeigned thanks to almighty God.

By the Cape of good hope and west of Africa he returned safe into England, and landed at * Plimouth, (being almost the first of those that made a thorowlight through the world ) having in his whole voyage, though a curious searcher after the time, lost one day through the variation of severall Climates. He feasted the Queen in his ship at Dartford, who Knighted him for his service: yet it grieved him not a little, that some prime * Courtiers refused the gold he offer'd them, as gotten by piracy. Some of them would have been loth to have been told, that they had *Aurum Tholosanum* in their own purses. Some think that they did it to shew that their envious pride was above their covetousnesse,

* *Novemb.* 3 1580.

* *Camb. Eliza. Anno ut priùs, pag.* 127.

T　　　　who

who of set purpose did blur the fair copy of his performance, because they would not take pains to write after it.

1585.    I passe by his next *West Indian voyage, wherein he took the Cities of S. Jago, S. Domingo, Carthagena, and S. Augustine in Florida: as also his service performed in 88, wherein he with many others helped to the waining of that half Moon, which sought to govern all the motion of our Sea. I hast to his last Voyage.

1595.    Queen Elizabeth perceiving that the onely way to make the Spaniard a criple for ever, was to cut his Sinews of warre in the West Indies, furnished S<sup>r</sup> Francis Drake, and S<sup>r</sup> John Hawkins with six of her own ships, besides 21 ships and Barks of their own providing, containing in all 2500 Men and Boyes, for some service on America. But, alas, this voyage was marr'd before begun. For so great preparations being too big for a cover, the King of Spain knew of it, and sent a Caravall of adviso to the West Indies, so that they had intelligence *three weeks before the Fleet set forth of England, either to fortifie, or remove their treasure; whereas in other of Drakes Voyages not two of his own men knew whither he went; and managing such a designe is like carrying a Mine in warre, if it hath any vent, all is spoyled. Besides, Drake and Hawkins being in joynt Commission hindred each other. The later took himself to be inferiour rather in successe then skill, and the action was unlike to prosper when neither would follow, and both could not handsomly go abreast. It vexed old Hawkins that his counsell was not followed, in present sayling to America, but that they spent time in vain in assaulting the Canaries; and the grief that his advice was slighted (say some) was the cause of his death. Others impute it to the sorrow he took, for the taking of his Bark called the Francis, which five Spanish Frigates had intercepted: But whē the same heart hath two mortall wounds given it together, 'tis hard to say which of them killeth. Drake

*Hacluits voyage, 3. vol. pag. 583.

Chap.21.   *The life of S^r. Francis Drake.*   139

Drake continued his courfe for Port-Rico, and riding within the roade, a fhot from the Caftle entred the fteerage of the fhip, took away the ftool from under him as he fate at fupper, wounded S^r Nicholas Clifford and Brute Brown to death. *Ah dear* * *Brute* (faid Drake) *I could grieve for thee. but now is no time for me to let down my fpirits.* And indeed a Souldiers moft proper bemoaning a friends death in warre is in revenging it. And fure, as if grief had made the Englifh furious, they foon after fired five Spanifh fhips of two hundred tunnes apiece, in defpight of the Caftle.

* *From the mouth of Henr. Drake Efquire there prefent, my dear and worthy parifhioner lately deceafed.*

America is not unfitly refembled to an Houre-glaffe, which hath a narrow neck of land (fuppofe it the hole where the fand paffeth) betwixt the parts thereof, Mexicana & Pervana. Now the Englifh had a defigne to march by land over this Ifthmus from Port-Rico to Panama, where the Spanifh treafure was layd up. S^r Thomas Baskervile, Generall of the land-forces, undertook the fervice with feven hundred and fifty armed men. They marched through deep wayes, the Spaniards much annoying them with fhot out of the woods. One fort in the paffage they affaulted in vain, and heard that two others were built to ftop them, befides Panama it felf. They had fo much of this breakfaft, they thought they fhould furfet of a dinner and fupper of the fame. No hope of conqueft, except with cloying the jaws of Death, and thrufting men on the mouth of the Canon. Wherefore fearing to find the Proverb true, That Gold may be bought too dear, they returned to their fhips. Drake afterwards fired Nombre de Dios, and many other petty Towns (whofe treafure the Spaniards had conveyed away) burning the empty casks, when their precious liquour was runne out before, and then prepared for their returning home.

Great was the difference betwixt the Indian cities

T 2   now

now from what they were when Drake first haunted these coasts: At first the Spaniards here were safe and secure, counting their treasure sufficient to defend it self, the remotenesse thereof being the greatest (almost onely) resistance, and the fetching of it more then the fighting for it. Whilest the King of Spain guarded the head and heart of his dominions in Europe, he left his long legs in America open to blows, till finding them to smart, being beaten black and blew by the English, he learned to arm them at last, fortifying the most important of them to make them impregnable.

Now began Sr Francis his discontent to feed upon him. He conceived that expectation, a mercilesse usurer, computing each day since his departure exacted an interest and return of honour and profit proportionable to his great preparations, and transcending his former atchievements. He saw that all the good which he had done in this voyage, consisted in the evill he had done to the Spaniards afarre off, whereof he could present but small visible fruits in England. These apprehensions accompanying if not causing the disease of the flux wrought his sudden * death. And sicknesse did not so much untie his clothes, as sorrow did rend at once the robe of his mortality asunder. He lived by the sea, died on it, and was buried in it. Thus an ex-tempore performance (scarce heard to be begun before we hear it is ended) comes off with better applause, or miscarries with lesse disgrace, then a long studied and openly premeditated action. Besides, we see how great spirits, having mounted to the highest pitch of performance, afterwards strain and break their credits in striving to go beyond it. Lastly, God oftentimes leaves the brightest men in an eclipse, to shew that they do but borrow their lustre from his reflection. We will not justifie all the actions of any man, though of a tamer profession then a

* *January* 28. 1595.

Sea-

Sea-Captain, in whom civility is often counted precisenesse. For the main, we say that this our Captain was a religious man towards God and his houses (generally sparing Churches where he came) chast in his life, just in his dealings, true of his word, and mercifull to those that were under him, hating nothing so much as idlenesse: And therefore lest his soul should rust in peace, at spare houres he brought fresh water to Plimouth. Carefull he was for posterity (though men of his profession have as well an ebbe of riot, as a flote of fortune) and providently raised a worshipfull Family of his kinred. In a word, should those that speak against him fast till they fetch their bread where he did his, they would have a good stomach to eat it.

## Chap. 22.

### The good Herald.

HE is a Warden of the temple of Honour. Mutuall necessity made mortall enemies agree in these Officers; the lungs of Mars himself would be burnt to pieces having no respiration in a truce. Heralds therefore were invented to proclaim peace or warre, deliver messages about summons of forts, ransoming of captives, burying the dead, and the like.

*He is grave and faithfull in discharging the service he is imployed in.* The names which Homer gives the Grecian Ceryces, excellently import their virtues in discharging their office: One was called Asphalio, *such an one as made sure work*; another Eurybates, *cunning and subtle*; a third Theotes, from his piety and godlinesse; a fourth Stentor, from his loud and audible pronouncing of messages. Therefore of every Heathen sacrifice the * tongue was cut out, and given to the Heralds, to shew that liberty of speech in all places was allowed them.

*Maxime* 1

\* Sr. Hen. Spelman Glossar. de verbo Herald.

2     *He imbitters not a distastfull message to a forrein Prince by his indiscretion in delivering it.* Commendable was the gravity of Guien King of arms in France, and Thomas Bevolt Clarenceaux of England, sent by their severall Princes to defie Charles the Emperour. For after leave demanded and obtained to deliver the message with safe conduct to their persons, they delivered the Emperour the lie in writing, and defying him were sent home safe with rewards. It fared worse with a foolish French Herald, sent from the Count of Orgell to challenge combat with the Count of Cardonna, Admiral of Arragon, where instead of wearing his Coat of Arms the Herald was attired in a long linen garment, painted with some dishonest actions, imputed to the said Count of Cardonna. But Ferdinand King of Arragon caused the Herald to be whipt naked through the streets * of Barcelona, as a punishment of his presumption. Thus his indescretion remitted him to the nature of an ordinary person, his Armour of proof of publick credence fell off, and he left naked to the stroke of justice, no longer a publick Officer, but a private offender. Passe we now from his use in warre to his imployment in peace.

*\* Span. Hist. in the life of Ferdinand.*

3     *He is skilfull in the pedigrees and descents of all ancient Gentry.* Otherwise, to be able onely to blazon a Coat doth no more make an Herald, then the reading the titles of Gally-pots makes a Physician. Bring our Herald to a Monument, *ubi jacet epitaphium,* and where the Arms on the Tombe are not onely crest-fallen, but their colours scarce to be discerned, and he will tell whose they be, if any certainty therein can be rescued from the teeth of Time. But how shamefull was the ignorance of the French * Heralds some fourty years since, who at a solemn entertainment of Queen Mary of Florence, wife to King Henrie the fourth, did falsly devise and blazon both the Arms of Florence, and the Arms of the Daulphin of France, now King thereof.

*\* Andr. Favin (a Parisian Advocate) in his Theatre of Honour, 1. book 4. chap. pag. 35*

He

### Chap. 22. *The good Herald.*

**4** *He carefully preserveth the memories of extinguish'd Families,* of such Zelophehads, who dying left onely daughters. He is more faithfull to many ancient Gentlemen then their own Heirs were, who sold their lands, and with them (as much as in them lay) their memories, which our Herald carefully treasureth up.

**5** *He restoreth many to their own rightfull Arms.* An Heir is a Phenix in a familie, there can be but one of them at the same time. Hence comes it often to passe, that younger brothers of gentile families live in low wayes, clouded often amongst the Yeomanry; and yet those under-boughs grow from the same root with the top-branches. It may happen afterwards that by industry they may advance themselves to their former lustre; and good reason they should recover their ancient ensignes of honour belonging unto them: For the river Anas in Spain, though running many miles under ground, when it comes up again is still the same river which it was before. And yet

**6** *He curbs their Vsurpation who unjustly entitle themselves to ancient Houses.* Hierophilus a *Ferrier in Rome pretended himself to be nephew to C. Marius, who had seven times been Consul, and carried it in so high a strain that many believed him, and some companies in Rome accepted him for their Patron. Such want not amongst us, who in spight of the stock will engraff themselves into noble bloods, and thence derive their pedegree. Hence they new mould their names, taking from them, adding to them, melting out all the liquid letters, torturing mutes to make them speak, and making vowels dumbe to bring it to a fallacious Homonomy at the last, that their names may be the same with those noble Houses they pretend to. By this trick (to forbear dangerous instances, if affinity of sound makes kinred) Lutulentus makes himself kinne to Luculentus, dirt to light, and Angustus to Augustus, some narrow-hearted Peasant, to some large-spirited Prince,

*\* Valer. Max. lib.9.cap.16.*

Prince, except our good Herald marre their mart, and discover their forgery. For well he knows where indeed the names are the same (though alter'd through variety of writing in severall ages, and disguis'd by the lisping of vulgar people, who miscall hard French Sirnames) and where the equivocation is untruly affected.

7. *He assignes honourable Arms to such as raise themselves by deserts.* In all ages their must be as well a beginning of new Gentry, as an ending of ancient. And let not *Linea*, when farre extended in length, grow so proud as to scorn the first *Punctum* which gave it the originall. Our Herald knows also to cure the surfet of Coats, and unsurcharge them, and how to wash out stained colours, when the merits of Posterity have outworn the disgraces of their Ancestours.

8. *He will not for any profit favour wealthy unworthinesse.* If a rich Clown (who deserves that all his shield should be the Base point) shall repair to the Herald-office, as to a drapers shop, wherein any Coat may be bought for money, he quickly finds himself deceived. No doubt if our Herald gives him a Coat, he gives him also a badge with it.

CHAP. 23.

Chap. 23. *The life of M*ʳ *W.* Cambden. 145

WILLIAM CAMBDEN Clarenciaux *king of*
Armes. *He dyed at Westminster Anno Dñi* 1623.
*Aged* 74 *yeares*
W *Marshall sculp* .

## Chap. 23.

### *The life of M*ʳ W. Cambden.

William Cambden was born *Anno* 1550 in old Baily, in the City of London. His Father, Sampſon Cambden, was deſcended of honeſt parentage in Staffordſhire; but by his Mothers ſide he was extracted from the worſhipfull family of the * Curwens in Cumberland.

He was brought up firſt in Chriſt-Church, then in Pauls School in London, and at fifteen years of age went

* A quibus nobis ( abſit invidia ) genus maternum, *Cambd. Brit. in Cumber.*

went to Magdalen Colledge in Oxford, and thence to *Broadgates Hall, where he first made those short Latine Graces, which the Servitours still use. From hence he was removed, and made student of Christ Church, where he profited to such eminency, that he was preferred to be Master of Westminster School, a most famous seminarie of learning.

*Ex Parentatione Degorii Wheat.

For whereas before, of the two grand Schools of England, one sent all her Foundation-scholars to Cambridge, the other all to Oxford, the good Queen (as the Head equally favouring both Breasts of Learning and Religion) divided her Scholars here betwixt both Universities, which were enriched with many hopefull plants sent from hence, through Cambdens learning, diligence, and clemency. Sure none need pity the beating of that Scholar, who would not learn without it under so meek a Master.

His deserts call'd him hence to higher employments. The Queen first made him Richmond Herald, and then Clarenceaux King of Arms. We reade how Dionysius first King of Sicily turn'd afterwards a Schoolmaster in his old age. Behold here Dionysius inverted, one that was a Schoolmaster in his youth become a King (of Arms) in his riper years, which place none ever did or shall discharge with more integrity. He was a most exact Antiquary, witnesse his worthy work, which is a comment on three kingdomes; and never was so large a text more briefly, so dark a text more plainly expounded. Yea what a fair garment hath been made out of the very shreds and Remains of that greater Work?

It is most worthy observation with what diligence he inquired after ancient places, making Hue and Crie after many a City which was run away, and by certain marks and tokens pursuing to find it; as by the situation on the *Romane high-wayes, by just distance from other ancient cities, by some affinity of name,

*Watlin } street
Ermin }

by

Chap. 23.  *The life of M*<sup>r</sup>. W. Cambden.  147

by tradition of the inhabitants, by Romane coyns digged up, and by some appearance of ruines. A broken urn is a whole evidence, or an old gate still surviving, out of which the city is run out. Besides, commonly some new spruce town, not farre off, is grown out of the ashes thereof, which yet hath so much naturall affection, as dutifully to own those reverend ruines for her Mother.

By these and other means he arrived at admirable knowledge, and restored Britain to her self. And let none tax him for presumption in conjectures where the matter was doubtfull; for many probable conjectures have stricken the fire, out of which Truths candle hath been lighted afterwards. Besides, conjectures, like parcells of unknown ore, are sold but at low rates : If they prove some rich metall, the buyer is a great gainer; if base, no looser, for he payes for it accordingly.

His candour and sweet temper was highly to be commended, gratefully acknowledging those by whom he was assisted in the work ( in such a case confession puts the difference betwixt stealing and borrowing ) and surely so heavy a log needed more levers then one. He honourably mentioneth such as differ from him in opinion; not like those Antiquaries, who are so snarling one had as good dissent a mile as an hairs breadth from them.

Most of the English ancient Nobility and Gentry he hath unpartially observed. Some indeed object that he * claws and flatters the Grandees of his own age, extolling some families rather great then ancient, making them to flow from a farre fountain because they had a great channell, especially if his private friends. But this cavil hath more of malice then truth : indeed 'tis pitty he should have a tongue, that hath not a word for a friend on just occasion; and justly might the stream of his commendations run broader, where meeting

* *Hugh Holland in the life of the Earl of Leicester.*

V 2                    with

with a confluence of desert and friendship in the same party. For the main, his pen is sincere and unpartiall, and they who complain that Grantham steeple stands awry will not set a straiter by it.

Some say that in silencing many gentile families, he makes baulks of as good ground as any he ploweth up. But these again acquit him, when they consider that it is not onely difficult but impossible to anatomize the English Gentry so exactly, as to shew where every smallest vein thereof runs. Besides, many Houses, conceived to be by him omitted, are rather rightly placed by him, not where they live, but whence they came. Lastly, we may perceive that he prepared another work on purpose for the English Gentry.

I say nothing of his learned Annalls of Queen Elizabeth, industriously performed. His very enemies (if any) cannot but commend him. Sure he was as farre from loving * Popery, as from hating Learning, though that aspersion be generall on Antiquaries; as if they could not honour hoary hairs, but presently themselves must doat.

*These words he wrote in the beginning of his Testament, Christi solius meritis & satisfactione spem omnem salutis meæ semper niti profiteor.

His liberality to Learning is sufficiently witnessed in his Founding of an History-Professour in Oxford, to which he gave the mannour of Bexley in Kent, worth in present a hundred and fourty pounds, but (some years expired) foure hundred pounds *per Annum*, so that he merited that distich,

 Est tibi pro Tumulo, Cambdene, Britannia tota,
 Oxonium vivens est Epigramma tibi.

The Military part of his office he had no need to imploy, passing it most under a peaceable Prince. But now having lived many years in honour and esteem, death at last, even contrarie to *Jus Gentium*, kill'd this worthy Herald, so that it seems, Mortality, the Law of Nature, is above the Law of Arms. He died *Anno* 1623. the ninth of November, in the seventie fourth yeare of his age.

CHAP. 24.

## Chap. 24.
### The true Gentleman.

WE will consider him in his Birth, Breeding, and Behaviour.

*He is extracted from ancient and worshipfull parentage.* [Maxime 1] When a Pepin is planted on a Pepin-stock, the fruit growing thence is called a *Renate, a most delicious apple, as both by Sire and Damme well descended. Thus his bloud must needs be well purified who is gentilely born on both sides.

*Draitons Polilbion, p.298.*

*If his birth be not, at leastwise his qualities are generous.* [2] What if he cannot with the Hevenninghams of Suffolk country *five and twenty Knights of his familie, or tell *sixteen Knights succesively with the Tilneys of Norfolk, or with the Nauntons shew where their Ancestours had *seven hundred pound a yeare before or at the conquest; yet he hath endeavoured by his own deserts to ennoble himself. Thus Valour makes him sonne to Cæsar, Learning entitles him kinsman to Tully, & Piety reports him nephew to godly Constantine. It graceth a Gentleman of low descent & high desert, when he will own the meannesse of his parentage. How ridiculous is it when many men brag, that their families are more ancient then the Moon, which all know are later then the starre which some seventy years since shined in Cassiopea. But if he be generously born, see how his parents breed him.

*Weavers fun. mon. pag. 854.*
*Idem. p.818.*
*Idem p.758.*

*He is not in his youth possest with the great hopes of his possession.* [3] No flatterer reads constantly in his ears a survey of the lands he is to inherit. This hath made many boyes thoughts swell so great they could never be kept in compasse afterwards. Onely his Parents acquaint him that he is the next undoubted Heir to correction, if misbehaving himself; and he finds no more favour from his Schoolmaster then his Schoolmaster

master finds diligence in him, whose rod respects persons no more then bullets are partiall in a battel.

**4** *At the University he is so studious as if he intended Learning for his profession.* He knowes well that cunning is no burthen to carry, as paying neither portage by land, nor poundage by sea. Yea though to have land be a good First, yet to have learning is the surest Second, which may stand to it when the other may chance to be taken away.

**5** *At the Innes of Court he applyes himself to learn the Laws of the kingdome.* Object not, Why should a Gentleman learn law, who if he needeth it may have it for his money, and if he hath never so much of his own, he must but give it away. For what a shame is it for a man of quality to be ignorant of Solon in our Athens, of Lycurgus in our Sparta? Besides, law will help him to keep his own, and besteed his neighbours. Say not, that there be enough which make this their set practice: for so there are also many masters of defence by their profession; and shall private men therefore learn no skill at their weapons.

As for the Hospitality, the Apparell, the Travelling, the Companie, the Recreations, the Marriage of Gentlemen, they are described in severall Chapters in the following Book. A word or two of his behaviour in the countrey.

**6** *He is courteous and affable to his neighbours.* As the sword of the best tempered mettall is most flexible; so the truly generous are most pliant and courteous in their behaviour to their inferiours.

**7** *He delights to see himself, and his servants well mounted:* therefore he loveth good Horsemanship. Let never any forrein Rabshakeh send that brave to our Jerusalem, offering *to lend her* \* *two thousand horses, if she be able for her part to set riders upon them.* We know how Darius got the Persian Empire from the rest of his fellow Peeres,

\* 2. Kings 18. 23.

Peeres, by the first neighing of his generous steed. It were no harm if in some needlesse suits of intricate precedencie betwixt equall Gentlemen, the priority were adjudged to him who keeps a stable of most serviceable horses.

*He furnisheth and prepareth himself in peace against time of warre.* Lest it be too late to learn when his skill is to be used. He approves himself couragious when brought to the triall, as well remembring the custome which is used at the Creation of Knights of the Bath, wherein the Kings Master-Cook * cometh forth, & presente his great knife to the new-made Knights, admonishing them to be faithfull and valiant, otherwise he threatens them that that very knife is prepared to cut off their spurres.

8

* M. Selden in his titles of Honour, pag. 820

*If the Commission of the Peace finds him out, he faithfully discharges it.* I say, Finds him out; for a publick Office is a guest which receives the best usage from them who never invited it. And though he declined the Place, the countrey knew to prize his worth, who would be ignorant of his own. He compounds many petty differences betwixt his neighbours, which are easier ended in his own Porch then in Westminster-hall: for many people think, if once they have fetched a warrant from a Justice, they have given earnest to follow the suit, though otherwise the matter be so mean that the next nights sleep would have bound both parties to the peace, and made them as good friends as ever before. Yet

9

*He connives not at the smothering of punishable faults.* He hates that practice, as common as dangerous amongst countrey people, who having received again the goods which were stollen from them, partly out of foolish pity, and partly out of covetousnesse to save charges in prosecuting the law, let the thief escape unpunished. Thus whilest private losses are repaired, the wounds to the Commonwealth ( in the breach of the Laws )

10

Laws) are left uncured: And thus petty Larceners are encouraged into Felons, and afterwards are hang'd for pounds, because never whipt for pence, who, if they had felt the cord, had never been brought to the halter.

11

*Acts 14.12.

*If chosen a Member of Parliament he is willing to do his Countrey service.* If he be no Rhetorician to raise affections, (yea Barnabas was a * greater speaker then S. Paul himself) he counts it great wisdome to be the good manager of Yea and Nay. The slow pace of his judgement is recompenced by the swift following of his affections, when his judgement is once soundly inform'd. And here we leave him in consultation, wishing him with the rest of his honourable Society all happy successe.

# The Holy State.

## THE THIRD BOOK.
## Containing Generall Rules.

### Chap. I.
### *Of Hospitality.*

Hospitality is threefold: for ones familie; this is of Necessity: for strangers; this is Courtesie: for the poore; this is Charity. Of the two latter.

*To keep a disorderly house is the way to keep neither house nor lands.* For whilest they keep the greatest roaring, their state steals away in the greatest silence. Yet when many consume themselves with secret vices, then Hospitality bears the blame: whereas it is not the Meat but the Sauce, not the Supper but the Gaming after it, doth undoe them. *Maxime* 1.

*Measure not thy entertainment of a guest by his estate, but thine own.* Because he is a Lord, forget not that thou art but a Gentleman: otherwise if with feasting him thou breakest thy self, he will not cure thy rupture, and (perchance) rather deride then pitie thee. 2.

*When provision (as we say) groweth on the same, it is miraculously multiplied.* In Northamptonshire all the rivers of the County are bred in it, besides those (Ouse and Charwell) it lendeth and sendeth into other shires: So the good Housekeeper hath a fountain of wheat in his field, mutton in his fold, &c. both to serve himself, 3.

and

4     *Mean mens palates are best pleased with fare rather plentifull then various, solid then dainty.* Dainties will cost more, and content lesse, to those that are not Criticall enough to distinguish them.

5     *Occasionall entertainment of men greater then thy self is better then solemn inviting them.* Then short warning is thy large excuse: whereas otherwise, if thou dost not overdo thy estate, thou shalt underdo his expectation, for thy feast will be but his ordinary fare. A King of France was often pleased in his hunting wilfully to lose himself, to find the house of a private Park-keeper; where going from the School of State-affairs, he was pleased to make a play-day to himself. He brought sauce (Hunger) with him, which made course meat dainties to his palate. At last the Park-keeper took heart, and solemnely invited the King to his house, who came with all his Court, so that all the mans meat was not a morsell for them: *Well* (said the Park-keeper) *I will invite no more Kings*; having learnt the difference between Princes when they please to put on the visard of privacie, and when they will appear like themselves, both in their Person and Attendants.

6     *Those are ripe for charitie which are withered by age or impotencie.* Especially if maimed in following their calling; for such are Industries Martyrs, at least her Confessours. Adde to these those that with diligence fight against poverty, though neither conquer till death make it a drawn battel. Expect not, but prevent their craving of thee; for God forbid the heavens should never rain till the earth first opens her mouth, seing some grounds will sooner burn then chap.

7     *The House of correction is the fittest Hospital for those Cripples, whose legs are lame through their own lazinesse.* Surely King Edward the sixth was as truly charitable in granting

Bridewell

Bridewell for the punishment of sturdy Rogues, as in giving S. Thomas Hospitall for the relief of the Poore. I have done with the subject, onely I desire rich men to awaken Hospitality, which * one saith since the yeare 1572 hath in a manner been laid asleep in the grave of Edward Earl of Darby.

*Cambd. Elis. Anno 1573.*

## Chap. 2.

## Of Jesting.

Harmlesse mirth is the best cordiall against the consumption of the spirits: wherefore Jesting is not unlawfull if it trespasseth not in Quantity, Quality, or Season.

*It is good to make a Jest, but not to make a trade of Jesting.* The Earl of Leicester, knowing that Queen Elizabeth was much delighted to see a Gentleman dance well, brought the Master of a dancing-school to dance before her: *Pish* (said the Queen) *it is his profession, I will not see him.* She liked it not where it was a Master-quality, but where it attended on other perfections. The same may we say of Jesting.

*Maxime 1.*

*Jest not with the two-edged* sword *of Gods Word.* Will nothing please thee to wash thy hands in, but the Font? or to drink healths in, but the Church Chalice? And know the whole art is learnt at the first admission, and profane Jests will come without calling. If in the troublesome dayes of King Edward the fourth a Citizen in Cheap-side was executed as a traitour, for saying he would make his sonne heir to the * Crown, though he onely meant his own house, having a Crown for the signe; more dangerous it is to wit-wanton it with the Majestie of God. Wherefore if without thine intention, and against thy will, by chancemedly thou hittest Scripture in ordinary discourse, yet fly to the city of refuge, and pray to God to forgive thee.

2
* Μάχαιραν δίστομον, Heb. 4.11.

* Speed in Edward the 4.

*Wanton Jests make fools laugh, and wise men frown.*

3

Seeing

Seeing we are civilized English men, let us not be naked Salvages in our talk. Such rotten speeches are worst in withered age, when men runne after that sinne in their words which flieth from them in the deed.

4. *Let not thy Jests like mummie be made of dead mens flesh.* Abuse not any that are departed; for to wrong their memories is to robbe their ghosts of their winding-sheets.

5. *Scoff not at the naturall defects of any which are not in their power to amend.* Oh 'tis crueltie to beat a cripple with his own crutches. Neither flout any for his profession if honest though poore and painfull. Mock not a Cobler for his black thumbes.

6. *He that relates another mans wicked Jest with delight, adopts it to be his own.* Purge them therefore from their poyson. If the prophanenesse may be sever'd from the wit, it is like a Lamprey, take out the string in the back, it may make good meat: But if the staple conceit consists in prophanenesse, then it is a viper, all poyson, and meddle not with it.

7. *He that will lose his friend for a Jest deserves to die a begger by the bargain.* Yet some think their conceits, like mustard, not good except they bite. We reade that all those who were born in England the yeare after the beginning of the great mortality * 1349. wanted their foure Cheek-teeth. Such let thy Jests be, that they may not grind the credit of thy friend, and make not Jests so long till thou becomest one.

* *Tho. Walsingam in eodem anno.*

8. *No time to break Jests when the heart-strings are about to be broken.* No more shewing of wit when the head is to be cut off. Like that dying man, who, when the Priest coming to him to give him extreme unction, asked of him where his feet were, answered, *at the end of my legs.* But at such a time Jests are an unmannerly *crepitus ingenii*: And let those take heed who end here with Democritus, that they begin not with Heraclitus hereafter.

CHAP. 3.

## Chap. 3.
## Of Self-prayſing.

HE *whoſe own worth doth ſpeak need not ſpeak his own worth.* Such boaſting ſounds proceed from emptineſſe of deſert: whereas the Conquerours in the Olympian games did not put on the Laurells on their own heads, but waited till ſome other did it. Onely Anchorets that want company may crown themſelves with their own commendations. *Maxime* 1

*It ſheweth more wit but no leſſe vanity to commend ones ſelf not in a ſtrait line but by reflection.* Some ſail to the port of their own praiſe by a ſide-wind: as when they diſpraiſe themſelves, ſtripping themſelves naked of what is their due, that the modeſty of the beholders may cloth them with it again; or when they flatter another to his face, toſſing the ball to him that he may throw it back again to them; or when they commend that quality, wherein themſelves excell, in another man (though abſent) whom all know farre their inferiour in that faculty; or laſtly (to omit other ambuſhes men ſet to ſurpriſe praiſe) when they ſend the children of their own brain to be nurſed by another man, and commend their own works in a third perſon, but if chalenged by the company that they were Authours of them themſelves, with their tongues they faintly deny it, and with their faces ſtrongly affirm it. 2

*Self-praiſing comes moſt naturally from a man when it comes moſt violently from him in his own defence.* For though modeſty binds a mans tongue to the peace in this point, yet being aſſaulted in his credit he may ſtand upon his guard, and then he doth not ſo much praiſe as purge himſelf. One braved a Gentleman to his face that in skill and valour he came farre behind him; *Tis true* (ſaid the other) *for when I fought with you, you ran* 3 *ran away before me.* In such a case, it was well return'd, and without any just aspersion of pride.

4  He that falls into sin is a man; that grieves at it, is a saint; that boasteth of it, is a devil. Yet some glory in their shame, counting the stains of sin the best complexion for their souls. These men make me believe it may be true what Mandevil writes of the Isle of Somabarre, in the East Indies, that all the Nobility thereof brand their faces with a hot iron in token of honour.

5  He that boasts of sinnes never committed is a double devil. Many brag how many gardens of virginity they have defloured, who never came near the walls thereof, lying on those with whom they did never lie, and with slanderous tongues committing rapes on chaste womens reputations. Others ( who would sooner creep into a scabbard then draw a sword ) boast of their robberies, to usurp the esteem of valour: Whereas first let them be well whipt for their lying, and as they like that, let them come afterward and entitle themselves to the gallows.

## Chap. 4.
### Of Travelling.

IT is a good accomplishment to a man, if first the stock be well grown whereon Travell is graffed, and these rules observed Before, In, and After his going abroad.

Maxime 1.  *Travell not too early before thy judgement be risen;* left thou observest rather shews then substance, marking alone Pageants, Pictures, beautifull Buildings, &c.

2  *Get the Language (in part) without which key thou shalt unlock little of moment.* It is a great advantage to be ones own interpreter. Object not that the French tongue learnt in England must be unlearnt again in France; for it is easier to adde then begin, and to pronounce then to speak.

*Be*

# Chap. 4.   *Generall Rules.*   159

3. *Be well settled in thine own Religion*, lest, travelling out of England into Spain, thou goest out of Gods blessing into the warm Sunne. They that go over maids for their Religion, will be ravish'd at the sight of the first Popish Church they enter into. But if first thou be well grounded, their fooleries shall rivet thy faith the faster, and Travell shall give thee Confirmation in that Baptisme thou didst receive at home.

4. *Know most of the rooms of thy native countrey before thou goest over the threshold thereof.* Especially seeing England presents thee with so many observables. But late Writers lack nothing but age, and home-wonders but distance to make them admired. 'Tis a tale what * Josephus writes of the two pillars set up by the sonnes of Seth in Syria, the one of brick, fire-proof; the other of stone, water-free, thereon engraving many heavenly matters to perpetuate learning in defiance of time. But it is truly moralized in our Universities, Cambridge ( of Brick ) and Oxford ( of Stone ) wherein Learning and Religion are preserved, and where the worst Colledge is more sight-worthy then the best Dutch Gymnasium. First view these, and the rest home-rarities; not like those English, that can give a better account of Fountain-bleau then Hampton-Court, of the Spaw then Bath, of Anas in Spain then Mole in Surrey.

\* *Antiqu. Jud. lib. 1. cap. 3.*

5. *Travell not beyond the Alps.* Mr. * Ascham did thank God that he was but nine dayes in Italie, wherein he saw in one citie ( Venice ) more liberty to sinne, then in London he ever heard of in nine years. That some of our Gentry have gone thither, and returned thence without infection, I more praise Gods providence then their adventure.

\* *In his preface to his Schoolmaster.*

6. *To travell from the sunne is uncomfortable.* Yet the northern parts with much ice have some crystall, and want not their remarkables.

7. *If thou wilt see much in a little, travell the Low countreys.* Holland is all Europe in an Amsterdam-print,

for

for Minerva, Mars, and Mercurie, Learning, Warre, and Traffick.

8. *Be wise in choosing Objects, diligent in marking, carefull in remembring of them*: yet herein men much follow their own humours. One askt a Barber, who never before had been at the Court, what he saw there? *Oh* (said he) *the King was excellently well trimm'd!* Thus Merchants most mark forrein Havens, Exchanges, and Marts; Souldiers note Forts, Armories, and Magazines; Scholars listen after Libraries, Disputations, and Professours; Statesmen observe Courts of justice, Counsells, &c. Every one is partiall in his own profession.

9. *Labour to distill and unite into thy self the scatter'd perfections of severall Nations.* But (as it was said of one, who with more industry then judgement frequented a Colledge-Library, and commonly made use of the worst notes he met with in any Authours, *that he weeded the Library*) many weed forrein Countries, bringing home Dutch Drunkennes, Spanish Pride, French Wantonnesse and Italian Atheisme. As for the good herbs, Dutch Industry, Spanish Loyalty, French Courtesie, and Italian Frugality, these they leave behind them. Others bring home just nothing; and because they singled not themselves from their Countreymen, though some years beyond Sea, were never out of England.

10. *Continue correspondency with some choyce forrein friend after thy return.* As some Professour or Secretary, who virtually is the whole University, or State. 'Tis but a dull Dutch fashion, their *Albus Amicorum*, to make a dictionary of their friends names: But a selected familiar in every Countrey is usefull, betwixt you there may be a Letter-exchange. Be sure to return as good wares as thou receivest, and acquaint him with the remarkables of thy own Countrey, and he will willingly continue the trade, finding it equally gainfull.

*Let*

*Let discourse rather be easily drawn, then willingly flow from thee.* That thou mayest not seem weak to hold, or desirous to vent news, but content to gratifie thy friends. Be sparing in reporting improbable truths, especially to the vulgar, who insteed of informing their judgements will suspect thy credit. Disdain their pevish pride who rail on their native land (whose worst fault is that it bred such ungratefull fools) and in all their discourses preferre forrein countreys, herein shewing themselves of kinne to the wild Irish in loving their Nurses better then their Mothers.

## Chap. 5.
## Of Company.

COmpanie is one of the greatest pleasures of the nature of man. For the beams of joy are made hotter by reflection, when related to another; and otherwise gladnesse it self must grieve for want of one to expresse it-self to.

*It is unnaturall for a man to court and hug solitarinesse.* It is observed, that the farthest Ilands in the world are so seated that there is none so remote but that from some shore of it another Iland or Continent may be discerned: As if hereby Nature invited countreys to a mutuall commerce one with another. Why then should any man affect to environ himself with so deep and great reservednesse, as not to communicate with the societie of others? And though we pity those who made solitarinesse their refuge in time of persecution, we must condemne such as chuse it in the Churches prosperity. For well may we count him not well in his wits, who will live alwayes under a bush, because others in a storm shelter themselves under it.

*Yet a desert is better then a debauch'd companion.* For the wildnesse of the place is but uncheerfull, whilest the wildnesse

wildnesse of bad persons is also infectious. Better therefore ride alone then have a thief's company. And such is a wicked man, who will rob thee of pretious time, if he doth no more mischief. The Nazarites who might drink no wine were also forbidden ( Numb. 6. 3. ) to eat grapes, whereof wine is made. We must not onely avoid sinne it self, but also the causes and occasions thereof: amongst which bad company (the limetwigs of the devil) is the chiefest, especially, to catch those natures which like the good-fellow planet Mercury are most swayed by others.

4 *If thou beest cast into bad company, like Hercules, thou must sleep with thy club in thine hand, and stand on thy guard.* I mean if against thy will the tempest of an unexpected occasion drives thee amongst such rocks; then be thou like the river * Dee in Merionethshire in Wales, which running through Pimble meere remains entire, and mingles not her streames with the waters of the lake. Though with them, be not of them; keep civil communion with them, but separate from their sinnes. And if against thy will thou fall'st amongst wicked men, know to thy comfort thou art still in thy calling, and therefore in Gods keeping, who on thy prayers will preserve thee.

*Cambd. Brit. in Merioneth.*

5 *The company he keeps is the comment, by help whereof men expound the most close and mysticall man;* understanding him for one of the same religion, life, and manners with his associates. And though perchance he be not such an one, 'tis just he should be counted so for conversing with them. Augustus Cesar came thus to discern his two daughters inclinations : for being once at a publick Shew, where much people was present, he * observed that the grave Senatours talked with Livia, but loose Youngsters and riotous persons with Julia.

*Sueton. in August. Cæs.*

9 *He that eats cherries with Noblemen shall have his eyes spirted out with the stones.* This outlandish Proverb hath in it an English truth, that they who constantly converse

verse with men farre above their estates shall reap shame and losse thereby: If thou payest nothing, they will count thee a sucker, no branch; a wen, no member of their companie: If in payments thou keepest pace with them, their long strides will soon tire thy short legs. The Bevers in New England, when some ten of them together draw a stick to the building of their lodging, set the *weakest Bevers to the lighter end of the log, and the strongest take the heaviest part thereof: whereas men often lay the greatest burthen on the weakest back; and great persons, to teach meaner men to learn their distance, take pleasure to make them pay for their companie. I except such men, who having some excellent qualitie are gratis very welcome to their betters; such a one, though he payes not a penny of the shot, spends enough in lending them his time and discourse.

*Wood in his description of New England.*

7. *To affect alwayes to be the best of the companie argues a base disposition.* Gold alwayes worn in the same purse with silver loses both of the colour and weight; and so to converse alwayes with inferiours degrades a man of his worth. Such there are that love to be the Lords of the companie, whilest the rest must be their Tenants: as if bound by their lease to approve, praise, and admire, whatsoever they say. These knowing the lownesse of their parts love to live with dwarfs, that they may seem proper men. To come amongst their equalls, they count it an abbridgement of their freedome, but to be with their betters, they deem it flat slavery.

8. *It is excellent for one to have a Library of Scholars, especially if they be plain to be read.* I mean of a communicative nature, whose discourses are as full as fluent, and their judgements as right as their tongues ready: such mens talk shall be thy Lectures. To conclude, Good Company is not onely profitable whilest a man lives, but sometimes when he is dead. For he that was buried

with the bones of *Elisha, by a Posthumous miracle of that Prophet, recovered his life by lodging with such a grave-fellow.

*2. Kings. 13. 21.

## Chap. 6.
### Of Apparell.

Clothes are for Necessity; warm cloths for Health; cleanly for Decency; lasting for Thrift; and rich for Magnificence. Now there may be a fault in their Number, if too various; Making, if too vain; Matter, if too costly; and Mind of the wearer, if he takes pride therein. We come therefore to some generall directions.

**Maxime 1**

*It's a chargeable vanity to be constantly clothed above ones purse, or place.* I say Constantly; for perchance sometimes it may be dispensed with. A Great man, who himself was very plain in apparell, checkt a Gentleman for being over fine: who modestly answered, *Your Lordship hath better clothes at home, and I have worse.* But sure no plea can be made when this Luxury is grown to be ordinary. It was an arrogant act of *Hubert Archbishop of Canterbury, who, when King John had given his Courtiers rich Liveries, to Ape the Lion, gave his servants the like, wherewith the King was not a little offended. But what shall we say to the riot of our age, wherein (as Peacocks are more gay then the Eagle himself) subjects are grown braver then their Sovereigne?

* Math. Paris in Joan. Anno. 1201.

**2**

*'Tis beneath a wise man alwayes to wear clothes beneath men of his rank.* True, there is a state sometimes in decent plainnesse. When a wealthy Lord at a great Solemnity had the plainest apparell, *O* (said one) *if you had markt it well his sute had the richest pockets.* Yet it argues no wisdome, in clothes alwayes to stoop beneath his condition. When Antisthenes saw Socrates in a torn coat, he shewed a hole thereof to the people; *And loe*
(quoth

(quoth he) *through this I see Socrates his pride.*

*He shews a light gravity who loves to be an exception from a generall fashion.* For the received custome in the place where we live is the most competent judge of decency; from which we must not appeal to our own opinion. When the French Courtiers mourning for their King * Henrie the second had worn cloth a whole yeare, all silks became so vile in every mans eyes, that if any was seen to wear them, he was presently accounted a Mechanick or Countrey-fellow.

*It's a folly for one Proteus-like never to appear twice in one shape.* Had some of our Gallants been with the * Israelites in the wildernesse, when for fourty years their clothes waxed not old, they would have been vexed, though their clothes were whole, to have been so long in one fashion. Yet here I must confesse, I understand not what is reported of Fulgentius, that he used the same garment Winter and Summer, and never alter'd his * clothes, *etiam in Sacris peragendis.*

*He that is proud of the russling of his silks, like a mad man, laughs at the ratling of his fetters.* For indeed, Clothes ought to be our remembrancers of our lost innocency. Besides, why should any brag of what's but borrowed? Should the Estrige snatch off the Gallants feather, the Beaver his hat, the Goat his gloves, the Sheep his sute, the Silk-worm his stockings, and Neat his shoes (to strip him no farther then modesty will give leave) he would be left in a cold condition. And yet 'tis more pardonable to be proud, even of cleanly rags, then (as many are) of affected slovennesse. The one is proud of a molehill, the other of a dunghill.

To conclude, Sumptuary laws in this land to reduce apparell to a set standard of price, and fashion, according to the severall states of men, have long been wish'd, but are little to be hoped for. Some think private mens superfluity is a necessary evill in a State,

*Mont. 1. book, chap. 4.*

*Deuterono. 29. 5.*

*Vincentius. Spec. lib. 10. cap. 105.*

the floting of fashions affording a standing maintenance to many thousands which otherwise would be at a losse for a livelihood, men maintaining more by their pride then by their charitie.

## Chap. 7.
## Of Building.

HE that alters an old house is tied as a translatour to the originall, and is confin'd to the phancie of the first builder. Such a man were unwise to pluck down good old building, to erect (perchance) worse new. But those that raise a new house from the ground are blame worthy if they make it not handsome, seeing to them Method and Confusion are both at a rate. In building we must respect Situation, Contrivance, Receipt, Strength, and Beauty. Of Situation.

*Maxime* 1. *Chiefly choose a wholesome aire.* For aire is a dish one feeds on every minute, and therefore it need be good. Wherefore great men (who may build where they please, as poore men where they can) if herein they preferre their profit above their health, I referre them to their Physicians to make them pay for it accordingly.

2. *Wood and water are two staple commodities where they may be had.* The former I confesse hath made so much iron, that it must now be bought with the more silver, and grows daily dearer. But 'tis as well pleasant as profitable to see a house cased with trees, like that of Anchises in Troy.

\*  *Virgil* 2. *Æneid.* 32.
----------\* *quanquam secreta parentis Anchisæ domus arboribusq; obtecta recessit.*

\* *Camb. Brit. in Cambridgeshire.*
The worst is, where a place is bald of wood, no art can make it a periwig. As for water, begin with Pindars beginning, ἄριϛον μὲν ὕδωρ. The fort of \* Gogmagog Hills nigh Cambridge is counted impregnable but for want of water, the mischief of many

Chap. 7.   *Generall Rules.*   167

ny houses where servants must bring the well on their shoulders.

*Next a pleasant prospect is to be respected.* A medly view (such as of water and land at Greenwich) best entertains the eyes, refreshing the wearied beholder with exchange of objects. Yet I know a more profitable prospect, where the owner can onely see his own land round about.

*A fair entrance with an easie ascent gives a great grace to a building*: where the Hall is a preferment out of the Court, the Parlour out of the Hall; not (as in some old buildings) where the doores are so low Pygmies must stoop, and the rooms so high that Giants may stand upright. But now we are come to Contrivance.

*Let not thy common rooms be severall, nor thy severall rooms be common.* The Hall (which is a Pandocheum) ought to lie open, and so ought Passages and Stairs (provided that the whole house be not spent in paths) Chambers and Closets are to be private and retired.

*Light (Gods eldest daughter) is a principall beauty in a building*: yet it shines not alike from all parts of Heaven. An East-window welcomes the infant beams of the Sun, before they are of strength to do any harm, and is offensive to none but a sluggard. A South-window in summer is a chimny with a fire in't, and needs the schreen of a curtain. In a West-window in summer time towards night, the Sun grows low and over familiar with more light then delight. A North-window is best for Butteries and Cellars, where the beere will be sower for the Suns smiling on it. Thorow-lights are best for rooms of entertainment, and windows on one side for dormitories. As for Receipt,

*A house had better be too little for a day then too great for a yeare.* And it's easier borrowing of thy neighbour a brace of chambers for a night, then a bag of money for a twelvemonth. It is vain therefore to proportion the receipt to an extraordinary occasion, as those who

by

by overbuilding their houses have dilapidated their lands, and their states have been press'd to death under the weight of their house. As for Strength,

8 *Countrey-houses must be Substantives, able to stand of themseves.* Not like City-buildings supported by their neighbours on either side. By Strength we mean such as may resist Weather and Time, not Invasion, Castles being out of date in this peaceable age. As for the making of motes round about, it is questionable whether the fogs be not more unhealthfull, then the fish brings profit, or the water defence. Beauty remains behind as the last to be regarded, because houses are made to be lived in not lookt on.

9 *Let not the Front look asquint on a stranger, but accost him right at his entrance.* Uniformity also much pleaseth the eye; and 'tis observed that free-stone, like a fair complexion, soonest waxeth old, whilest brick keeps her beauty longest.

10 *Let the office-houses observe the due distance from the mansion-house.* Those are too familiar which presume to be of the same pile with it. The same may be said of stables and barns; without which a house is like a city without outworks, it can never hold out long.

11 *Gardens also are to attend in their place*: When God (Genesis 2. 9) planted a garden Eastward, he made to grow out of the ground every tree pleasant to the sight, and good for food. Sure he knew better what was proper to a garden then those, who nowadayes therein only feed the eyes, and starve both tast and smell.

To conclude, in Building rather believe any man then an Artificer in his own art for matter of charges, not that they cannot but will not be faithfull. Should they tell thee all the cost at the first, it would blast a young Builder in the budding, and therefore they sooth thee up till it hath cost thee something to confute them. The spirit of Building first possessed people after the floud,

floud, which then caused the confusion of languages, and since of the estate of many a man.

## Chap. 8.

### *Of Anger.*

ANger is one of the sinews of the soul; he that wants it hath a maimed mind, and with Jacob sinew-shrunk in the hollow of his thigh must needs halt. Nor is it good to converse with such as cannot be angry, and with the Caspian sea never ebbe nor flow. This Anger is either Heavenly, when one is offended for God: or Hellish, when offended with God and Goodnes: or Earthly, in temporall matters. Which Earthly Anger (whereof we treat) may also be Hellish, if for no cause, no great cause, too hot, or too long.

*Be not angry with any without a cause.* If thou beest, thou must not onely, as the Proverb saith, be appeas'd without amends (having neither cost nor damage given thee) but, as our Saviour* saith, be in danger of the judgement. | Maxime 1.

*Matth 5.22.

*Be not mortally angry with any for a veniall fault.* He will make a strange combustion in the state of his soul, who at the landing of every cockboat sets the beacons on fire. To be angry for every toy debases the worth of thy anger; for he who will be angry for any thing, will be angry for nothing. | 2

*Let not thy anger be so hot, but that the most torrid zone thereof may be habitable.* Fright not people from thy presence with the terrour of thy intolerable impatience. Some men like a tiled house are long before they take fire, but once on flame there is no coming near to quench them. | 3

*Take heed of doing irrevocable acts in thy passion.* As the revealing of secrets, which makes thee a bankrupt for society ever after: neither do such things which done once are done for ever, so that no bemoaning can | 4

Z amend

amend them. Sampsons hair grew again, but not his eyes: Time may restore some losses, others are never to be repaird. Wherefore in thy rage make no Persian decree which cannot be revers'd or repeald; but rather Polonian laws which (they say) last but three dayes: Do not in an instant what an age cannot recompence.

5 *Exod.16.24. *Ephes.4.26.
*Anger kept till the next morning, with* Manna, doth putrifie and corrupt.* Save that Manna corrupted not at all, and anger most of all, kept the next Sabbath. S. Paul *saith, *Let not the Sunne go down on your wrath*; to carry news to the Antipodes in another world of thy revengefull nature. Yet let us take the Apostles meaning, rather then his words, with all possible speed to depose our passion, not understanding him so literally that we may take leave to be angry till Sunset: then might our wrath lengthen with the dayes; and men in Greenland, where day lasts above a quarter of a yeare, have plentifull scope of revenge. And as the English (by command from William the Conquerer) always raked up their fire, and put out their candles, when the * Curfew-bell was rung; let us then also quench all sparks of anger and heat of passion.

*Cowels Interpreter out of Stows Annals.

6 *Ephes. 4.27.
*He that keeps anger long in his bosome giveth place to the* devil.* And why should we make room for him, who will crowd in too fast of himself? Heat of passion makes our souls to chappe, and the devil creeps in at the cranies; yea a furious man in his fits may seem possess'd with a devil, fomes, fumes, tears himself, is deaf, and dumbe in effect, to heare or speak reason: sometimes wallows, stares, stamps, with fiery eyes and flaming cheeks. Had Narcissus himself seen his own face when he had been angry, he could never have fallen in love with himself.

CHAP. 9.

## Chap. 9.
### Of Expecting Preferment.

THere are as many severall tenures of Expectation as of Possession, some nearer, some more remote, some grounded on strong, others on weaker reasons. (As for a groundlesse Expectation, it is a wilfull self-delusion.) We come to instructions how men should manage their hopes herein.

*Hope not for impossibilities.* For though the object of hope be *Futurum possibile*, yet some are so mad as to feed their Expectation on things, though not in themselves, yet to them impossible, if we consider the weaknesse of the means whereby they seek to attain them. He needs to stand on tiptoes that hopes to touch the moon; and those who expect what in reason they cannot expect, may expect. *Maxime 1.*

*Carefully survey what proportion the means thou hast bear to the end thou expectest.* Count not a Courtiers promise of course a specialty that he is bound to preferre thee: Seeing Complements oftentimes die in the speaking, why should thy hopes (grounded on them) live longer then the hearing? perchance the text of his promise intended but common courtesies, which thy apprehension expounds speedy and speciall favours. Others make up the weaknesse of their means with conceit of the strength of their deserts, foolishly thinking that their own merits will be the undoubted Patrons to present them to all void Benefices. 2

*The heir apparent to the next preferment may be disinherited by an unexpected accident.* A Gentleman, servant to the Lord Admirall Howard, was suiter to a Lady above his deserts, grounding the confidence of his successe on his relation to so honourable a Lord; which Lord gave the Anchor as badge of his office, and therefore this suiter wrote in a window, 3

> If I be bold,
> The anchor is my hold.

But his corrivall to the same Mistris coming into the same room wrote under,

> Yet fear the worst:
> What if the Cable burst?

Thus uselesse is the Anchor of hope (good for nothing but to deceive those that relie on it) if the cable or small cords of means and causes whereon it depends fail and miscarry. Daily experience tenders too many examples. A Gentleman who gave a Basilisk for his Arms or Crest promised to make a young kinsman of his his heir, which kinsman to ingratiate himself painted a Basilisk in his study, and beneath it these verses,

> *Falleris asspectu Basiliscum occidere, Plini,*
> *Nam vitæ nostræ spem Basiliscus alit.*
> The Basilisk's the onely stay,
> My life preserving still;
> Pliny, thou li'dst when thou didst say
> The Basilisk doth kill.

But this rich Gentleman dying frustrated his expectation, and bequeathed all his estate to another, whereupon the Epigram was thus altered,

> *Certe aluit, sed spe vana, spes vana venenum:*
> *Ignoscas, Plini, verus es Historicus.*
> Indeed vain hopes to me he gave,
> Whence I my poison drew:
> Pliny, thy pardon now I crave,
> Thy writings are too true.

4. *Proportion thy expences to what thou hast in possession, not to thy expectancies.* Otherwise he that feeds on wind must needs be griped with the Collick at last. And if the Ceremoniall law forbad the Jews to seeth a kid in the mothers milk, the law of good husbandry forbids us to eat a kid in the mothers belly, spending our pregnant hopes before they be delivered.

| Chap. 9. | *Generall Rules.* | 173 |

*Imbrue not thy soul in bloudy wishes of his death who parts thee and thy preferment.* A murther the more common, because one cannot be arraigned for it on earth. But those are charitable murtherers which wish them in heaven, not so much that they may have ease at their journeys end, but because they must needs take death in the way.

*In earthly matters expectation takes up more joy on trust, then the fruition of the thing is able to discharge.* The Lion is not so fierce as painted, nor are matters so fair as the pencill of the expectant limmes them out in his hopes. They forecount their wives fair, fruitfull, and rich, without any fault; their children witty, beautifull, and dutifull, without any frowardnesse: and as S. Basil held that roses in paradise before mans fall grew without prickles, they abstract the pleasures of things from the troubles annexed to them, which when they come to enjoy, they must take both together. Surely a good unlook'd for is a virgin happinesse; whereas those who obtain what long they have gazed on in expectation, onely marry what themselves have defloured before.

*When our hopes break let our patience hold:* relying on Gods providence without murmuring, who often provides for men above what we can think or desire. When Robert * Holgate could not peaceably enjoy his small living in Lincolneshire, because of the litigiousnesse of a neighbouring Knight, coming to London to right himself he came into the favour of King Henrie the eighth, and got by degrees the Archbishoprick of York. Thus God sometimes defeats our hopes, or disturbs our possession of lesser favours, thereby to bestow on his servants better blessings, if not here, hereafter.

\* *Godwin in his Catal. of Archbishops of York.*

Z 3     Chap. 10.

## Chap. 10.
### Of Memory.

IT is the treasure-house of the mind, wherein the monuments thereof are kept and preserved. Plato makes it the mother of the Muses. *Aristotle sets it one degree further, making Experience the mother of Arts, Memory the parent of Experience. Philosophers place it in the rere of the head; and it seems the mine of Memory lies there, because there naturally men dig for it, scratching it when they are at a losse. This again is twofold: one, the simple retention of things; the other, a regaining them when forgotten.

*Metaphys. lib. 1 cap. 1.*

**Maxime 1** *Brute creatures equall, if not exceed, men in a bare retentive Memory.* Through how many labyrinths of woods, without other clue of threed then naturall instinct, doth the hunted hare return to her muce? How doth the little bee, flying into severall meadows and gardens, sipping of many cups, yet never intoxicated, through an ocean (as I may say) of air, steddily steer her self home, without help of card or compasse. But these cannot play an aftergame, and recover what they have forgotten, which is done by the mediation of discourse.

**2** *Artificiall memory is rather a trick then an art, and more for the gain of the teacher then profit of the learners.* Like the tossing of a pike, which is no part of the postures and motions thereof, and is rather for ostentation then use, to shew the strength and nimblenesse of the arm, and is often used by wandring Souldiers as an introduction to beg. Understand it of the artificiall rules which at this day are delivered by Memory-mountebanks; for sure an art thereof may be made (wherein as yet the world is defective) and that no more destructive to naturall Memory then spectacles are to eyes, which girls in Holland wear from 12 years of age. But till this

# Chap. 10.    Generall Rules.    175

this be found out, let us observe these plain rules.

*First soundly infix in thy mind what thou desirest to remember.* What wonder is it if agitation of businesse jog that out of thy head, which was there rather tack'd then fastned? whereas those notions which get in by *violenta possessio* will abide there till *ejectio firma*, sicknesse or extreme age, dispossesse them. It is best knocking in the nail overnight, and clinching it the next morning.

*Overburthen not thy Memory to make so faithfull a servant a slave.* Remember Atlas was weary. Have as much reason as a Camell, to rise when thou hast thy full load. Memory, like a purse, if it be over full that it cannot shut, all will drop out of it: Take heed of a gluttonous curiositie to feed on many things, lest the greedinesse of the appetite of thy Memory spoyl the digestion thereof. Beza's case was peculiar and memorable; being above fourescore years of age he perfectly could say by heart any Greek Chapter in * S. Pauls Epistles, or any thing else which he had learnt long before, but forgot whatsoever was newly told him; his Memory like an inne retaining old guests, but having no room to entertain new.

*Spoyl not thy Memory with thine own jealousie, nor make it bad by suspecting it.* How canst thou find that true which thou wilt not trust? S. Augustine tells us of his friend Simplicius, who being ask'd, could tell all Virgills verses backward and forward, and yet the same party, * vowed to God, that he knew not that he could do it till they did try him. Sure there is conceal'd strength in mens Memories, which they take no notice of.

*Marshall thy notions into a handsome method.* One will carrie twice more weight trust and pack'd up in bundles, then when it lies untowardly flapping and hanging about his shoulders. Things orderly fardled up under heads are most portable.

*Adventure not all thy learning in one bottom, but divide it betwixt*

3

4

* *Thuan. obit. doct. virorum. pag. 384.*

5

* *Testatus est Deum, nescisse se hoc posse ante illud experimentum,* August. Tom. 7. lib. de anima & ejus orig. cap. 7.

6

7

*betwixt thy Memory and thy Note-books.* He that with Bias carries all his learning about him in his head will utterly be beggerd and bankrupt, if a violent disease, a mercilesse thief, should rob and strip him. I know some have a Common-place against Common-place-books, and yet perchance will privately make use of what publickly they declaim against. A Common-place-book contains many Notions in garison, whence the owner may draw out an army into the field on competent warning.

*Moderate diet and good aire preserve Memory*; but what aire is best I dare not define, when such great ones differ. *Some say a pure and subtle aire is best, another commends a thick and foggy aire. For the *Pisans sited in the fennes and marish of Arnus have excellent memories, as if the foggy aire were a cap for their heads.

*Thankfulnesse to God for it continues the Memory*: whereas some proud people have been visited with such oblivion, that they have forgotten their own names. Staupitius Tutour to Luther, and a godly man, in a vain ostentation of his memory repeated Christs Genealogie (Matth. 1.) by heart in his Sermon, but being out about the Captivity of Babylon, *I see* (saith *he) *God resisteth the proud*, and so betook himself to his book. Abuse not thy Memory to be Sinnes Register, nor make advantage thereof for wickednesse. Excellently * Augustine, *Quidam vero pessimi memoria sunt mirabili, qui tanto pejores sunt, quanto minus possunt, quæ male cogitant, oblivisci.*

## 8

*Plato, Aristotle, Tully.
*Singulari valent memoriâ quo urbs crassiore fruatur aere, Mercat. Atlas in Tussia.

## 9

* Melchior Adamus in vita Staupitii, pag. 20.

* De civ. Dei lib. 7. cap. 3.

## Chap. II.
## Of Phancie.

IT is an inward Sense of the soul, for a while retaining and examining things brought in thither by the Common sense. It is the most boundles and restlesse faculty of the soul: for whilest the Understanding and the Will are kept as it were in *Libera Custodia* to their objects of *Verum* & *Bonum*, the Phancie is free from all engagements: it digs without spade, sails without ship, flies without wings, builds without charges, fights without bloudshed, in a moment striding from the centre to the circumference of the world, by a kind of omnipotencie creating and annihilating things in an instant; and things divorced in Nature are married in Phancie as in a lawlesse place. It is also most restlesse: whilest the Senses are bound, and Reason in a manner asleep, Phancie like a sentinell walks the round, ever working, never wearied. The chief diseases of the Phancie are, either that they are too wild and high-soaring, or else too low and groveling, or else too desultory and overvoluble. Of the first.

*If thy Phancie be but a little too rank, age it self will correct it.* To lift too high is no fault in a young horse, because with travelling he will mend it for his own ease. Thus lofty Phancies in young men will come down of themselves, and in processe of time the overplus will shrink to be but even measure. But if this will not do it, then observe these rules. — Maxime 1

*Take part alwayes with thy Judgement against thy Phancie in any thing wherein they shall dissent.* If thou suspectest thy conceits too luxuriant, herein account thy suspicion a legall conviction, and damne whatsoever thou doubtest of. Warily Tullie, *Bene monent, qui vetant quicquam facere, de quo dubitas, æquum sit an iniquum.* — 2

*Take the advise of a faithfull friend, and submit thy inventions* — 3 to his censure. When thou penneſt an oration, let him have the power of *Index expurgatorius*, to expunge what he pleaſeth; and do not thou like a fond mother crie if the child of thy brain be corrected for playing the wanton. Mark the arguments and reaſons of his alterations, why that phraſe leaſt proper, this paſſage more cautious and adviſed, and after a while thou ſhalt perform the place in thine own perſon, and not go out of thy ſelf for a cenſurer. If thy Phancie be too low and humble,

4. *Let thy judgement be King but not Tyrant over it, to condemne harmleſſe yea commendable conceits.* Some for fear their orations ſhould giggle will not let them ſmile. Give it alſo liberty to rove, for it will not be extravagant. There is no danger that weak folks if they walk abroad will ſtraggle farre, as wanting ſtrength.

5. *Acquaint thy ſelf with reading Poets, for there Phancie is in her throne*; and in time the ſparks of the Authours wit will catch hold on the Reader, and inflame him with love, liking, and deſire of imitation. I confeſſe there is more required to teach one to write then to ſee a coppy: however there is a ſecret force of faſcination in reading Poems to raiſe and provoke Phancie. If thy Phancie be over voluble, then

6. *Whip this vagrant home to the firſt object whereon it ſhould be ſettled.* Indeed nimbleneſſe is the perfection of this faculty, but levity the bane of it. Great is the difference betwixt a ſwift horſe, and a skittiſh, that will ſtand on no ground. Such is the ubiquitary Phancie, which will keep long reſidence on no one ſubject, but is ſo courteous to ſtrangers that it ever welcomes that conceit moſt which comes laſt; and new ſpecies ſupplant the old ones, before ſeriouſly conſidered. If this be the fault of thy Phancie, I ſay whip it home to the firſt object, whereon it ſhould be ſettled. This do as often as occaſion requires, and by degrees the fugitive ſervant will learn to abide by his work without running away.

7. *Acquaint thy self by degrees with hard and knotty studies*, as School-divinity, which will clog thy overnimble Phancie. True, at the first it will be as welcome to thee as a prison, and their very solutions will seem knots unto thee. But take not too much at once, lest thy brain turn edge. Taste it first as a potion for Physick, and by degrees thou shalt drink it as beer for thirst: Practice will make it pleasant. Mathematicks are also good for this purpose: If beginning to try a Conclusion, thou must make an end, lest thou losest thy pains that are past, and must proceed seriously and exactly. I meddle not with those Bedlam-phancies, all whose conceits are antiques, but leave them for the Physician to purge with hellebore.

8. *To clothe low-creeping matter with high-flown language is not fine Phancie, but flat foolerie.* It rather loads then raises a Wren, to fasten the feathers of an Estridge to her wings. Some mens speeches are like the high mountains in Ireland, having a durty bog in the top of them; the very ridge of them in high words having nothing of worth, but what rather stalls then delights the Auditour.

9. *Fine Phancies in manufactures invent engines rather pretty then usefull*; and commonly one trade is too narrow for them. They are better to project new wayes then to prosecute old, and are rather skilfull in many mysteries then thriving in one. They affect not voluminous inventions, wherein many years must constantly be spent to perfect them, except there be in them variety of pleasant employment.

10. *Imagination (the work of the Phancie) hath produc'd reall effects*. Many serious and sad examples hereof may be produced: I will onely insist on a merry one. A Gentleman having led a company of children beyond their usuall journey, they began to be weary, and joyntly cried to him to carry them; which because of their multitude he could not do, but told them he would

Aa 2 provide

provide them horses to ride on. Then cutting little wands out of the hedge as nagges for them, and a great stake as a gelding for himself, thus mounted Phancie put mettall into their legs, and they came cheerfully home.

11 *Phancie runs most furiously when a guilty Conscience drives it.* One that owed much money, and had many Creditours, as he walked London-streets in the evening, a tenterhook catch'd his cloak. *At whose suit?* said he, conceiving some Bailiff had arrested him. Thus guilty Consciences are afraid where no fear is, and count every creature they meet a Serjeant sent from God to punish them.

## Chap. 12.
### Of Naturall Fools.

They have the cases of men, and little else of them besides speech and laughter. And indeed it may seem strange that *Risibile* being the propertie of man alone, they who have least of man should have most thereof, laughing without cause or measure.

Maxime 1  *Generally Nature hangs out a sygne of simplicity in the face of a Fool;* and there is enough in his countenance for an Hue and Crie to take him on suspicion: or else it is stamped on the figure of his body; their heads sometimes so little, that there is no room for wit; sometimes so long, that there is no wit for so much room.

2  *Yet some by their faces may passe currant enough till they cry themselves down by their speaking.* Thus men know the bell is crackt, when they heare it toll'd; yet some that have stood out the assault of two or three questions, and have answered pretty rationally, have afterwards of their own accord betrayed and yielded themselves to be fools.

3  *The oathes and railing of Fools is oftentimes no fault of theirs but their teachers.* The Hebrew word *Barac* signifies to blesse,

blesse, and to curse; and 'tis the speakers pleasure if he use it in the worst acception. Fools of themselves are equally capable to pray and to swear; they therefore have the greatest sinne who by their example or otherwise teach them so to do.

*One may get wisdome by looking on a Fool.* In beholding him, think how much thou art beholden to him that suffered thee not to be like him: Onely Gods pleasure put a difference betwixt you. And consider that a Fool and a Wiseman are alike both in the starting-place, their birth, and at the post, their death; onely they differ in the race of their lives.

*It is unnaturall to laugh at a Naturall.* How can the object of thy pity be the subject of thy pastime? I confesse sometimes the strangenesse, and, as I may say, witty simplicity of their actions may extort a smile from a serious man, who at the same time may smile at them and sorrow for them. But it is one thing to laugh at them *in transitu*, a snap and away, and another to make a set meal in jeering them, and as the Philistines to send for Sampson to make them sport.

*To make a trade of laughing at a Fool is the highway to become one.* Tullie confesseth that whilest he laughed at one * Hircus a very ridiculous man, *dum illum video pene factus sum ille*: And one telleth us of Gallus Vibius, a man first of great eloquence, and afterwards of great madnesse, which seized not on him so much by accident as his own affectation, so long * mimically imitating mad men that he became one.

*Epist. lib. 2. Epist. 9.*

*Dum insanos imitatur, quod assimulabat ad vivum redegit, Rhodiginus Antiq. lib. 11. c. 13.*

*Many have been the wise speeches of fools, though not so many as the foolish speeches of wise men.* Now the wise speeches of these silly souls proceed from one of these reasons: Either because talking much, and shooting often, they must needs hit the mark sometimes, though not by aim, by hap: Or else because a Fools *mediocriter* is *optime*; Sense from his mouth, a Sentence; and a tolerable

rable speech cri'd up for an Apothegme: Or lastly, because God may sometimes illuminate them, and (especially towards their death) admit them to the possession of some part of reason. A poore begger in Paris being very hungry stayed so long in a Cooks shop, who was dishing up of meat, till his stomach was satisfied with the onely smell thereof. The cholerick covetous Cook demanded of him to pay for his breakfast. The pooreman denyed it, and the controversie was referr'd to the deciding of the next man that should passe by, which chanced to be the most notorious Idiot in the whole City. He on the relation of the matter determined that the poore mans money should be put betwixt two empty dishes, and the Cook should be recompenced with the gingling of the poore mans money, as he was satisfied with the onely smell of the Cooks meat. And this is affirmed by * credible Writers, as no fable but an undoubted fact. More waggish was that of a rich landed Fool, whom a Courtier had begg'd, and carried about to wait on him. He coming with his master to a Gentlemans house where the picture of a Fool was wrought in a fair suit of arras, cut the picture out with a penknife. And being chidden for so doing, *You have more cause* (said he) *to thank me, for if my master had seen the picture of the Fool, he would have begg'd the hangings of the King as he did my lands.* When the standers by comforted a Naturall which lay on his death-bed, and told him that foure proper fellows should carry his body to the Church: *Yea* (quoth he) *but I had rather by half go thither my self*; and then prayed to God at his last gasp not to require more of him then he gave him.

As for a Changeling, which is not one child changed for another, but one child on a sudden much changed from it self; and for a Jester, which some count a necessary evil in a Court (an office which none but he that hath wit can perform, and none

* *Jo. And. Panor. Barba. & alii inde ad nostram. Hiero. Franc. in lib. furios. de reg. juris ff. Boer. decis. 23 n 58. Mantic. de conject. ult. v. lib. 2. Tit. 5. n. 8. Corset. sing. verbi Testamentum.*

and none but he that wants wit will perform) I conceive them not to belong to the present subject.

## Chap. 13.
### Of Recreations.

REcreation is a second Creation, when wearinesse hath almost annihilated ones spirits. It is the breathing of the soul, which otherwise would be stifled with continuall businesse. We may trespasse in them, if using such as are forbidden by the Lawyer, as against the statutes; Physician, as against health; Divine, as against conscience.

*Be well satisfied in thy Conscience of the lawfulnesse of the recreation thou usest.* Some fight against Cockfighting, and bait Bull and Bearbaiting, because man is not to be a common Barretour to set the creatures at discord; and seeing Antipathy betwixt creatures was kindled by mans sinne, what pleasure can he take to see it burn? Others are of the contrary opinion, and that Christianity gives us a placard to use these sports; and that mans Charter of dominion over the creatures enables him to employ them as well for pleasure as necesity. In these, as in all other doubtfull recreations, be well assured first of the legality of them. He that sinnes against his Conscience sinnes with a witnesse. *Maxime* 1

*Spill not the morning (the quintessence of the day) in recreations.* For sleep it self is a recreation; adde not therefore sauce to sauce; and he cannot properly have any title to be refresh'd, who was not first faint. Pastime, like wine, is poyson in the morning. It is then good husbandry to sow the head, which hath lain fallow all night, with some serious work. Chiefly intrench not on the Lords day to use unlawfull sports; this were to spare thine own flock, and to sheere Gods lambe. 2

*Let thy recreations be ingenious, and bear proportion with thine age.* If thou saist with Paul, *When I was a child I did* 3

*as*

*as a child*, say also with him, *But when I was a man I put away childish things.* Wear also the childs coat, if thou usest his sports.

4. *Take heed of boisterous and overviolent exercises.* Ringing oftentimes hath made good musick on the bells, and put mens bodies out of tune, so that by overheating themselves they have rung their own passing-bell.

5. *Yet the ruder sort of people scarce count any thing a sport which is not loud and violent.* The Muscovite women esteem none loving husbands except they beat their wives. 'Tis no pastime with country Clowns that cracks not pates, breaks not shins, bruises not limbes, tumbles and tosses not all the body. They think themselves not warm in their geeres, till they are all on fire; and count it but dry sport, till they swim in their own sweat. Yet I conceive the Physicians rule in exercises, *Ad ruborem* but *non ad sudorem,* is too scant measure.

6. *Refresh that part of thy self which is most wearied.* If thy life be sedentary, exercise thy body; if stirring and active, recreate thy mind. But take heed of cousening thy mind, in setting it to do a double task under pretence of giving it a play-day, as in the labyrinth of Chesse, and other tedious and studious Games.

7. *Yet recreations distastfull to some dispositions rellish best to others.* Fishing with an angle is to some rather a torture then a pleasure, to stand an houre as mute as the fish they mean to take : yet herewithall * Doctour Whitaker was much delighted. When some Noble-men had gotten William Cecill Lord Burleigh and Treasurer of England to ride with them a hunting, & the sport began to be cold; What call you this, said the Treasurer? Oh now said they the dogs are at a fault. Yea quoth the Treasurer, take me again in such a fault, and Ile give you leave to punish me. Thus as soon may the same meat please all palats, as the same sport suit with all dispositions.

8. *Running, Leaping, and Dancing,* the descants on the plain
song

* *In his life writ by Mr. Ashton.*

*song of walking*, are all excellent exercises. And yet those are the best recreations which besides refreshing enable, at least dispose, men to some other good ends. Bowling teaches mens hands and eyes Mathematicks, and the rules of Proportion: Swimming hath sav'd many a mans life, when himself hath been both the wares, and the ship: Tilting and Fencing is warre without anger; and manly sports are the Grammer of Military performance.

But above all Shooting *is a noble recreation, and an half Liberall art*. A rich man told a poore man that he walked to get a stomach for his meat: And I, said the poore man, *walk to get meat for my stomach*. Now Shooting would have fitted both their turns; it provides food when men are hungry, and helps digestion when they are full. King Edward the sixth (though he drew no strong bow) shot very well, and when once John Dudley Duke of Northumberland commended him for hitting the mark; *You shot better* (quoth the King) *when you shot off my good uncle Protectours head*. But our age sees his Successour exceeding him in that art, whose eye like his judgement is clear and quick to discover the mark, and his hands as just in Shooting as in dealing aright.

Some *sports being granted to be lawfull, more propend to be ill then well used*. Such I count Stage-playes, when made alwayes the Actours work, and often the Spectatours recreation. * Zeuxis the curious picturer painted a boy holding a dish full of grapes in his hand, done so lively that the birds being deceived flew to peck the grapes. But Zeuxis in an ingenious choller was angry with his own workmanship *Had I* (said he) *made the boy as lively as the grapes the birds would have been afraid to touch them*. Thus two things are set forth to us in Stage-playes: some grave sentences, prudent counsells, and punishment of vitious examples: and with these desperate oathes, lustfull talk, and riotous acts are so per-

9

10

* Plin. na. Hist. lib. 35. cap. 10.

B b              sonated

sonated to the life, that wantons are tickled with delight, and feed their palats upon them. It seems the goodnesse is not portrayed out with equall accents of livelinesse as the wicked things are: otherwise men would be deterr'd from vitious courses, with seeing the wofull successe which follows them. But the main is, wanton speeches on stages are the devils ordinance to beget badnesse; but I question whether the pious speeches spoken there be Gods ordinance to increase goodnesse, as wanting both his institution and benediction.

11. *Choak not thy soul with immoderate pouring in the cordiall of pleasures.* The Creation lasted but six dayes of the first week: Prophane they whose Recreation lasts seven dayes every week. Rather abbridge thy self of thy lawfull liberty herein; it being a wary rule which S. * Gregory gives us, *Solus in illicitis non cadit, qui se aliquando & a licitis caute restringit.* And then Recreations shall both strengthen labour, and sweeten rest, and we may expect Gods blessing and protection on us in following them, as well as in doing our work: For he that saith grace for his meat, in it prayes also to God to blesse his sauce unto him. As for those that will not take lawfull pleasure, I am afraid they will take unlawfull pleasure, and by lacing themselves too hard grow awry on one side.

* *Lib. 5. moral. & Homil. 35. supra Evang.*

CHAP. 14.

## Chap. 14.
## Of Tombes.

Tombes are the clothes of the dead: a Grave is but a plain suit, and a rich Monument is one embroyder'd. Most moderate men have been carefull for the decent interment of their corps. Few of the fond mind of Arbogastus an Irish Saint, and Bishop of Spires in Germany, who would be buried near the *Gallows in imitation of our Saviour, whose grave was in mount Calvary near the place of execution.

*Warræus de Scriptor. Hiber. pag. 26.

*Tis a provident way to make ones Tombe in ones life-time*; both hereby to prevent the negligence of heirs, and to mind him of his mortality. * Virgil tells us that when bees swarm in the aire, and two armies meeting together fight as it were a set battel with great violence, cast but a little dust upon them and they will be quiet,

Maxime 1

*Georgic. lib. 4.

 *Hi motus animorum, atque hæc certamina tanta*
 *Pulveris exigui jactu compressa quiescunt.*
 These stirrings of their minds and strivings vast,
 If but a little dust on them be cast,
 Are straitwayes stinted, and quite overpast.

Thus the most ambitious motions and thoughts of mans mind are quickly quell'd when dust is thrown on him, whereof his fore-prepared Sepulchre is an excellent remembrancer.

*Yet some seem to have built their Tombes, therein to bury their thoughts of dying*, never thinking thereof, but embracing the world with greater greedinesse. A Gentleman made choice of a fair stone, and intending the same for his Grave-stone, caused it to be pitched up in a field a pretty distance from his house, and used often to shoot at it for his exercise. *Yea but* (said a wag that stood by) *you would be loath Sir to hit the mark*: And so are many unwilling to die who notwithstanding have erected their Monuments.

2

    Bb 2       Tombes

3

*Lucian. περὶ εἰκόνων.

*Hector Booth in the life of King Reutha.

4

*J. Speed in the end of Henry the 5.
*In the descript. of London, Broadstreet-ward, pag. 184.

*Si nimirum sepulchrorum dissolutorem esse probaverit, Kirkman. de funer. Roman. lib. 3. c. 26. ex cod. de repudiis.

*Tombes ought in some sort to be proportioned not to the wealth but deserts of the party interred.* Yet may we see some rich man of mean worth loaden under a tombe big enough for a Prince to bear. There were Officers appointed in the * Grecian Games, who alwayes by publick authority did pluck down the Statues erected to the Victours, if they exceeded the true symmetrie and proportion of their bodies. We need such nowadayes to order Monuments to mens merits, chiefly to reform such depopulating Tombes as have no good fellowship with them, but engrosse all the room, leaving neither seats for the living, nor graves for the dead. It was a wise and thrifty law which * Reutha King of Scotland made, That Noblemen should have so many pillars, or long pointed stones set on their sepulchres, as they had slain enemies in the warres. If this order were also enlarged to those who in peace had excellently deserved of the Church or Commonwealth, it might well be revived.

*Overcostly Tombes are onely baits for Sacriledge.* Thus Sacriledge hath beheaded that peerelesse Prince King Henrie the fift, the body of whose Statue on his Tombe in Westminster was covered over with silver plate guilded, and his head of * massy silver; both which now are stollen away: Yea hungry palats will feed on courser meat. I had rather *Mr Stow then I should tell you of a Nobleman who sold the monuments of Noblemen, in S. Augustines Church in Broadstreet, for an hundred pound, which cost many thousands, and in the place thereof made fair stabling for horses; as if Christ who was born in a stable should be brought into it the second time. It was not without cause in the Civill Law that a wife might be divorc'd from her husband, if she could prove him to be one that had * broken the Sepulchres of the dead: For it was presum'd he must needs be a tyrannicall husband to his wife, who had not so much mercy as to spare the ashes of the departed.

The

*The shortest, plainest, & truest Epitaphs are best.* I say, the Shortest; for when a Passenger sees a Chronicle written on a Tombe, he takes it on trust, some Great man lies there buried, without taking pains to examine who he is. M^r Cambden in his Remains presents us with examples of Great men that had little *Epitaphs. And when once I ask'd a witty Gentleman, an honoured friend of mine, what Epitaph was fittest to be written on M^r Cambdens Tombe. Let it be, said he,
CAMBDENS REMAINS.

I say also the Plainest; for except the sense lie above ground, few will trouble themselves to dig for't. Lastly, it must be True: Not as as in some Monuments, where the red veins in the marble may seem to blush at the falshoods written on it. He was a witty man that first taught a stone to speak, but he was a wicked man that taught it first to lie.

*To want a Grave is the cruelty of the living, not the misery of the dead.* An English Gentleman not long since did lie on his death-bed in Spain, and the Jesuites did flock about him to pervert him to their Religion. All was in vain. Their last argument was, If you will not turn Romane Catholick, then your body shall be unburied. *Then* (answered he) *I'le stink*, and so turned his head and dyed. Thus love, if not to the dead, to the living will make him, if not a grave, a hole: and it was the Beggers Epitaph,

*Nudus eram vivus, mortuus ecce tegor.*
Naked I liv'd, but being dead,
Now behold I'm covered.

*A good Memory is the best Monument.* Others are subject to Casualty and Time, and we know that the Pyramids themselves doting with age have forgotten the names of their Founders. To conclude, Let us be carefull to provide rest for our souls, and our bodies will provide rest for themselves. And let us not be herein like unto Gentlewomen, which care not to

*as, Fui Caius. Scaligeri quod reliquum est. Depositum Cardinalis Poli, &c.

keep the inside of the orenge, but candy and preserve onely the outside thereof.

## Chap. 15.
### Of Deformitie.

Deformitie is either Naturall, Voluntary, or Adventitious, being either caused by Gods unseen Providence (by men nicknamed, Chance) or by mans Cruelty. We will take them in order.

*Maxime* 1. *If thou beest not so handsome as thou wouldest have been thank God thou art no more unhandsome then thou art.* 'Tis his mercie thou art not the mark for passengers fingers to point at, an Heteroclite in Nature, with some member defective or redundant. Be glad that thy clay-cottage hath all the necessary rooms thereto belonging, though the outside be not so fairly playstered as some others.

2. *Yet is it lawfull and commendable by Art to correct the defects and deformities of Nature.* Ericthonius being a goodly man from the girdle upwards, but, as the Poets feigne, having downwards the body of a * Serpent (moralize him to have had some defect in his feet) first invented charets, wherein he so sate that the upper parts of him might be seen, and the rest of his body concealed. Little heed is to be given to his * lying pen, who maketh Anna Bollen, Mother to Queen Elizabeth, the first finder out and wearer of Ruffes, to cover a wen she had in her neck. Yet the matter's not much, such an addition of Art being without any fraud or deceit.

*Mock not at those who are misshapen by Nature.* There is the same reason of the poore and of the deformed; he that despiseth them despiseth God that made them. A poore man is a picture of Gods own making, but set in a plain frame, not guilded: a deformed man is also his workmanship, but not drawn with

* *Servius in illud Virgilii lib. 3. Georg Primus Ericthonius, &c.*

* *Sanders de schism. Anglic. lib. 1. pag. 17.*

## Chap. 15.     Generall Rules.

with even lines and lively colours: The former, not for want of wealth, as the latter not for want of skill, but both for the pleasure of the maker. As for *Aristotle, who would have parents expose their deformed children to the wide world without caring for them, his opinion herein, not onely deform'd but most monstrous, deserves rather to be exposed to the scorn and contempt of all men.

* Lib. 7. Polit. ca 16.

*Some people handsome by Nature have wilfully deformed themselves.* Such as wear Bacchus his colours in their faces, arising not from having, but being, bad livers. When the woman (the first of Kings, the 3. and 21.) considered the child that was laid by her, *Behold*, said she, *it was not my sonne which I did bear*. Should God survey the faces of many men and women, he would not own and acknowledge them for those which he created: many are so altered in colour, and some in sex, women to men, and men to women in their monstrous, fashions, so that they who behold them cannot by the evidence of their apparell give up their verdict of what sex they are. It is most safe to call the users of these hermaphroditicall fashions, Francisses, and Philips, names agreeing to both sexes.

4

*Confessours which wear the badges of truth are thereby made the more beautifull;* though deformed in time of Persecution for Christs sake through mens malice. This made Constantine the Great to * kisse the hole in the face of Paphnutius, out of which the Tyrant Maximinus had bored his eye for the profession of the faith, the good Emperour making much of the socket even when the candle was put out. Next these, wounds in warre are most honourable: Halting is the stateliest march of a Souldier; and 'tis a brave sight to see the flesh of an Ancient as torn as his Colours. He that mocks at the marks of valour in a Souldiers face, is likely to live to

5

* Ruffin. lib. 1. cap. 4.

to have the brands of justice on his own shoulders.

6  *Nature oftentimes recompenceth deform'd bodies with excellent wits.* Witnesse Æsop, then whose Fables children cannot reade an easier, nor men a wiser book; for all latter Morallists do but write comments upon them. Many jeering wits who have thought to have rid at their ease on the bowed backs of some Cripples, have by their unhappy answers been unhors'd and thrown flat on their own backs. A jeering Gentleman commended a Begger who was deformed and little better then blind for having an excellent eye, *True* (said the Begger) *for I can discern an honest man from such a knave as you are.*

7  *Their souls have been the Chappells of sanctity, whose bodies have been the Spitolls of deformity.* An * Emperour of Germany coming by chance on a Sunday into a Church, found there a most misshapen Priest, *pene portentum Naturæ*, insomuch as the Emperour scorn'd and contemn'd him. But when he heard him reade those words in the Service, *For it is he that made us and not we our selves*, the Emperour check'd his own proud thoughts, and made inquiry into the quality and condition of the man, and finding him on examination to be most learned and devout, he made him Archbishop of Colen, which place he did excellently discharge.

*Guliel.Malm. lib. 2. cap. 10.*

CHAP. 16.

## Chap. 16.
## Of Plantations.

PLantations make mankind broader, as Generation makes it thicker. To advance an happy Plantation the Undertakers, Planters, and Place it self must contribute their endeavours.

*Let the prime Undertakers be men of no shallow heads, nor narrow fortunes.* Such as have a reall Estate, so that if defeated in their adventure abroad, they may have a retreating place at home, and such as will be contented with their present losse to be benefactours to posterity. But if the Prince himself be pleased not onely to wink at them with his permission, but also to smile on them with his encouragement, there is great hope of successe: for then he will grant them some immunities and priviledges. Otherwise ( Infants must be swathed not laced ) young Plantations will never grow, if straitned with as hard Laws as settled Common-wealths. *Maxime 1*

*Let the Planters be honest, skilfull, and painfull people.* For if they be such as leap thither from the gallows, can any hope for cream out of scumme? when men send ( as I may say ) Christian Savages to Heathen Savages. It was rather bitterly then falsely spoken concerning one of our Western Plantations ( consisting most of dissolute people ) *That it was very like unto England, as being spit out of the very mouth of it.* Nor must the Planters be onely honest but industrious also. What hope is there that they who were drones at home will be bees abroad, especially if farre off from any to oversee them. 2

*Let the place be naturally strong, or at leastwise capable of fortification.* For though at the first Planters are sufficiently fenced with their own povertie, and though at the beginning their worst enemies will spare them out 3 of pity to themselves, their spoyl not countervailing the cost of spoyling them; yet when once they have gotten wealth, they must get strength to defend it. Here know Ilands are easily shut, whereas Continents have their doores ever open, not to be bolted without great charges. Besides, unadvised are those Planters, who having choice of ground, have built their Towns in places of a servile nature, as being overawed and constantly commanded by some hills about them.

4. *Let it have a Self-sufficiency, or some Staple commoditie to ballance traffique with other countreys.* As for a Self-sufficiencie few countreys can stand alone, and such as can for matter of want, will for wantonnesse lean on others. Staple commodities are such as are never out of fashion, as belonging to a mans Being, Being with comfort, Being with delight, the Luxury of our age having made superfluities necessary. And such a place will thrive the better, when men may say with Isaac, * *Rehoboth, Now the Lord hath made room for us*, when new Colonies come not in with extirpation of the Natives; for this is rather a Supplanting then a Planting.

*Gen. 26. 22.*

5. *Let the Planters labour to be loved and feard of the Natives.* With whom let them use all just bargaining, being as naked in their dealings with them as the other in their going, keeping all covenants, performing all promises with them: Let them embrace all occasions to convert them, knowing that each Convert is a conquest; and it is more honour to overcome Paganisme in one, then to conquer a thousand Pagans. As for the inscription of a Deity in their hearts it need not be new written, but onely new scowred in them.. I am confident that America ( though the youngest sister of the foure ) is now grown marriageable, and daily hopes to get Christ to her husband, by the Preaching of the Gospel. This makes me attentively to listen after some Protestant first-fruits, in hope the harvest will ripen afterwards.

CHAP. 17.

## Chap. 17.
## Of Contentment.

IT is one property which (they say) is required of those who seek for the Philosophers stone, that they must not do it with any covetous desire to be rich; for otherwise they shall never find it. But most true it is that whosoever would have this jewell of Contentment (which turns all into Gold, yea Want into Wealth) must come with minds devested of all ambitious and covetous thoughts, else are they never likely to obtain it. We will describe Contentment first negatively:

*It is not a senselesse stupidity what becomes of our outward estates.* God would have us take notice of all accidents which from him happen to us in worldly matters. Had the Martyrs had the dead palsie before they went to the stake to be burnt, their suffrings had not been so glorious.    *Maxime 1*

*It is not a word-braving, or scorning of all wealth in discourse.* Generally those who boast most of Contentment have least of it. Their very boasting shews that they want something, and basely beg it, namely Commendation. These in their language are like unto kites in their flying, which mount in the aire so scornfully, as if they disdaind to stoop for the whole earth, fetching about many stately circuits: but what is the Spirit these conjurers with so many circles intend to raise? a poore chicken, or perchance a piece of carrion: And so the height of the others proud boasting will humble it self for a little base gain.    2

*But it is an humble and willing submitting our selves to Gods pleasure in all conditions.* One observeth (how truly I dispute not) that the French naturally have so elegant and gracefull a carriage, that what posture of body soever in their salutations, or what fashion of attire soe-    3 ver they are pleased to take on them it doth so beseem them, that one would think nothing can become them better. Thus Contentment makes men carry themselves gracefully in wealth, want, in health, sicknesse, freedome, fetters, yea what condition soever God allots them.

4. *It is no breach of Contentment for men to complain that their suffrings are unjust, as offered by men*: provided they allow them for just, as proceeding from God, who useth wicked mens injustice to correct his children. But let us take heed that we bite not so high at the handle of the rod, as to fasten on his hand that holds it; our discontentments mounting so high as to quarrell with God himself.

5. *It is no breach of Contentment for men by lawfull means to seek the removall of their miserie, and bettering of their estate.* Thus men ought by industrie to endeavour the getting of more wealth, ever submitting themselves to Gods will. A lazy hand is no argument of a Contented heart. Indeed he that is idle, and followeth after vain persons shall have enough, but how? Prov. 28. 19. *Shall have poverty enough.*

6. *Gods Spirit is the best Schoolmaster to teach Contentment*: A Schoolmaster who can make good Scholars, and warrant the successe as well as his endeavour. The School of Sanctified afflictions is the best place to learn Contentment in: I say, Sanctified; for naturally, like resty horses, we go the worse for the beating, if God blesse not afflictions unto us.

7. *Contentment consisteth not in adding more fuell, but in taking away some fire*: not in multiplying of wealth, but in substracting mens desires. Worldly riches, like nuts, teare many clothes in getting them, spoil many teeth in cracking them, but fill no belly with eating them, obstructing onely the stomach with toughnes, and filling the guts with windinesse: Yea our souls may sooner surfet then be satisfied with earthly things. He that at first

first thought ten thousand pound too much for any one man, will afterwards think ten millions too little for himself.

Men create more discontents to themselves, then ever happened to them from others. We reade of our Saviour that at the buriall of Lazarus, John 11. 33. Ἐτάραξεν ἑαυτὸν, *He troubled himself*, by his spirit raising his own passions, though without any ataxie or sinfull disturbance. What was an act of power in him, is an act of weaknesse in other men : *Man disquieteth himself in vain*, with many causelesse and needlesse afflictions.

*Pious meditations much advantage Contentment in adversitie.* Such as these are, to consider first, that more are beneath us then above us ; secondly, many of Gods dear Saints have been in the same condition ; thirdly, we want rather superfluities then necessities ; fourthly, the more we have the more we must account for ; fifthly, earthly blessings through mans corruption are more prone to be abused then well used. In some fenny places in England, where they are much troubled with gnats, they use to hang up dung in the midst of the room for a bait for the gnats to flie to, and so catch them with a net provided for the purpose. Thus the devil ensnareth the souls of many men by alluring them with the muck and dung of this world, to undo them eternally ; sixthly, we must leave all earthly wealth at our death, *and riches avail not in the day of wrath*. But as some use to fill up the stamp of light gold with dirt, thereby to make it weigh the heavier ; so it seems some men load their souls with thick clay, to make them passe the better in Gods ballance, but all to no purpose ; seventhly, the lesse we have, the lesse it will grieve us to leave this world ; lastly, it is the will of God, and therefore both for his glory and our good, whereof we ought to be assured. I have heard how a Gentleman travelling in a misty morning ask'd of a Shepherd ( such men being

being generally skill'd in the Physiognomie of the Heavens) what weather it would be? *It will be,* said the Shepherd, *what weather shall please me*: and being courteously requested to expresse his meaning, *Sir* ( saith he ) *it shall be what weather pleaseth God, and what weather pleaseth God, pleaseth me.* Thus Contentment maketh men to have even what they think fitting themselves, because submitting to Gods will and pleasure.

To conclude, A man ought to be like unto a cunning Actour, who if he be enjoyned to represent the person of some Prince or Nobleman, does it with a grace and comlinesse; if by and by he be commanded to lay that aside, and play the Begger, he does that as willingly and as well. But as it happened in a Tragedy ( to spare naming the Person and Place ) that one being to act Theseus, in *Hercules Furens,* coming out of Hell, could not for a long time be perswaded to wear old sooty clothes proper to his part, but would needs come out of Hell in a white Satin doublet: so we are generally loath, and it goes against flesh and blood, to live in a low and poore estate, but would fain act in richer and handsomer clothes, till Grace, with much adoe, subdues our rebellious stomachs to Gods will.

CHAP. 18.

## Chap. 18.
## Of Books.

SOlomon saith truly, *Of making many Books there is no end*, so insatiable is the thirst of men therein: as also endles is the desire of many in buying and reading them. But we come to our Rules.

*It is a vanity to perswade the world one hath much learning by getting a great library.* As soon shall I believe every one is valiant that hath a well furnish'd armoury. I guesse good housekeeping by the smoking, not the number of the tunnels, as knowing that many of them (built merely for uniformity) are without chimnies, and more without fires. Once a dunce, void of learning but full of Books, flouted a library-lesse Scholar with these words, *Salve Doctor sine libris*: But the next day the Scholar coming into this jeerers study crowded with Books, *Salvete libri* (saith he) *sine Doctore*. {Maxime 1}

*Few Books well selected are best*. Yet as a certain Fool bought all the pictures that came out, because he might have his choice; such is the vain humour of many men in gathering of Books: yet when they have done all, they misse their end, it being in the Editions of Authours as in the fashions of clothes, when a man thinks he hath gotten the latest and newest, presently another newer comes out. {2}

*Some Books are onely cursorily to be tasted of*. Namely first Voluminous Books, the task of a mans life to reade them over; secondly, Auxiliary Books, onely to be repair'd to on occasions; thirdly, such as are mere pieces of Formality, so that if you look on them you look thorow them; and he that peeps thorow the casement of the Index sees as much as if he were in the house. But the lazinesse of those cannot be excused who perfunctorily passe over Authours of consequence, and onely trade in their Fables and Contents. These like City- {3}

City-Cheaters having gotten the names of all countrey Gentlemen, make silly people believe they have long lived in those places where they never were, and flourish with skill in those Authours they never seriously studied.

4. *The Genius of the Authour is commonly discovered in the Dedicatory epistle.* Many place the purest grain in the mouth of the sack for chapmen to handle or buy: And from the dedication one may probably guesse at the Work, saving some rare and peculiar exceptions. Thus when once a Gentleman admired how so pithy, learned, and witty a dedication was match'd to a flat, dull, foolish book; In truth, said another, *they may be well match'd together, for I professe they are nothing a kinne.*

5. *Proportion an houres meditation to an houres reading of a staple Authour.* This makes a man master of his learning, and dispirits the book into the Scholar. The King of Sweden never * filed his men above six deep in one company, because he would not have them lie in uselesse clusters in his Army, but so that every particular Souldier might be drawn out into service. Books that stand thinne on the shelves, yet so as the owner of them can bring forth every one of them into use, are better then farre greater libraries.

* *Wards Animadver. of warre sect. 17 lib. 2. cap. 5.*

6. *Learning hath gained most by those books by which the Printers have lost.* Arius Montanus in printing the Hebrew Bible (commonly called the Bible of the King of Spain) much wasted himself, and was accused in the Court of Rome for his good deed, and being cited thither, * *Pro tantorum laborum præmio vix veniam impetravit.* Likewise Christopher Plantin by printing of his curious interlineary Bible in Anwerp, through the unseasonable * exactions of the Kings Officers, sunk and almost ruin'd his estate. And our worthy English Knight, who set forth the golden-mouth'd Father in a silver print, was a looser by it.

* *Thuanus obit. vir. Doct. Anno 1598.*

* *Idem in eodem oper. Anno 1589.*

7. *Whereas foolish Pamphlets prove most beneificall to the Printers.*

ters. When a French Printer complain'd that he was utterly undone by Printing a solid serious book of Rablais concerning Physick, Rablais to make him recompence made that his jesting scurrilous Work which repair'd the Printers losse with advantage. Such books the world swarms too much with. When one had set out a witlesse Pamphlet, writing *Finis* at the end thereof, another wittily wrote beneath it,

——————*Nay there thou li st, my friend,*
*In writing foolish books there is no end.*

And surely such scurrilous scandalous papers do more then conceivable mischief. First their lusciousnesse puts many palats out of taste, that they can never after rellish any solid and wholsome Writers: secondly, they cast dirt on the faces of many innocent persons, which dryed on by continuance of time can never after be washed off: thirdly, the Pamphlets of this age may passe for Records with the next (because publickly uncontrolled) and what we laugh at, our children may believe: fourthly, grant the things true they jeer at, yet this musick is unlawfull in any Christian Church, to play upon the sinnes and miseries of others, the fitter object of the Elegies then the Satyrs of all truly religious.

But what do I speaking against multiplicity of books in this age, who trespasse in this nature my self? What was a * learned mans complement may serve for my confession and conclusion, *Multi mei similes hoc morbo laborant, ut cum scribere nesciant tamen à scribendo temperare non possint.*

* *Erasmus in præfat. in 3. seriem 4. Tomi Hieron. pag.* 408.

CHAP. 19.

## Chap. 19.
### Of Time-serving.

THere be foure kinds of Time-serving: first, out of Christian discretion, which is commendable; second, out of humane infirmity, which is more pardonable; third, and fourth, out of ignorance, or affection, both which are damnable: of them in order.

*Maxime 1* — *He is a good Time-server that complyes his manners to the severall ages of this life*: pleasant in youth, without wantonnesse; grave in old age without frowardnesse. Frost is as proper for winter, as flowers for spring. Gravity becomes the ancient; and a green Christmas is neither handsome nor healthfull.

*2* — *He is a good Time-server that finds out the fittest opportunity for every action.* God hath made a time for every thing under the sunne, save onely for that, which we do at all times, to wit Sinne.

*3* — *He is a good Time-server that improves the present for Gods glory, and his own salvation.* Of all the extent of time, onely the instant is that which we can call ours.

*4* — *He is a good Time-server that is pliant to the times in matters of mere indifferency.* Too blame are they whose minds may seem to be made of one entire bone without any joynts: they cannot bend at all, but stand as stiffly in things of pure indifferency, as in matters of absolute necessity.

*5* — *He is a good Time-server that in time of persecution neither betrayes Gods cause, nor his own safety.* And this he may do,

   1 By lying hid both in his person and practice: though he will do no evil he will forbear the publick doing of some good. He hath as good cheer in his heart, though he keeps not open house, and will not publickly broch his Religion,

on, till the palat of the times be better in taste to rellish it. The *Prudent shall keep silence in that time, for it is an evil time. Though according to S. Peters command we are to give a *reason of our hope to every one that asketh; namely, that asketh for his instruction, but not for our destruction, especially if wanting lawfull Authority to examine us. *Ye shall be brought saith Christ ( no need have they therefore to run ) before Princes for my sake.

*Annos. 5. v. 13.
*1. Pet. 3. 15.
*Matth. 10. 18.

2 By flying away: if there be no absolute necessity of his staying, no scandall given by his flight; if he wants strength to stay it out till death; and lastly, if God openeth a fair way for his departure: otherwise, if God bolts the doores and windows against him, he is not to creep out at the top of the chimney, and to make his escape by unwarrantable courses. If all should flie, Truth would want champions for the present; if none should flie, Truth might want champions for the future. We come now to Time-servers out of infirmity.

*Heart of oke hath sometimes warp'd a little in the scorching heat of persecution.* Their want of true courage herein cannot be excused. Yet many censure them for surrendring up their forts after a long siege, who would have yielded up their own at the first summons. Oh, there is more required to make one valiant, then to call Cranmer or Jewell Coward, as if the fire in Smithfield had been no hotter, then what is painted in the Book of Martyrs.

6

*Yet afterwards they have come into their former straightnesse & stiffnesse.* The troops which at first rather wheel'd about then ran away have come in seasonable at last. Yea their constant blushing for shame of their former cowardlinesse hath made their souls ever after look more modest and beautifull. Thus Cranmer ( who subscribed to Popery ) grew valiant afterwards, and

7

D d 2             thrust

thrust his right hand which subscribed first into fire, so that that hand dyed (as it were) a malefactour and all the rest of his body dyed a martyr.

8. *Some have served the times out of mere Ignorance.* Gaping for company, as others gap'd before them, *Pater noster,* or, Our Father. I could both sigh and smile at the witty simplicity of a poore old woman who had lived in the dayes of Queen Marie, and Queen Elizabeth, and said her prayers dayly both in Latine and English, and *Let God,* said she, *take to himself which he likes best.*

9. *But worst are those who serve the times out of mere Affectation.* Doing as the times do, not because the times do as they should do, but merely for sinister respects, to ingratiate themselves. We reade of an Earl of * Oxford fined by King Henrie the seventh fifteen thousand marks for having too many Retainers. But how many Retainers hath Time had in all ages? and Servants in all offices? yea and Chaplains too?

*\* Lord Bacon in Henry seventh, p. 211.*

10. *It is a very difficult thing to serve the times;* they change so frequently, so suddenly, and sometimes so violently from one extreme to another. The times under Dioclesian were Pagan; under Constantine, Christian; under Constantius, Arian; under Julian, Apostate; under Jovian, Christian again, and all within the age of man, the term of seventie years. And would it not have wrench'd and spraind his soul with short turning, who in all these should have been of the Religion for the time being?

11. *Time-servers are oftentimes left in the lurch.* If they do not onely give their word for the times in their constant discourses, but also give their bands for them, and write in their defence. Such, when the times turn afterwards to another extreme, are left in the briers, and come off very hardly from the bill of their hands; If they turn again with the times none will trust them; for who will make a staff of an osier?

12. *Miserable will be the condition of such Time-servers when their*

their *Master is taken from them.* When as the Angel swore Rev. 10. 6. that *Time shall be no longer.* Therefore is it best serving of him who is eternity, a Master that can ever protect us.

To conclude, he that intends to meet with one in a great Fair, and knows not where he is, may sooner find him by standing still in some principall place there, then by traversing it up and down. Take thy stand on some good ground in Religion, and keep thy station in a fixed posture, never hunting after the times to follow them, and an hundred to one, they will come to thee once in thy lifetime.

## Chap. 20.
### Of Moderation.

Moderation is * *the silken string running through the pearl-chain of all virtues.* It appears both in Practice, and Judgement: we will insist on the latter, and describe it first negatively:

* *Bishop Hall of Christian Moderation, pag. 6.*

*Moderation is not an halting betwixt two opinions, when the through-believing of one of them is necessary to salvation.* no pity is to be shown to such voluntary cripples. We reade ( Acts 27. 12. ) of an Haven in Crete *which lay towards the South-West, and towards the North-West*: strange, that it could have part of two opposite points, North and South, sure, it must be very winding. And thus some mens souls are in such intricate postures, they lay towards the Papists, and towards the Protestants; such we count not of a moderate judgement, but of an immoderate unsettlednesse.

Maxime 1

*Nor is it a lukewarmnesse in those things wherein Gods glory is concernd.* Herein it's a true Rule, * *Non amat qui non zelat.* And they that are thus lukewarm here shall be too hot hereafter in that oven wherein *Dow-bak'd cakes* shall be burnt.

2
* *Augustin. contra Adamant. cap. 13.*

*But it is a mixture of discretion and charity in ones judgement.*

3

Discretion

Discretion puts a difference betwixt things absolutely necessary to salvation to be done and believed, and those which are of a second sort and lower form, wherein more liberty and latitude is allowed. In maintaining whereof, the stiffnesse of the judgement is abated, and supled with charity towards his neighbour. The lukewarm man eyes onely his own ends, and particular profit; the moderate man aims at the good of others, and unity of the Church.

**4**
*\*Irenæus lib. 5.*

Yet such moderate men are commonly crush'd betwixt the extreme parties on both sides. But what said Ignatius ? * *I am Christs wheat, and must be ground with the teeth of beasts, that I may be made Gods pure manchet.* Saints are born to suffer, and must take it patiently. Besides, in this world generally they get the least preferment; it faring with them as with the guest that sat in the midst of the table, who could reach to neither messe, above or beneath him:

*Esuriunt Medii, Fines bene sunt saturati;*
*Dixerunt stulti, Medium tenuere beati.*
Both ends o'th' table furnish'd are with meat,
Whilst they in middle nothing have to eat.
They were none of the wisest well I wist,
Who made blisse in the middle to consist.

Yet these temporall inconveniences of moderation are abundantly recompenced with other better benefits : for

*\* Diog. Laert in fine Prooemii.*

1  A well inform'd judgement in it self is a preferment. Potamon began a sect of Philosophers called * Ἐκλέκτικοι, who wholly adher'd to no former sect, but chose out of all of them what they thought best. Surely such Divines, who in unimporting controversies extract the probablest opinions from all Professions, are best at ease in their minds.

2  As the moderate mans temporall hopes are not great so his fears are the lesse. He fears not to have

have the splinters of his party (when it breaks) flie into his eyes, or to be buried under the ruines of his side if suppreft. He never pinn'd his religion on any mans sleeve, no, not on *the Arme of flesh*, and therefore is free from all dangerous engagements.

3 His conscience is clear from raising Schismes in the Church. The Turks did use to wonder much at our English men for *pinking or cutting their clothes, counting them little better then mad for their pains to make holes in whole cloth, which time of it self would tear too soon. But grant men may doe with their own garments, as their phancy adviseth them: yet woe be to such who willingly cut and rend the seamlesse Coat of Christ with dissentions.

* *Bidulph. in his travell to Jerusalem, pag. 98.*

4 His religion is more constant and durable; being here, *in via*, in his way to Heaven, and jogging on a good Travellers pace he overtakes and out-goes many violent men, whose overhot ill-grounded Zeal was quickly tired.

5 In matters of moment indeed none are more Zealous. He thriftily treasur'd up his spirits for that time, who if he had formerly rent his lungs for every trifle, he would have wanted breath in points of importance.

6 Once in an age the moderate man is in fashion, Each extreme courts him, to make them friends; and surely he hath a great advantage to be a Peace-maker betwixt opposite parties. Now whilest, as we have said, moderate men are constant to themselves,

*Violent men reel from one extremity to another.* Who would think that the East and West Indies were so near together, whose names speak them at diametricall opposition? And yet their extremities are either the same Continent, or parted with a very narrow Sea.

As

As the world is round, so we may observe a circulation in opinions, and Violent men turn often round in their tenets.

*Pride is the greatest enemy to Moderation.* This makes men stickle for their opinions, to make them fundamentall: Proud men having deeply studied some additionall point in Divinity, will strive to make the same necessary to salvation, to enhanse the value of their own worth and pains; and it must be fundamentall in religion, because it is fundamentall to their reputation. Yea as love doth descend, and men doat most on their Grandchildren, so these are indulgent to the deductions of their deductions, and consequentiall inferences to the seventh generation, making them all of the foundation, though scarce of the building of religion. * Ancient Fathers made the Creed *symbolum*, the shot and totall summe of Faith. Since which how many arrearages, and after-reckonings have men brought us in? to which if we will not pay our belief, our souls must be arrested without bail upon pain of damnation. Next to Pride popular Applause is the greatest foe Moderation hath, and sure they who sail with that wind have their own vain glory for their Haven.

To close up all, Let men on Gods blessing soundly, yet wisely, whip and lash Lukewarmnesse and Timeserving, their thongs will never flie in the face of true Moderation, to do it any harm; for however men may undervalue it, that * Father spake most truly, *Si virtutum finis ille sit maximus, qui plurimorum spectat profectum, Moderatio prope omnium pulcherrima est.*

*marginalia:*
* Irenæus cap. 2. 5.
Tertull. de virgin. velan.
Hilarius ad Constant. August.
Taur. Maxim. Serm. de symbolo.
August. Serm. 2. & 1081. De Tempore.

* Ambros. de pœniten. contra Novat. lib. 1. cap. 1

CHAP. 21.

## Chap. 21.
## Of Gravity.

Gravity is the ballast of the soul, which keeps the mind steddy. It is either true, or counterfeit.

*Maxime 1*

*Naturall dulnesse, and heavinesse of temper, is sometimes mistaken for true Gravity.* In such men in whose constitutions one of the tetrarch Elements *fire* may seem to be omitted. These sometimes not onely cover their defects, but get praise:

*Sæpe latet vitium proximitate boni.*

They do wisely to counterfeit a reservednesse, and to keep their chests always lock'd, not for fear any should steal treasure thence, but lest some should look in, and see that there is nothing within them. But they who are born Eunuchs deserve no such great commendation for their chastity. Wonder not so much that such men are grave, but wonder at them if they be not grave.

*Affected Gravity passes often for that which is true:* I mean with dull eyes, for in it self nothing is more ridiculous. When one shall use the preface of a mile, to bring in a furlong of matter, set his face and speech in a frame, and to make men believe it is some pretious liquour, their words come out drop by drop: Such mens visards do sometimes fall from them, not without the laughter of the beholders. One was called *Gravity* for his affected solemnesse, who afterwards being catch'd in a light prank was ever after to the day of his death called *Gravity-levity*.

2

*True Gravity expresseth it self in Gate, Gesture, Apparell, and Speech. Vox* * *quædam est animi, corporis motus.* As for Speech, Gravity enjoyns it,

3
* *Ambros. de offic. lib. 1. cap. 18.*
* *Prov. 10. 19.*

1 Not to be over much. *In* * *the multitude of words there wanteth not sinne.* For of necesity many of them must be idle, whose best commendation is that they

they are good for nothing. Besides, * *Dum otiosa verba cavere negligimus, ad noxia pervenimus.* And great talkers discharge too thick to take alwayes true aim; besides, it is odious in a company. A man full of words, who took himself to be a Grand wit, made his brag that he was the leader of the discourse in what company soever he came, and *None*, said he, *dare speak in my presence, if I hold my peace. No wonder,* answered one, *for they are all struck dumbe at the miracle of your silence.*

* Greg. moral. lib. 7. cap. 17.

2 To be wise and discreet, Colossians 4. 6. *Let your speech be alwayes with grace, seasoned with salt.* Alwayes, not onely sometimes in the company of godly men. * Tindals being in the room hindred a juggler that he could not play his feats: (A Saints presence stops the devils elbow-room to do his tricks) and so some wicked men are awed into good discourse, whilest pious people are present. But it must be alwayes *seasoned with salt,* which is the *primum vivens & ultimum moriens* at a feast, first brought, and last taken away, and set in the midst as most necessary thereunto. *With salt,* that is with wisdome and discretion, *non salibus, sed sale;* nor yet with smarting jeeres, like those whose discourse is *fire-salt,* speaking constant satyrs to the disgrace of others.

* Fox Martyrs, pag. 1079.

4 *That may be done privately without breach of Gravity, which may not be done publickly.* As when a father makes himself his childs rattle, sporting with him till the father hath devour'd the wiseman in him.

*Equitans in arundine longa.*
In stead of stately steed,
Riding upon a reed.

Making play unto him, that one would think he kill'd his own discretion, to bring his child asleep. Such cases are no trespasse on Gravity, and married men may claim their priviledge, *to be judged by their Peeres*

*Peeres*, and may herein appeal from the cenſuring verdict of batchelours.

*Nature in men is ſometimes unjuſtly taxed for a treſpaſſe againſt Gravity.* Some have active ſpirits, yea their ordinary pace is a race. Others have ſo ſcornfull a carriage, that he who ſeeth them once may think them to be all pride, whileſt he that ſeeth them often knows them to have none. Others have perchance a misbeſeeming garb in geſture which they cannot amend; that fork needing ſtrong tines wherewith one muſt thruſt away nature. A fourth ſort are of a merry cheerfull diſpoſition; and God forbid all ſuch ſhould be condemned for lightneſſe. O let not any envious eye diſinherit men of that which is their * *Portion in this life,* comfortably to enjoy the bleſsings thereof. Yet Gravity muſt prune though not root out our mirth.

*Gratious deportment may ſometimes unjuſtly be accuſed of lightneſſe.* Had one ſeen David * dancing before the Ark, * Eliah in his praying-poſture when he put his head betwixt his legs, perchance he might have condemn'd them of unfitting behaviour. Had he ſeen * Peter and John poſting to Chriſts grave, * Rhodia running into the houſe, he would have thought they had left their Gravity behind them. But let none blame them for their ſpeed untill he knows what were their ſpurres, and what were the motives that urged them to make ſuch haſte. Theſe their actions were the true concluſions, following from ſome inward premiſſes in their own ſouls; and that may be a ſyllogiſme in grace, which appears a ſoleciſme in manners.

*In ſome perſons Gravity is moſt neceſſary.* Viz. in Magiſtrates and Miniſters. One * Palevizine an Italian Gentleman, and kinſman to Scaliger, had in one night all his haire chang'd from black to gray. Such an alteration ought there to be in the heads of every one that enters into Holy Orders, or Publick

5

* *Eccles* 7.18.

6
* 2. *Sam.* 6. 16.
* 1. *Kings* 18. 42.

* *John* 20. 14.
* *Acts* 12. 14

7
* *Scaliger de ſubtil. pag.* 18.

Ee 2       lick

lick Office, metamorphos'd from all lightnesse to Gravity.

8

*God alone is the giver of true Gravity.* No man wants so much of any grace as he hath to spare; and a constant impression of Gods omnipresence is an excellent way to fix mens souls. Bishop Andrews ever placed the picture of* Mulcaster his Schoolmaster over the doore of his study (whereas in all the rest of his house you should scarce see a picture) as to be his Tutour and Supervisour. Let us constantly apprehend Gods being in presence, and this will fright us into staied behaviour.

\* Vid. in the funerall serm. on him, pag. 18.

## Chap. 22.

### Of Marriage.

Some men have too much decried Marriage, as if she the mother were scarce worthy to wait on Virginity her daughter, and as if it were an advancement for Marriage to be preferr'd before fornication, and praise enough for her to be adjudged lawfull. Give this holy estate her due, and then we shall find,

Maxime 1

*Though batchelours be the strongest stakes, married men are the best binders in the hedge of the Commonwealth.* 'Tis the Policy of the Londoners when they send a ship into the Levant or Mediterranean sea, to make every marriner therein a merchant, each seaman adventuring somewhat of his own, which will make him more wary to avoid, and more valiant to undergo dangers. Thus married men, especially if having posterity, are the deeper sharers in that state wherein they live, which engageth their affections to the greater loyalty.

2

*It is the worst clandestine marriage when God is not invited to it.* Wherefore beforehand beg his gratious assistance. Marriage shall prove no lottery to thee, when the hand

hand of providence chuseth for thee, who, if drawing a blank, can turn it into a prize by sanctifying a bad wife unto thee.

*Deceive not thy self by overexpecting happinesse in the married estate.* Look not therein for contentment greater then God will give, or a creature in this world can receive, namely to be free from all inconveniences. Marriage is not like the hill Olympus, ὅλος λαμπρὸς, *wholly clear*, without clouds; yea expect both wind and storms sometimes, which when blown over, the aire is the clearer, and wholsomer for it. Make account of certain cares and troubles which will attend thee. Remember the nightingales which sing onely some moneths in the spring, but commonly are silent when they have hatch'd their egges, as if their mirth were turned into care for their young ones. Yet all the molestations of Marriage are abundantly recompenced with other comforts which God bestoweth on them, who make a wise choice of a wife, and observe the following rules.

*Let Grace and Goodnesse be the principall loadstone of thy affections.* For love which hath ends will have an end, whereas that which is founded in true virtue will alwayes continue. Some hold it unhappy to be married with a diamond ring, perchance (if there be so much reason in their folly) because the diamond hinders the roundnesse of the ring, ending the infinitenesse thereof, and seems to presage some termination in their love, which ought ever to endure, and so it will, when it is founded in religion.

*Neither chuse all, nor not at all for Beauty.* A cried-up Beauty makes more for her own praise then her husbands profit. They tell us of a floting Iland in Scotland: but sure no wise pilot will cast anchor there, lest the land swimme away with his ship. So are they served (and justly enough) who onely fasten their love on fading Beauty, and both fail together.

Ee 3 *Let*

**6**

*Let there be no great disproportion in age.* They that marry ancient people merely in expectation to bury them, hang themselves in hope that one will come and cut the halter. Nor is Gods ordinance but mans abusing thereof taxed in this homely expression, used by the Apostle himself. If Virginity enforced above the parties power be* termed by S. Paul 1. Cor. 7. 35. a *snare or halter*, marriage is no better when against ones will, for private respects.

*\*Οὐχ ἵνα βρόχον ὑμῖν ἐπιβάλω, 1. Cor. 7. 35.*

**7**

*Let wealth in its due distance be regarded.* There be two towns in the land of Liege called Bovins and Dinant, the inhabitants whereof bear almost an incredible hatred one to another, and yet notwithstanding their children usually marry together; and the * reason is, because there is none other good town, or wealthy place near them. Thus parents for a little pelf often marry their children to those whose persons they hate; and thus union betwixt families is not made, but the breach rather widened the more.

*\*Phil.Com. lib. 2. cap. 1.*

This shall serve for a Conclusion. A Batchelour was saying, *Next to no wife, a good wife is best.* Nay, said a Gentlewoman, *next to a good wife, no wife is the best.* I wish to all married people the outward happinesse which* *Anno* 1605 happened to a couple in the city of Delph in Holland, living most lovingly together seventy five years in wedlock, till the man being one hundred and three, the woman ninety nine years of age, died within three houres each of other, and were buried in the same grave.

*\* Thuan. de obit. vir doct. in eod. Anno. pag. 385.*

CHAP. 23

## Chap. 23.
### Of Fame.

FAme is the echo of actions, resounding them to the world, save that the echo repeats onely the last part, but Fame relates all and often more then all.

*Fame sometimes hath created something of nothing.* She hath made whole countreys more then ever Nature did, especially near the Poles, and then hath peopled them likewise with inhabitants of her own invention, Pygmies, Giants, and Amazons: Yea Fame is sometimes like unto a kind of Mushrom, which * Pliny recounts to be the greatest miracle in nature, because growing and having no root, as Fame no ground of her reports.

*Maxime* 1

\* *In miraculis vel maximum est Tubera nasci & vivere sine ulla radice, Plin. Nat. Hist. lib. 19. cap. 2.*

*Fame often makes a great deal of a little.* Absalom kill'd one of Davids sonnes, and * Fame kill'd all the rest; and generally she magnifies and multiplies matters. Loud was that lie which that bell told hanging in a clock-house at Westminster, and usually rung at the Coronation and Funeralls of Princes, having this inscription about it,

2

\* 2. *Sam.* 13. 30.

 *King Edward made me*
 *thirty thousand and three,*
 *Take me down and weigh me*
 *and more shall you find me.*

But when this bell was taken down at the doomsday of Abbeys, this and two more were found not to weigh * twenty thousand. Many relations of Fame are found to shrink accordingly.

\* *Stowes survey of London, pag.* 528.

*Some Fames are most difficult to trace home to their form*: and those who have sought to track them, have gone rather in a circle then forward, and oftentimes through the doubling of reports have return'd back again where they began. Fame being a bastard or *filia populi*, 'tis very hard to find her father, and ofttimes she hath

3

hath rather all then any for her first Authours.

**4**  Politicians *sometimes raise Fames on purpose.* As that such things are done already, which they mean to do afterwards. By the light of those false fires they see into mens hearts, and these false rumours are true scouts to discover mens dispositions. Besides, the deed (though strange in it self) is done afterwards with the lesse noise, men having vented their wonder beforehand, and the strangenesse of the action is abated, because formerly made stale in report. But if the rumour startles men extremely, and draws with it dangerous consequences, then they can presently confute it, let their intentions fall and prosecute it no further.

**5**  *The Papall side of all Fame-merchants drive the most gainfull trade*, as that worthy * Knight hath given us an exact survey thereof. But long before them, strange was that plot of Stratocles, who gave it out that he had gotten a victory, and the constant report thereof continued three dayes, and then was confuted; and Stratocles being charged with abusing his people with a lie, *Why* (said * he) *are ye angry with me for making you passe three dayes in mirth and jollity more then otherwise you should?*

* S. Edward Sandys view of the West Religions, pag. 100.

* Plutarchs Πολίτικα. παραγγέλματα.

**6**  *Incredible is the swiftnesse of Fame in carrying reports.* First she creeps thorow a village, then she goes thorow a town, then she runs thorow a city, then she flyes thorow a countrey, still the farther the faster. Yea Christ who made the dumbe speak, made not tell-tale Fame silent, though charging those he cured to hold their peace, * *but so much the more went there a Fame abroad of him.* Yea some things have been reported soon as ever they were done at impossible distance. The overthrow of Perseus was brought out of Macedon to Rome in * foure dayes. And in Domitians time a report was brought two thousand five hundred miles in one day. In which accidents,

* Luke 5. 15.

* Livy. lib.45. juxta princip.

1 *Fame takes post on some other advantage.* Thus the

the overthrow of the Sabines was known at Rome *prius pene quam nunciari possit*, by the means of the * arms of the Sabines drowned in the river of Tiber, and carried down by the tide to Rome. And thus *Anno* * 1568 the overthrow which the Spaniards gave the Dutch at the river of Ems was known at Grunning before any horseman could reach thither, by the multitude of the Dutch caps which the river brought down into the city. But these conveiances are but slugs to make such miraculous speed: wherefore sometimes reports are carried,

* *Livy, lib. 1.*

*Famian. Strada de Bello Belgic. lib. 5. pag. 456.*

2 By the ministration of Spirits. The devils are well at leisure to play such pranks, and may do it in a frolick. And yet they would scarce be the carriers except they were well payed for the portage, getting some profit thereby ( doing of mischief is all the profit they are capable of) and do harm to some by the suddennesse of those reports. Or else

3 The Fame is antedated and rais'd before the fact, being related at guesse before 'twas acted. Thus some have been causlessely commended for early rising in the morning, who indeed came to their journeys end over night. If such foremade reports prove true, they are admired and registred; if false, neglected and forgotten: as those onely which escaped shipwrack hung up *votivas tabulas*, tablets with their names in those Haven-towns where they came ashore. But as for those who are drowned, their memorialls are drowned with them.

*Generall reports are seldome false. Vox populi vox Dei.* A body of that greatnesse hath an eye of like clearnesse, and it is impossible that a wanderer with a counterfeit passe should passe undiscovered.

7

*A fond Fame is best confuted by neglecting it.* By *Fond* un-

8

F f               derstand

derstand such a report as is rather ridiculous then dangerous if believed. It is not worth the making a Schisme betwixt News-mongers to set up an antifame against it. Yea seriously and studiously to endeavour to confute it, will grace the rumour too much, and give suspicion that indeed there is some reality in it. What madnesse were it to plant a piece of ordinance to beat down an aspen leaf, which having always the palsie, will at last fall down of it self. And Fame hath much of the scold in her ; the best way to silence her is to be silent, and then at last she will be out of breath with blowing her own trumpet.

9    *Fame sometimes reports things lesse then they are.* Pardon her for offending herein, she is guilty so seldome. For one kingdome of Scotland, which (they say) Geographers describe an hundred miles too short, most Northern countreys are made too large. Fame generally overdoes, underdoes but in some particulars. The Italian proverb hath it, *There is lesse honesty, wisdome, and money in men then is counted on*: yet sometimes a close churl, who locks his coffers so fast Fame could never peep into them, dyeth richer then he was reported when alive. None could come near to feel his estate; it might therefore cut fatter in his purse, then was expected. But Fame falls most short in those Transcendents, which are above her Predicaments ; as in * Solomons wisdome : *And behold one half was not told me : thy wisdome and prosperity exceedeth the Fame that I heard.* But chiefly in fore-reporting the Happinesse in heaven, which eye hath not seen, nor ear heard, neither hath it entred into the heart of man to conceive.

\* 1 Kings. 10. 7.

CHAP. 24.

# Chap. 24.

## Of the Antiquity of Churches and Necessity of them.

WE will consider their Antiquity amongst the Jews, Heathen, and Christians. Now Temples amongst the Jews were more or lesse ancient as the acception of the word is straiter or larger.

*Take Temple for a covered standing structure,* and the Jews had none till the time of Solomon, which was from the beginning of the * world about two thousand nine hundred thirty two years: till then they had neither leave nor libertie to build a Temple. For the Patriarchs, Abraham, Isaac, and Jacob, lived in Pilgrimage; their posterity in Egypt in persecution; their children in the Wildernesse in constant travelling; their Successours in Canaan in continuall warrefare, till the dayes of Solomon.

*Take* Templum *for* tectum * amplum, *a large place covered to serve God therein,* and the Tabernacle was a moveable Temple, built by Moses in the wildernesse about the yeare of the world two thousand foure hundred fiftie five. Yea we find Gods Spirit styling this Tabernacle a Temple, 1. Sam. 1. 9. *Ely the Priest sate upon a seat by a pillar of the Temple.* 1. Sam. 3. 3. *Before the lamp of the Lord went out in the Temple.* Such a portable Church Constantine * had carried about with him when he went to warre.

Gods children had places with Altars to serve God in before they had any Temples. Such Altars seem as ancient as Sacrifices, both which are twins; and in Relatives find one and find both. Indeed the first Altar we reade of in Scripture is that which Noah built after the Flood: But heare what a * Learned man saith thereof, *Non tamen existimandum toto illo tempore, quo ante diluvium pii homines*

*Maxime* 1

* *Vid. Chron. Helvici.*

2
* *Isidorus lib. 15. cap 14.*

* *Socrates lib. 1. cap. 14. & Sozomen. lib. 1. cap. 8.*

3

* *Rivet. in Genes. pag. 275.*

Ff 2 *Deo*

*Deo sacrificarunt Altarium usum fuisse incognitum. Potius id credendum, Noachum sequutum fuisse exemplum eorum, qui eum præcesserant, imo morem inolitum.*

4   The *Jews* besides the Temple had many other *Synagogues*, serving instead of Chappells of ease to the mother Church at Jerusalem. In the new Testament (the Temple yet standing) 'tis plain that Christ often graced such Synagogues with his presence and preaching; and 'tis * probable they were in use ever since Josuahs time, when the land was first inhabited with Israelites, and that the Levites dispersed all over the land did teach the people therein: Otherwise Palestine was a great Parish, and some therein had an hundred miles to Church; besides, peoples souls were poorely fed having but three meals in a yeare, being but thrice to appear at Jerusalem.

\* *Hospinian. de orig. Temp c.4.*

5   *Many Heathen Temples were ancienter then that of Solomons.* Amongst which Pagan Temples there is much justling for precedency, though some think that of Apis in Egypt shews the best evidence for her seniority, wherein was worshipped an Oxe, of whose herd (not to say breed) was the Calf which the Israelites worshipped in the wildernesse, being made in imitation thereof. But the Heathen had this grosse conceit that their Gods were affixt to their Statues, as their Statues were confin'd in their Temples: So that in effect they did not so much build Temples for their Gods, as thereby lay Nets to catch them in, inviting them thither as into a Pallace, and then keeping them there as in a Prison.

6   *Most civilized Heathen Nations had Temples for their Gods.* I say, *Most*, for the Persians are said to have none at all. Perchance it was because they chiefly worshipped the Sunne, and then according to the generall opinion of fixing Deities to their Temples, it was in vain to erect any structure therein to restrain and keep his Ubiquitary beams. And yet that the Persians were wholly Temple-

Temple-lesse will hardly be believed, seeing the Assyrians on this side (* Senacherib was killed worshipping in the house of Nisroch his God) and the Indians on the other side of them had their Temples erected, as some will have it, by Bacchus their Dionysius: yea we find a Temple in Persia dedicated to * Nanea in the time of Antiochus, and though it may be pretended that the influence of the Grecian Empire on the Persians had then spiced them with a smack of Grecisme, yet Nanea will scarce be proved any Grecian Deity: not to say any thing of the Temple of Bell. *Civilized*: for as for the Scythian wandring Nomades, Temples sorted not with their condition, as wanting both civility and settlednesse: and who can expect Churches from them, who had no houses for themselves? Lastly I say, *Nation*: for the Stoicks onely, a conceited sect, forbad any building of Temples, either out of derision of the common conceit that Deities were kept in durance in their Temples; or else out of humour, because they counted the generall practice of other men a just ground for their contrary opinion. And now we come to the Antiquity of Christian Churches, and crave leave of the Reader, that we may for a while dissolve our continued discourse into a dialogue.

* 2 *Kings* 19. 37.

* 2. *Maccabees* 1. 13. *vide etiam*. 1. *Maccab.* 6. 2.

*A.* I am much perplexed to find the beginning of Christian Churches in the Scripture. There I find the Saints meeting *in the house of Marie the mother of Mark*; *in the School of Tyrannus*; *in an upper Chamber*; but can see no foundation of a Church, I mean of a place and structure separated and set apart solely for Divine Service.

*B.* That the Saints had afterwards Churches in your sense is plain: 1. Cor. 11. 22. *Have ye not Houses to eat and drink in, or despise ye the Church of God, and shame them that have not?* Here the opposition is a good exposition of the Apostles meaning, and the Antithesis betwixt *Houses* and *Church*

Ff 3 speaks

speaks them both to be locall; so that S. Paul thought their materiall Church *despised*, that is abused and unreverenc'd, by their lay-meetings of Love-feasts therein.

*A.* By your favour, S^r, the Apostle by *Church* meaneth there the assembly or society of Gods servants, as appears by what followeth, *or despise ye the Church of God, and shame them that have not ? Them*, and not *that*, not speaking of the Place but Persons: The latter words of the Apostle comment on the former, shewing how to shame those who had not ( that is, to neglect and upbraid the poore ) is *to despise the Church of God*.

*B.* Pardon me S^r: for the Apostle therein accuseth the Corinthians of a second fault. *Imprimis* he chargeth them for despising Gods materiall Church; *Item*, for shaming their poore brethren in their Love-feasts. The particle *And* sheweth the addition of a new charge, but no expounding or amplifying of the former. But, S^r, suspending our judgements herein, let us descend to the Primitive times before Constantine, we shall there find Churches without any contradiction.

*A.* Not so neither: Herein also the trumpet of Antiquity giveth a very uncertain sound: Indeed we have but little left of the story of those times wherein Christian books were as much persecuted as men, and but a few Confessour-records escaping martyrdome are come to our hands. Yea God may seem to have permitted the suppression of primitive History, lest men should be too studious in reading, and observant in practising the customes of that age, even to the neglecting and undervaluing of his written Word.

*B.* Yet how slenderly soever those Primitive times are

are ftoried, there is enough in them to prove the Antiquity of Churches. I will not inftance on the decrees of Evariftus, Hyginus, and other Popes in the firft three hundred years about the confecrating of Churches, becaufe their authority is fufpected as antedated; and none are bound to believe that the Gibeonites came from fo far a Countrey as their mouldy bread & clouted fhoes did pretend. Churches are plainly to be found in Tertullian, two hundred years after Chrift; and Eufebius * witneffeth that before the time of Dioclefian the Chriftians had Churches, which the Tyrant caufed to be deftroyed.

*A.* But * Origen, Minutius Felix, Arnobius, and Lactantius, being preff'd by the Heathen that Chriftians had no Churches, anfwered by way of confefsion, yielding that they had none. This is the difficulty perplexeth me. It was a bloody fpeech of Abner, *Let the young men rife up and play before us* : But worfe is their cruelty who make fport at the falling out of the old men, when the reverend brows of Antiquity knock one againft another, and Fathers thus extremely differ in matters of fact.

*B.* Why, S*r* ? A charitable diftinction may reconcile them : if by *Churches*, ftately magnificent Fabricks be meant, in that acception the Chriftians had no Churches ; but fmall Oratories and Prayer-places they then had, though little, low and dark, being fo fearfull of perfecution they were jealous the Sunne-beams fhould behold them : and indeed ftately Churches had but given a fairer aim to their Enemies malice to hit them. Such an homely place learned S*r* Henrie Spelman * prefents us with, which was firft founded at Glaftenbury, thatched and wattled :
And

*\* Hift. Eccles. lib. 8. c. 1, & 2.*
*\* Origen. lib. 4. contra Celfum, Objicit nobis Celfus quod non habeamus Imagines aut Aras aut Templa. Idem lib. 8. contra Celfum, Celfus & Aras & Simulacra & Delubra ait nos diffugere quo minùs fundentur. Arnobius lib. 4 contra Gen. Accufatis nos quòd nec Templa habeamus, nec Imagines nec Aras. Minut. Felix pag. 73. Putatis autem nos occultare quod colamus fi Delubra et Aras non habemus. Lactantius, Quid fibi Templa, quid Aræ volunt, quid denique ipfa Simulacra, &c.*
*\* De Conciliis Brittan. pag. 11.*

And let not our Churches now grown men look with a scornfull eye on their own picture, when babes in their swadling clothes. And no wonder if Gods House

*Erubuit domino cultior esse suo*,
The Church did blush more glory for to have
Then had her Lord. He begg'd, should she be brave?
Christ himself being then cold, and hungry, and naked in his afflicted members. Such a mean Oratory Tertullian calls * *Triclinium Christianorum*, the Parlour or Three-bed-room of the Christians.

*\* Adversus Gentes, cap. 3. 9.*

A. But it seems not to consist with Christian ingenuity for the fore-named Fathers absolutely to deny their having of Churches, because they had onely poore ones.

B. Take then another Answer, namely in denying they had no Temples, they meant it in the same notion wherein they were interrogated, to wit, they had no Temples like the Pagans for Heathen Gods, no *claustra Numinum*, wherein the Deity they served was imprisoned. Or may we not say that in that age the Christians had no Churches generally, though they might have them in some places ? the elevation of their happinesse being varied according to severall climates : And Christendome then being of so large an extent, it might be stormy with persecution in one countrey, and fair weather in another. We come now to the Necessity.

7

*There is no absolute necessity that Christians should have Churches.* No necessity at all in respect of God, no absolute necessity in respect of men, when persecution hinders the erecting of them : In such a case any place is made a Church for the time being, as any private house where the King and his Retinue meet is presently made the Court.

*Christians*

Christians have no direct precept to build Churches under the Gospel. I say *direct*: For the Law of God, which commands a publick Sanctification of a Sabbath, must needs, by * way of necessary consequence, imply a set, known, and publick Place. Besides, Gods command to Moses and Solomon to build a Temple in a manner obligeth us to build Churches. In which command observe the body and the soul thereof. The body thereof was Ceremoniall and mortall, yea dyed, and is buried in our Saviours grave: The soul thereof is Morall and eternall, as founded in Nature, and is always to endure. Thus S. Paul finds a constant bank for Ministers Maintenance lockt up in a Ceremoniall Law, *Thou shalt not muzzle the mouth of the Ox that treadeth out the corn.* The Apostle on the Morality couched therein founded the *Charter of endowment* for Ministers in the Gospel. Besides, God hath left a warrant dormant with his Church, *Let all things be done decently and in order.* And this ties Christians to the building of Churches for their publick Assemblies, whereby not onely Decency but Piety is so much advanced, especially in these three respects:

8

\* Ut communes fidelibus preces Deus verbo suo edicit, sic & Templa publica ipsis peragendis destinata esse oportet, *Calvin. instit. lib. 3. cap. 20. num. 30.*

1. Hereby the same meat serves to feed many guests, one Pastour instructing many people in the same place.
2. Devotion is increased with company. Their praises are the louder; and musick is sweetest in a full consort: their prayers are the stronger, besetting God as it were in a round, and not suffering him to depart till he hath blessed them.* *Hæc vis grata deo.*

\**Tertull. Apol.*

3. The very Place it self, being dedicated to Gods service, is a Monitour to them *Hoc agere*, & stirres up pious thoughts in them. Say not, it is but lame Devotion that cannot mount without the help of such a wooden stock; rather 'tis lame indeed which is not rais'd though having the advantage thereof.

G g

*Those*

9 *Those that may, must frequent the publick Churches.* Such as nowadayes are ambitious of conventicles are deeply guilty: for as it had been desperate madnesse in time of persecution publickly to resort to Divine Service, so it is no lesse unthankfulnesse to God now to serve him in woods and holes, not taking notice of the liberty of the Gospel, which he gratiously hath vouchsafed; yea such people in effect deny the King to be Defender of the Faith, but make him a Persecuter rather, in that they dare not avouch the truth in the face of his Authority. If it be good they do (thanks be to God) it may be done any where; if bad, it must be done no where. Besides, by their voluntary private meetings, they give occasions to many to supect their actions there: And grant them unjustly traduced for their behaviour therein, yet can they not justly be excused, because they invite slaunderous tongues to censure them, in not *providing for honest things in the sight of men*, and clearing Gods service as well from the suspicion as from the guilt of any dishonesty.

We should now come to speak of the Holinesse, Reverence, Decency, and Magnificencie of Churches: But herein I had rather heare the judgements of other men. Let it serve instead of a conclusion to observe that Solomons Temple was the statelyest structure that ever was or shall be in the world; built by the wealthyest, contrived by the wisest King in seven years (now counted the life of a man) by an army of Workmen, no fewer then * one hundred fourtie three thousand three hundred, of the soundest timber, most pretious stones, most proper metall, as the nature of the things required; either the strongest, Brasse; or the richest, Gold: In a word, Earth gave it most costly matter, and Heaven it self most curious workmanship, God directing them. And though Solomon had no mines of Gold and Silver in his own land, yet had he the spoils and gifts of the neighbouring nations, and once

* 1. Kings 5. 15, 16.

once in three years the golden land of Ophir came fwimming to Hierufalem. God being the Landlord of the earth, Solomon was then his Receiver, to whom the World payed in her rent, to build his Temple. And was not he a moſt wealthy King, *in whoſe dayes ſilver was nothing accounted of;* ſeeing in our dayes the commander of both Indyes hath ſo much braſſe coin currant in his Court? As for Joſephus his conceit, that the ſecond edition of the Temple by Zorobabel, as it was new forrelled and filleted with gold by Herod, was a ſtatelier volume then that firſt of Solomon, it is too weak a ſurmiſe to have a confutation faſtned to it.

And yet we will not deny but the world hath ſeen greater buildings for the Piles and Fabricks, as may appear by this parrallel.

| 1 | 2 | 3 |
|---|---|---|
| Gods Temple, built at Hieruſalem by Solomon. | Diana's Temple, built at Epheſus by the Kings of Aſia. | Sepulcher Church, built on Mount Calvary by Constantine. |
| Long 60 [a] Broad 20 cubits. High 30 | Long 425 [b] Broad 220 foot. High 60 | Long [c] We find no ſet dimenſion but hyperbolicall expreſſions of it. Broad High |
| 4 | 5 | 6 |
| S. Sophia's Church, built at Conſtantinople by Juſtinian. | S. Pauls Church, built at London by King Ethelbert. | Turkiſh Mosque, built at Fez. |
| Long 260 [d] Broad 75 foot. High 180 | Long 690 [e] Broad 130 foot. High 102 | Long 150 [f] Broad 80 Florentine High Cubits. |

[a] 2. Chron. 3.3.
[b] Plin. nat. Hiſt. lib. 36. cap. 14.
[c] Euſebius lib. 3 de vit. Conſtantini, c. 24. ἡγίω ἐπτεῖον μῶνου ὅτι πλάϊος ἐυρυνδ-ὕηεν.
[d] Evagrius lib. 4. cap. 30.
[e] Namely in the body of the Church beſides the ſteeple, Cambd. Britt. in Middleſex.
[f] The height we find not, but it is a mile and half in compaſſe, Leo Africanus, lib. 3. pag. 126.

But when the Reader hath with his eyes ſurveyed theſe Temples, and findeth them to exceed Solomons, yet let him remember, firſt, that there is nothing more uncertain then the meaſures uſed in ſeverall countreys; one countreys ſpan may be another countreys cubit, and

and the toe of one countrey as big as the foot of another: secondly, that in Solomons Temple great Cubits were meant *Primæ mensuræ*, 2. Chron. 3. 3. thirdly, that we see most of these structures onely through the magnifying glasse of Fame, or else by the eyes of Travellers, who usually count the best they ever saw to be the best was ever seen, yea in charity will lend a Church some hundreds of feet to help out the dimension thereof, as Bellonius a modern eye-witnesse counteth * three hundred sixtie five doores in the present Church of Sophia, which hath but foure, as an exact * Traveller hath observed. Lastly, whilest humane Historians will overlash for the honour of their own Nations, we know it must needs be true what Truth hath written of Solomons Temple.

*\*Lib. 1. observ. cap. 76.*

*\* G. Sandys Travells, pag. 32.*

## Chap. 25.

### Of Ministers maintenance.

MAintenance of Ministers ought to be Plentifull Certain, and in some sort Proportionable to their deserts. It should be Plentifull, because

*Maxime 1*

*Their education was very chargeable to fit them for their profession*, both at School, and in the Universisty: their books very dear, and those which they bought in Folio shrink quickly into Quarto's, in respect of the price their executours can get for them. Say not that Scholars draw needlesse expences on themselves by their own lavishnesse, and that they should rather lead a Fashion of thrift, then follow one of riot; for let any equall man tax the bill of their necessary charges, and it amounts to a great Summe, yea though they be never so good husbands. Besides, the prizes of all commodities daily rise higher; all persons and professions are raised in their manner of living: Scholars therefore, even against their wills, must otherwhiles be involved in the generall expensivenesse of the times, it being impossible

possible that one spoke should stand still when all the wheel turns about.

*Ob.* But many needlessely charge themselves in living too long in the University, sucking so long of their Mother, they are never a whit the wiser for it; whilest others not staying there so long, nor going through the porch of humane Arts, but entring into Divinity at the postern, have made good Preachers, providing their people wholsome meat, though not so finely drest.

*Answ.* Much good may it do their very hearts that feed on it. But how necessary a competent knowledge of those Sciences is for a perfect Divine, is known to every wise man. Let not mens suffering be counted their fault, nor those accused to *stand idle in the market whom no man hath hired.* Many would leave the University sooner, if called into the countrey on tolerable conditions.

*Because Ministers are to subsist in a free, liberal, & comfortable way.* Balaam the false Prophet rode with his * two men; Gods Levite had * one man: Oh let not the Ministers of the Gospel be slaves to others, and servants to themselves! They are not to prie into gain through every small chink. It becomes them rather to be acquainted with the natures of things, then with the prizes, and to know them rather as they are in the world then as they are in the market. Otherwise, if his means be small, and living poore, necessity will bolt him out of his own study, and send him to the barn, when he should be at his book, or make him study his Easter-book more then all other Writers. Hereupon some wanting what they should have at home, have done what they should not abroad.

*Because Hospitality is expected at their hands.* The poore come to their houses, as if they had interest in them, and the Ministers can neither receive them nor refuse them.

2
* Numb. 22. 22.
* Judges. 19. 11.

3

them. Not to relieve them, were not Christianity, and to relieve them, were worse then Infidelity, because therein they wrong their providing for their own family. Thus sometimes are they forced to be Nabals against their will; yet it greiveth them to send away the people empty. But what shall they do, seeing they cannot multiply their loaves and their fishes? Besides, Clergie-men are deeply rated to all payments. Oh that their profession were but as highly prized, as their estate is valued.

4. *Because they are to provide for their Posterity*, that after the death of their parents they may live, though not in an high, yet in an honest fashion, neither leaving them to the wide world, nor to a narrow cottage.

5. *Because the Levites in the Old Testament had plentifull provision.* Oh 'tis good to be Gods Pensioner, for he giveth his large allowance. They had Cities and Suburbs (houses and glebeland) Tithes, Freewill-offerings, and their parts in First-fruits, and Sacrifices. Do the Ministers of the Gospel deserve worse wages for bringing better tidings? Besides, the Levites places were hereditary, and the Sonne sure of his Fathers house and land without a Faculty *ad succedendum patri*.

6. *Because the Papists in time of Popery gave their Priests plentifull means.* Whose Benefactours, so bountifull to them, may serve to condemne the covetousnesse of our age towards Gods Ministers, in such who have more knowledge, and should have more religion.

*Ob.* But the great means of the Clergie in time of Popery was rather wrested then given. The Priests melted mens hearts into charity with the Scare-fire of Purgatory: And for justice now to give back what holy fraud had gotten away, is not Sacriledge but Restitution. And when those grand and vast Donations were given to the Church,

Church, there was ( as some say ) a voyce of Angels heard from heaven, saying, *Hodie venenum in Ecclesiam Christi cecidit.*

*Answ.* If poyson then fell into the Church, since hath there a strong antidote been given to expell it, especially in Impropriations. Distinguish we betwixt such Donations given to uses in themselves merely unlawfull and superstitious, as Praying for the dead, and the like; and those which *in Genere* were given to Gods Service, though *in Specie* some superstitious end were annexed thereto. And grant the former of these to be void in their very granting, yet the latter ought to be rectified and reduced to the true use, and in no case to be alienated from God. Plato saith that in his time it was a Proverb amongst Children, Τῶν ὀρθῶς δοθέντων οὐκ ἔστιν ἀφαίρεσις, *Things that are truly given must not be taken away again.* Sure, as our Saviour set a child in the midst of his Disciples to teach them humility, so nowadayes a child need be set in the midst of some men to teach them justice. Excellently * Luther, *Nisi superesset spolium Aegypti, quod rapuimus Papae, omnibus Ministris Verbi fame pereundum esset; quod si sustentandi essent de contributione populi, misere profecto ac duriter viverent. Alimur ergo de spoliis Aegypti collectis sub Papatu, & hoc ipsum tamen quod reliquum est diripitur à Magistratu: spoliantur Parochiae & Scholae, non aliter ac si fame necare nos velint.*

*Ob.* But in the pure Primitive times the Means were least, and Ministers the best: And nowadayes, does not wealth make them lazy, and poverty keep them painfull? like Hawks they flie best when sharp. The best way to keep the stream of the Clergie sweet and clear is to fence out the tide of wealth from coming unto them.

*Answ.*

* *In his Comment on the 47. of Genes. pag. 631.*

*Answ.* Is this our thankfulnesse to the God of heaven, for turning persecution into peace, in pinching his poore Ministers? When the Commonwealth now makes a feast, shall neither Zadok the Priest, nor Nathan the Prophet, be invited to it? that so the footsteps of Primitive persecution may still remain in these peaceable times, amongst the Papists, in their needlesse burning of candles; and amongst the Protestants, in the poore means of their Ministers. And what if some turn the spurres unto Virtue into the stirrups of Pride, grow idle, and insolent? let them soundly suffer for it themselves on Gods blessing; but let not the bees be sterved that the drones may be punished.

7. *Ministers Maintenance ought to be certain*; lest some of them meet with Labans for their Patrons and parishioners; changing their wages ten times; and at last, if the fear of God doth not fright the, send them away empty.

8. *It is unequall that there should be an equality betwixt all Ministers Maintenance.* Except that first there were made an equality betwixt all their Parts, Pains, and Piety. Parity in means will quickly bring a levell and flat in Learning; and few will strive to be such spirituall Musicians, to whom David directeth many Psalms, *To him that excelleth*, but will even content themselves with a Canonicall sufficiency, and desiring no more then what the Law requires: More learning would be of more pains, and the same profit, seeing the *mediocriter* goeth abreast with *optime*.

*Ob.* But neither the best, nor the most painfull and learned get the best preferment. Sometimes men of the least, get Livings of the best worth; yea such as are not worthy to be the curates to their curates, and *crassa Ingenia* go away with *opima Sacerdotia*.

*Answ.* Thus it ever was, and will be. But is this dust onely to be found in Churches, and not in Civill

Civill Courts? Is merit everywhere elſe made the exact ſquare of preferment? or did ever any urge, that all Offices ſhould be made champian for their profits, none higher then other? ſuch corruption will ever be in the Church, except there were a Law (ridiculous to be made, and impoſsible to be kept) that men ſhould be no men, but that all Patrons or people in their Election or Preſentations of Miniſters ſhould wholly deveſt themſelves of by-reſpects of kinred, friendſhip, profit, affection, and merely chuſe for deſert: and then ſhould we have all things ſo well ordered, ſuch Paſtours and ſuch people, the Church in a manner would be Triumphant, whileſt Militant. Till then, though the beſt livings light not alwayes on the ableſt men, yet as long as there be ſuch preferments in the Church, there are ſtill encouragements for men to endeavour to excell, all hoping, and ſome hapning on advancement.

*Ob.* But Miniſters ought to ſerve God merely for love of himſelf; and pity but his eyes were out that ſquints at his own ends in doing Gods work.

*Anſw.* Then ſhould Gods beſt Saints be blind; for Moſes himſelf had *an eye to the recompence of reward.* Yea Miniſters may look not onely on their eternall but on their temporall reward, as motives to quicken their endeavours. And though it be true, that grave and pious men do ſtudy for learning ſake, and embrace virtue for it ſelf, yet it is as true that youth (which is the ſeaſon when learning is gotten) is not without ambition, nor will ever take pains to excell in any thing, when there is not ſome hope of excelling others in reward and dignity. And what reaſon is it that whileſt Law and Phyſick bring great portions to ſuch as

H h  marry

marry them, Divinity their elder sister should onely be put off with her own beauty? In after-ages men will rather bind their sonnes to one gainfull, then to seven liberall Sciences: onely the lowest of the people would be made Ministers, which cannot otherwise subsist; and it will be bad when Gods Church is made a Sanctuary onely for men of desperate estates to take refuge in it.

However, let every Minister take up this resolution, *To preach the word, to be instant in season, out of season, reprove, rebuke, exhort with all long-suffering and doctrine.* If thou hast competent means comfortably to subsist on, be the more thankfull to God the fountain, to man the channell; painfull in thy place, pitifull to the poore, cheerfull in spending some, carefull in keeping the rest. If not, yet tire not for want of a spurre: do something for love, and not all for money; for love of God, of goodnesse, of the godly, of a good conscience. Know 't is better to want means, then to detain them; the one onely suffers, the other deeply sinnes: and it is as dangerous a persecution to religion, to draw the fewell from it, as to cast water on it. Comfort thy self that another world will pay this worlds debts, *and great is thy reward with God in heaven.* A reward, in respect of his promise; a gift, in respect of thy worthlesnesse: And yet the lesse thou lookest at it, the surer thou shalt find it, if labouring with thy self to serve God for himself, in respect of whom even heaven it self is but a sinister end.

To

## To the Reader.

THese Generall Rules we have placed in the middle, that the Books on both sides may equally reach to them; because all Persons therein are indifferently concerned.

# The Holy State.

## THE FOURTH BOOK.

### Chap. I.
### *The Favourite.*

A Favourite is a Court-diall, whereon all look whilest the King shines on him, and none, when it is night with him. A Minion differs from a Favourite: for He acts things by his own will and appetite, as a Favourite by the judgement and pleasure of his Prince. These again are twofold: either such as relie wholly on their Kings favour, or such as the King partly relies on their wisdome, loving them rather for use then affection. The former are like pretty wands in a Princes hand, for him to play with at pleasure; the latter, like staves, whereon he leans and supports himself in State-affairs.

*God is the originall Patron of all preferment, all dignities being in his disposall. Promotion* (\* saith David) *comes neither from the East, nor from the West, nor yet from the South.* The word here translated *South,* in the Hebrew signifies the Desert; and such a course list bounded Palestine both on the South and \* North, so that in effect preferment bloweth from no point of the Compasse. True, every man is, *fortunæ suæ faber,* the Smith to beat out his own fortunes; 

Maxime 1
\* *Psal.* 75. 7.

\**Tremellius on the verse.*

fortunes; but God first doth give him coals, iron, and anvil before he can set up his trade.

2. *The first inlet into a Princes knowledge is half way into his favour.* Indeed the heat of the sunne pierceth into the innermost bowells of the earth, but onely the surface thereof is guilded with his beams: So though the influence of the Princes protection reacheth the utmost and obscurest man in his dominions, yet onely some few, who lie on the top of the heap of his subjects, can be graced with his favour. He therefore that is known to his Prince, starts in the half way of his race to honour. A notable fellow, and a souldier to Alexander, finding this first admission to be the greatest difficulty, put feathers into his nose and eares, and danced about the Court in an antique fashion, till the strangenesse of the Shew brought the King himself to be a spectatour. Then this Mimick throwing off his disguize, S$^e$ (said he to the King) *thus I first arrive at your Majesties notice in the fashion of a fool, but can do you service in the place of a wise-man, if you please to employ me.*

3. *'Tis the easier for them to leap into preferment, who have the rise of noble bloud*: such get their honour with more ease, and keep it with lesse envie, which is busiest in maligning of upstarts. Nor is it any hinderance unto him, but rather an advantage, if such a Nobleman be of an ancient family, decayed in estate through the fault of his Ancestours; for such, Princes count the object as well of their pity as favour, and it an act as well of charity as bounty to relieve and raise them: But those are in some sort born Favourites, and succeed by descent to a Princes affection (rather as a debt then a gift) whose parents have formerly suffered in the Princes or his predecessours behalf. This made Queen Elizabeth first reflect on the Lord Norris, (for in the peaceable beginning of her reigne the Martiall spirits of his sonne were not yet raised) because his father dyed her mothers Martyr, to attest her innocencie in the reigne of King Henry the eighth.

*Severall*

## Chap. 1.   *The Favourite.*

**4** *Severall doores open to preferment, but the King keeps the key of them all.* Some have been advanced for their Faces, their Beauty; their Heads, their Wisdome; their Tongues, their Eloquence; their Hands, their Valour; their Bloud, their Nobility; their Feet, their Nimblenesse, and Comlinesse in dancing; but all is ultimately resolv'd on the Princes pleasure.

**5** *Happy the Favourite that is raised without the rune of another*: as those which succeed in a dead place, who draw lesse envy of competitours, in keeping others out of the Kings favour, then those that cast one out of the possession thereof. Also he that climbeth up by degrees stands more firmly in favour, as making his footing good as he goes.

**6** *Sometimes the Princes favour is all the known worth in the Favourite.* I say, *known*: for he is an Infidel that believes not more then he sees, and that a rationall Prince will love where he sees no lovelinesse. Surely Charles the ninth of France beheld some worth in Albertus Tudius (an Hucksters sonne, to whom in five years, besides other honours, he gave six hundred thousand crowns) though some affirm all the good the King got by him, was to learn to * swear by the Name of God. Except we will say, that Kings desire in some to shew as the absolutenesse of their power, to raise them from nothing, so of their will also, to advance them for nothing. But Princes have their grounds reard above the flats of common men, and who will search the reasons of their actions must stand on an equall basis with them.

* *Camerarius, med. Hist. cap. 4.*

**7** *Some Kings to make a jest have advanced a man in earnest.* When amongst many Articles exhibited to King Henrie the seventh by the Irish against the Earl of Kildare, the last was, * *Finally, all Ireland cannot rule this Earl.* Then (quoth the King) *shall this Earl rule all Ireland*; and made him Deputie thereof. But such accidents are miraculous; and he shall sterve that will not eat till such Manna is dropt into his mouth.

* *Camb. Rem. pag. 271.*

But

8    *But by what lawfull means soever he hath gotten his advancement, he standeth but in a slippery place* ; and therefore needs constantly to wear ice-spurres, for he rather glides then goes, and is in continuall fear to be crush'd from above by his Princes anger, and undermin'd from beneath by his fellow-subjects envie. Against both which see how he fenceth himself.

9    *He prayseth God for preferring him, and prayeth to him to preserve him.* His Greatnesse must needs fall which is not founded in Goodnesse. First he serveth his God in heaven, and then his Master on earth. The best way to please all, or to displease them with least danger, is to please him who is all in all.

10    *Next he studieth the alphabet of his Princes disposition*: whose inclination when found out is half fitted. Then he applyes himself to please his naturall, though not vitious, humours, never preferring himself before his Prince in any thing, wherein he desires or conceiveth himself to excell. Nero, though indeed but a Fidler, counted himself as well Emperour of Musick as of Rome; and his Followers too grossely did sooth him up in the admiration of his skill in that Art. But the most temperate Princes love to taste the sweetnesse of their own praises (if not overluscious with flattery) where their own deserts lay the groundwork, and their Favourites give the varnish to their commendations.

11    *Bluntnesse of speech hath becom'd some, and made them more acceptable*: Yea this hath been counted Freeheartednesse, in Courtiers; Conscience and Christian simplicity, in Clergiemen; Valour, in Souldiers. *I love thee the better* (said Queen Elizabeth to Archbishop Grindall) *because you live unmarried*. And I, Madam, (replyed Grindall) *because you live unmarried love you the worse*. But those, who make musick with so harsh an instrument, need have their bow well rosend before, and to observe Time and Place, lest that gall which would tickle at other times.

*He*

*He leaveth his Prince alwayes with an appetite, and never gluts him with his company.* Sometimes taking occasion to depart, whilest still his staying might be welcome. Such intermissions render him more gratious; yet he absents himself neither farre, nor long, lest he might seem to neglect. Though he doth not alwayes spurre up close to the Kings side (to be constantly in his presence) he never lagges so farre behind, as to be out of distance. Long absence hath drawn the curtain betwixt a Favourite and his Sovereigne, and thereby hath made room for others to step in betwixt them.

*He doth not boldly engrosse and limit his Masters favour to himself.* He is willing his Prince should shine beside him, but especially thorow him, on others. Too covetous are they who, not content to be sole heirs to their Princes favour, grudge that any pensions should be allotted to their younger brethren. Why should it not as well be Treason to confine a Princes affection, as to imprison his person?

*He makes provident yet moderate use of his Masters favour.* Especially if he be of a various nature, and loveth exchange, counting it not to stand with the state of a King to wear a Favourite thredbare. Too blame they, who thinking it will be continuall summer with them (as in the countrey under the Æquator) will not so much as frostnip their souls with a cold thought of want hereafter, and provide neither to oblige others, nor to maintain themselves: As bad they on the other side, who like those who have a lease, without impeachment of waste, speedily to expire, whip and strip, and rap and rend, whatsoever can come to their fingers.

*He makes his estate invisible by purchasing reversions, and in remote countreys.* He hath a moderate estate in open view, that the world may settle their looks on't (for if they see nothing they will suspect the more) and the rest farre off and hereafter. The eyes of envy can never bewitch

witch that which it doth not see. These Reversions will be ripe for his heir, by that time his heir shall be ripe for them, and the money of distracted revennues will meet entirely in one purse.

6. *Having attained to a competent height, he had rather grow a buttresse broader, then a storie higher.* He fortifieth himself by raising outworks, and twisting himself by inter-marriages of his kinred into noble Families: his Countenance will give all his Kinswomen beauty. Some Favourites, whose heels have been tript up by their adversaries, have with their hands held on their Allies, till they could recover their feet again.

17. *He makes not Great men dance envidious attendance to speak with him.* Oh whilest their heels cool how do their hearts burn? Wherefore in the midst of the Term of his businesse he makes himself a vacation to speak with them. Indeed some difficulty of accesse and conference begets a reverence towards them in common people (who will suspect the ware not good if cheap to come by) and therefore he values himself in making them to wait: Yet he loves not to over-linger any in an afflicting hope, but speedily dispatcheth the fears or desires of his expecting Clients.

18. *He loveth a good name, but will not wooe or court it otherwise, then as it is an attendant on honesty and virtue.* But chiefly he avoydeth the sweet poyson of Popularity, wherewith some have swollen till they have broken. Especially, he declines the entertainment of many Martialists, the harsh counsell of souldiers being commonly untunable to the Court-way. The immoderate resorting of military men to a Favourite (chiefly if by any palliation he pretends to the Crown) is like the flocking of so many ravens and vulturs which foretell his funerall.

19. *He preserves all inferiour Officers in the full rights and priviledges of their places.* Some are so boysterous, no severals will hold them, but lay all Offices common to their

their power, or else are so busie, that making many circles in other mens professions, they raise up ill spirits in them, and for every finger they needlessely thrust into other mens matters, shall find an hand against them, when occasion shall serve. As bad are they, who leaping over meaner persons to whom the businesse is proper, bring it *per saltum* to themselves, not suffering matters to run along in a legall channell, but in a by-ditch of their own cutting, so drawing the profit to themselves, which they drein from others.

*If accused by his adversaries, he flies with speed to his Princes person.* No better covert for a hunted Favourite to take to: where if innocent, with his loyall breath he easily dispels all vapours of ill suggestions; if guilty, yet he is half acquitted, because judged by the Prince himself, whose compassion he moves by an ingenuous confession. But if this Sanctuary-doore be bolted against him, then his ruine is portended, and not long after.

*He is a fish on the dry shore when the tide of his Masters love hath left him;* so that if he be not the more wise, he will be made a prey to the next that finds him. Severall are the causes of Favourites falls, proceeding either from the Kings pleasure, their enemies malice, or their own default: different the degrees and manner of their ruine: some when grown too great are shifted under honourable colours of employment into a forrein aire, there to purge and lessen; others receive their condemnation at home. But how bad soever his cast be, see how he betters it by good playing it.

*He submits himself, without contesting, to the pleasure of his Prince.* For being a Tenant at will to the favour of his Sovereigne, it is vain to strive to keep violent possession when his Landlord will out him. Such struggling makes the hook of his enemies malice strike the deeper into him. And whilest his adversaries spurre him with injuries on purpose to make him spring out into rebellious practices, he reins in his passions with the stronger patience.

23. *If he must down, he seeks to fall easily, and if possible, to light on his legs.* If stript out of his robes, he strives to keep his clothes; loosing his honour, yet to hold his lands, if not them, his life; and thanks his Prince for giving him whatsoever he takes not away from him.

To conclude, A Favourite is a trade, whereof he that breaks once seldome sets up again. Rare are the examples of those who have compounded and thrived well afterwards. Mean men are like underwood, which the Law calls *sylva cædua, quæ* * *succisa renascitur*, being cut down it may spring again, but Favourites are like okes, which scarce thrive after ( to make timber) being lopt, but if once cut down never grow more. If we light on any who have flourished the second time, impute it to their Princes pleasure to crosse the common observation, and to shew that nothing is past cure with so great a chirurgion, who can even set a broken Favourite.

Now to shew the inconstancie of Greatnesse not supported with virtue, we will first insist in a remarkable pattern in holy Scripture. Next will we produce a parallel of two Favourites in our English Court, living in the same time, and height of honour with their Sovereigne, the one through his vitiousnesse ending in misery, the other by his virtuous demeanour shining bright to his death: for I count it a wrong to our Countrey to import presidents out of forrein Histories, when our home-Chronicles afford us as plentifull and proper examples.

* *Lynwood lib. 3. cap.* Quanquam exsolventibus.

CHAP. 2.

## Chap. 2.
### The life of HAMAN.

Haman the sonne of Amedatha, of the kinred of Agag, and people of Amalek, was highly favoured by Ahasuerus Emperour of Persia. I find not what pretious properties he had, sure he was a pearl in the eye of Ahasuerus, who commanded all his subjects to do lowly reverence unto him: onely Mordecai the Jew excepted himself from that rule, denying him the payment of so humble an observance.

I fathome not the depth of Mordecai's refusall: perchance Haman interpreted this reverence farther then it was intended, as a divine honour, and therefore Mordecai would not blow wind into so empty a bladder, and be accessary to puff him up with self-conceit; or because Amalek was the devils first-fruits, which first brake the peace with Israel, and God commanded an antipathy against them; or he had some private countermand from God not to reverence him. What ever it was, I had rather accuse my self of ignorance, then Mordecai of pride.

Haman swells at this neglect. Will not his knees bow? his neck shall break with an halter. But oh, this was but poore and private revenge: one lark will not fill the belly of such a vultur. What if Mordecai will not stoop to Haman, must Haman stoop to Mordecai to be revenged of him alone? wherefore he plotteth with the Kings sword to cut off the whole Nation of the Jews.

Repairing to Ahasuerus, he requested that all the Jews might be destroyed. He backs his petition with three arguments: first, It was a scattered Nation; had they inhabited one entire countrey, their extirpation would have weakned his empire, but being dispersed, though kill'd every where, they would have been missed no where; secondly, his Empire would be more uniform when this irregular people, not obferving his Laws, were taken away ; thirdly, ten thoufand talents Haman would pay into the bargain into the Kings Treafure.

What, out of his own purfe ? I fee his pride was above his covetoufneffe; and fpightfull men count their revenge a purchafe which cannot be overbought : or perchance this money fhould arife out of the confifcation of their goods. Thus Ahafuerus fhould lock all the Jews into his cheft, and by help of Hamans Chymiftry convert them into filver.

See how this grand deftroyer of a whole Nation pleads the Kings profit. Thus our punie depopulatours alledge for their doings the Kings and countreys good; and we will believe them, when they can perfwade us that their private coffers are the Kings exchequer. But never any wounded the Commonwealth, but firft they kiff'd it, pretending the publick good.

Hamans filver is droffe with Ahafuerus : onely his pleafure is currant with him. If Haman will have it fo, fo it fhall freely be; he will give him and not fell him his favour. 'Tis wofull when great Judges fee parties accufed by other mens eyes, but condemne them by their own mouthes : and now Pofts were fent thorow out all Perfia to execute the Kings cruell decree.

I had almoft forgotten how before this time Mordecai had difcovered the treafon, which two of the Kings Chamberlains had plotted againft him; which good fervice of his, though not prefently paid, yet was fcored up in the Chronicles, not rewarded but recorded, where it flept till a due occafion did awake it. Perchance Hamans envy kept it from the Kings knowledge; and Princes fometimes to reward the defert of men want not mind, but minding of it

To proceed : See the Jews all pitifully penfive, and fafting fasting in sackcloth and ashes, even to Queen Esther her self, which (unknown to Haman) was one of that nation. And to be brief, Esther invites Ahasuerus and Haman to a banquet (whose life shall pay the reckoning) and next day they are both invited to a second entertainment.

Mean time Haman provides a gallows of fifty cubits high to hang Mordecai on. Five cubits would have serv'd the turn; and had it took effect, the height of the gallows had but set his soul so much the farther on his journey towards heaven. His stomach was so sharp set, he could not stay till he had din'd on all the Jews, but first he must break his fast on Mordecai; and fit it was this bell-weather should be sacrificed before the rest of the flock: wherefore he comes to the Court to get leave to put him to death.

The night before Ahasuerus had passed without sleep. The Chronicles are called for, either to invite slumber, or to entertain waking with the lesse tediousnesse. Gods hand in the margin points the Reader to the place where Mordecai's good service was related; and Ahasuerus asketh Haman (newly come into the presence) what shall be done to the man whom the King will honour?

Haman being now (as he thought) to measure his own happinesse, had been much too blame if he made it not of the largest size. He cuts out a garment of honour, royall both for matter and making, for Mordecai to wear. By the Kings command he becomes Mordecai's Herauld and Page, lacquying by him riding on the Kings steed (who he hoped by this time should have mounted the wooden horse) and then pensive in heart hasts home to bemoan himself to his friends. Hamans wife proves a true Prophetesse, presaging his ruine. If the feet of a Favourite begin to slip on the steep hill of Honour, his own weight will down with him to the bottom: once past noon with him, it is presently night. For

For at the next feast Ahasuerus is mortally incens'd against him for plotting the death of Esther, with the rest of her people. (For had his project succeeded, probably the Jew had not been spared for being a Queen, but the Queen had been killed for being a Jew.) Haman in a carelesse sorrowfull posture, more minding his life then his lust, had cast himself on the Queens bed. *Will he force the Queen also* (said Ahasuerus) *before me in the house?* These words rang his passing-bell in the Court, and according to the Persian fashion they covered his face, putting him in a winding sheet that was dead in the Kings favour. The next news we hear of him is, that by exchange Haman inherits the gibbet of Mordecai, and Mordecai the house and greatnesse of Haman, the decree against the Jews being generally reversed.

CHAP. 3.

Chap. 3.　　*The life of Card.* Wolsey.　　249

THOMAS WOLSEY Arch-Bishop *of Yorke*, Chancelovr *of England* Cardinal *and* Legate de Latere He Died at Leicester Abby. *Anno Dñi* 1529. the 29th *of November*.　　W.M.sculp:

## Chap. 3.

### *The life of Card.* Wolsey.

THomas Wolsey was born at Ipswich in Suffolk, whose father was a Butcher, and an * honest man, and was there brought up at school, where afterwards he built a beautifull Colledge. From Ipswich he went to Oxford, and from thence was preferred to be Schoolmaster to the Marques of Dorset's children, where he first learnt to be imperious over Noble bloud. By the stairs of a Parsonage or two he climbed

* Parentem habuit virum probum at Ianium, Pol. Virgil. pag. 6, 3.

K k　　　　up

up at last into the notice of Fox, Bishop of Winchester, and was received to be his Secretary.

There was at that time a faction at Court betwixt Bishop Fox and Thomas Howard, Earl of Surrey. The Bishop being very old was scarce able to make good his party; yet it grieved him not so much to stoop to Nature as to the Earl his Corrivall: wherefore not able to manage the matter himself, he was contented to be the stock whereon Wolsey should be graffed, whom he made heir to his favour, commending him to King Henrie the seventh for one fit to serve a King, and command others: And hereupon he was entertained at Court.

Soon after, when Henrie his sonne came to the Crown, Wolsey quickly found the length of his foot, and fitted him with an easie shoe. He perswaded him that it was good accepting of pleasure whilest youth tender'd it: let him follow his sports, whilest Wolsey would undertake every night briefly to represent unto him all matters of moment which had passed the Counsell-table. For Princes are to take State-affairs not in the masse and whole bulk of them, but onely the spirits thereof skilfully extracted. And hereupon the King referred all matters to Wolsey's managing, on whom he conferr'd the Bishopricks of Duresme, Winchester, and York, with some other spirituall promotions.

Nothing now hindred Wolsey's prospect to overlook the whole Court but the head of Edward Stafford Duke of Buckingham, who was high in birth, honour, and estate. For as for Charles Brandon, Duke of Suffolk, he stood not in Wolsey's way, but rather besides then against him: Brandon being the Kings companion in pleasures, Wolsey his counsellour in policy; Brandon Favourite to Henrie, Wolsey to the King. Wolsey takes this Buckingham to task, who (otherwise a brave Gentleman) was proud and popular; and
that

that tower is easily undermin'd whose foundation is hollow. His own folly with Wolsey's malice overthrew him. Vainglory ever lyeth at an open guard, and giveth much advantage of play to her enemies. The Duke is condemned of high treason, though rather corrivall with the King for his Clothes then his Crown, being excessively brave in apparell.

The ax that kills Buckingham frights all others, who turn contesting into complying with our Archbishop, now Cardinall, Legate *à latere*, and Lord-Chancellour. All the Judges stood at the barre of his devotion. His displeasure more feared then the Kings, whose anger though violent was placable; the Cardinalls of lesse furie, but more malice: yet in matters of Judicature he behaved himself commendably. I heare no widows sighes, nor see orphans tears in our Chronicles caused by him: sure in such cases wherein his private ends made him not a party, he was an excellent Justicer, as being too proud to be bribed, and too strong to be overborn.

Next he aspires to the Triple Crown; he onely wants Holinesse, and must be Pope. Yet was it a great labour for a Tramountain to climbe over the Alps to S. Peters Chair; a long leap from York to Rome, and therefore he needed to take a good rise. Besides he used Charles the fift, Emperour, for his staff, gold he gave to the Romish Cardinalls, and they gave him golden promises, so that at last Wolsey perceived, both the Emperour and the Court of Rome delay'd and deluded him.

He is no fox whose den hath but one hole: Wolsey finding this way stopt, goes another way to work, and falls off to the French King, hoping by his help to obtain his desires. However if he help not himself, he would hinder Charles the Emperours designes; and revenge is a great preferment. Wherefore covertly he seeks to make a divorce betwixt Queen Katharine,

Dowager, the Emperours Aunt, and King Henrie the eighth his Master.

Queen Katharines age was above her Husbands, her gravity above her age; more pious at her beads then pleasant in her bed, a better woman then a wife, and a fitter wife for any Prince then King Henrie. Wolsey by his instruments perswades the King to put her away, pleading they were so contiguous and near in kinred, they might not be made continuous (one flesh) in marriage, because she before had been wife to Prince Arthur the Kings brother. Besides, the King wanted a male heir, which he much desired.

Welcome whisperings are quickly heard. The King embraceth the motion: the matter is enter'd in the Romish Court, but long delayed; the Pope first meaning to divorce most of the gold from England in this tedious suit. But here Wolsey miscarried in the Masterpiece of his policy. For he hoped upon the divorce of King Henrie from Queen Katharine his wife (which with much adoe was effected) to advance a marriage betwixt him and the King of France his sister, thinking with their nuptiall ring to wed the King of France eternally to himself, and mould him for farther designes: whereas contrary to his expectation King Henrie fell in love with Anna Bullen, a Lady whose beauty exceeded her birth (though honourable) wit her beauty, piety all; one for his love not lust, so that there was no gathering of green fruit from her till marriage had ripened it: whereupon the King took her to wife.

Not long after followed the ruine of the Cardinall, caused by his own vitiousnesse, heightned by the envy of his Adversaries. He was caught in a Premunire for procuring to be Legate *de latere*, and advancing the Popes power against the Laws of the Realm; and eight other Articles were framed against him, for which we report the Reader to our * Chronicles. The main

* *Fox Acts & Monuments, p. 996.*

main was, his *Ego & Rex meus*, wherein he remembred his old profession of a Schoolmaster, and forgot his present estate of a Statesman. But as for some things laid to his charge, his friends plead, that where potent malice is Promoter, the accusations shall not want proof, though the proof may want truth. Well, the broad seal was taken from him, and some of his spirituall Preferments. Yet was he still left Bishop of Winchester, and Archbishop of York, so that the Kings goodnesse hitherto might have seemd rather to ease him of burthensome greatnesse, then to have deprived him of wealth or honour: which whether he did out of love to Wolsey, or fear of the Pope, I interpose no opinion.

Home now went Wolsey into Yorkshire, and lived at his Mannour of Cawood, where he wanted nothing the heart of man could desire for contentment. But great minds count every place a prison, which is not a Kings Court; and just it was that he which would not see his own happinesse, should therefore feel his own misery. He provided for his enstalling Archbishop State equivalent to a Kings Coronation, which his ambition revived other of his misdemeanours, and by command from the King he was arrested by the Earl of Northumberland, and so took his journeys up to London. By the way his soul was rackt betwixt different tidings; now hoysed up with hope of pardon, then instantly let down with news of the Kings displeasure, till at Leicester his heart was broken with these sudden and contrary motions. The Storie goes that he should breath out his soul with speeches to this effect, *Had I been as carefull to serve the God of Heaven, as I have to comply to the will of my earthly King, God would not have left me in mine old age, as the other hath done.*

His body swell'd after his death, as his mind did whilest he was living, which with other symptomes gave the suspicion that he poysoned himself. It will suffice

suffice us to observe, If a Great man much beloved dyeth suddenly, the report goes that others poysoned him: If he be generally hated, then that he poysoned himself. Sure never did a Great man fall with lesse pity. Some of his own servants with the feathers they got under him flew to other Masters. Most of the Clergy (more pitying his Profession then Person) were glad that the felling of this oke would cause the growth of much underwood.

 Let Geometricians measure the vastnesse of his mind by the footsteps of his Buildings, Christ-Church White-Hall, Hampton-Court: And no wonder if some of these were not finished, seeing his life was rather broken off then ended. Sure King Henrie lived in two of his houses, and lies now in the third, I mean his Tombe at Windsor. In a word, in his prime he was the bias of the Christian world, drawing the bowl thereof to what side he pleased.

## Chap. 4.
### *The life of* Charles Brandon, *Duke of Suffolk.*

Charles Brandon was sonne to S<sup>r</sup>. William Brandon, Standerd-bearer to King Henry the seaventh, in whose quarrell he was slain in Bosworth field; wherefore the King counted himself bound in honour and conscience to favour young Charles, whose father spent his last breath to blow him to the haven of victory, and caused him to be brought up with Prince Henrie, his second sonne.

 The intimacy betwixt them took deep impression in their tender years, which hardned with continuance of time proved indeleble. It was advanced by the sympathy of their active spirits (men of quick and large-striding minds loving to walk together) not to say, that the loosenesse of their youthfull lives made
them

them the faster friends. Henry, when afterwards King, heaped honours upon him, created him Viscount Lisle, and Duke of Suffolk.

Not long after some of the English Nobility got leave to go to the publick Tilting in Paris, and there behav'd themselves right valiantly, though the sullen French would scarce speak a word in their praise. For they conceived it would be an eternall impoverishing of the credit of their Nation, if the honour of the day should be exported by foreiners. But Brandon bare away the credit from all, fighting at Barriers with a giant Almain, till he made an earth-quake in that mountain of flesh, making him reel and *stagger, and many other courses at Tilt he performed to admiration. Yea, the Lords beheld him not with more envious, then the Ladies with gracious eyes, who darted more glaunces in love, then the other ranne spears in anger against him; especially Mary the French Queen, and sister to King Henry the eighth, who afterward proved his wife.  *Hollinshed, pag 833.

For after the death of Lewis the twelfth her husband, King Henry her brother imployed Charles Brandon to bring her over into England; who improved his service so well that he got her good will to marrie her. Whether his affections were so ambitious to climbe up to her, or hers so courteous as to descend to him (who had been *twice a widower before) let youthfull pennes dispute it: it sufficeth us, both met together. Then wrote he in humble manner to request King Henries leave to marrie his sister; but knowing that matters of this nature are never sure till finisht, and that leave is sooner got to do such attempts when done already; and wisely considering with himself that there are but few dayes in the Almanack, wherein such *Marriages come in*, and subjects have opportunity to wed Queens, he first married her *privately in Paris.  *First married to Margaret Nevil, after to Anne, daughter to S<sup>r</sup> Anthony Brown.

*Hollinshed, pag.836.

King Henrie after the acting of some anger, and shewing

shewing some state-discontent, was quickly contented therewith; yea the world conceiveth that he *gave this woman to be married to this man*, in sending him on such an imployment. At Calis they were afterward re-married, or if you will their former private marriage publickly solemniz'd, and coming into England liv'd many years in honour and esteem, no lesse dear to his fellow-subjects then his Sovereigne. He was often imployed Generall in Martiall affairs, especially in the warres betwixt the English and French, though the greatest performance on both sides was but mutuall indenting the Dominions each of other with inrodes.

When the divorce of King Henry from Queen Katharine was so long in agitation, Brandon found not himself a little agrieved at the Kings expence of time and money: for the Court of Rome in such matters, wherein money is gotten by delays, will make no more speed then the beast in Brasil, which the Spaniards call *Pigritia*, which goes no farther in a fortnight then a man will cast a stone. Yea Brandon well perceived that Cardinall Campeius and Wolsey in their Court at Bridewell, wherein the divorce was judicially handled, intended onely to produce a solemn Nothing, their Court being but the clock set according to the diall at Rome, and the instructions received thence. Wherefore knocking on the table, in the presence of the two Cardinalls, he bound it with an oath, That *It was never well in England since Cardinalls had any thing to do therein*: And from that time forward, as an active instrument, he indeavoured the abolishing of the Popes power in England.

\* *Sanders. de Schismate Anglicano,p. 108.*

For he was not onely (as the Papists complain \* of him) a principall agent in that Parliament, *Anno.* 1534. wherein the Popes supremacy was abrogated, but also a main means of the overturning of Abbeys, as conceiving that though the head was struck off, yet as long as as that neck and those shoulders remained there would be a continuall appetite of reuniting themselves. Herein his thoughts were more pure from the mixture of covetousnesse then many other imployed in the same service: For after that our eyes, justly dazled at first with the brightnesse of Gods Justice on those vitious fraternities, have somewhat recovered themselves, they will serve us to see the greedy appetites of some instruments to feed on Church-morsels.

He lived and dyed in the full favour of his Prince, though as Cardinall Pool observed, they who were highest in this Kings favour, their heads were nearest danger. Indeed King Henrie was not very tender in cutting off that joynt, and in his Reigne the ax was seldome wiped, before wetted again with Noble bloud. He dyed *Anno* 1544. much beloved, and lamented of all, for his bounty, humility, valour, and all noble virtues, since the heat of his youth was tamed in his reduced age, and lies buried at Windsor.

## Chap. 5.

### *The wise Statesman.*

TO describe the Statesman at large, is the subject rather of a Volume then a Chapter, and is as farre beyond my power, as wide of my profession. We will not lanch into the deep, but satisfie our selves to sail by the shore, and briefly observe his carriage towards God, his King, himself, home-persons, and forein Princes.

*He counts the fear of God the beginning of wisdome;* and therefore esteemeth no project profitable, which is not lawfull; nothing politick, which crosseth piety. Let not any plead for the contrary Hushai's dealing with Absalom, which strongly savour'd of double-dealing; for what is a question cannot be an argument, seeing

*Maxime* 1

the lawfulnesse of his deed therein was never decided; and he is unwise that will venter the state of his soul on the litigious title of such an example. Besides, we must live by Gods precepts, not by the godlies practice. And though God causeth sometimes the sunne of successe to shine as well on bad as good projects, yet commonly wicked actions end in shame at the last.

2. *In giving counsell to his Prince, he had rather displease then hurt him.* Plain-dealing is one of the daintiest rarities can be presented to some Princes, as being novelty to them all times of the yeare. The Philosopher could say,[*] *Quid omnia possidentibus deest? Ille qui verum dicat.* Wherefore our Statesman seeks to undeceive his Prince from the fallacies of flatterers, who by their plausible perswasions have bolster'd up their crooked counsells, to make them seem straight in the Kings eyes.

[*] Seneca de benefic. lib. 3. c. 30.

3. *Yet if dissenting from his Sovereigne, he doth it with all humility and moderation.* It is neither manners nor wit to crosse Princes in their game, much lesse in their serious affairs. Yea, it may be Rebellion in a subject to give his Sovereigne loyall counsell, if proceeding from a spirit of contradiction and contempt, and uttered in audacious language. What do these but give wholsome Physick, wrapt up in poysoned papers?

4. *He is constant, but not obstinate in the advice he gives.* Some think it beneath a wise man to alter their opinion: A maxime both false and dangerous. We know what worthy Father wrote his own Retractation; and it matters not though we go back from our word, so we go forward in the truth and a sound judgement. Such a one changeth not his main opinion, which ever was this, to embrace that course which upon mature deliberation shall appear unto him the most advised. As for his carriage towards himself,

5. *He taketh an exact survey of his own defects and perfections.* As for the former, his weaknesses and infirmities he doth carefully and wisely conceal: sometimes he covers

covers them over with a cautious confidence, and presents a fair hilt, but keeps the sword in the sheath which wanteth an edge. But this he manageth with much art, otherwise, being betray'd, it would prove most ridiculous, and it would make brave musick to his enemies, to heare the hissing of an empty bladder when it is prick'd.

*His known perfections he seeks modestly to cloud and obscure.* 6
It is needlesse to shew the sunne shining, which will break out of it self. Not like our Phantasticks, who having a fine watch draw all occasions to draw it out to be seen. Yea, because sometimes he concealeth his sufficiency in such things, wherein others know he hath ability, he shall therefore be thought at other times to have ability in those matters wherein indeed he wants it, men interpreting him therein rather modestly to dissemble, then to be defective. Yet when just occasion is offer'd, he shews his perfections soundly, though seldome, and then graceth them out to the best advantage.

*In discourse he is neither too free, nor overreserv'd, but observes a mediocrity.* 7
His hall is common to all comers, but his closet is lock'd. Generall matters he is as liberall to impart, as carefull to conceal importancies. Moderate liberty in speech inviteth and provoketh liberty to be used again, where a constant closenesse makes all suspect him: and his company is burthensome that liveth altogether on the expences of others, and will lay out nothing himself. Yea, who will barter intelligence with him, that returns no considerable ware in exchange?

*He trusteth not any with a secret which may endanger his estate.* 8
For if he tells it to his servant, he makes him his master; if to his friend, he enables him to be a foe, and to undo him at pleasure, whose secrecy he must buy at the parties own price, and if ever he shuts his purse, the other opens his mouth. Matters of inferiour conse-

Ll 2                    quence

quence he will communicate to a fast friend, and crave his advice; for two eyes see more then one, though it be never so big, and set (as in Polyphemus) in the middest of the forehead.

**9**

*Lib. 2. de offic. cap. 112.*

*He is carefull and provident in the managing of his private estate.* Excellently * Ambrose, *An idoneum putabo qui mihi det consilium, qui non dat sibi?* Well may Princes suspect those Statesmen not to be wise in the businesse of the Common-wealth, who are fools in ordering their own affairs. Our Politician, if he enlargeth not his own estate, at least keeps it in good repair. As for avaricious courses, he disdaineth them. S<sup>r</sup> Thomas More, though some years Lord-Chancellour of England, scarce left his sonne * five and twenty pounds ayeare more then his father left him. And S<sup>r</sup> Henrie Sidney (father to S<sup>r</sup> Philip) being Lord President of Wales and Ireland, got not * one foot of land in either Countrey, rather seeking after the common good then his private profit. I must confesse the last age produced an English Statesman, who was the picklock of the cabinets of forein Princes, who, though the wisest in his time and way, died poore and indebted to private men, though not so much as the whole Kingdome was indebted to him. But such an accident is rare; and a small Hospitall will hold those Statesmen who have impaired their means, not by their private carelesnesse, but carefulnesse for the publick. As for his carriage towards Home-persons,

*Sanders. de Schism. Anglic. pag. 118.*

*Henry Lho'd, in the beginning of his Welch Chronicle.*

**10**

*He studieth mens natures, first reading the Title-pages of them by the report of Fame:* but credits not Fames relations to the full. Otherwise, as in London-exchange one shall overbuy wares, who gives half the price at first demanded, so he that believeth the moity of Fame may believe too much. Wherefore to be more accurate,

**11**

*He reads the Chapters of mens natures* ( *chiefly his concurrents and competitours* ) *by the reports of their friends and foes,*

making

making allowance for their engagements, not believing all in the masse, but onely what he judiciously extracteth. Yet virtues confess'd by their foes, and vices acknowledged by their friends, are commonly true. The best intelligence, if it can be obtained, is from a fugitive Privado.

*But the most legible Character and truest Edition wherein he reads a man is in his own occasionall openings*: And that in these three cases.

1. When the party discloses himself in his wine: for though it be unlawfull to practise on any to make them drunk, yet no doubt one may make a good use of another mans abusing himself. What they say of the herb Lunaria ceremoniously gathered at some set times, that laid upon any lock, it makes it flie open, is most true of drunkennesse, unbolting the most important secrets.

2. When he discovereth himself in his passions. Physicians to make some small veins in their Patients arms plump and full, that they may see them the better to let them bloud, use to put them into hot water: so the heat of passion presenteth many invisible veins in mens hearts to the eye of the beholder; yea the sweat of anger washeth off their paint, and makes them appear in their true colours.

3. When accidentally they bolt out speeches unawares to themselves. More hold is then to be taken of a few words casually uttered, then of set solemn speeches, which rather shew mens arts then their natures, as endited rather from their brains then hearts. The drop of one word may shew more then the stream of an whole oration; and our Statesman by examining such fugitive passages (which have stollen on a sudden out of the parties mouth) arrives at his best intelligence.

**13**

*Pere de Lancre, of the uncertainty of things, lib. 2. fourth discourse*

*In Court-factions he keeps himself in a free neutrality.* Otherwise to engage himself needlessely were both folly and danger. When Francis the first, King of France, was consulting with his Captains how to lead his army * over the Alps into Italy, whether this way or that way, Amarill his fool sprung out of a corner, where he sate unseen, and bade them rather take care which way they should bring their army out of Italy back again. Thus is it easie for one to interest and embarque himself in others quarrells, but much difficulty it is to be disengaged from them afterwards. Nor will our Statesman entitle himself a party in any feminine discords, knowing that *womens jarres breed mens warres.*

**14**

*Prov. 26. 17.*

*Yet he counts neutrality profanenesse in such matters wherein God, his Prince, the Church, or State are concern'd.* Indeed, *He that meddleth with strife not belonging unto him is like one that taketh a dog by the eares.* Yet if the dog worrieth a sheep, we may, yea ought to rescue it from his teeth, and must be champions for innocence when it is overborn with might. He that will stand neuter in such matters of moment, wherein his calling commands him to be a party, with Servilius in Rome, will please neither side: Of whom the Historian sayes, *P. Servilius medium se gerendo, nec plebis vitavit odium, nec apud Patres gratiam inivit.* And just it is with God, that they should be strained in the twist, who stride so wide as to set their legs in two opposite sides. Indeed an upright shoe may fit both feet, but never saw I glove that would serve both hands. Neutrality in matters of an indifferent nature may fit well, but never suit well in important matters, of farre different conditions.

**15**

*He is the centre wherein lines of intelligence meet from all forein countreys.* He is carefull that his outlandish instructions be full, true, and speedy; not with the sluggard telling for news at noone, that the sunne is risen.

sen. But more largely hereof in the Embassadour hereafter.

*He refuseth all underhand pensions from forein Princes.* Indeed honourary rewards received with the approbation of his Sovereigne may be lawfull, and lesse dangerous. For although even such gifts tacitly oblige him by way of gratitude to do all good offices to that forein Prince whose Pensioner he is; yet his counsells passe not but with an open abatement, in regard of his known engagements, and so the State is armed against the advice of such, who are well known to lean to one side. But secret pensions which flow from forein Princes, like the river Anas in Spain, under ground, not known or discerned, are most mischievous. The receivers of such will play under-board at the Counsell-table; and the eating and digesting of such outlandish food will by degrees fill their veins with outlandish bloud, even in their very hearts.

*His Master-piece is in negotiating for his own Master with forein Princes.* At Rhodes there was a contention betwixt Apelles and Protogenes, corrivalls in the Mystery of Limming. Apelles with his pencill drew a very slender even line; Protogenes drew another more small and slender in the midst thereof with another colour: Apelles again with a third line of a different colour drew thorow the midst of that Protogenes had made, * *Nullum relinquens amplius subtilitati locum.* Thus our Statesman traverseth matters, doubling and redoubling in his forein negotiations with the Politicians of other Princes, winding, and entrenching themselves mutually within the thoughts each of other, till at last our Statesman leaves no degree of subtlety to go beyond him.

\* *Plin. nat. Hist. lib.* 34. *cap.* 10.

To conclude: Some plead that dissembling is Lawfull in the State-craft, upon the presupposition that men must meet with others which dissemble. Yea they hold, that thus to counterfeit, *se defendendo,* against a crafty corrivall, is no sinne, but a just punishment on our adversary, who first began it. And therefore Statesmen sometimes must use crooked shoes, to fit hurl'd feet. Besides, the honest Politician would quickly be begger'd, if, receiving black money from cheatours, he payes them in good silver, and not in their own coin back again. For my part, I confesse that herein I rather see what then whither to flie; neither able to answer their arguments, nor willing to allow their practice. But what shall I say? They need to have steddy heads who can dive into these gulfs of policy, and come out with a safe conscience. I'le look no longer on these whirl-pools of State, lest my pen turn giddy.

CHAP. 6.

WILLIAM CECIL Baron of Burgleigh & Lord Treafurer of England. He dyed Anno 1598. Aged 77 yeares.

W. Marshall sculp:

## Chap. 6.

### The life of William Cecil Lord Burleigh.

William Cecil born at Bourn in Lincolnſhire, deſcended from the ancient and worſhipfull Family of the Sitſilts or Cecils of Alterynnis in Herefordſhire, on the confines of Wales; a name which a great[*] Antiquary thinks probably derived from the Romane *Cecilii.* No credit is to be given to their pens, who tax him with meanneſſe of birth, and whoſe malice is ſo generall againſt all goodneſſe, that it had been

[*] *Verſtegan, reſtitut. of decaid intelligence, pag. 312.*

a slander if this worthy man had not been slandred by them: The servant is not above his master; and we know what aspersions their malice sought to cast on the Queen her self.

He being first bred in S. Johns Colledge in Cambridge, went thence to Grayes Inne (and used it as an Inne indeed, studying there in his Passage to the Court) where he attained good learning in the Laws: yet his skill in fencing made him not daring to quarrell, who in all his life-time neither* sued any, nor was sued himself. He was after Master of the Requests (the first that ever bare that office) unto the Duke of Sommerset, Lord Protectour, and was knighted by King Edward the sixth.

*Cambd. Elizab. in Anno 1598.

One * challengeth him to have been a main contriver of that act, and unnaturall will of King Edward the sixth, wherein the King passing by his sisters, Marie and Elizabeth, entailed the Crown on Queen Jane; and that he furnished that act with reasons of State, as Judge Montague filled it with arguments of Law. Indeed his hand wrote it, as Secretary of State, but his heart consented not thereto; yea he openly * opposed it, though at last yielding to the greatnesse of Northumberland, in an age wherein it was present drowning, not to swim along with the stream. But as the * Philosopher tells us, that though the Planets be whirled about daily from East to West by the motion of the *Primum mobile*, yet have they also a contrary proper motion of their own, from West to East, which they slowly yet surely move at their leisures: so Cecill had secret counter-endeavours against the strain of the Court herein, and privately advanced his rightfull intentions against the foresaid Dukes ambition; and we see that afterward Queen Marie not onely pardoned but employ'd him; so that towards the end of her reigne he stood in some twilight of her favour.

*S*r*. John Hayward in his Edward sixth, p.417.

*Cambden, ut prius.

*Aristot. lib. 2. de caelo cap. 4. & 10.

As for S*r*. Edward Montague Lord chief Justice, what

what he did was by command againſt his own will, as appears by his written proteſtation at his death, ſtill in the hands of his honourable poſterity. But whileſt in this army of offenders, the Nobility in the front made an eſcape for themſelves, Queen Maries diſpleaſure overtook the old Judge in the rere, the good old man being not able with ſuch ſpeed to provide for himſelf; yea though he had done nothing but by generall conſent and command, the reſt of the Lords laid load on him, deſirous that the Queens anger ſhould ſend him on an errand to the priſon, and thence to the ſcaffold, to excuſe themſelves from going on the ſame meſſage. However, after ſome impriſonment he was pardon'd; a ſufficient argument, that the Queen conceived him to concurre paſsively in that action.

In Queen Elizabeths dayes he was made Secretary of State, Maſter of the Wards, Lord Treaſurer, and at laſt after long ſervice Baron of Burleigh. For the Queen honoured her honours in conferring them ſparingly, thereby making Titles more ſubſtantiall, wherewith ſhe payed many for their ſervice. The beſt demonſtration of his care in ſtewarding her Treaſure was this, that the Queen, vying gold and ſilver with the King of Spain, had money or credit, when the other had neither; her Exchequer, though but a pond in compariſon, holding water, when his river, fed with a ſpring from the Indies, was dreined dry.

In that grand faction betwixt Leiceſter and Suſſex, he meddled not openly, though 'tis eaſie to tell whom he wiſh'd the beſt to. Indeed this cunning Wreſtler would never catch hold to grapple openly with Leiceſter (as having ſomewhat the diſadvantage of him both in height and ſtrength) but as they ran to their ſeverall goles, if they chanced to meet, Burleigh would fairly give him a trip, and be gone; and the Earl had many a rub laid in his way, yet never ſaw who put it there.

'Tis true, the Sword-men accus'd him as too cold in the Queens credit, and backward in fighting against forein enemies. Indeed he would never engage the State in a warre, except necessity, or her Majesties honour, sounded the alarm: But no reason he should be counted an enemie to the Sparks of Valour, who was so carefull to provide them fewel, and pay the Souldier. Otherwise, in vain do the brows frown, the eyes sparkle, the tongue threaten, the fist bend, and the arm strike, except the belly be fed.

The Queen reflected her favour highly upon him, counting him both her Treasurer, and her principall Treasure. She would cause him always to sit down in her presence, because troubled with the gout, and used to tell him: *My Lord, we make much of you, not for your bad legs, but for your good head.* This caused him to be much envied of some great ones at Court; and at one time no fewer then the * Marquesse of Winchester, Duke of Norfolk, Earls of Arundel, Northumberland, Westmerland, Pembroke and Leicester combining against him, taking advantage about his making over some moneys beyond sea to the French Protestants, and on some other occasions; S. Nicholas Throgmorton advised them first to clap him up in prison, saying, that if he were once shut up, men would open their mouths to speak freely against him. But the Queen understanding hereof, and standing, as I may say, in the very prison-doore, quash'd all their designes, and freed him from the mischief projected against him.

He was a good friend to the Church, as then established by Law; he used to advise his eldest sonne Thomas never to bestow any great cost, or to build any great house on an Impropriation, as fearing the foundation might fail hereafter. A Patron to both Universities, chiefly to Cambridge, whereof he was Chancellour; and though Rent-corn first grew in the head

\* *Cambden, Elizab. Anno* 1579.

head of S^r Thomas Smith, it was ripened by Burleighs afsiftance, whereby though the rents of Colledges ftand ftill, their revennues increafe.

No man was more pleafant and merry at meals; and he had a pretty wit-rack in himfelf, to make the dumbe to fpeak, to draw fpeech out of the moft fullen and * filent gueft at his table, to fhew his difpofition in any point he fhould propound. For forein intelligence, though he traded fometimes on the ftock of Secretary Walfingham, yet wanted he not a plentifull bank of his own. At night when he put off his gown, he ufed to fay, *Lie there*, *Lord Treafurer*, and bidding adieu to all State-affairs, difpofed himfelf to his quiet reft.

*  *Hottoman in defcrip. of the Embaffadour witneffeth fo much, who had been at his table.*

Some looking on the eftate he left, have wondered that it was fo great, and afterwards wondred more that it was fo little, having confidered what Offices he had, and how long he enjoyed them. His harveft lafted every day for above thirty years together, wherein he allowed fome of his fervants the fame courtefie Boaz granted to Ruth, to glean even among the fheaves, and to fuffer fome handfulls alfo to fall on purpofe for them, whereby they raifed great eftates.

To draw to a conclufion: There arofe a great queftion in State, whether warre with Spain fhould be continued, or a peace drawn up? The Sword and Gown-men brought weighty arguments on both fides, ftamping alfo upon them with their private interefts, to make them more heavy: Burleigh was all againft warre, now old, being defirous to depart in peace, both private in his Confcience, and publick in the State. But his life was determined before the queftion was fully decided. In his ficknefſe the Queen often vifited him, a good plaifter to affwage his pain, but unable to prolong his life; fo that, *Cum fatis naturæ, fatisque gloriæ, patriæ autem non fatis vixiffet*, in the feventy feventh yeare of his age, *Anno* 1598. he exchanged this life

life for a better. God measured his outward happinesse not by an ordinary standard: How many great Undertakers in State set in a cloud, whereas he shined to the last? Herein much is to be ascribed to the Queens constancy, who to confute the observation of Feminine ficklenesse, where her favour did light it did lodge; more to his own temper and moderation, whereas violent & boysterous meddlers in State cripple themselves with aches in their age; most to Gods goodnesse, who honoureth them that honour him. He saw Thomas his eldest sonne richly married to an honourable coheir; Robert, able to stand alone in Court, having a competent portion of favour, which he knew thriftily to improve, being a pregnant proficient in State-discipline.

## Chap. 7.
### The good Judge.

*Lib. 2.cap.1.*

THe good Advocate, whom we * formerly described, is since by his Princes favour, and own deserts, advanced to be a Judge: which his place he freely obtained with S$^r$. Augustine * Nicolls, whom King James used to call *the Judge that would give no money.* Otherwise they that buy Justice by wholesale, to make themselves savers must sell it by retail.

*Bolton in his funer. notes on him.*

Maxime 1

*He is patient and attentive in hearing the pleadings on both sides;* and hearkens to the witnesses, though tedious. He may give a waking testimony who hath but a dreaming utterance; and many countrey people must be impertinent, before they can be pertinent, and cannot give evidence about an hen, but first they must begin with it in the egge. All which our Judge is contented to hearken to.

2

*He meets not a testimony half-way, but stayes till it come at him.* He that proceeds on half-evidence, will not do quarter-justice. Our Judge will not go till he is lead.

If

If any shall brow-beat a pregnant witnesse, on purpose to make his proof miscarry, he checketh them, and helps the witnesse that labours in his delivery. On the other side, he nips those Lawyers, who under a pretence of kindnesse to lend a witnesse some words, give him new matter, yea clean contrary to what he intended.

 *Having heard with patience, he gives sentence with uprightnesse.*    3
For when he put on his robes, he put off his relations to any; and like Melchisedech becomes without pedigree. His private affections are swallowed up in the common cause, as rivers lose their names in the ocean. He therefore allows no noted favourites, which cannot but cause multiplication of fees, and suspicion of by-wayes.

 He silences that Lawyer who seeks to set the neck of a bad    4
cause, once broken with a definitive sentence; and causeth that contentious suits be spued out, as the surfets of Courts.

 *He so hates bribes, that he is jealous to receive any kindnesse*    5
*above the ordinary proportion of friendship;* lest like the Sermons of wandring Preachers, they should end in begging. And surely Integrity is the proper portion of a Judge. Men have a touch-stone whereby to try gold, but gold is the touch-stone whereby to trie men. It was a shrewd gird which Catulus gave the Romane Judges for acquitting Clodius a great malefactour, when he met them going home well attended with Officers; *You do well* (quoth he) *to be well \* guarded for your safety, lest the money be taken away from you, you took for bribes.* Our Judge also detesteth the trick of Mendicant Friers, who will touch no money themselves, but have a boy with a bag to receive it for them.

\* *Plutar. in the life of Cicero, pag. 871.*

 *When he sits upon life, in judgement he remembreth mercy.*    6
Then (they say) a butcher may not be of the Jurie, much lesse let him be the Judge. Oh let him take heed how he strikes, that hath a dead hand. It was the

charge

charge Queen Marie gave to Judge Morgan, chief Justice of the common Pleas, that notwithstanding the old * errour amongst Judges did not admit any witnesse to speak, or any other matter to be heard in favour of the adversary, her Majestie being party; yet her Highnesse pleasure was that whatsoever could be brought in the favour of the Subject should be admitted and heard.

* Holinshed in Queen Marie, pag. 1112.

7 *If the cause be difficult, his diligence is the greater to sift it out.* For though there be mention, Psal. 37. 6. of righteousnesse as clear as the noon-day, yet God forbid that that innocency which is no clearer then twilight should be condemned. And seeing ones oath commands anothers life, he searcheth whether malice did not command that oath: yet when all is done, the Judge may be deceived by false evidence. But blame not the hand of the diall, if it points at a false houre, when the fault's in the wheels of the clock which direct it, and are out of frame.

8 *The sentence of condemnation he pronounceth with all gravity.* 'Tis best when steep'd in the Judges tears. He avoideth all jesting on men in misery: easily may he put them out of countenance, whom he hath power to put out of life.

9 *Such as are unworthy to live, and yet unfitted to die, he provides shall be instructed.* By Gods mercy, and good teaching, the reprive of their bodies may get the pardon of their souls, and one dayes longer life for them here may procure a blessed eternity for them hereafter, as may appear by this memorable Example. It happened about the yeare one thousand five hundred and fiftie six in the town of *Weissenstein in Germany that a Jew for theft he had comitted, was in this cruell manner to be executed: He was hang'd by the feet with his head downwards betwixt two dogs, which constantly snatch'd and bit at him. The strangenesse of the torment moved Jacobus Andreas ( a grave, moderate, and

* Melchior Adamus in vit. Jac. Andreæ, pag. 639.

and learned Divine as any in that age ) to go to behold it. Coming thither he found the poore wretch, as he hung, repeating Verses out of the Hebrew Psalmes, wherein he cryed out to God for mercy. Andreas hereupon took occasion to counsell him to trust in Jesus Christ the true Saviour of mankind: The Jew embracing the Christian Faith, requested but this one thing, that he might be taken down and be baptized, though presently after he were hanged again ( but by the neck as Christian malefactours suffered ) which was accordingly granted him.

10. *He is exact to do justice in civill Suits betwixt Sovereigne and Subject.* This will most ingratiate him with his Prince at last. Kings neither are, can, nor should be Lawyers themselves, by reason of higher State-employments, but herein they see with the eyes of their Judges, and at last will break those false spectacles which ( in point of Law ) shall be found to have deceived them.

11. *He counts the Rules of State and the Laws of the Realm mutually support each other.* Those who made the Laws to be not onely disparate, but even opposite terms to maximes of Government, were true friends neither to Laws nor Government. Indeed *Salus Reip.* is *Charta maxima*: extremity makes the next the best remedy. Yet though hot waters be good to be given to one in a swound, they will burn his heart out who drinks them constantly, when in health. Extraordinary courses are not ordinarily to be used, when not enforced by absolute necessity.

And thus we leave our good Judge to receive a just reward of his integrity from the Judge of Judges, at the great Assize of the world.

CHAP. 8.

## Chap. 8.

### The life of Sr. JOHN MARKHAM.

JOhn Markham was born at Markham in Nottinghamshire, descended of an ancient and worthy familie. He employed his youth in the studying of the Municipall Law of this realm, wherein he attained to such eminencie, that King Edward the fourth Knighted him, and made him Lord chief * Justice of the Kings Bench in the place of Sr John Fortescue, that learned and upright Judge, who fled away with King Henrie the sixth.

*13. Maii. 1. Edwardi. 4.*

Yet Fortescue was not miss'd, because Markham succeeded him: and that losse, which otherwise could not be repair'd, now could not be perceiv'd. For though these two Judges did severally lean to the sides of Lancaster and York, yet both sate upright in matters of Judicature.

We will instance and insist on one memorable act of our Judge, which though single in it self, was plurall in the concernings thereof. And let the Reader know, that I have not been carelesse to search, though unhappy not to find, the originall Record, perchance abolished on purpose, and silenced for telling tales to the disgrace of great ones. We must now be contented to write this Story out of the English Chronicles; * and let him die of drought without pity, who will not quench his thirst at the river, because he cannot come at the fountain.

*Fabian. pag. 497 &c. Holinshed pag. 670. and Stow in 12. of Edward the fourth.*

King Edward the fourth having married into the family of the Woodvills (Gentlemen of more antiquity then wealth, and of higher spirits then fortunes) thought it fit for his own honour to bestow honour upon them: But he could not so easily provide them of wealth, as titles. For honour he could derive from himself, like light from a candle, without any diminishing

nishing of his own lustre; whereas wealth flowing from him, as water from a fountain, made the spring the shallower. Wherefore he resolved to cut down some prime subjects, and to engraff the Queens kinred into their estates, which otherwise like suckers must feed on the stock of his own Exchequer.

There was at this time one S^r Thomas Cook, late Lord Maior of London, and Knight of the Bath, one who had well lick'd his fingers under Queen Margaret (whose Wardroper he was, and customer of Hampton) a man of a great estate. It was agreed that he should be accused of high Treason, and a Commission of Oyer and Terminer granted forth to the Lord Maior, the Duke of Clarence, the Earl of Warwick, the Lord Rivers, S^r. John Markham, S^r. John Fogg, &c. to try him in Guild Hall: And the King by private instructions to the Judge appear'd so farre, that Cook, though he was not, must be found guilty, and if the Law were too short, the Judge must stretch it to the purpose.

The fault laid to his charge was for lending moneys to Queen Margaret, wife to King Henrie the sixth; the proof, was the confession of one Hawkins, who being rack'd in the Tower had confessed so much. The Counsell for the King, hanging as much weight on the smallest wier as it would hold, aggravated each particular, & by their Rhetoricall flashes blew the fault up to a great height. S^r Thomas Cook pleaded for himself, that Hawkins indeed upon a season came to him, and requested him to lend one thousand marks, upon good security. But he desired first to know for whom the money should be: and understanding it was for Queen Margaret, denyed to lend any money, though at last the said Hawkins descended so low as to require but one hundred pounds, and departed without any peny lent him.

Judge Markham in a grave speech did recapitulate,

select and collate the materiall points on either side, shewing that the proof reached not the charge of high Treason, and misprision of Treason was the highest it could amount to, and intimated to the Jurie, to be tender in matter of life, and discharge good consciences.

The Jurie being wise men ( whose apprehensions could make up an whole sentence of every nod of the Judge ) saw it behoved them to draw up Treason into as narrow a compasse as might be, lest it became their own case; for they lived in a troublesome world, wherein the cards were so shuffled, that two Kings were turn'd up trump at once, which amazed men how to play their games. Whereupon they acquitted the prisoner of high Treason, and found him guilty, as the Judge directed.

Yet it cost S$^r$ Thomas Cook, before he could get his libertie, eight hundred pounds to the Queen, and eight thousand pounds to the King: A summe in that age more sounding like the ransome of a Prince, then the fine of a Subject. Besides, the Lord Rivers ( the Queens Father ) had, during his Imprisonment, despoyled his houses, one in the city, another in the countrey of plate and furniture, for which he never received a penie recompence. Yet God righted him of the wrongs men did him, by blessing the remnant of his estate to him, and his posterity, which still flourish at Giddy Hall in Essex.

As for S$^r$ John Markham, the Kings displeasure fell so heavy on him, that he was outed of his place, and S$^r$ Thomas Billing put in his room, though the one lost that Office with more honour then the other got it; and gloried in this, that though the King could make him no Judge, he could not make him no upright Judge. He lived privately the rest of his dayes, having ( besides the estate got by his practice ) fair lands by Margaret his wife, daughter and coheir

to

to Sʳ Simon Leak * of Cotham in Nottinghamshire, whose Mother Joan was daughter and heir of Sʳ John Talbot, of Swannington in Leicestershire.

*Burtons Lecestershire, pag. 577.*

## Chap. 9.

### The good Bishop.

HE is an Overseer of a Flock of Shepherds, as a Minister is of a Flock of Gods sheep. Divine providence and his Princes bounty advanced him to the Place, whereof he was no whit ambitious: Onely he counts it good manners to sit there where God hath placed him, though it be higher then he conceives himself to deserve, and hopes that he who call'd him to the Office hath or will in some measure fit him for it.

*His life is so spotlesse, that Malice is angry with him, because she cannot be angry with him*: because she can find no just cause to accuse him. And as * Diogenes confuted him who denyed there was any motion, by saying nothing but walking before his eyes; so our Bishop takes no notice of the false accusations of people disaffected against his order, but *walks* on *circumspectly* in his calling, really refelling their cavils by his conversation. A Bishops bare presence at a marriage in his own diocesse, is by the Law interpreted for a licence; and what actions soever he graceth with his company, he is conceived to priviledge them to be lawfull, which makes him to be more wary in his behaviour.

*Maxime* 1

*Diogen. Laert. lib. 6. pag. 212. in vit. Diogenis.*

*With his honour, his holinesse and humility doth increase.* His great Place makes not his piety the lesse: farre be it from him that the glittering of the candlestick should dimme the shining of his candle. The meanest Minister of Gods word may have free accesse unto him: whosoever brings a good cause brings his own welcome with him. The pious poore may enter in at his wide gates,

2

Nn 3

gates, when not so much as his wicket shall be open to wealthy unworthinesse.

**3**

*He is diligent and faithfull in preaching the Gospel*: either by his pen, *Evangelizo manu & scriptione*, saith a strict * Divine; or by his vocall Sermons (if age and other indispensable occasions hinder him not) teaching the Clergie to preach, and the Laity to live, according to the ancient * Canons. Object not that it is unfitting he should lie Perdue, who is to walk the round, and that Governing as an higher employment is to silence his Preaching: For Preaching is a principall part of Governing, and Christ himself ruleth his Church by his Word. Hereby Bishops shall govern hearts, and make men yield unto them a true and willing obedience, reverencing God in them. Many in consumptions have recover'd their healths by returning to their native aire wherein they were born: If Episcopacy be in any declination or diminution of honour, the going back to the painfulnesse of the primitive Fathers in Preaching, is the onely way to repair it.

* *Reinold de Idol. Rom. Eccles. Epist. dedicat.*

* *Concil. Toëtan. 2. Cap. 2. Tom. 4. pag. 820. Concil. Constant. 6. Can. 19. Tom. 5. pag. 328. Concil. Aurel. Can. 33. pag. 723. and lately, Concil Trident. Sess 24. Can. 4*

**4**

*Painfull, pious, and peaceable Ministers are his principall Favourites.* If he meets them in his way (yea he will make it his way to meet them) he bestoweth all grace and lustre upon them.

**5**

*He is carefull that Church-censures be justly and solemnly inflicted*: namely,

1. Admonition, when the Church onely chideth, but with the rod in her hand.
2. Excommunication, the Mittimus whereby the Malefactour is sent to the gaolour of hell, and *delivered to Satan*.
3. Aggravation, whereby for his greater contempt, he is removed out of the gaole into the dungeon.
4. Penance, which is or should be inward repentance, made visible by open confession, whereby the Congregation is satisfied for the publick offense given her.       5 Absolution,

5 Absolution, which fetcheth the penitent out of hell, and opens the doore of heaven for him, which Excommunication had formerly lock'd, and Aggravation bolted against him.

As much as lies in his power, he either prevents or corrects those too frequent abuses, whereby offenders are not *prick'd to the heart*, but let bloud in the purse; and when the Court hath her costs, the Church hath no damage given her, nor any reparation for the open scandall she received by the parties offence. Let the memory of Worthy Bishop Lake ever survive, whose hand had the true seasoning of a Sermon with Law and Gospel, and who was most fatherly grave in inflicting Church-censures: Such offenders as were unhappy in deserving, were happy in doing penance in his presence.

* Acts 2. 37.

*He is carefull and happy in suppressing of Heresies and Schismes.* He distinguisheth of Schismaticks, as Phisicians do of Leprous people: Some are infectious, * others not; Some are active to seduce others, others quietly enjoy their opinions in their own consciences. The latter by his mildnesse he easily reduceth to the truth; whereas the Chirurgeons rigourously handling it, often breaks that bone quite off, which formerly was but out of joynt: Towards the former he useth more severity, yet endeavouring first to inform him aright, before he punisheth him. To use force first before people are fairly taught the truth, is to knock a nail into a board, without wimbling a hole for it, which then either not enters, or turns crooked, or splits the wood it pierceth.

6

* The Leprosy Elephantiasis not infectious to the company.

*He is very mercifull in punishing offenders*; both in matters of life and livelyhood, seing in S. Johns Language the same word * Bios signifies both. He had rather draw tears, then bloud. It was the honour of the Romane State, as yet being Pagan, * *In hoc gloriari licet, nulli Gentium mitiores placuisse pœnas*: Yea for the first seventy years

7

* Iohn. 3 17.
* Livius lib. 1. pag. 20.

years (till the reigne of Ancus Martius) they were without a prison. Clemency therefore in a Christian Bishop is most proper: O let not the *Starres of our Church* be herein turn'd to Comets, whose appearing in place of judicature presageth to some death or destruction. I confesse that even Justice it self is a kind of mercy: But God grant that my portion of mercy be not paid me in that coin. And though the highest detestation of sinne best agreeth with Clergy-men, yet ought they to cast a severe eye on the vice and example, and a mercifull eye on the person.

**8**
*\* Cambd Elizab.in Anno 1588. p. 538.*

*None more forward to forgive a wrong done to himself.* Worthy Archbishop *Whitgift interceded to Queen Elizabeth for remitting of heavie fines laid on some of his Adversaries (learning from Christ his Master to be a mediatour for them) till his importunity had angred the Queen, yea and till his importunity had pleas'd her again, and gave not over till he got them to be forgiven.

**9**

*\* Socrat. Ecclef. Hist. lib. 5. cap. 20.*

*He is very carefull on whom he layeth hands in Ordination;* lest afterwards he hath just cause to beshrew his fingers, and with Martianus, a Bishop of Constantinople (who made Sabbatius a Jew and a turbulent man Priest) wish he had then rather laid his hand on the * briers, then such a mans head. For the sufficiency of Scholarship he goeth by his own eye; but for their honest life, he is guided by other mens hands, which would not so oft deceive him, were Testimonialls a matter of lesse courtesie and more conscience. For whosoever subscribes them enters into bond to God and the Church, under an heavy forfeiture, to avouch the honestie of the party commended; and, as Judah for Benjamin, they become *sureties for the young man unto his father*. Nor let them think to void the band and make it but a blank with that clause, *so farre forth as we know*, or words to the like effect: For what saith the Apostle? *God is not mocked.*

He

*He meddleth as little as may be with Temporall matters*: having little skill in them, and lesse will to them. Not that he is unworthy to manage them, but they unworthy to be managed by him. Yea generally the most dexterous in spirituall matters are left-handed in temporall businesse, and go but untowardly about them. Wherefore our Bishop, with reverend * Andrews, *meddleth little in civill affairs, being out of his profession and element.* Heaven is his vocation, and therefore he counts earthly employments avocations: except in such cases which lie (as I may say) in the Marches of Divinity, and have connexion with his calling; or else when temporall matters meddle with him, so that he must rid them out of his way. Yet he rather admireth then condemneth such of his brethren, who are strengthned with that which would distract him, making the concurrence of spirituall and temporall power in them support one another, and using worldly businesse as their recreation to heavenly employment.

*\* Funerall Serm. on him, pag. 19.*

*If call'd to the Court he there doth all good offices,* betwixt Prince and people, striving to remove all misprisions & disaffections, & advancing unity and concord. They that think the Church may flourish when the Common-wealth doth wither may as well conceive that the brains may be sound when *pia mater* is perished. When in the way of a Confessour he privately tells his Prince of his faults, he knows by Nathans parable, to go the nearest way home by going farre about.

*He improves his power with his Prince for the Churches good,* in maintaining both true religion and the maintenance thereof; lest some pretending with pious Ezechiah to beat down the brazen serpent, the occasion of Idolatry, do indeed with sacrilegious Ahaz take away the brazen bulls from the Laver, and set it on a pavement of stone. He jointly advanceth the pains and gains, the work and wages of Ministers, which going together make a flourishing Clergy, with Gods blessing, and without mans envy.

13     *His mortified mind is no whit moved with the magnificent vanities of the Court*: no more then a dead corps is affected with a velvet herse-cloth over it. He is so farre from wondring at their pomps, that though he looks daily on them, he scarce sees them, having his eyes taken up with higher objects; and onely admires at such, as can admire such low matters. He is loved and feared of all; and his presence frights the Swearer either out of his oathes or into silence, and he stains all other mens lives with the clearnesse of his own.

14     *Yet he daily prayeth God to keep him in so slippery a place.* Elisha prayed that a double portion of Eliahs Spirit might rest upon him. A Father descanteth hereon, that a double portion of grace was necessary for Elisha, who was gratious at Court, lived in a plentifull way, and favoured of the Kings of Israel; whereas Eliah lived poorely, and privately: And more wisdome is requisite to manage prosperity then affliction.

15     *In his grave writings he aims at Gods glory, and the Churches peace*, with that worthy Prelate, the second Jewell of Salisbury, whose Comments and Controversies will transmit his memory to all Posterity:

    Whose dying pen did write of *Christian Union,*
    How Church with Church might safely keep *Communion.*
    Commend his care, although the cure do misse;
    The woe is ours, the happinesse is his:
    Who finding discords daily to encrease,
    Because he could not live, would die, in peace.

16     *He ever makes honourable mention of forein Protestant Churches;* even when he differs and dissents from them. The worst he wisheth the French Church is a Protestant King: not giving the left hand of Fellowship to them, and reserving his right for some other. Cannot Christs coat be of different colours, but also it must be of severall seams? railing one on another, till these Sisters, by bastardizing one another, make the Popish Church

Church the sole heir to all truth. How often did reverend *Whitgift (knowing he had the farre better cheere) send a messe of meat from his own table to the Ministers of Geneva? relieving many of them by bountifull contributions. Indeed English charity to forein Protestant Churches in some respect is payment of a debt: their children deserve to be our welcome guests, whose Grandfathers were our loving hosts in the dayes of Queen Mary.

*S. G. Paul. in his life, pag. 63, 64.

17. *He is thankfull to that Colledge whence he had his education.* He conceiv'd himself to heare his Mother-Colledge alwayes speaking to him in the language of Joseph to Pharaohs Butler, * *But think on me, I pray thee, when it shall be well with thee.* If he himself hath but little, the lesse from him is the more acceptable: A drop from a spunge is as much as a tunne of water from a Marish. He bestows on it Books, or Plate, or Lands or Building; and the Houses of the Prophets rather lack watering then planting, there being enough of them, if they had enough.

* Gen. 40. 14.

18. *He is hospitable in his housekeeping according to his estate.* His bounty is with discretion to those that deserve it: Charity mistaken, which relieves idle people, like a dead corps, onely feeds the vermin it breeds. The ranknesse of his housekeeping produceth no riot in his Family. S. Paul calls a Christian Family well ordered, * *a Church in their house.* If a private mans house be a Parochiall, a Bishops may seem a Cathedrall Church, as much better as bigger, so decently all things therein are disposed.

* Rom. 6. 5. Theoph. in locum.

We come now to give a double Example of a godly Bishop: the first out of the Primitive times, the second out of the English Church since the Reformation, both excellent in their severall wayes.

CHAP. 10.

St. AVGVSTINE the Learned and painfull Bishop of Hippo, in Africa, for the space of 40 yeares where he dyed, in the 70th. yeare of His Age, about ye yeare of or Lord 430.

W. Marshall sculp.

## Chap. II.
### The life of S. Augustine.

Augustine was born in the City of Tagasta in Africa, of Gentile parentage, Patricius and Monica, though their means bore not proportion to their birth, so that the breeding of their sonne at Learning much weakned their estate, in so much as Romanian a noble gentleman ( all the world is bound to be thankfull to S. Augustines Benefactour) bountifully advanced his education.

It

It will be needlesse to speak of his youth, vitious in manners and erroneous in doctrine, especially seeing he hath so largely accus'd himself in his *Confessions*. 'Tis tyranny to trample on him that prostrates himself; and whose sinnes God hath gratiously forgotten, let no man despightfully remember.

Being made a Presbyter in the Church of Hippo, this great favour was allowed him, to preach constantly, though in the presence of * Valerius the Bishop: whereas in that age to heare a Priest preach when that a Bishop was in the Church, was as great a wonder as the Moon shining at mid-day. Yea godly Valerius, one that could do better then he could speak, and had a better heart then tongue, (being a Grecian, and therefore not well understood of the Africans) procured Augustine in his life-time to be designed Bishop of Hippo, and to be joyned * fellow-Bishop with himself, though it was flatly against the Canons.

* *Posidonius in vit. August. cap 5.*

* *Idem. cap. 8.*

For a Coadjutour commonly proves an hinderer, and by his envious clashing doth often dig his Partners grave with whom he is joyn'd; besides that such a superinstallation seems an unlawfull bigamy, marrying two husbands at the same time to the same Church. Yea, S. Augustine himself, afterwards understanding that this was against the Constitutions of the Church, was sorry thereat (though others thought his eminency above Canons, and his deserts his dispensation) and desiring that his ignorance herein should not misguide others, obtained that the Canons (then not so hard to be kept as known, because obscure and scattered) were compiled together and published, that the Clergy might know what they were bound to observe.

Being afterwards sole Bishop, he was diligent in continuall preaching, and beating down of Hereticks especially the Manicheans, in whose Fence-school he was formerly brought up, and therefore knew best how

how to hit them, and guard himself; also the Pelagians, the duellists against Grace, and for Freewill, which till S. Augustines time was never throughly sifted, points in Divinity being but slenderly fenced till they are assaulted by Hereticks. He was also the hammer of the Donatists, Hereticks who did scatter more then they did devoure, and their Schisme was more dangerous then their *Doctrine.

*See their Tenets at large in our fifth book.

He went not so willingly to a feast as to a conference, to reduce any erroneous persons: once he disputed with Pascentius the Arian, who requested that what passed betwixt them might not be written, and afterwards gave out his *bragges that he had worsted Augustine in the dispute, which report was believed of all who desired it.

*August. Tom. 2. Ep. 174.

In other battels, if the conquered side should be so impudent as to boast of the victory, it will ere long be confuted by the number of their men slain, ensignes and wagons taken, with their flight out of the field. It is not thus in the tongue-combats of disputes, wherein no visible wounds are given, and wherein bold men (though inwardly convinced with force of reason) count not themselves conquered till they confesse it; so that in effect none can be overcome except they will themselves: For some are so shamelesse that they count not their cause *wrackt* as long as any thing alive comes to the Land, so long as they have breath to talk though not to answer, and employ their hands not to untie their Adversaries arguments, but onely obstinately to lay hold on their own opinions; yea after the conference ended they cry *victoria* in all companies wherein they come, whilest their Auditours, generally as engaged as the Disputants, will succour their Champion with partiall relations, as the Arians did in this case of Pascentius.

But their false cavills have done the Church this true

true courtesie, that ever after S. Augustine set down his disputations in writing, that so the eye of the Reader might more steddily behold his arguments presented fixed in black and white, then when they were onely *in fluxu*, as passing in his words.

His clothes were neither *brave, nor base, but comely: As for the black Cowl of the Augustinians, which they pretend from his practice, it seemeth rather ( if so ancient ) to be cut with the sheeres, or by the pattern, of Augustine the Monk. He would not receive gifts to the Church from those who had poore kinred of their own: Divinitie saith, that mercy is better then sacrifice; and the Law provides, that debts are to be paid before legacies.

* *Vestis nec nitida nimium, nec abjecta plurimùm, Possidon. cap. 22.*

In case of great want he would sell the very Ornaments of the Church, and bestow the money on the poore, contrary to the * opinion of many ( the thorn of Superstition began very soon to prick ) who would not have such things in any case to be alienated. Sure a Communion-table will not catch cold with wanting a rich carpet, nor stumble for lack of the candles thereon in silver candlesticks. Besides, the Church might afterwards be seasonably replenished with new furniture, whereas if the poore were once sterved, they could not be revived again. But let not Sacriledge in the disguize of Charity make advantage hereof, & Covetousnesse, which is ever hungry till it surfets, make a constant ordinary on Church-bread, because David in necesity fed one meal thereon. His diet was very cleanly and sparing, yet hospitable in the entertaining of others, and had this distich wrote on his table,

*De vasis Dominicis, propter captivos quamplurimos indigentes, frangi & conflari jubebat, & indigentibus dispensari: quod non commemorassem, nisi contra carnalem sensum quorundam fieri perviderem, Possidon. in vit. August. cap. 24.*

*Quisquis amat dictis absentum rodere famam,*
*Hanc mensam indignam noverit esse sibi.*

He that doth love on absent friends to jeere
May hence depart, no room is for him here.

His family was excellently well ordered, and ten of those Scholars which were brought up under him came afterwards to be Bishops.

To come to his death. It happened that the Northern countreys, called by * some *Vagina gentium*, the Sheath of people (though more properly they may be termed, *Ensis dei, the Sword of God*) sent forth the Vandalls, Albans, and Gothes, into the Southern parts, God punishing the pride of the Roman Empire to be confounded by Barbarous enemies. Out of Spain they came into Africa, and massacred all before them. The neighbouring villages like little children did flie to Hippo the mother-City for succour: thirteen moneths was Hippo besieged by the Gothes, and S. Augustine being therein prayed to God either to remove the siege, or to give the Christians therein patience to suffer, or to take him out of this miserable world, which he obtained, and dyed in the third moneth of the siege.

*\* Methodius Martyr & Paul. Diacon.*

Falling very sick (besides the disease of age and grief) he lay languishing a pretty time, and took order that none should come to him save when his meat was brought, or Physicians visited him, that so he might have elbow-room the more freely to put off the clothes of his mortality.

The motion of Piety in him (by custome now made naturall) was *velocior in fine*, daily breathing out most pious Ejaculations. He died intestate, not for lack of time to make a will, but means to bestow, having formerly passed his soul to God, whilest his body of course bequeathed it self to the earth. As for the books of his own making, a treasure beyond estimation, he carefully consigned them to severall Libraries. He dyed in the seventy sixth yeare of his age, having lived a Bishop almost fourty years. Thus a Saint of God, like an oke, may be cut down in a moment; but how many years was he a growing! Not long after his death the City of Hippo was sack'd by the Gothes, it being no wonder if Troy was taken, when the Palladium was first fetch'd away from it.

CHAP. II.

NICHOLAS RIDLEY Bishop of LONDON.
He died a constant Martyr for the Truth, and was burnt at Oxford the 16th of Octob: 1555.   W. Marshall sculp:

## CHAP. II.
### The life of Bishop RIDLEY.

Nicholas Ridley born in the Bishoprick of Duresme, but descended from the ancient and worshipfull familie of the Ridleys of Willimotes-wike in Northumberland. He was brought up in Pembroke-hall in Cambridge, where he so profited in generall Learning, that he was chosen Fellow of the Colledge, and *Anno* 1533 was Proctour of the University.

At which time two Oxford men, George Throgmorton,

ton, and John Ashwell, came to Cambridge, and in the publick Schools challenged any to dispute with them on these questions,

An {*Jus civile sit medicina præstantius?* (*denda?*
{*Mulier condemnata, bis ruptis laqueis, sit tertio suspen-*

It seems they were men of more brow then brain, being so ambitious to be known, that they had rather be hiss'd down then not come upon the stage. Sure Oxford afforded as many more able disputants, as Civill Law yielded more profound and needfull questions. Throgmorton had the fortune of daring men, to be worsted, being so pressed by John Redman and Nicholas * Ridley the opponents, that his second refused at all to dispute.

*\* Caius de Antiquit. Cant. Acad. p. 19. 20.*

Indeed an University is an onely fit match for an University; and any private man who in this Nature undertakes a whole body, being of necessity put to the worst, deserves not Phaetons Epitaph, *magnis,* but *stultis tamen excidit ausis.* And though* one objects, *Neminem Cantabrigiensium constat Oxonienses unquam ad certamen provocasse*; yet lesse learning cannot be inferred from more modestie. The best is, the two Sisters so well agree together that they onely contend to surpasse each other in mutuall kindnesse, and forbidding all duells betwixt their children, make up their joint forces against the common foe of them and true Religion.

*\* Brian Twine pag. 336.*

He was after chosen Master of Penbroke Hall, and kept the same whilest Bishop of Rochester and London, till outed in the first of Queen Marie. Not that he was covetous to hold his place in the Colledge, but the Colledge ambitious to hold him; as who would willingly part with a jewell. He was in good esteem with Henrie the eighth, and in better with pious King Edward the sixth, and was generally beloved of all the Court, being one of an handsome person, comelie presence, affable speech, and courteous behaviour.

But before I go further, Reader, pardon a digression, and

Chap. 11.    *The life of Bishop* Ridley.

and yet is it none, for 'tis necessary. I have within the narrow scantling of my experimentall remembrance observed strange alteration in the worlds valuing of those learned men which lived in that age ; and take it plainly without welt or gard, for he that smarts for speaking truth hath a playster in his own conscience.

When I was a child I was possessed with a reverend esteem of them, as most holy and pious men, dying Martyrs in the dayes of Queen Marie for profession of the truth ; which opinion having from my Parents taken quiet possession of my soul, they must be very forcible reasons which eject it.

Since that time they have been much cried down in the mouthes of many, who making a *Coroners enquest* upon their death, have found them little better then *Felons de se*, dying in their own bloud, for a mere formality, *de modo*, of the manner of the Presence, and a Sacrifice in the Sacrament, who might easily with one small distinction have knockt off their fetters, & saved their lives. By such the Coronet of Martyrdome is pluckt off from their memories ; and others more moderate equally part their death betwixt their enemies cruelty, and their own over-forwardnesse.

Since that, one might have expected that these worthy men should have been re-estated in their former honour, whereas the contrary hath come to passe. For some who have an excellent facultie in uncharitable Synecdoches, to condemne a life for an action, & taking advantage of some faults in them do much condemne them. And * one lately hath traduced them with such language, as neither beseemed his parts ( whosoever he was ) that spake it, nor their piety of whom it was spoken. If pious Latimer, whose bluntnesse was incapable of flattery, had his simplicity abused with false informations, he is called *another Doctour Shaw, to divulge in his Sermon forged accusations*. Cranmer and Ridley for some failings styled, *the common stales to countenance*

* *Authour of the book lately printed of Causes hindring Reformation in England, lib. 1. pag. 10.*

P p 2    *with*

with their prostituted gravities every politick fetch which was then on foot, as oft as the potent Statists pleased to employ them. And, as it follows not farre after, *Bishop Cranmer*, one of *King Henries* Executours, and the other *Bishops*, none refusing ( lest they should resist the Duke of *Northumberland* ) could find in their consciences to set their hands to the disenabling and defeating of the *Princesse Marie*, &c. Where Christian ingenuity might have prompted unto him to have made an intimation, that *Cranmer* ( with pious Justice *Hales* in *Kent*) was last and least guilty, much refusing to subscribe; and his long resisting deserved as well to be mentioned, as his yielding at last. Yea, that very Verse, which Doctour *Smith* at the burning of *Ridley* used against him, is by the foresaid Authour ( though not with so full a blow, with a slenting stroke ) applyed to those Martyrs, *A man may give his body to be burnt, and yet have not charity*.

*pag. 11.*

Thus the prices of Martyrs ashes rise and fall in *Smithfield* market. However their reall worth flotes not with peoples phancies, no more then a rock in the sea rises and falls with the tide : S. *Paul* is still S. *Paul*, though the *Lycaonians* now would sacrifice to him, and presently after would sacrifice him: These Bishops, Ministers, and Lay-people, which were put to death in Queen *Maries* dayes, were worthy Saints of God, holy and godly men, but had their faults, failings, and imperfections. Had they not been men they had not burn't; yea had they not been more then men ( by Gods assistance ) they had not burn't. Every true Christian should, but none but strong Christians will, die at the stake.

But to return to *Ridley* : One of the greatest things objected against him, was his counsell to King *Edward* ( which the good Prince wash'd away with his tears ) about tolerating the Masse for Princesse *Mary*, at the intercession of *Charles* the fifth Emperour, which how great it was, let the indifferent party give

judgement,

Chap. 11.   *The life of Bishop* Ridley.   293

judgement, when the * Historian hath given his evidence, *The Bishops*, of Canterbury, London, Rochester, *gave their opinion, that to give licence to sinne, was sinne, but to connive at sinne, might be allowed, in case it were neither too long, nor without hope of reformation.*

* Haywards Edward sixth pag. 291.

Another fault, wherewith he was charged, was that wofull and unhappy discord betwixt him and reverend Bishop Hooper, about the wearing of some Episcopall garments at his consecration ( then in use ) which Ridley press'd, and Hooper refused with equall violence, as being too many, rather loading then gracing him; and so affectedly grave, that they were light again. All we will say is this, that when worthy men fall out, onely one of them may be faulty at the first, but if such strifes continue long, commonly both become guilty: But thus Gods diamonds often cut one another, and good men cause afflictions to good men.

It was the policy of the * Lacedemonians alwayes to send two Embassadours together, which disagreed amongst themselves, that so mutually they might have an eye on the actions each of other: Sure I am that in those Embassadours, the Ministers, which God sendeth to men, God suffereth great discords betwixt them, ( Paul with Barnabas, Jerome with Ruffin, and Augustine, and the like ) perchance because each may be more cautious and wary of his behaviour in the view of the other. We may well behold mens weaknesse in such dissentions, but better admire Gods strength and wisdome in ordering them to his glory, and his childrens good. Sure it is, Ridley and Hooper were afterwards cordially reconciled; and let not their discords pierce farther then their reconciliation : The worst is, mens eyes are never made sound with the clearnesse, but often are made sore with the bleernesse of other mens eyes in their company. The virtues of Saints are not so attractive of our imitation, as their vices and infirmities are prone to infect.

* *Arist. polit. lib. 2. cap. 7.*

P p 3   Ridley

[margin: <sup>a</sup> *Hayward Edward 6. p. 407. & sequent.*]

\*Ridley was very gracious with King Edward the sixth, and by a Sermon he preach'd before him so wrought upon his pious disposition, whose Princely charity rather wanted a directour then a perswader, that the King at his motion gave to the city of London,

1. Greyfriers, now called Christ-Church, for impotent, fatherlesse, decrepid people by age or nature to be educated or maintained.
2. S. Bartholomews near Smithfield, for poore by faculty, as wounded souldiers, diseas'd and sick persons to be cur'd and relieved.
3. Bridewell, the ancient Mansion of the English Kings, for the poore by idlenesse or unthriftynesse, as riotous spenders, vagabonds, loyterers, strumpets to be corrected and reduc'd to good order.

[margin: *\* Fr. Quarles Enchirid. pag. 1.*]

I like that Embleme of Charity which * one hath expressed *in a naked child, giving honey to a Bee without wings*; onely I would have one thing added, namely holding *a whip in the other hand to drive away the drones*: So that King Edwards bounty was herein perfect and complete.

To return to Ridley: His whole life was a letter written full of learning and religion, whereof his death was the seal. Brought he was with Cranmer and Latimer to Oxford to dispute in the dayes of Queen Mary, though before a Syllogisme was form'd, their deaths were concluded on, and as afterwards came to passe, being burnt the sixteenth of October *Anno* 1555. in the ditch over against Balioll Colledge.

[margin: *\* Fox. Acts Mon: An: 1555. Octob.*]

He came to the * stake in a fair black gown furr'd and fac'd with foins, a Tippet of velvet, furr'd likewise, about his neck, a velvet night-cap upon his head, and a corner'd cap upon the same.

Doctour Smith preacht a Sermon at their burning; a Sermon which had nothing good in it but the text (though misapplyed) and the shortnesse, being not above

Chap. 11.    *The life of Bishop* Ridley.

above a quarter of an houre long. Old Hugh Latimer was Ridleys partner at the stake, sometimes Bishop of Worcester, who crauled thither after him, one who had lost more learning then many ever had, who flout at his plain Sermons, though his down-right style was as necessary in that ignorant age, as it would be ridiculous in ours. Indeed he condescended to peoples capacity; and many men unjustly count those low in learning, who indeed do but stoop to their Auditours. Let me see any of our sharp Wits do that with the edge, which his bluntnesse did with the back of the knife, and perswade so many to restitution of ill-gotten goods. Though he came after Ridley to the stake, he got before him to heaven: his body, made tinder by age, was no sooner touch'd by the fire, but instantly this old Simeon had his *Nunc dimittis*, and brought the news to heaven that his brother was following after.

But Ridley suffered with farre more pain, the fire about him being not well made: And yet one would think that age should be skilfull in making such bonefires, as being much practised in them. The Gunpowder that was given him did him little service, and his Brother-in-law, out of desire to rid him out of pain, encreased it, (great grief will not give men leave to be wise with it) heaping fewell upon him to no purpose; so that neither the fagots which his enemies anger, nor his Brothers good will cast upon him, made the fire to burn kindly.

In like manner, not much before, his dear friend Master * Hooper suffered with great torment, the wind (which too often is the bellows of great fires) blowing it away from him once, or twice. Of all the Martyrs in those dayes, these two endured most pain, it being true that each of them,

> *Quærebat in ignibus ignes* :
> And still he did desire,
> For fire in midd'st of fire.

* *See Mr Fox Acts and Mon. on Hoopers death.*

Both

Both desiring to burn, and yet both their upper parts were but Confessours, when their lower parts were Martyrs, and burnt to ashes: Thus God, where he hath given the stronger faith, he layeth on the stronger pain. And so we leave them going up to Heaven, like Eliah, in a chariot of fire.

## Chap. 12.

### The true Nobleman.

HE is a Gentleman in a Text Letter, because bred, and living in an higher and larger way. Conceive him when young brought up at School, *in ludo literario*, where he did not take *ludus* to himself, and leave *literarius* to others, but seriously applyed himself to learning, and afterwards coming to his estate, thus behaves himself.

*Maxime* 1 — *Goodnesse sanctifies his Greatnesse, and Greatnesse supports his Goodnesse.* He improves the upper ground whereon he stands, thereby to do God the more glory.

2 — *He counts not care for his Countreys good to be beneath his state.* Because he is a great pillar, shall he therefore bear the lesse weight? never meddling with matters of Justice. Can this be counted too low for a Lord, which is high enough for a King? our Nobleman freely serves his Countrey, counting his very work a sufficient reward. (As by our *Laws no Duke, Earl, Baron, or Baronet, though Justices of Peace, may take any wages at the Sessions.) Yea he detesteth all gainfull wayes, which have the least blush of dishonour: For the Merchant Nobility of Florence and Venice (how highly soever valued by themselves) passe in other countreys with losse and abatement of repute; as if the scarlet robes of their honour had a stain of the stamell die in them.

*Statute 14. of Ric. 2. c. 11.

3 — *He is carefull in the thrifty managing of his estate.* Gold, though the most solid and heavy of metalls, yet may be

be beaten out so thin, as to be the lighteft and flighteft of all things. Thus Nobility, though in it self moft honourable, may be so attenuated through the fmalneffe of means as thereby to grow neglected. Which makes our Nobleman to practice Solomons precept, * *Be diligent to know the ftate of thy flocks, and look well to thine herds; for the Crown doth not endure to every generation.* If not the *Crown* much leffe the *Coronet*; and good husbandry may as well ftand with great honour, as breadth may confift with height.

*Prov. 27. 23.

*If a weak estate be left him by his Ancefters, he feeks to repair it,* by wayes thrifty, yet noble: as by travelling, sparing abroad, till his ftate at home may outgrow debts and penfions: Hereby he gains experience, and saves expence, sometimes living private, sometimes shewing himself at an half light, and sometimes appearing like himself as occafion requires; or elfe by betaking himself to the warres: Warre cannot but in thankfulneffe grace him with an Office, which graceth her with his perfon; or elfe by warlike sea-adventures wifely undertaken, and providently managed: otherwise, this courfe hath emptied more full, then filled empty purfes, and many thereby have brought a Galeon to a Gally; or laftly by match with wealthy Heirs, wherein he is never fo attentive to his profit, but he liftens alfo to his honour.

4

*In proportion to his means, he keeps a liberall houfe.* This much takes the affections of countrey people, whofe love is much warmed in a good kitchin, and turneth much on the hinges of a buttery-doore often open. Francis Ruffell, second Earl of Bedford of that firname, was fo bountifull to the poore, that Queen Elizabeth would merrily complain of him, that he made all the beggers: sure 'tis more honourable for Noblemen to make beggers by their liberality, then by their oppreffion. But our Nobleman is efpecially carefull to fee all things difcharged which he taketh up. When the corps

5

of Thomas Howard second Duke of Norfolk were carried to be interred in the Abbey of Thetford, *Anno* 1524. no person could demand of him one * groat for debt, or restitution for any injury done by him.

*marginal note:* * Weavers fun. Mon. p. 839.

**6** *His servants are best known by the coat and cognizance of their civill behaviour.* He will not entertain such ruffian-like men, who know so well who is their Master, that they know not who they are themselves, and think their Lords reference is their innocence, to bear them out in all unlawfull actions. But our Lords house is the Colledge wherein the children of the neighbouring Gentry and Yeomanry are bred, and there taught by serving of him to rule themselves.

**7** *He hateth all oppression of his tenants and neighbours;* disdaining to crush a mean Gentleman for a meaner offense; and counts it no conquest but an execution from him, who on his side hath the oddes of height of place, strength of arme, and length of weapon. But as the Proverb saith, *No grasse grows where the grand Seignieurs horse sets his feet;* so too often nothing but grasse grows where some Great men set their footing, no towns or tillage, for all must be turn'd into depopulating pastures, and commons into enclosures. Nigh the city of Lunenberg in Germany flowed a plentifull salt spring, till such time as the rich men, engrossing all the profit to themselves, would not suffer the poore to make any salt thereof; whereupon God and Nature being offended at their covetousnesse, the spring * ceased and ran no more for a time. Thus hath Gods punishment overtaken many great men, and stopp'd his blessing towards them, which formerly flowed plentifully unto them, for that they have wronged poore people of their commonage, which of right belonged unto them.

*marginal note:* * Morisons Travells, chap. 1. Part. 1. pag. 5. Yet afterward upon readmission of the poore to it it ran again.

**8** *In his own pleasures he is carefull of his neighbours profit.* Though his horses cannot have wings like his hawks to spoil no grasse or grain as he passeth, yet he is very

carefull

## Chap. 12.   *The true Noblemam.*   299

carefull to make as little waste as possible may be: his horses shall not trample on loaves of bread as he hunteth, so that whilest he seeks to gather a twig for himself he breaks the staff of the commonwealth.

*All the countrey are his Retainers in love and observance.* When they come to wait on him, they leave not their hearts at home behind them, but come willingly to tender their respects. The holding up of his hand is as good as the displaying of a banner; thousands will flock to him, but it must be for the Kings and Countreys service. For he knows that he who is more then a Lord, if his cause be loyall, is lesse then a private man, if it be otherwise: with S. *Paul, he can do nothing against the truth, but for the truth.* Thus Queen Elizabeth Christ=ned the youngest daughter of Gilbert Talbot Earl of Shrewsbury (now Countesse of Arundell) *Aletheia, Truth,* out of true * consideration and judgement that the house of the Talbots was ever loyall to the Crown.

*Some priviledges of Noblemen he endeavours to deserve:* namely such priviledges as are completely Noble, that so his merits as well as the Law should allow them unto him. He conceives this word, *On mine Honour*, wraps up a great deal in it; which unfolded and then measured, will be found to be a large attestation, and no lesse then an eclipticall oath, calling God to witnesse, who hath bestowed that Honour upon him. And seeing the State is so tender of him, that he shall not be forced to swear in matters of moment in Courts of Justice, he is carefull not to swear of his own accord in his sports and pleasures. Other priviledges of Noblemen he labours not to have need of, namely such as presuppose a fault, are but honourable penalties, and excuse from shamefull punishments. Thus he is not to be *bound to the * peace.* And what needs he; who hath the peace alwayes bound to him, being of his own accord alwayes carefull to preserve it, and of so noble a disposition, he will never be engaged in any braules or contentions.

9

* 2. Cor. 13. 8.

*Vincents discov. of Brooks Errours, p. 470.*

10

*Lamb. Justice of peace pag. 83.*

To give an instance of such a Nobleman seems to be needlesse, hoping that at this time in one city of this Realm, and in one room of that city, many such Noblemen are to be found together.

## Chap. 13.

### The Court-Lady.

To describe an Holy State without a virtuous Lady therein, were to paint out a yeare without a Spring: we come therefore to her Character.

*Maxime* 1. *She sets not her face so often by her glasse, as she composeth her soul by Gods word.* Which hath all the excellent qualities of a glasse indeed.

1. It is clear: in all points necessary to Salvation, except to such whose eyes are blinded.
2. It is true: not like those false glasses some Ladyes dresse themselves by. And how common is flattery at Court, when even glasses have learnt to be parasites?
3. It is large; presenting all spots Cap-a-pe, behind and before, within and without.
4. It is durable: though in one sense it is broken too often (when Gods Laws are neglected) yet it will last to break them that break it, and *one tittle thereof shall not fall to the ground.*
5. This glasse hath power to smooth the wrinkles, cleanse the spots, and mend the faults it discovers.

2. *She walks humbly before God in all religious duties.* Humbly: For she well knows that the strongest Christian is like the city of Rome, which was never besieged but it was taken, and the best Saint without Gods assistance would be as often foyled as tempted. She is most constant and diligent at her houres of private prayer. Queen Katharine Dowager never kneeld on a cushion

# Chap. 13.   *The Court-Lady.*   301

*cushion when she was at her devotions: This matters not at all; our Lady is more carefull of her heart then of her knees, that her soul be settled aright.

*She is carefull and most tender of her credit and reputation.* There is a tree in *Mexicana which is so exceedingly tender, that a man cannot touch any of his branches but it withers presently. A Ladyes credit is of equall nicenesse, a small touch may wound and kill it; which makes her very cautious what company she keeps. The Latine tongue seems somewhat injurious to the feminine sex; for whereas therein *Amicus* is a friend, *Amica* alwayes signifies a Sweetheart, as if their sex in reference to men were not capable of any other kind of familiar friendship but in way to marriage, which makes our Lady avoid all privacie with suspicious company.

*Yet is she not more carefull of her own credit then of Gods glory*; and stands up valiantly in the defence thereof. She hath read how at the Coronation of King Richard the second, Dame *Margaret Dimock, wife to Sʳ John Dimock, came into the Court and claimed the place to be the Kings Champion, by the virtue of the tenure of her Mannour of Scrinelby in Lincolnshire, to challenge and defie all such as opposed the Kings right to the Crown. But if our Lady heares any speaking disgracefully of God or Religion, she counts her self bound by her tenure (whereby she holds possession of grace here, and reversion of glory hereafter.) to assert and vindicate the honour of the King of Heaven, whose Champion she professeth to be. One may be a lambe in private wrongs, but in hearing generall affronts to goodnesse, they are asses which are not lions.

*She is pitifull and bountifull to people in distresse.* We reade how a daughter of the Duke of Exeter invented a brake or cruel rack to torment people withall, to which purpose it was long reserved and often used in the

Tower

---

*Sanders. de Schism. Anglic. lib. 1. pag. 5.*

3
*Doctour Heylens Microcos. pag. 783.*

4

*She claimed the place, but her husband performed the office, Lelands Colle. Tit. 1. pag. 299.*

5

Tower of London, and commonly called (was it not fit so pretty a babe should bear her mothers name?) The * Duke of Exeters' daughter. Me thinks the finding out of a salve to ease poore people in pain had born better proportion to her Ladiship then to have been the inventer of instruments of cruelty.

<small>* Vid. Stowes Chron. in the reigne of King Edward the fourth.</small>

6. *She is a good scholar, and well learned in usefull Authours.* Indeed as in purchases an house is valued at nothing, because it returneth no profit, and requires great charges to maintain it; so for the same reasons, Learning in a woman is but little to be prized. But as for great Ladyes, who ought to be a confluence of all rarities and perfections, some Learning in them is not onely usefull but necessary.

7. *In discourse her words are rather fit then fine, very choice and yet not chosen.* Though her language be not gaudy, yet the plainnesse thereof pleaseth, it is so proper, and handsomly put on. Some having *a set of fine phrases* will hazard an impertinency to use them all, as thinking they give full satisfaction for dragging in the matter by head and shoulders, if they dresse it in queint expressions. Others often repeat the same things: the Platonick yeare of their discourses being not above three dayes long, in which term all the same matter returns over again, threadbare talk ill suiting with the variety of their clothes.

8. *She affects not the vanity of foolish fashions;* but is decently apparelled according to her state and condition. He that should have guessed the bignesse of Alexanders souldiers by their shields left in India, would much overproportion their true greatnesse. But what a vast overgrown creature would some guesse a woman to be, taking his aim by the multitude and variety of clothes and ornaments, which some of them use: insomuch as the ancient Latines called a womans wardrope *Mundus, a World*, wherein notwithstanding was much *terra incognita* then undiscovered, but since found

# Chap. 13.   The Court-Lady.

found out by the curiosity of modern Fashion-mongers. We find a mappe of this world drawn by Gods Spirit, Isaiah the third, wherein one and twenty womens ornaments (all superfluous) are reckoned up, which at this day are much encreased. The *moons, there mentioned, which they wore on their heads, may seem since grown to the full in the luxury of after-ages.

*Isaiah.3.18.

*She is contented with that beauty which God hath given her.* If very handsome, no whit the more proud, but farre the more thankfull: If unhandsome, she labours to better it in the virtues of her mind, that what is but plain cloth without may be rich plush within. Indeed such naturall defects as hinder her comfortable serving of God in her calling may be amended by art; and any member of the body being defective, may thereby be lawfully supplied. Thus glasse-eyes may be used, though not for seeing, for sightlinesse. But our Lady detesteth all adulterate complexions, finding no president thereof in the Bible save one, and her so bad, that Ladyes would blush through their paint to make her the pattern of their imitation. Yet are there many that think the grossest fault in painting is to paint grossely (making their faces with thick daubing not onely new pictures, but new statues) and that the greatest sinne therein, is to be discover'd.

9

*In her marriage she principally respects virtue and religion,* and next that, other accomodatious, as we have *formerly discours'd of. And she is carefull in match not to bestow her self unworthily beneath her own degree to an ignoble person, except in case of necessity. Thus the Gentlewomen in *Champaigne in France some three hundred years since were enforced to marry Yeomen and Farmers, because all the Nobility in that countrey were slain in the warres in the two voyages of King Lewis to Palestine: and thereupon ever since by custome and priviledge the Gentlewomen of Champaigne

10
*Vid. 3. Book chap. of Marriage.

*Andr. Favin in his Theater of Honour, 1. Book, chap. the 6.

Champaigne and Brye ennoble their husbands and give them honour in marrying them, how mean soever before.

11 *Though pleasantly affected she is not transported with Court-delights*: as in their statelie Masques and Pageants. Seeing Princes cares are deeper then the cares of private men, it is fit their recreations also should be greater, that so their mirth may reach the bottome of their sadnesse: yea God allows to Princes a greater latitude of pleasure. He is no friend to the tree, that strips it of the bark; neither do they mean well to Majesty, which would deprive it of outward shews, and State-solemnities, which the servants of Princes may in loyalty and respect present to their Sovereigne; however, our Lady by degrees is brought from delighting in such Masques, onely to be contented to see them, and at last (perchance) could desire to be excused from that also.

12 *Yet in her reduced thoughts she makes all the sport she hath seen earnest to her self*: It must be a dry flower indeed out of which this bee sucks no honey: they are the best Origens who do allegorise all earthly vanities into heavenly truths. When she remembreth how suddenly the Scene in the Masque was altered (almost before moment it self could take notice of it) she considereth, how quickly mutable all things are in this world, God *ringing the changes* on all accidents, and making them tunable to his glorie: The lively representing of things so curiously, that Nature her self might grow jealous of Art, in outdoing her, minds our Lady to make sure work with her own soul, seeing hypocrisie may be so like to sincerity. But O what a wealthy exchequer of beauties did she there behold, severall faces most different, most excellent, (so great is the variety even in bests) what a rich mine of jewells above ground, all so brave, so costly! To give Court-masques their due, of all the bubbles in this world they have the greatest variety

riety of fine colours. But all is quickly ended: this is the spight of the world, if ever she affordeth fine ware, she alwayes pincheth it in the measure, and it lasts not long: But oh, thinks our Lady, how glorious a place is Heaven, *where there are joyes for evermore*. If an herd of kine should meet together to phancy and define happinesse, they would place it to consist in fine pastures, sweet grasse, clear water, shadowie groves, constant summer, but if any winter, then warm shelter and dainty hay, with company after their kind, counting these low things the highest happinesse, because their conceit can reach no higher. Little better do the Heathen Poets describe Heaven, paving it with pearl, and roofing it with starres, filling it with Gods and Goddesses, and allowing them to drink (as if without it no Poets Paradise) Nectar and Ambrosia; Heaven indeed being *Poetarum dedecus*, the shame of Poets, and the disgrace of all their Hyperboles, falling as farre short of truth herein, as they go beyond it in other Fables. However the sight of such glorious earthly spectacles advantageth our Ladyes conceit by infinite multiplication thereof to consider of Heaven.

*She reades constant lectures to her self of her own mortality.* 13
To smell to a turf of fresh earth is wholsome for the body; no lesse are thoughts of mortality cordiall to the soul. *Earth thou art, to earth thou shalt return*: The sight of death when it cometh will neither be so terrible to her, nor so strange, who hath formerly often beheld it in her serious meditations. With * Job she  \* *Job.* 17. 14.
saith to the worm, *Thou art my sister*: If fair Ladyes scorn to own the worms their kinred in this life, their kinred will be bold to challenge them when dead in their graves: for when the soul (the best perfume of the body) is departed from it, it becomes so noysome a carcasse, that should I make a description of the lothsomnesse thereof, some dainty dames would hold their noses in reading it.

R r To

To conclude: We reade how Henry a Germain Prince was admonished by revelation to search for a writing in an old wall, which should nearly concern him, wherein he found onely these two words written, * POST SEX, AFTER SIX. Whereupon Henry conceived that his death was foretold, which after six dayes should ensue, which made him passe those dayes in constant preparation for the same. But finding the six dayes past without the effect he expected, he successively persevered in his godly resolutions six weeks, six moneths, six years, and on the first day of the seventh yeare the Prophecie was fulfill'd, though otherwise then he interpreted it ; for thereupon he was chosen Emperour of Germany, having before gotten such an habit of piety that he persisted in his religious course for ever after. Thus our Lady hath so inur'd her self *all the dayes of her appointed time to wait till her change cometh*, that expecting it every houre, she is alwayes provided for that, then which nothing is more certain or uncertain.

* *Surius in vita Sancti Henr. July 14. & Baronius in Anno 1007.*

CHAP. 14.

JANE GRAY *proclaimed* Queen of England *wife to the* Lord GILFORD DUDLEY. *She was beheaded on* Tower-hill *in* London *Februarie y̆ 12. 1553. at 18 yeares of Age.*
W:M: *sculp*

## CHAP. 14.
### *The life of Ladie* Jane GREY.

JAne Grey, eldeſt daughter of Henry Grey Marqueſſe of Dorſet, and Duke of Suffolk, by Francis Brandon eldeſt daughter of Charles Brandon Duke of Suffolk, and Mary his wife youngeſt daughter to King Henry the ſeventh, was by her parents bred according to her high birth in Religion and Learning. They were no whit indulgent to her in her childhood, but extremely ſevere, more then needed to ſo ſweet a temper;

temper; for what need iron inſtruments to bow wax?

But as the ſharpeſt winters (correcting the rankneſſe of the earth) cauſe the more healthfull and fruitfull ſummers; ſo the harſhneſſe of her breeding compacted her ſoul to the greater patience and pietie, ſo that afterwards ſhe proved the miroir of her age, and attained to be an excellent Scholar through the teaching of M$^r$ Elmer her Maſter.

Once M$^r$ Roger Aſcham, coming to wait on her at Broad-gates in Leiceſterſhire, found her in her chamber reading * Phœdon-Platonis in Greek, with as much delight as ſome Gentleman would have read a merry tale in Bocchace, *Whileſt the Duke her father with the Dutcheſſe and all their houſhold were hunting in the Park*: He askt of her, how ſhe could loſe ſuch paſtime? who ſmiling anſwered, *I wiſſe all the ſport in the Park is but the ſhadow of what pleaſure I find in this book*, adding moreover, that one of the greateſt bleſsings God ever gave her, was in ſending her ſharp parents, and a gentle Schoolmaſter, which made her take delight in nothing ſo much as in her ſtudies.

* *Aſcham's Schoolmaſter, lib. 1. fol. 10.*

About this time John Dudley Duke of Northumberland projected for the Engliſh Crown: But being too low to reach it in his own perſon, having no advantage of royall birth, a match was made betwixt Guilford his fourth ſonne, and this Lady Jane; the Duke hoping ſo to reigne in his daughter-in-law, on whom King Edward the ſixth by will, paſsing by his own ſiſters, had entayled the Crown: And not long after that godly King, who had ſome defects, but few faults (and thoſe rather in his age then perſon) came to his grave: it being uncertain whether he went, or was ſent thither. If the latter be true, *the crying of this Saint under the Altar*, beneath which he was buried in King Henries Chappell (without any other monument, then that of his own virtues) hath been heard long ſince for avenging his bloud. Preſently

Presently after Lady Jane was proclaimed Queen of England. She lifted not up her least finger to put the Diadem on her self, but was onely contented to sit still, whilest others endeavoured to Crown her; or rather was so farre from biting at the bait of Sovereignty, that unwillingly she opened her mouth to receive it.

Then was the Duke of Northumberland made Generall of an Army, and sent into Suffolk to suppresse the Lady Marie, who there gathered men to claim the Crown. This Duke was appointed out of the policie of his friend-seeming enemies for that employment: For those who before could not endure the scorching heat of his displeasure at the Counsell-table, durst afterwards oppose him, having gotten the skreen of London-walls betwixt him and them. They also stinted his journeys every day (thereby appointing the steps by which he was to go down to his own grave) that he should march on very slowly, which caused his confusion. For lingring doth tire out treacherous designes, which are to be done all on a sudden, and gives breath to loyalty to recover it self.

His army like a sheep left part of his fleece on every bush it came by, at every stage and corner some conveying themselves from him, till his Souldiers were wash'd away before any storm of warre fell upon them. Onely some few, who were chain'd to the Duke by their particular engagements, and some great Persons hopelesse to conceal themselves, as being too bigge for a cover, stuck fast unto him. Thus those enterprises need a strong hand which are thrown against the bias of peoples hearts and consciences. And not long after the Norfolk and Suffolk Protestant Gentry (Loyalty alwayes lodgeth in the same breast with true Religion) proclaimed and set up Queen Marie, vvho got the Crown by *Our Father*, and held it by *Pater noster*.

Then was the late Queen, now Lady Jane Grey, brought from a Queen to a prisoner, and committed to the Tower. She made misery it self amiable by her pious and patient behaviour: Adversity, her night-clothes, becoming her as well as her day-dressing, by reason of her pious deportment.

During her imprisonment many moved her to alter her religion, and especially M^r Fecnam sent unto her by Queen Mary: but how wisely and religiously she answer'd him, I referre the Reader to M^r Fox,* where it is largely recorded.

*Acts & Monum. pag. 1419 & deinceps.*

And because I have mentioned that Book, wherein this Ladyes virtues are so highly commended, I am not ignorant that of late great disgrace hath been thrown on that Authour, and his worthy Work, as being guilty of much falsehood: chiefly because sometimes he makes Popish Doctours, well known to be rich in learning, to reason very poorely, and the best Fencers of their Schools worsted and put out of their play by some countrey poore Protestants. But let the cavillers hereat know, that it is a great matter to have the oddes of the weapon, Gods word on their side; not to say any thing of supernaturall assistance given them. Sure for the main, his Book is a worthy work (wherein the Reader may rather leave then lack) and seems to me, like Ætna, always burning, whilest the smoke hath almost put out the eyes of the adverse party, and these *Foxes firebrands* have brought much annoyance to the *Romish Philistines*. But it were a miracle if in so voluminous a work there were nothing to be justly reproved; so great a Pomgranate not having any rotten kernell must onely grow in paradise. And though perchance he held the beam at the best advantage for the Protestant party to weigh down, yet generally he is a true Writer, and never wilfully deceiveth, though he may sometimes be unwillingly deceived.

## Chap. 14.  *The life of* Jane Grey.

To return to the Lady Jane : Though Queen Marie of her own disposition was inclined finally to pardon her, yet necessity of State was such, as she must be put to death. Some report her to have been with child when she was beheaded ( cruelty to cut down the tree with blossomes on it ) and that that which hath saved the life of many women hastned her death ; but God onely knows the truth hereof. On Tower-hill she most patiently, Christianly, and constantly yielded to God her soul, which by a bad way went to the best end. On whom the foresaid Authour ( whence the rest of her life may be supplied ) bestows these verses, 1553. Feb. 12.

*Nescio tu quibus es, Lector lecturus ocellis :*
  *Hoc scio, quod siccis scribere non potui.*

What eyes thou readst with, Reader, know I not:
Mine were not dry, when I this story wrote.

She had the innocency of childhood, the beauty of youth, the solidity of middle, the gravity of old age, and all at eighteen : the birth of a Princesse, the learning of a Clerk, the life of a Saint, yet the death of a Malefactour, for her parents offenses. I confesse, I never read of any canonized Saint of her name, a thing whereof some Papists are so scrupulous, that they count it an unclean and unhallowed thing to be of a name whereof never any Saint was : which made that great Jesuit Arthur Faunt ( as his *kinsman tell's us ) change his Christian name to Laurence. But let this worthy Lady passe for a Saint ; and let all great Ladyes, which bear her name, imitate her virtues, to whom I wish her inward holinesse, but farre more outward happinesse.

*Burton of Leicestershire pag. 105.

Yet lest Goodnesse should be discouraged by this Ladyes infelicity, we will produce another example, which shall be of a fortunate virtue.

CHAP. 15.

ELIZABETH Queen of England, She dyed at Richmond the 24.th of March 1602. in the 44.th yeare of Her Raign and 70.th of Her Life.

W. Marshall sculp:

## Chap. 15.

### The life of Queen Elisabeth.

WE intermeddle not with her description as she was a Sovereigne Prince, too high for our pen, and performed by others already, though not by any done so fully, but that still room is left for the endeavours of Posterity to adde thereunto. We consider her onely as she was a worthy Lady, her private virtues rendring her to the imitation, and her publick to the admiration of all.

Her

## Chap. 15.  *The life of* Queen Elizabeth.

Her royall birth by her Fathers side doth comparatively make her Mother-descent seem low, which otherwise considered in it self was very noble and honourable. As for the bundle of scandalous aspersions by some cast on her birth, they are best to be buried without once *opening of them. For as the basest rascall will presume to miscall the best Lord, when farre enough out of his hearing; so slanderous tongues think they may run riot in railing on any, when once got out of the distance of time, and reach of confutation.

* *See these slanders plainly confuted in Anti-Sander. Dialog. 2. pag. 125. & deinceps.*

But Majesty which dyeth not will not suffer it self to be so abused, seeing the best assurance which living Princes have, that their memories shall be honourably continued, is founded ( next to their own deserts ) in the maintaining of the unstained reputation of their Predecessours. Yea divine Justice seems herein to be a compurgatour of the parents of Queen Elizabeth, in that Nicholas Sanders, a Popish Priest, the first raiser of these wicked reports, was accidentally famished as he roved up and down in Ireland; either because it was just he should be sterved that formerly surfeted with lying, or because that Iland out of a naturall antipathy against poysonous creatures would not lend life to so venemous a slanderer.

Under the reigne of her Father, and Brother King Edward the sixth, ( who commonly called her his Sister Temperance ) she lived in a Princely fashion. But the case was altered with her when her Sister Mary came to the Crown, who ever look'd upon her with a jealous eye and frowning face: chiefly, because of the difference betwixt them in religion. For though Queen Mary is said of her self not so much as to have bark'd, yet she had under her those who did more then bite; and rather her religion then disposition was guilty in countenancing their cruelty by her authority.

This antipathy against her Sister Elizabeth was encreased with the remembrance how Katharine Dowager, Queen Maries Mother, was justled out of the bed of Henry the eighth by Anna Bullen, Mother to Queen Elizabeth: so that these two Sisters were born, as I may say, not onely in severall but opposite horizons, so that the elevation and bright appearing of the one inferr'd the necessary obscurity and depression of the other; & still Qu. Mary was troubled with this *fit of the Mother*, which incensed her against this her half Sister.

To which two grand causes of opposition, this third may also be added, because not so generally known, though in it self of lesser consequence. Queen Mary had released Edward Courtney Earl of Devonshire out of the Tower, where long he had been detained prisoner, a Gentleman of a beautifull body, sweet nature, and royall descent, intending him, as it was generally conceived, to be an husband for her self. For when the said Earl petitioned the Queen for leave to travel she advised him rather to marry, ensuring him that no Lady in the land, how high soever, would refuse him for an husband; and urging him to make his choyce where he pleased, she pointed her self out unto him as plainly as might stand with the modesty of a maid, and Majesty of a Queen. Hereupon the young Earl (whether because that his long durance had some influence on his brain, or that naturally his face was better then his head, or out of some private phancie and affection to the Lady Elizabeth, or out of loyall bashfulnesse, not presuming to climbe higher, but expecting to be call'd up) is said to have requested the Queen for leave to marry her Sister the Lady Elizabeth, unhappy that his choyce either went so high or no higher: For who could have spoken worse Treason against Mary (though not against the Queen) then to preferre her Sister before her? and she, innocent Lady, did afterwards dearly pay the score of this Earls indiscretion.

For

### Chap. 15.     *The life of* Queen Elisabeth.

For these reasons Lady Elizabeth was closely kept and narrowly sifted all her Sisters reigne, Sʳ Bedenifield her keeper using more severity towards her then his place required, yea more then a good man should, or a wiseman would have done. No doubt the least tripping of her foot should have cost her the losing of her head, if they could have caught her to be privy to any conspiracies.

This Lady as well deserved the title of Elizabeth *the Confessour* as ever Edward her ancient predecessour did. Mʳ Ascham was a good Schoolmaster to her, but affliction was a better, so that it is hard to say whether she was more happy in having a Crown so soon, or in having it no sooner, till affliction had first laid in her a low (and therefore sure) foundation of humility, for highnesse to be afterwards built thereupon.

We bring her now from the Crosse to the Crown; and come we now to describe the rare endowments of her mind, when behold her virtues almost stifle my pen, they crowd in so fast upon it.

She was an excellent Scholar, understanding the Greek, and perfectly speaking the Latine: witnesse her extempore speech in answer to the Polish Embassadour, and another at Cambridge, *Et si fœminilis iste meus pudor* (for so it began) elegantly making the word * *Fœminilis*: and well might she mint one new word, who did * refine so much new gold and silver. Good skill she had in the French, and Italian, using Interpreters not for need but state. She was a good Poet in English, and fluently made verses. In her time of persecution, when a Popish Priest pressed her very hardly to declare her opinion concerning the presence of Christ in the Sacrament, she truly and warily presented her judgement in these verses,

> 'Twas God the word that spake it,
> He took the bread and brake it;
> And what the word did make it,
> That I believe and take it.

* *See her oration at large in Holinshead, p. 1026.*
* *Moneta ad suum valorem reducta is part of the Epitaph on her Tombe.*

And though perchance some may say this was but the best of shifts, and the worst of answers, because the distinct manner of the Presence must be believed; yet none can deny it to have been a wise return to an adversary who lay at wait for all advantages. Nor was her Poetick vein lesse happy in Latine. When a little before the Spanish Invasion in eighty eight, the Spanish Embassadour ( after a larger representation of his Masters demands ) had summed up the effect thereof in a Tetrastich, she instantly in one verse rejoined her answer. We will presume to English both, though confessing the Latine loseth lustre by the Translation.

> *Te veto ne pergas bello defendere Belgas :*
> *Quæ Dracus eripuit nunc restituentur oportet :*
> *Quas Pater evertit jubeo te condere cellas :*
> *Relligio Papæ fac restituetur ad unguem.*

> These to you are our commands,
> Send no help to th' Netherlands :
> Of the treasure took by Drake,
> Restitution you must make :
> And those Abbies build anew,
> Which your Father overthrew :
> If for any peace you hope,
> In all points restore the Pope.

The Queens extempore return,

> *Ad Græcas, bone Rex, fient mandata calendas.*

> Worthy King, know this your will
> At latter lammas wee'l fulfill.

Her piety to God was exemplary, none more constant or devout in private prayers; very attentive also at Sermons, wherein she was better affected with soundnesse of matter, then queintnesse of expression: She could not well digest the affected over-elegancy of such as prayed for her by the title of *defendresse of the faith* and not the *Defender*, it being no false construction to apply a masculine word to so heroick a spirit.

She was very devout in returning thanks to God for her

her constant and continuall preservations; for one traitours stabbe was scarce put by, before another took aim at her: But as if the poysons of treason by custome were turn'd naturall unto her, by Gods protection they did her no harm. In any designe of consequence she loved to be long, and well advised; but where her resolutions once seis'd, she would never let go her hold, according to her motto, *Semper eadem*.

By her Temperance she improved that stock of health which Nature bestowed on her, using little wine, and lesse Physick. Her Continence from pleasures was admirable, and she the Paragon of spotlesse chastity, what ever some Popish Priests (who count all virginity hid under a Nunnes veil) have feigned to the contrary. The best is, their words are no slander, whose words are all slander, so given to railing, that they must be dumbe if they do not blaspheme Magistrates. * One Jesuit made this false Anagram on her name,

Elizabeth.<br>* Jezabel.

false both in matter and manner. For allow it the abatement of H, (as all Anagrams must sue in Chancery for moderate favour) yet was it both unequall and ominous that T, a solid letter, should be omitted, the presage of the gallows whereon this Anagrammatist was afterwards justly executed.

Yea let the testimony of Pope * Sixtus Quintus himself be believed, who professed that amongst all the Princes in Christendome he found but two which were worthy to bear command, had they not been stained with heresie, namely Henry the fourth, King of France, and Elizabeth Queen of England. And we may presume that the Pope, if commending his enemy, is therein infallible.

We come to her death, the discourse whereof was more welcome to her from the mouth of her private Confessour, then from a publick Preacher; and she loved

*marginalia:*
* *Edmond Campian.*
* *Our English Bibles call her Jezabel.*
* *Thuan. Hist. lib. 82.*

loved rather to tell her self, then to be told of her mortality, becauſe the open mention thereof made (as ſhe conceived) her ſubjects divide their loyalty betwixt the preſent and the future Prince. We need look into no other cauſe of her ſickneſſe then old age, being ſeventy years old (Davids age) to which no King of England ſince the Conqueſt did attain. Her weakneſſe was encreaſed by her removall from London to Richmond in a cold winter day, ſharp enough to pierce thorow thoſe who were arm'd with health and youth. Alſo melancholy (the worſt naturall Paraſite, whoſoever feeds him ſhall never be rid of his company) much afflicted her, being given over to ſadneſſe and ſilence.

Then prepared ſhe her ſelf for another world, being more conſtant in prayer, and pious exerciſes then ever before: yet ſpake ſhe very little to any, ſighing out more then ſhe ſaid, and making ſtill muſick to God in her heart. And as the red roſe, though outwardly not ſo fragrant, is inwardly farre more cordiall then the damask, being more thrifty of its ſweetneſſe, and reſerving it in it ſelf; ſo the religion of this dying Queen was moſt turn'd inward in ſoliloquies betwixt God and her own ſoul, though ſhe wanted not outward expreſsions thereof. When her ſpeech fail'd her, ſhe ſpake with her heart, tears, eyes, hands, and other ſignes, ſo commending herſelf to God the beſt interpreter, who underſtands what his Saints deſire to ſay. Thus dyed Queen Elizabeth, whileſt living, the firſt maid on earth, and when dead, the ſecond in heaven.

Surely the kingdome had dyed with their Queen, had not the fainting ſpirits thereof been refreſh'd by the coming in of gratious King James.

She was of perſon, tall; of hair and complexion, fair, well-favoured, but high-noſed; of limbes and feature, neat; of a ſtately and **majeſtick** deportment.

She

She had a piercing eye wherewith she used to touch what metall strangers were made of, which came into her presence. But as she counted it a pleasant conquest with her Majestick look to dash strangers out of countenance, so she was mercifull in pursuing those whom she overcame, and afterwards would cherish and comfort them with her smiles, if perceiving towardlinesse, and an ingenuous modesty in them. She much affected rich and costly apparell; and if ever jewells had just cause to be proud, it was with her wearing them.

## Chap. 16.
### *The Embassadour.*

HE is one that represents his King in a forrein countrey ( as a Deputy doth in his own Dominions ) under the assurance of the publick faith, authorized by the Law of Nations. He is either Extraordinary for some one affair with time limited, or Ordinary for generall matters during his Princes pleasure, commonly called a Legier.

*He is born, made, or at leastwise qualified honourably*, both for the honour of the sender, and him to whom he is sent; especially if the solemnity of the action wherein he is employed consisteth in ceremony and magnificence. Lewis the eleventh King of France is sufficiently condemn'd by Posterity for sending Oliver his Barber in an Embassage to a Princesse, who so trimly dispatch'd his businesse, that he left it in the suddes, and had been well wash'd in the river * at Gant for his pains, if his feet had not been the more nimble.

*Maxime* 1

\* *Comin. lib.* 5. *cap.* 14.

*He is of a proper, at least passable person.* Otherwise if he be of a contemptible presence, he is absent whilest he is present; especially if employed in love-businesses to advance a marriage. Ladyes will dislike the body for a deformed shadow. The jest is well known: When the

2

the State of Rome sent*two Embassadours, the one having scarres on his head, the other lame in his feet, *Mittit populus Romanus legationem quæ nec caput habet, nec pedes*, The people of Rome send an Embassy without head or feet.

<small>* Some say they sent three, and one of them a fool, and that Cato should say they sent an Embassy without head, heart, or feet. See Plutarchs Lives.</small>

3. *He hath a competent estate whereby to maintain his port*: for a great poverty is ever suspected; and he that hath a breach in his estate lies open to be assaulted with bribes. Wherefore his means ought at least to be sufficient both to defray set and constant charges, as also to make sallies and excursions of expenses on extraordinary occasions, which we may call Supererogations of State. Otherwise if he be indigent and succeed a bountifull Predecessour, he will seem a fallow field after a plentifull crop.

4. *He is a passable scholar, well travell'd in Countreys and Histories*; well studyed in the Pleas of the Crown, I mean not such as are at home, betwixt his Sovereigne and his subjects, but abroad betwixt his and forrein Princes; to this end he is well skill'd in the Emperiall Laws. Common Law it self is outlawed beyond the seas; which though a most true, is too short a measure of right, and reacheth not forrein kingdomes.

5. *He well understandeth the language of that countrey to which he is sent*; and yet he desires rather to seem ignorant of it (if such a simulation which stands neuter betwixt a Truth and a Lie be lawfull) and that for these reasons: first, because though he can speak it never so exactly, his eloquence therein will be but stammering, compar'd to the ordinary talk of the Natives: secondly, hereby he shall in a manner stand invisible, and view others; and as Josephs deafnesse heard all the dialogues betwixt his brethren, so his not owning to understand the language, shall expose their talk the more open unto him: thirdly, he shall have the more advantage to speak and negotiate in his own language, at the least wise, if he cannot make them come over to him, he

may

may meet them in the midway, in the Latine, a speech common to all learned Nations.

*He gets his Commission and instructions well ratified and confirm'd before he sets forth.* Otherwise it is the worst prison to be commission-bound. And seeing he must not jet out the least penthouse beyond his foundation, he had best well survey the extent of his authority.

*He furnisheth himself with fit Officers in his family.* Especially he is carefull in choosing

1. A Secretary, honest and able, carefull to conceal counsels, and not such a one as will let drop out of his mouth whatsoever is poured in at his eare: Yea the head of every Embassadour sleeps on the breast of his Secretary.
2. A Steward, wise and provident, such as can temper magnificence with moderation, judiciously fashioning his ordinary expences with his Masters estate, reserving a spare for all events and accidentall occasions, and making all things to passe with decency, without any rudenesse, noise, or disorder.

*He seasonably presents his Embassage, and demands audience.* Such is the fresh nature of some Embassages, if not spent presently, they sent ill. Thus it is ridiculous to condole griefs almost forgotten, for (besides that with a cruell courtesie it makes their sorrows bleed afresh) it foolishly seems to teach one to take that, which he hath formerly digested. When some Trojane Embassadours came to comfort Tiberius Cesar for the losse of his sonne, dead well nigh a twelvemoneth before; *And I* (said the Emperour) *am very sorry for your grief for the death of your Hector, slain by Achilles a thousand years since.* [Suetonius in Tiberio.]

*Coming to have audience, he applyeth himself onely to the Prince to whom he is sent.* When Chancellour Morvill, Embassadour from the French King, delivering his message to Philip Duke of Burgundy was interrupted by by Charles the Dukes * sonne, *I am sent* ( said he ) *not to treat with you, but with your father.* And our Mʳ Wade is highly commended that being sent by Queen Elizabeth to Philip King of Spain, he would not be turned * over to the Spanish Privy Counsel ( whose greatest Grandees were dwarfs in honour to his Queen ) but would either have audience from the King himself, or would return without it. And yet afterwards our Embassadour knows ( if desirous that his businesse should take effect ) how, and when to make his secret and underhand addresses to such potent Favourites as strike the stroke in the State; it often hapning in Commonwealths, that the Masters mate steers the ship thereof, more then the Master himself.

*\* Comin. lib. 1.*

*\* Cambd. Eliz. in Anno 1584. pag. 380.*

10. *In delivering his message he complies with the garb and guise of the countrey*; either longer, briefer, more plain, or more flourishing, as it is most acceptable to such to whom he directs his speech. The Italians ( whose countrey is called *the countrey of good words* ) love the circuits of courtesie, that an Embassadour should not as a sparrow-hawk flie outright to his prey, and meddle presently with the matter in hand, but with the noble falcon mount in language, soar high, fetch compasses of complement, and then in due time stoop to game, and seise on the businesse propounded. Clean contrary the Switzers ( who sent word to the King of France, not to send them an Embassadour with store of words, but a Treasurer with plenty of money) count all words quite out, which are not straight on, have an antipathy against eloquent language; the flowers of Rhetorick being as offensive to them, as sweet perfumes to such as are troubled with the Mother. Yea generally great souldiers have their stomachs sharp set to feed on the matter, lothing long speeches, as wherein they conceive themselves to lose time, in which they could conquer half a countrey, and, counting bluntnesse their best eloquence, love to be accosted in their own kind.

He

## Chap. 16.   *The Embassadour.*

*He commands himself not to admire any thing presented unto him.* He looks, but not gazeth, on forrein magnificence (as countrey clowns on a city) beholding them with a familiar eye, as challenging old acquaintance having known them long before. If he be surprised with a sudden wonder, he so orders it, that though his soul within feels an admiration, none can perceive it without in his countenance. For

1. It is inconsistent with the steddinesse of his gravity to be startled with a wonder.
2. Admiration is the daughter of ignorance: whereas he ought to be so read in the world as to be posed with no rarity.
3. It is a tacit confession (if he wonders at State, Strength, or Wealth) that herein his own Masters kingdome is farre surpass'd. And yet he will not slight and neglect such worthy sights as he beholds, which would savour to much of sullennesse and self-addiction, things ill beseeming his noble spirit.

*He is zealous of the least puntillo's of his Masters honour.* Herein 'tis most true, the Law of honour *servanda in apicibus*: Yea a toy may be reall, and a point may be essentiall to the sense of some sentences, and worse to be spared then some whole letter. Great Kings wrestle together by the strength and nimblenesse of their Embassadours; wherefore Embassadours are carefull to afford no advantages to the adverse party: and mutually no more hold is given, then what is gotten, lest the fault of the Embassadour be drawn into president to the prejudice of his Master. He that abroad will lose an hair of his Kings honour deserves to lose his own head when he comes home.

*He appears not violent in desiring any thing he would effect;* but with a seeming carelesnesse most carefully advanceth his Masters businesse. If employed to conclude a Peace, he represents his Master as indifferent therein for his own part, but that desiring to spare Christian bloud, preponderates him for Peace, whose conscience, not purse or arms are weary of the warre: He entreats not, but treats for an accord, for their mutuall good. But if the Embassadour declareth himself zealous for it, perchance he may be forced to buy those conditions, which otherwise would be given him.

14. *He is constantly and certainly inform'd of all passages in his own Countrey.* What a shame is it for him to be a stranger to his native affairs? Besides, if gulls and rumours from his Countrey be raised on purpose to amuse our Embassadour, he rather smiles then starts at these false vizards, who by private instructions from home knows the true face of his Countrey-estate. And lest his Masters Secretary should fail him herein, he counts it thrift to cast away some pounds yearly to some private friend in the Court to send him true information of all home-remarkables.

15. *He carefully returns good intelligence to his Master that employeth him.*
 1. Speedy. Not being such a sluggard as to write for news at noon, That the Sunne is risen.
 2. True; so farre forth as may be: else he stamps it with a mark of uncertainty or suspicion.
 3. Full: not filling the paper, but informing those to whom it is written.
 4. Materiall: not grinding his advises too small, to frivolous particulars of love-toyes, and private brawls, as * one layeth it to the charge of Francis Guicciardines Historie, *Minutissima quæque narrat, parum ex lege aut dignitate Historiæ.* And yet such particulars which are too mean to be served up to the Counsel-Table, may make a feast for Ladies, or other his friends; and therefore to such our Embassadour relates them by his private letters.
 5. Methodi-

* *Lipsius in the end of his Politicks, in his censure of Historians.*

5. Methodicall: not running on all in a continued strain, but stopping at the stages of different businesses to breath himself and the Reader, and to take and begin a new sentence.

6. Well-penned, clear and plain, not hunting after language, but teaching words their distance to wait on his matter, intermingling sententious speeches sparingly, lest seeming affected. And if constrained twice to write the same matter, still he varieth his words, lest he may seem to write like Notaries by presidents.

*He will not have his house serve as a retreating-place for people suspected and odious*, in that State wherein he is employed. Much lesse shall his house be a Sanctuary for Offenders, seeing the very horns of Gods Altar did push away from them such notorious Malefactours as did flie unto them for protection.

*He is cautious not to practice any treacherous act against the Prince under whom he lives*: lest the Shield of his Embassy prove too small to defend him from the Sword of Justice, seeing that for such an offense an Embassadour is resolved into a private man, and may worthily be punished, as in the cases of Bernardinus Mendoza and the Bishop of * Rosse. Yea he will not so much as break forth publickly into any discourse which he knows will be distastfull in that Countrey wherein he is employed. Learned Bodin, who some seventy years since waited on Monsieur into England, was here, though highly admired for his learning, condemned much for his indiscretion, if his *corrivals pen may be credited. For being feasted at an English Lords table, he fell into the odious discourse, That a Princesse, meaning Mary Queen of Scots, was after Queen Elizabeth the presumptive Inheritrix of the English Crown, notwithstanding an English Law seemed to exclude those which are born out of the land; *And yet*, said he, *I know not where this Law is, for all*

16

17

\* *Set his case largely discussed in Cambd. Elizab. by the best Civilians, Anno 1571.*

\* *Francisc. Hottoman in his Treatise of an Embass. fol. 42.*

the diligence that I have used to find it out: To whom it was suddenly replyed by the Lord, that entertain'd him, *You shall find it written on the backside of your Salick Law*: a judicious and biting rebound.

**18**

He is carefull of suspicious complying with that Prince to whom he is sent: as to receive from him any extraordinary gifts, much lesse pensions, which carry with them more then an appearance of evil. S^r* Amias Paulet was so scrupulous herein, that being Embassadour in France in the dayes of Queen Elizabeth he would not at his departure receive from the French King the chain of gold (wich is given of course) till he was half a league out of the city of Paris.

*Idem. fol. 23, 24.*

**19**

If he hath any libera mandata, *unlimited instructions*, herein his discretion is most admirable.

But what go I about to do? hereof enough already, if not too much: it better complying with my profession to practice S. Pauls precept to mine own parishioners, * *Now then we are Embassadours for Christ, as though God did beseech you by us, we pray you in Christs stead, be reconciled to God.*

*2. Cor. 5. 20.*

## Chap. 17.

### The good Generall.

THe Souldier, whom we formerly described, hath since by the stairs of his own deserts climb'd up to be a Generall, and now we come, to character him.

*Maxime* 1

*He is pious in the ordering of his own life.* Some falsely conceive that Religion spoyleth the spirit of a Generall, as bad as a rainy day doth his plume of feathers, making it droop, and hang down; whereas indeed Piety onely begets true Prowesse.

**2**

*He acknowledgeth God the Generalissimo of all armies;* who in all battels, though the number be never so unequall,

quall, reserves the casting voice for himself. Yet can I scarce believe what * one tells us, how Walter Pletemberg, Master of the Teutonick order, with a small number slew in a battel an hundred thousand Muscovite enemies with the losse of but one man on his side.

*Tilman Bredenbach .de bello Livon. & Fitz Herbert of Policy & Religion, part. 1. cap. 14.*

*He hath gained skill in his place by long experience*: not beginning to lead others before himself ever knew to follow, having never before (except in Cockmatches) beheld any battels. Surely they leap best in their providence forward, who fetch their rise farthest backward in their experience.

*He either is, or is presumed valiant.* Indeed courage in him is necessary, though some think that a Generall is above valour, who may command others to be so. As if it were all one whether courage were his naturally, or by adoption, who can make the valiant deeds of others seem his own; and his reputation for personall manhood once rais'd, will bear it self up; like a round body, some force is required to set it, but a touch will keep it agoing. Indeed it is extreme indiscretion (except in extremities) for him to be prodigall of his person.

*He is cheerfull and willing in undergoing of labour.* Admirable are the miracles of an industrious armie, witnesse the mighty ditch in Cambridge-shire made by the East-Angles, commonly call'd *Devils-ditch*, as if the Pioners thereof came from hell. Thus the effeminatenesse of our age, defaming what it should imitate, falsely traduces the monuments of their Ancestours endeavours.

*He loves, and is beloved of his souldiers.* Whose good will he attaineth,

1. By giving them good words in his speeches unto them. When wages have sometimes accidentally fallen short, souldiers have accepted the payment in the fair language and promises of their Generall. 2. By

2. By partaking with his souldiers in their painfull employments. When the English, at the Spanish Fleets approch in eightie eight, drew their ships out of Plimouth haven, the Lord Admirall Howard himself* towed a cable, the least joynt of whose exemplarie hand drew more then twentie men besides.

*Cambden. Elizab. Anno 1588.*

3. By sharing with them in their wants. When victuals have grown scant, some Generalls have pinched themselves to the same fare with their souldiers, who could not complain that their messe was bad, whilest their Generall was Fellow-commoner with them.

4. By taking notice, and rewarding of their deserts; never disinheriting a worthy souldier of his birthright, of the next Office due unto him. For a worthy man is wounded more deeply by his own Generalls neglect, then by his enemies sword: The latter may kill him, but the former deads his courage, or, which is worse, mads it into discontent; Who had rather others should make a ladder of his dead corps to scale a city by it, then a bridge of him whilest alive for his punies to give him the *Goe-by*, and passe over him to preferment. For this reason chiefly ( beside some others ) a great and valiant English Generall in the daies of Queen Elizabeth was hated of his souldiers, because he disposed Offices by his own absolute will, without respect of orderly advancing such as deserved it, which made a Great man once salute him with this letter: *S<sup>r</sup>, if you will be pleased to bestow a Captains place on the bearer hereof, being a worthy Gentleman, he shall do that for you which never as yet any souldier did, namely pray to God for your health and happinesse.*

7. *He is fortunate in what he undertakes.* Such a one was Julius Cesar, who in * Brittain, a countrey undiscovered,

*Cæsar. Comment. lib. 4.*

# Chap. 17. *The good Generall.* 329

vered, peopled with a valiant Nation, began a warre in Autumne, without apparent advantage, not having any intelligence there, being to passe over the sea into a colder climate (an enterprise, saith * one, well worthy the invincible courage of Cesar, but not of his accustomed prudence) and yet returned victorious. Indeed God is the sole disposer of successe: Other gifts he also scattereth amongst men, yet so that they themselves scramble to gather them up; whereas successe God gives immediately into their hands, on whom he pleaseth to bestow it.

*The Duke of Rohan in the complete Captain, pag. 19.

   *He tryeth the forces of a new enemy before he encounters him.* Sampson is half conquered, when it is known where his strength lies; and skirmishes are scouts for the discovery of the strength of an army, before battel be given.

8

   *He makes his flying enemy a bridge of gold*, and disarms them of their best weapon, which is necessity to fight whether they will or no. Men forced to a battel against their intention often conquer beyond their expectation: stop a flying coward, and he will turn his legges into arms, and lay about him manfully; whereas open him a passage to escape, and he will quickly shut up his courage.

9

   But I dare dwell no longer on this subject. When the Pope earnestly wrote to King Richard the first, not to detain in prison *his dear sonne*, the Martiall Bishop of Beavois, the King sent the Pope back the armour wherein the Bishop was taken, with the words of Jacobs sonnes to their Father, *See whether or no this be the coat of thy sonne.* Surely a corslet is no canonicall coat for me, nor suits it with my Clergy-profession to proceed any further in this warlike description; onely we come to give an example thereof.

V v        CHAP. 18.

330            *The Holy State.*          Book IV.

GUSTAVUS Adolphus the pious and Valiant King of Sweden. He was slaine in the Battell at Lutzen the 16 of November 1632. Aged 38 yeares

W. M. sculp:

## Chap. 18.

### The life of Gustavus Adolphus King of Sweden.

Gustavus Adolphus King of Sweden, born *Anno Domini* 1594 had princely education both for Arts and Armes. In Italie he learnt the Mathematicks, and in other places abroad, the French, Italian, and Germane tongues, and after he was King, he travelled under the name of M.<sup>r</sup> * G. A. R. S. being the foure initiall letters of his name, and title.

He

*\* Gustavus Adolph. Rex Suecorum D<sup>e</sup>. Wats in charact. ad finem 3. part. p. 183.*

## Ch. 18. *The life of* G. Adolph. K. *of Sweden.*

He was but seventeen years old at his Fathers death, being left not onely a young King, but also in a young kingdome; for his title to the Crown of Sweden was but five years old, to wit since the beginning of his Fathers reigne. All his bordering Princes ( on the North nothing but the North bounded on him ) were his enemies; the Duke-Emperour of Muscovy on the East, the King of Denmark on the West, and of Poland on the South: The former two laid claim to parcels, the latter, to all his kingdome. Yet was he too great for them in his minority, both defending his own, and gaining on them. *Wo be to the kingdome whose King is a child,* yet blessed is that kingdome whose King, though a child in age, is a man in worth.

These his first actions had much of glory, and yet somewhat of possibility and credit in them. But Chronicle and belief must strain hard to make his Germane Conquest probable with posterity; coming in with eleven thousand men, having no certain confederates, but some of his alliance, whom the Emperour had outed of all their estates: And yet in two years and foure moneths he left the Emperour in as bad a case almost, as he found those Princes in.

Gods Providence herein is chiefly to be admired, who to open him a free entrance into Germany, diverted the Imperiall and Spanish forces into Italy, there to scramble against the French for the Dukedome of Mantua. For heaven onely knows how much Protestant flesh the Imperialists had devoured, if that bone had not stuck in their teeth.

If we look on second causes, we may ascribe his victories to this Kings piety, wisedome, valour, and other virtues. His piety to God was exemplary, being more addicted to prayer then to fight, as if he would rather conquer Heaven then Earth. He was himself exceeding temperate, save onely too much given to anger, but afterwards he would correct himself, and be cholerick with his choler, shewing himself a man in the one, and a Saint in the other.

He was a strict observer of Martiall discipline, the life of Warre, without which an Army is but a crowd (not to say herd) of people. He would march all day in complete armour, which was by custome no more burthen to him then his armes, and to carry his helmet, no more trouble then his head; whilest his example made the same easie to all his souldiers. He was a strict punisher of misdemeanours and wanton intemperance in his camp: And yet let me relate this story from one present therein.

When first he entred Germany, he perceived how that many women followed his souldiers, some being their wives, and some wanting nothing to make them so but marriage, yet most passing for their landresses, though commonly defiling more then they wash. The King coming to a great river, after his men and the wagons were passed over, caused the bridge to be broken down, hoping so to be rid of these feminine impediments; but they one a sudden lift up a panick schrick which pierced the skies, and the souldiers hearts on the other side of the river, who instantly vowed not to stirre a foot farther, except with baggage, and that the women might be fetch'd over, which was done accordingly. For the King finding this ill humour so generally disperst'd in his men, that it was dangerous to purge it all at once, smiled out his anger for the present, and permitted what he could not amend: yet this abuse was afterwards reformed by degrees.

He was very mercifull to any that would submit. And as the iron gate miraculously opened to S. Peter of its own accord, so his mercy wrought miracles, making many city-gates open to him of themselves, before he ever knock'd at them to demand entrance, the inhabitants desiring to shroud themselves under his protection. Yea he was mercifull to those places

which

which he took by assault, ever detesting the bloudinesse of Tilly at Magdenburg, under the ashes whereof he buried his honour, coming valiant thither, and departing cruell thence. In such cases he was mercifull to women ( not like those Generalls who know the differences of Sex in their lust, but not in their anger ) yea the very Jesuites themselves tasted of his courtesie, though merrily he laid to their charge, that they would neither *Preach faith* to, nor *keep faith* with others.

He had the true art ( almost lost ) of Encamping, where he would lie in his Trenches in despight of all enemies, keeping the clock of his own time, and would fight for no mans pleasure but his own. No seeming flight or disorder of his enemies should cousen him into a battel, nor their daring bravado's anger him into it, nor any violence force him to fight, till he thought fitting himself, counting it good manners in Warre to take all, but give no advantages.

It was said of his Armies, that they used to rise when the swallows went to bed, when winter began, his forces most consisting of Northern Nations, and *a Swede fights best when he can see his own breath.* He alwayes kept a long vacation in the dog-dayes, being onely a saver in the summer, and a gainer all the yeare besides. His best harvest was in the snow; and his souldiers had most life in the dead of winter.

He made but a short cut in taking of cities, many of whose fortifications were a wonder to behold; but what were they then to assault and conquer? at scaling of walls he was excellent for contriving, as his souldiers in executing: it seeming a wonder that their bodies should be made of aire, so light to climbe, whose armes were of iron, so heavy to strike. Such cities as would not presently open unto him, he shut them up, and having businesse of more importance then to imprison himself about one strength, he would consigne the besieging thereof to some other Captain. And indeed he wanted not his Joabs, who when they had reduced cities to terms of yielding knew ( with as much wisdome as loyalty ) to entitle their David to the whole honour of the action.

He was highly beloved of his souldiers, of whose deserts he kept a faithfull Chronicle in his heart, and advanced them accordingly. All valiant men were Swedes to him; and he differenced men in his esteem by their merits not their countrey.

To come to his death, wherein his reputation suffers in the judgements of some, for too much hazarding of his own person in the battel. But surely some conceived necessity thereof urged him thereunto. For this his third grand set battel in Germany, was the third and last asking of his banes to the Imperiall Crown; and had they not been forbidden by his death, his marriage in all probability had instantly followed. Besides, * *Never Prince hath founded great Empire, but by making warre in person, nor hath lost any, but when he made warre by his lieutenants*: which made this King the more adventurous.

*Duke of Rohan, in his complete Captain cap. 22.*

His death is still left in uncertainty, whether the valour of open enemies, or treachery of false friends caused it. His side *won the day*, and yet *lost the sunne* that made it; and as one saith,

Upon this place the great *Gustavus* dy'd,
Whilest *victory* lay bleeding by his side.

Thus the readiest way to lose a jewell is to overprise it: for indeed many men so doted on this worthy Prince, and his victories ( without any default of his, who gave God the glory ) that his death in some sort seemed necessary to vindicate Gods honour, who usually maketh that prop of flesh to break whereon men lay too great weight of their expectation.

After his death, how did men struggle to keep him alive in their reports? partly out of good will, which
made

## Ch. 18. *The life of G. Adolph. K. of Sweden.*

made them kindle new hopes of his life at every spark of probability, partly out of infidelity that his death could be true. First they thought so valiant a Prince could not live on earth; and when they saw his life, then they thought so valiant a Prince could never die, but that his death was rather a concealment for a time, dayly expecting when the politickly dead should have a Resurrection in some noble exploit.

I find a most * learned pen applying these Latine verses to this noble Prince, and it is honour enough for us to translate them:

*In Templo plus quam Sacerdos.*
*In Republica plus quam Rex.*
*In sententia dicenda plus quam Senator.*
*In Judicio plus quam Jurisconsultus.*
*In Exercitu plus quam Imperator.*
*In Acie plus quam Miles.*
*In adversis perferendis injuriisque condonandis plus quam vir.*
*In publica libertate tuenda plus quam Civis.*
*In Amicitia colenda plus quam Amicus.*
*In convictu plus quam familiaris.*
*In venatione ferisque domandis plus quam Leo.*
*In tota reliqua vita plus quam Philosophus.*

More then a Priest he in the Church might passe.
More then a Prince in Commonwealth he was.
More then a Counseller in points of State.
More then a Lawyer matters to debate.
More then a Generall to command outright.
More then a Souldier to perform a fight.
More then a man to bear affliction strong.
More then a man good to forgive a wrong.
More then a Patriot countrey to defend.
True friendship to maintain, more then a Friend.
More then familiar sweetly to converse.
And though in sports more then a Lion fierce,
To hunt and kill the game; yet he exprest
More then Philosopher in all the rest.

* Dr. *Hakewill in his Apologie for divine Providence, lib. 4. cap. 11. p. 546.*

*Descript.Bell. Suecici, per Aut. Anonymum, pag. 186.

The Jesuites made him to be the * Antichrist, and allowed him three years and an half of reigne and conquest: But had he lived that full term out, the true Antichrist might have heard further from him, and Romes Tragedy might have had an end, whose fift and last Act is still behind. Yet one * Jesuite, more ingenuous then the rest, gives him this testimony, that, *save the badnesse of his cause and religion, he had nothing defective in him which belonged to an excellent King, and a good Captain.*

* Silvester Petra Sancta in his book against Du Moulin.

Thus let this our poore description of this King serve like a flat grave-stone or plain pavement for the present; till the richer pen of some Grotius or Heinsius shall provide to erect some statelyer Monument unto his Memory.

## Chap. 19.

### The Prince or Heir apparent to the Crown.

HE is the best pawn of the future felicity of a kingdome. His Fathers Subjects conceive they take a further estate of happinesse in the hopes of his Succession.

Maxime 1

*In his infancy he gives presages of his future worth.* Some first-fruits are dispatch'd before, to bring news to the world of the harvest of virtues which are ripening in him: his own Royall spirit prompts him to some speeches and actions wherein the standers by will scarce believe their own eares and eyes, that such things can proceed from him: And yet no wonder if they have light the soonest, who live nearest the East, seeing Princes have the advantage of the best birth and breeding. The Gregorian account goes ten dayes before the computation of the English calendar: but the capacity of Princes goes as many years before private mens of the same age.

*Ante-*

*Antevenit sortem meritis, virtutibus, annos.*
His worth above his wealth appears,
And virtues go beyond his years.

*He is neither kept too long from the knowledge, nor brought too soon to the acquaintance with his own Greatnesse.* To be kept too long in distance from himself, would breed in him a soul too narrow for his place: On the other side, he needs not to be taught his Greatnesse too soon, who will meet with it everywhere. The best of all is when his Governours open him to himself by degrees, that his soul may spread according to his age.

*He playeth himself into Learning before he is aware of it.* Herein much is to be ascribed to the wisdome of his Teachers, who alwayes present Learning unto him (as Angels are painted) smiling, and candy over his sourest studies with pleasure and delight, observing seasonable time, and fit method. Not like many countrey Schoolmasters, who in their instructions spill more then they fill, by their overhasty pouring of it in.

*He sympathizeth with him that by a Proxie is corrected for his offense:* yea sometimes goeth further, and (above his age) considereth, that it is but an Embleme, how hereafter his people may be punished for his own fault. He hath read how the Israelites, the second of Sam. 24. 17. were plagued for Davids numbring of them. And yet withall he remembreth how in the first verse of the same chapter, *The wrath of the Lord was kindled against Israel, and he* (by permitting of Satan the instrument 1. Chron. 21. 1.) *moved David to number them.* And as the stomach and vitall parts of a man are often corroded with a rheume falling from the head, yet so that the disaffection of the stomach first caused the breeding of the same offensive distillation; so our young Prince takes notice of a reciprocation of faults and punishments betwixt King and Kingdome (both making up the same body) yea that sometimes the

King is corrected for the peoples offenses, and so *è contra*: Indeed in Relatives neither can be well, if both be not.

5. *He is most carefull in reading, and attentive in hearing Gods word.* King Edward the sixth (who, though a Sovereigne, might still in age passe for a Prince) accurately noted the dayes, Texts, and names of Ministers, that preached before him. Next to Gods word, our Prince studies *Basilicon Doron*, that Royall gift, which onely King James was able to give, and onely King James his sonne worthy to receive.

6. *He is carefull in chusing and using his recreations,* refusing such which in their very posture and situation are too low for a Prince. In all his exercises he affects comlinesse, or rather a kind of carelesnesse in shew, to make his activities seem the more naturall, & avoids a toyling and laborious industry, especially seeing each drop of a Princes sweat is a pearl, and not to be thrown away for no cause. And Princes are not to reach, but to trample on recreations, making them their footstool to heighten their souls for seriousnesse, taking them in passage thereunto.

7. *His clothes are such as may beseem his Greatnesse*: especially when he solemnly appears, or presents himself to forrein Embassadours. Yet he disdains not to be plain at ordinary times. The late \*Henrie, Prince of Wales, being tax'd by some for his too long wearing of a plain sute of Welch frize; *Would* (said he) *my countrey cloth would last for ever.*

\* S<sup>t</sup>. *Fr. Nethersol, in the fun. orat. of him, pag.* 16.

8. *He begins to study his own countrey, and the people therein*: what places are, what may be fortified; which can withstand a long siege, and which onely can make head against a present insurrection. If his land accosteth the sea, he considereth what Havens therein are barr'd, whose dangerous chanells fence themselves, and their rocks are their blockhouses; what Keys are rusty with sands and shelves, and what are

scoured

scoured with a free and open tide, with what serviceable ships belong thereunto. He takes notice also of the men in the land, and disdains his soul should be blurred with unjust prejudices, but fairly therein writes every one in order, as they are ranked by their own deserts.

*Hence he looks abroad to see how his countrey stands in relation to forrein Kingdomes*; how it is friended with Confederates, how oppos'd with Enemies. His little eyes can cast a soure glance on the suspicious greatnesse of any near borderer; for he conceives others weakned by their own distance. He considers forrein Kingdomes, and States, whether they stand on their own strength, or lean on the favour of friends, or onely hang by a Politicall Geometry, equally poysing themselves betwixt their neighbours, like Lucca and Geneva, the multitude of enemies mouthes keeping them from being swallowed up. He quickly perceives that Kings, how nearly soever allied, are most of kinne to their own interest; and though the same Religion be the best bond of forrein affection, yet even this breaks too often: and States when wonded, will cure themselves with a plaister made of the heart-blood of their best friends.

9

*He tunes his soul in consort to the disposition of his King-father*. Whatsoever his desire be, the least word, countenance, or signe given, of his fathers disallowance makes him instantly desist from further pursuit thereof with satisfaction, in regard he understands it disagreeing to his Majesties pleasure, and with a resolution not to have the least semblance of being discontented: He hath read how such Princes which were undutifull to their Parents either had no children, or children worse then none, which repai'd their disobedience. He is also kind to his Brothers, and Sisters, whose love and affection he counteth the bulwarks and redouts for his own safety and security.

10

X x 2 *When*

11. *When grown to keep a Court by himself, he is carefull in well ordering it.* The foresaid Prince Henries Court consisted of few lesse then five hundred persons, and yet his grave and Princely aspect gave temper to them all, so that in so numerous a familie, not so much as any * blows were given.

* S*r*. William Cornwallis in the life of Prince Henry.

12. *With a frowning countenance he brusheth off from his soul all Court-mothes of flattery*: especially he is deaf to such as would advise him, without any, or any just grounds, when he comes to the Crown, to runne counter to the practice of his Father; and who knowing that muddy water makes the strongest beere, may conceive the troubling and embroyling of the State will be most advantagious for their active spirits. Indeed seldome two succesive Kings tread in the same path: if the former be Martiall, though the warre be just, honourable, and profitable, yet some will quarrell with the time present, not because *it is bad*, but because *it is*, and put a Prince forward to an alteration. If the former King were peaceable, yet happinesse it self is unhappy in being too common, and many will desire warre (conceited sweet to every palate which never tasted it) and urge a Prince thereunto. But our Prince knows to estimate things by their true worth and value, and will not take them upon the credit, whereon others present them unto him.

'Ἀεὶ τὸ παρὸν βαρύ.

13. *He conceives they will be most loving to the branch, which were most loyall to the root*, and most honour'd his father. We reade how Henry the fifth (as yet Prince of Wales) intending to bear out one of his servants for a misdemeanour, reviled S*r* William Gascoine Lord chief Justice of the Kings Bench to his face in open court. The aged Judge considered how this his action would beget an immortall example, and the echo of his words (if unpunished) would be resounded for ever to the disgrace of Majesty, which is never more on its throne, then when either in person, or in his substitutes, sitting

on

on the bench of Justice; and thereupon commanded the Prince to the prison, till he had given satisfaction to his father for the affront offered. Instantly down fell the heart of great Prince Henry, which (though as hard as rock) the breath of Justice did easily shake, being first undermin'd with an apprehension of his own guiltinesse: And King Henry the fourth his father is reported greatly to rejoyce, that he had a Judge who knew how to command by, and a Sonne who knew how to submit to his Laws. And afterward this Prince when King (first conquering himself, and afterwards the French) reduced his Court from being a forrest of wild trees, to be an orchard of sweet fruit, banishing away his bad companions, and appointing and countenancing those to keep the key of his honour, who had lock'd up his fathers most faithfully.

14. *He shews himself to the people on fit occasions.* It is hard to say whether he sees or is seen with more love and delight. Every one that brings an eye to gaze on him, brings also an heart to pray for him. But his subjects in reversion most rejoyce to see him in his military exercises, wishing him as much skill to know them, as little need to use them, seeing peace is as farre to be preferred before victory it self, as the end is better then the means.

15. *He values his future sovereignty, not by impunity in doing evil, but by power to do good.* What now his desire is, then his ability shall be; and he more joyes, that he is a member of the true Church, then the second in the land. Onely he fears to have a Crown too quickly, and therefore lengthens out his fathers dayes with his prayers for him, and obedience to him. And thus we leave Solomon to delight in David, David in Solomon, their people in both.

Xx 3     CHAP. 20.

EDWARD Prince of Wales, commonly called the black-Prince. He dyed at Canturbury june the 8th. 1326. Aged 46 yeares.

W. Marshall sculp:

## Chap. 20.

### The life of Edvvard the Black Prince.

Edward the Black Prince ( so called from his dreaded acts and not from his * complexion ) was the eldest sonne to Edward the third by Philippa his Queen. He was born *Anno* 1329, on the fifteenth of June, being friday, at Woodstock in Oxfordshire. His Parents perceiving in him more then ordinary naturall perfections, were carefull to bestow on him such education in Piety, and Learning, agreeable to his high birth.

*For King Ed. his father called him his Fair Sonne, Speed p. 579.

## Ch. 20. *The life of* Edward *the Black Prince.* 343

birth. The Prince met their care with his towardlinesse, being apt to take fire, and blaze at the least spark of instruction put into him.

We find him to be the first Prince of Wales, whose * Charter at this day is extant, with the particular rites of investiture, which were the Crownet, and Ring of gold, with a rod of silver, worthily bestowed upon him, who may passe for a miroir of Princes whether we behold him in Peace or in Warre. He in the whole course of his life manifested a singular observance to his Parents, to comply with their will and desire; nor lesse was the tendernesse of his affection to his Brothers and Sisters, whereof he had many.

* *See the copy thereof in Mr. Seldens titles of Honour, pag. 595.*

But as for the Martiall performances of this Prince, they are so many and so great that they would fill whole volumes: we will onely insist on three of his most memorable atchievements, remitting the Reader for the rest to our English Historians. The first shall be his behaviour in the battel of *Cressy, against the French, wherein Prince Edward, not fully eighteen years old, led the fore front of the English.

* *1346 in the twenty yeare of Ed. the third.*

There was a causlesse report (the beginning of a rumour is sometimes all the ground thereof) spread through the French army, that the English were fled: whereupon the French posted after them, not so much to overcome (this they counted done) but to overtake them, preparing themselves rather to pursue then to fight. But coming to the town of Cressy, they found the English fortified in a wooddy place, and attending in good array to give battel. Whereat the French falling from their hopes were extremely vext (a fools paradise is a wisemans hell) finding their enemies faces to stand where they look'd for their backs. And now both armies prepared to fight, whilest behold flocks of ravens and vulturs in the aire flew thither; bold guests to come without an invitation: But these smell-feast birds when they saw the cloth laid (the tents of two

armies

armies pitch'd) knew there would be good cheere, and came to feed on their carcases.

The English divided themselves into three parts: The formost consisting most of Archers, led by the Black Prince; the second, by the Earl of Northampton; the third, commanded by King Edward in person. The French were treble in number to the English, and had in their army the three Kings, of France, Bohemia, and Majorca: Charles Duke of Alenson, with John the Bohemian King, led the vanguard; the French King Philip, the main battel; whilest Amie Duke of Savoy brought up the rere.

The Genoan Archers in the French forefront, wearied with marching, were accus'd for their slothfulnesse, and could neither get their wages nor good words, which made many of them cast down their bows, and refuse to fight; the rest had their bowstrings made uselesse, being wetted with a sudden showre which fell on their side: But Heavens smiling offended more then her weeping, the sunne suddenly shining out in the face of the French, gave them so much light that they could not see.

However Duke Charles, breaking through the Genoans, furiously charged the fronts of the English, and joyned at hand-strokes with the Princes battel, who though fighting most couragiously was in great danger: Therefore King Edward was sent unto (who hitherto hovered on a hillock, judiciously beholding the fight) to come and rescue his sonne. The King apprehending his case dangerous but not desperate, and him rather in need then extremity, told the messenger, *Is my sonne alive, let him die or conquer, that he may have the honour of the day.*

The English were vext, not at his deniall, but their own request; that they should seem to suspect their Kings fatherly affection, or Martiall skill, as needing a remembrancer to tell him his time. To make amends, they

they laid about them manfully, the rather because they knew that the King looked on, to testifie their valour, who also had the best cards in his own hand, though he kept them for a revie.

The victory began to incline to the English, when, rather to settle then get the conquest, the King (hitherto a spectatour) came in to act the Epilogue. Many English with short knifes for the nonce stabb'd the bellies of their enemies, cut the throats of more, letting out their souls wheresoever they could come at their bodies: and to all such as lay languishing, they gave a short acquittance, that they had paid their debt to nature. This makes French Writers complain of the English cruelty, and that it had been more honour to the Generall, and profit to the souldiers to have drawn lesse bloud, and more money in ransoming captives, especially seeing many French Noblemen, who fought like lions, were kill'd like calves. Others plead that in Warre all wayes and weapons are lawfull, where it is the greatest mistake not to take all advantages.

Night came on, and the King commanded no pursuit should be made for preventing of confusion; for souldiers scarce follow any order, when they follow their flying enemy; and it was so late, that it might have proved too soon to make a pursuit.

The night proved exceeding dark (as mourning for the bloud shed) nor was the next morning comforted with the rising of the sun, but remained sad and gloomy, so that in the mist many French men lost their way, and then their lives, falling into the hands of the English: so that next dayes gleanings for the number, though not for the quality of the persons slain, exceeded the harvest of the day before. And thus this victory, next to Gods Providence, was justly ascribed to the Black Princes valour, who there wonne and wore away the Estridge feathers, then the Arms of John King of Bohemia, there conquer'd and kill'd, and therefore since

since made the *hereditary Emblemes of honour to the Princes of Wales.

* Vid. Cambd. Remains pag. 344.

The battel of Poictiers followed ten years after, which was fought betwixt the foresaid Black Prince, and John King of * France. Before the battel began the English were reduced to great straits, their enemies being six to one. The French conceived the victory, though not in hand, yet within reach, and their arm must be put out not to get but take it. All articles with the English they accounted alms, it being great charity but no policy to compound with them. But what shall we say? warre is a game wherein very often that side loseth which layeth the oddes. In probability they might have famished the English without fighting with them, had not they counted it a lean conquest so to bring their enemies to misery, without any honour to themselves.

*September 19. 1356.

The conclusion was, that the French would have the English lose their honour to save their lives, tendring them unworthy conditions, which being refused, the battel was begun. The French King made choice of three hundred prime horsmen to make the first assault on the English; the election of which three hundred made more then a thousand * heartburnings in his army: every one counted his loyalty or manhood suspected, who was not chosen into this number; and this took off the edge of their spirits against their enemies, and turned it into envy and disdain against their friends.

* Paulus Æmil. in the life of King John, pag. 286.

The French horse charged them very furiously, whom the English entertain'd with a feast of arrows, first, second, third course, all alike. Their horses were galled with the bearded piles, being unused to feel spurres in their breasts and buttocks. The best horses were worst wounded, for their mettall made one wound many; and that arrow which at first did but pierce, by their struggling did tear and rend. Then would

would they know no riders, and the riders could know no ranks; and in such a confusion, an army fights against it self. One rank fell foul with another, and the rere was ready to meet with the front: and the valiant Lord Audley, charging them before they could repair themselves, overcame all the Horse, *Qua parte belli* (saith my Authour) *invicti Galli habebantur.* The Horse being put to flight, the Infantry consisting most of poore people (whereof many came into the field with conquered hearts, grinded with oppression of their Gentry) counted it neither wit nor manners for them to stay, when their betters did flie, and made post hast after them. Six thousand common souldiers were slain, fifty two Lords, and seventeen hundred Knights and Esquires; one hundred Ensignes taken, with John the French King, and two thousand prisoners of note.

The French had a great advantage of an after-game, if they had returned again, and made head, but they had more mind to make heels, and run away. Prince Edward, whose prowesse herein was conspicuous, overcame his own valour, both in his piety, devoutly giving to God the whole glory of the conquest, and in his courtesie, with stately humility entertaining the French Prisoner-King, whom he bountifully feasted that night, though the other could not be merry albeit he was supped with great cheere, and knew himself to be very welcome.

The third performance of this valiant Prince, wherein we will instance, was acted in Spain, on this occasion. Peter King of Castile was driven out of his kingdome by Henry his base Brother, and the assistance of some French forces. Prince Edward on this Peters petition, and by his own Fathers permission, went with an army into Spain, to re-estate him in his kingdome: For though this Peter was a notorious Tyrant, (if Authours in painting his deeds do not overshadow them, to make them blacker then they were) yet our Prince, not looking into his vices but his right, thought he was bound to assist him: For all Sovereignes are like the strings of a Basevioll equally tuned to the same height, so that by sympathy, he that toucheth the one moves the other. Besides, he thought it just enough to restore him, because the French helpt to cast him out; and though Spain was farre off, yet our Prince never counted himself out of his own countrey, whilest in any part of the world; valour naturalizing a brave spirit through the Universe.

With much adoe he effected the businesse through many difficulties, occasioned partly by the treachery of King Peter, who performed none of the conditions promised, and partly through the barrennesse of the countrey, so that the Prince was forced to sell all his own plate (Spain more needing meat then dishes) to make provision for his souldiers; but especially through the distemper of the climate, the aire (or fire shall I say) thereof being extreme hot, so that it is conceived to have caused this Princes death, which happened soon after his return. What English heart can hold from inveighing against Spanish aire which deprived us of such a jewell? were it not that it may seem since to have made us some amends, when lately the *breath of our nostrills* breathed in that climate, and yet by Gods providence was kept there, and returned thence in health and safety.

Well may this Prince be taken for a Paragon of his age, and place, having the fewest vices, with so many virtues. Indeed he was somewhat given to women, our Chronicles fathering two base children on him; so hard it is to find a Sampson without a Dalila. And seeing never King or Kings eldest sonne since the conquest before his time married a subject, I must confesse his Match was much beneath himself, taking the double reversion of a subjects bed,

marrying

Chap. 21.　　*The King.*　　　　349

marrying Joan Countesse of Salisbury, which had been twice a widow. But her surpasing beauty pleads for him herein, and yet her beauty was the meanest thing about her, being surpass'd by her virtues. And what a worthy woman must she needs be her self, whose very *garter* hath given so much honour to Kings and Princes?

He dyed at Canterbury, June the eighth 1376 in the fourty sixth yeare of his age: it being wittily * observed of the short lives of many worthy men, *fatuos a morte defendit ipsa insulsitas; si cui plus cæteris aliquantulum salis insit ( quod miremini ) statim putrescit.*

*\* Sr Francis Netherfole in his fun. orat. on Prince Henry, pag. 16.*

## Chap. 21.

### *The King.*

HE is a mortall God. This world at the first had no other Charter for its being, then Gods *Fiat*: Kings have the same in the Present tense, *I have said ye are Gods*. We will describe him, first as a good man ( so was Henry the third ) then as a good King ( so was Richard the third) both which meeting together make a King complete. For he that is not a *good man*, or *but a good man*, can never be a good Sovereigne.

*He is temperate in the ordering of his own life.* O the Mandate of a Kings example is able to do much! especially he is,

*Maxime 1*

1. Temperate in his diet. When Æschines commended Philip King of Macedon, for a joviall man that would drink freely, * Demosthenes answered, *that this was a good quality in a spunge, but not in a King.*

*\* Plutarch in the life of Demosthenes.*

2. Continent in his pleasures. Yea Princes lawfull children are farre easier provided for then the *rabida fames* of a spurious offspring can be satisfied, whilest their Paramors and Concubines ( counting

Yy 3

ing it their best manners to carve for themselves all they can come by) prove intolerably expensive to a State. Besides, many rebellions have risen out of the marriage-bed defiled.

2

*Dan. 4. 17.

*Irenæus l. 5.
*Tertull. Apol. pag. 6.5.

He holds his Crown immediately from the God of Heaven. * The most high ruleth in the kingdomes of men, and giveth them to whomsoever he will. Cujus jussu nascuntur homines, ejus jussu constituuntur Principes, saith a * Father: Inde illis potestas unde Spiritus, saith * another. And whosoever shall remount to the first originall of Kings, shall lose his eyes in discovering the top thereof, as past ken, and touching the heavens. We reade of a place in Mount Olivet (wherein the last footsteps, they say, of our Saviour before he ascended into heaven are to be seen) that it will ever lie open to the skies, and will not admit of any close or * covering to be made over it how costly soever. Farre more true is this of the condition of absolute Kings, who in this respect are ever *sub dio*, so that no superiour power can be interposed betwixt them and heaven. Yea the Character of loyalty to Kings so deeply impress'd in Subjects hearts shews that onely Gods finger wrote it there. Hence it is if one chance to conceive ill of his Sovereigne, though within the cabinet of his soul, presently his own heart grows jealous of his own heart, and he could wish the tongue cut out of his tell-tale thoughts, lest they should accuse themselves. And though sometimes Rebels (Atheists against the Gods on earth) may labour to obliterate loyalty in them, yet even then their conscience, the Kings Aturney, frames Articles against them, and they stand in daily fear lest Darius Longimanus (such a one is every King) should reach them, and revenge himself.

*Nullo modo contegi aut concamerari potest, sed transitus ejus à terra ad cœlum usque patet apertum, Adricom. de terra Sancta ex Hieron. & aliis Autoribus.

3

He claimeth to be supreme Head on earth over the Church in his Dominions. Which his power over all persons and causes Ecclesiasticall

1. Is given him by God, who alone hath the originall propriety thereof.

2. Is derived unto him by a prescription time out of mind in the Law of Nature, declared more especially in the Word of God.
3. Is cleared and averred by the private Laws and Statutes of that State wherein he lives. For since the Pope (starting up from being the Emperours Chaplain to be his Patron) hath invaded the rights of many earthly Princes, many wholsome Laws have been made in severall Kingdomes to assert and notifie their Kings just power *in Spiritualibus*.

Well therefore may our King look with a frowning face on such, whose tails meet in this firebrand (which way soever the prospect of their faces be) to deny Princes power in Church-matters. Two * Jesuites give this farre-fetch'd reason, why * Samuel at the Feast caused the shoulder of the Sacrifice to be *reserved and kept on purpose* for Saul to feed on; because, say they, *Kings of all men have most need of strong shoulders patiently to endure those many troubles and molestations they shall meet with*, especially, I may well adde, if all their Subjects were as troublesome and disloyall as the Jesuites. The best is, as God hath given Kings shoulders to bear, he hath also given them armes to strike such as deprive them of their lawfull Authority in Ecclesiasticall affairs.

* *Zanchez & Velasquez in their Comments on the Text.*
1. Sam. 9. 14.

4

*He improves his power to defend true Religion.* Sacerdotall Offices though he will not doe, he will cause them to be done. He will not offer to burn incense with Uzziah, yet he will burn Idolaters bones with Josiah, I mean advance Piety by punishing Profaneness. God* saith to his Church, *Kings shall be thy Nursing-fathers, and their Queens thy Nursing-mothers*. And oh let not Princes out of State refuse to be so themselves, and onely hire others, it belonging to Subjects to suck, but to Princes to suckle Religion by their authority. They ought to command Gods Word to be read and practised, wherein the blessed Memory of King James shall never

* *Isaiah. 49. 23.*

ver be forgotten. His Predecessour in England restored the Scripture to her Subjects, but he in a manner, restored the Scripture to it self in causing the *New Translation* thereof, whereby the meanest that can reade English, in effect understands the Greek and Hebrew. A Princely act, which shall last even when the lease of Time shall be expired: Verily I say unto you, wheresoever this Translation shall be read in the whole realm, there shall also this that this King hath done be told in memoriall of him.

5

* Prov. 16. 12.
* Prov. 20. 28.

*He useth Mercy and Justice in his proceedings against Offenders.* Solomon * saith, *The throne is established by Justice*: and Solomon * saith, *The throne is upholden by Mercy.* Which two Proverbs speak no more contradiction, then he that saith that the two opposite side-walls of an house hold up the same roof. Yea as some Astronomers (though erroneously) conceived the Crystalline Sphere to be made of water, and therefore to be set next the *Primum mobile* to allay the heat thereof, which otherwise by the swiftnesse of his motion would set all the world on fire; so Mercy must ever be set near Justice for the cooling and tempering thereof. In his mercy our King desires to resemble the God of heaven, who measureth his judgements by the ordinary cubit, but his kindnesses by the cubit of the Sanctuary, twice as big; yea all the world had been a hell without Gods mercy.

6

*He is rich in having a plentifull exchequer of his peoples hearts. Allow me,* said Archimedes, *to stand in the aire, and I will move the earth.* But our King having a firm footing in his Subjects affections, what may he do, yea what may he not do? making the coward valiant, the miser liberall; for love, the key of hearts, will open the closest coffers. Mean time how poore is that Prince amidst all his wealth, whose Subjects are onely kept by a slavish fear, the jaylour of the soul. An iron arm fastned with scrues may be stronger, but never so usefull,

because

because not so naturall, as an arm of flesh, joined with muscles & sinews. Loving Subjects are most serviceable, as being more kindly united to their Sovereigne then those which are onely knock'd on with fear and forcing. Besides, where Subjects are envassaled with fear, Prince and People mutually watch their own advantages, which being once offered them, 'tis wonderfull if they do not, and wofull if they do, make use thereof.

*He willingly orders his actions by the Laws of his realm.* Indeed some maintain that Princes are too high to come under the roof of any Laws, except they voluntarily of their goodnesse be pleased to bow themselves thereunto, and that it is Corban, a gift and courtesy, in them to submit themselves to their Laws. But whatsoever the Theories of absolute Monarchy be, our King loves to be legall in all his practices, and thinks that his power is more safely lock'd up for him in his Laws then kept in his own will; because God alone makes things lawfull by willing them, whilest the most calmest Princes have sometimes gusts of Passion, which meeting with an unlimited Authority in them may prove dangerous to them and theirs. Yea our King is so suspicious of an unbounded power in himself, that though the widenesse of his strides could make all the hedge stiles, yet he will not go over, but where he may. He also hearkneth to the advise of good Counsellers, remembring the speech of Antoninus the Emperour, *Aequius est ut ego tot taliumque amicorum consilium sequar, quam tot talesque amici meam unius voluntatem.* And yet withall our King is carefull to maintain his just Prerogative, that as it be not outstretched, so it may not be overshortned.

Such a gratious Sovereigne God hath vouchsafed to this Land. How pious is he towards his God! attentive in hearing the Word, preaching Religion with his silence, as the Minister doth with his speech! How loving to his Spouse, tender to his Children, faithfull to his servants whilest they are faithfull to their own innocence; otherwise leaving them to Justice under marks of his displeasure. How doth he with David walk in the *midst of his house* without partiality to any! How just is he in punishing wilfull murder! so that it is as easie to restore the murthered to life, as to keep the murtherer from death. How mercifull is he to such who not out of leigier malice, but sudden passion may chance to shed bloud! to whom his pardon hath allowed leisure to drop out their own souls in tears by constant repentance all the dayes of their lives. How many wholsome Laws hath he enacted for the good of his Subjects! How great is his humilitie in so great height! which maketh his own praises painfull for himself to heare, though pleasant for others to report. His Royall virtues are too great to be told, and too great to be conceal'd. All cannot, some must break forth from the full hearts of such as be his thankfull Subjects.

But I must either stay or fall. My sight fails me dazell'd with the lustre of Majestie: all I can do is pray.

Give the King thy judgements, O Lord, and thy righteousnesse to the Kings Sonne: smite through the loins of those that rise up against his Majestie, but upon him and his let the Crown flourish: Oh cause his Subjects to meet his Princely care for their good, with a proportionable cheerfulnesse and alacrity in his service, that so thereby the happinesse of Church and State may be continued. Grant this, O Lord, for Christ Jesus his sake our onely Mediatour and Advocate. Amen.

The

# THE PROFANE STATE.

BY
THOMAS FULLER, *B. D.*
and Prebendarie of
Sarum.

ISAIAH 32. 5.
*The vile person shall be no more called liberall, nor the churl said to be bountifull.*

EZEK. 44. 23.
*And they shall teach my people the difference betwixt the Holy and the Profane.*

CAMBRIDGE:
¶ Printed by ROGER DANIEL for
*John Williams*, and are to be sold at the signe
of the Crown in S. Pauls
Churchyard. 1642.
Zz 2

# The Profane State.

## THE FIFTH BOOK.

### Chap. I.
### *The Harlot*

IS one that her self is both merchant and merchandise, which she selleth for profit, and hath pleasure given her into the bargain, and yet remains a great loser. To describe her is very difficult, it being hard to draw those to the life, who never sit still: she is so various in her humours, and mutable, 'tis almost impossible to character her in a fixed posture; yea indeed some cunning Harlots are not discernable from honest women. Solomon saith, *she wipeth her mouth*; and who can distinguish betwixt that which was never foul, and that which is cleanly wiped.

*Her love is a blank, wherein she writeth the next man that tendreth his affection.* Impudently the Harlot lied ( Prov. 7.15.) *Therefore came I forth to meet thee, diligently to seek thy face, and I have found thee*: else understand her that she came forth to meet him, not *qua talis*, but *qua primus*, because he came first; for any other youngster in his place would have serv'd her turn: yet see how she makes his chance her courtesie, she affecting him as much

*Maxime* I

much above others, as the common road loves the next passenger best

2. *As she sees, so her self is seen by her own eyes.* Sometimes she stares on men with full fixed eyes; otherwhiles she squints forth glances, and contracts the beams in her burning glasses, to make them the hotter to inflame her objects; sometimes she dejects her eyes in a seeming civility, and many mistake in her a cunning for a modest look. But as those bullets which graze on the ground do most mischief to an army, so she hurts most with those glances which are shot from a down-cast eye.

3. *She writes characters of wantonnesse with her feet as she walks:* And what Potiphars wife said with her tongue, she saith unto the passengers with her gesture and gate, *Come lie with me*; and nothing angrieth her so much, as when modest men affect a deafnesse and will not heare, or a dulnesse and will not understand the language of her behaviour. She counts her house a prison, and is never well till gadding abroad: sure 'tis true of women what is observed of elm, if lying within doores dry, no timber will last sound longer, but if without doores expos'd to weather, no wood sooner rots and corrupts.

4. *Yet some Harlots continue a kind of strange coynesse even to the very last*: which coynesse differs from modesty as much as hemlock from parsely. They will deny common favours, because they are too small to be granted: They will part with all or none, refuse to be courteous, and reserve themselves to be dishonest; whereas women truly modest will willingly go to the bounds of free and harmlesse mirth, but will not be dragg'd any farther.

5. *She is commonly known by her whorish attire*: As crisping and curling, (making her hair as winding and intricate as her heart) painting, wearing naked breasts. The face indeed ought to be bare, and the haft should lie

out

Chap. 1.   *The Harlot.*   359

out of the sheath; but where the back and edge of the knife are shown, 'tis to be feared they mean to cut the fingers of others. I must confesse some honest women may go thus, but no whit the honester for going thus. The ship may have Castor and Pollux for the badge, and notwithstanding have S. Paul for the lading: yet the modesty and discretion of honest Matrons were more to be commended, if they kept greater distance from the attire of Harlots.

*Sometimes she ties her self in marriage to one, that she may the more freely stray to many*: and cares not though her husband comes not within her bed, so be it he goeth not out beyond the Foure-seas. She useth her husband as an hood, whom she casts off in the fair weather of prosperity, but puts him on for a cover in adversity, if it chance she prove with child.    6

*Yet commonly she is as barren as lustfull.* Yea who can expect that malt should grow to bring new increase. Besides, by many wicked devices she seeks on purpose to make her self barren (a retrograde act to set Nature back) making many issues, that she may have no issue, and an hundred more damnable devices,    7

*Which wicked projects first from hell did flow,*
*And thither let the same in silence go,*
*Best known of them who did them never know.*

And yet for all her cunning, God sometimes meets with her (who varieth his wayes of dealing with wantons, that they may be at a losse in tracing him) and sometimes against her will she proves with child, which though unable to speak, yet tells at the birth a plain story to the mothers shame.

*At last when her deeds grow most shamefull she grows most shamelesse.* So impudent, that she her self sometimes proves both the poyson and the antidote, the temptation and the preservative; young men distasting and abhorring her boldnesse. And those wantons, who perchance would willingly have gathered the fruit
from

fruit from the tree, will not feed on such fallings.

**9**

*Generally she dies very poore.* The wealth she gets is like the houses some build in Gothland, made of * snow, no lasting fabrick; the rather, because she who took money of those who tasted the top of her wantonnesse, is fain to give it to such who will drink out the dregs of her lust.

*Olaus magnus de Rit. Gent. sept. lib.1.c.23.*

**10**

*She dieth commonly of a lothsome disease.* I mean that disease, unknown to Antiquity, created within some hundreds of years, which took the name from Naples. When hell invented new degrees in sinnes, it was time for heaven to invent new punishments. Yet is this new disease now grown so common and ordinary, as if they meant to put divine Justice to a second task to find out a newer. And now it is high time for our Harlot, being grown lothsome to her self, to runne out of her self by repentance.

Some conceive that when King Henry the eighth destroyed the publick Stews in this Land (which till his time stood on the banks side on Southwark next the Bear-garden, beasts and beastly women being very fit neighbours) he rather scattered then quenched the fire of lust in this kingdome, and by turning the flame out of the chimney where it had a vent, more endangered the burning of the Commonwealth. But they are deceived: for whilest the Laws of the Land tolerated open uncleannesse, God might justly have made the whole State do penance for whoredome; whereas now that sinne though committed, yet not permitted, and though (God knows) it be too generall, it is still but personall.

CHAP. 2.

JOAN the first of that Name Queen of Naples, which for her Incontinency and other wicked Practises was put to Death. Anno 1381

Page 260.   W M sculp:

## Chap. 2.
## The life of JOAN Queen of Naples.

JOan, grandchild to Robert King of Naples by Charles his sonne, succeeded her grandfather in the Kingdome of Naples and Sicily, *Anno* 1343. a woman of a beautifull body and rare endowments of nature, had not the heat of her lust soured all the rest of her perfections, whose wicked life * and wofull death we now come to relate: And I hope none can justly lay it to my charge, if the foulnesse of her actions stain through the cleanest language I can wrap them in.

<sub>* Taken out of Brovius An. Eccle.an.1344. Petrarch.lib.5. Epist. & Summontius Hist. Neopol. lib. 3.</sub>

She was first married unto her cosen Andrew, a Prince of royall extraction, and of a sweet and loving disposition. But he being not able to satisfie her wantonnesse, she kept company with lewd persons, at first privately, but afterwards she presented her badnesse visible to every eye, so that none need look through the chinks where the doores were open.

Now Elizabeth Queen of Hungary, her husband Andrews mother, was much offended at the badnesse of her daughter-in-law, whose deeds were so foul she could not look on them, and so common she could not look besides them; wherefore in a matronly way she fairly advised her to reform her courses. For the lives of Princes are more read then their Laws, and generally more practised: Yea their example passeth as current as their coin, and what they do they seem to command to be done. Cracks in glasse though past mending are no great matter; but the least flaw in a diamond is considerable: Yea her personall fault was a nationall injury, which might derive and put the Sceptre into a wrong hand.

These her mild instructions she sharpned with severe threatnings: But no razor will cut a stony heart. Queen Joan imputed it to ages envy, old people perswading

swading youth to leave those pleasures, which have left themselves. Besides, a Mother-in-laws Sermon seldome takes well with an audience of Daughter-in-laws. Wherefore the old Queen finding the other past grace (that is never likely to come to it) resolved no longer to punish anothers sinne on her self, and vex her own righteous soul, but leaving Naples return'd into Hungary.

After her departure Queen Joan grew weary of her husband Andrew, complaining of his insufficiency, though those who have *caninum appetitum* are not competent judges what is sufficient food: And she caused her husband in the city of Aversa to be hung upon a beam and strangled in the night time, and then threw out his corps into a garden, where it lay some dayes unburied.

There goes a\* story that this Andrew on a day coming into the Queens chamber, and finding her twisting a thick string of silk and silver, demanded of her for what purpose she made it: She answered, *To hang you in it*, which he then little believed, the rather because those who intend such mischief never speak of it before. But such blows in jest-earnest are most dangerous, which one can neither receive in love, nor refuse in anger.

*\* Collenusius, l. 5. Regn. Neop.*

Indeed she sought in vain to colour the businesse, and to divert the suspicion of the murther from her self, because all the world saw that she inflicted no punishment on the actours of it which were in her power. And in such a case, when a murther is generally known, the sword of the Magistrate cannot stand neuter, but doth justify what it doth not punish.

Besides, his corps was not cold before she was hot in a new love, and married Lewis Prince of Tarentum, one of the beautifullest men in the world. But it was hard for her to please her love and her lust in the same person.

person. This Prince wasted the state of his body to pay her the conjugall debt, which she extorted beyond all modesty or reason, so unquenchable was the wild-fire of her wantonnesse.

After his death (she hating widowhood as much as Nature doth *vacuum*) maried James King of Majorca, and commonly styled Prince of Calabria. Some say he dyed of a naturall death: Others, that she beheaded him for lying with another woman (who would suffer none to be dishonest but her self) Others, that he was unjustly put to death, and forced to change worlds, that she might change husbands.

Her fourth husband was Otho of Brunswick, who came a Commander out of Germany, with a company of souldiers, and performed excellent service in Italy. A good souldier he was, and it was not the least part of his valour to adventure on so skittish a beast: But he hoped to feast his hungry fortune on this reversion. By all foure husbands she had no children; either because the drougth of her wantonnesse parched the fruit of her wombe; or else because provident Nature prevented a generation of Monsters from her.

By this time her sinnes were almost hoarse with crying to heaven for revenge. They mistake who think divine Justice sleepeth when it winks for a while at Offenders. Hitherto she had kept herself in a whole skin by the rents which were in the Church of Rome. For there being a long time a Schisme betwixt two Popes, Urban, and Clement, she so poysed herself between them both, that she escaped unpunished. This is that Queen Joan that gave Avignon in France (yet under a pretence of sale) to Pope Urban and his Successours: the stomach of his Holinesse not being so squeamish, but that he would take a good almes from dirty hands. It may make the chastity of Rome suspicious with the world that she hath had so good fortune to be a gainer by Harlots.

But see now how Charles Prince of Dyrachium, being next of kin to Prince Andrew that was murdered, comes out of Hungary with an army into Naples to revenge his uncles bloud. He was received without resistance of any, his very name being a Petrard to make all the city-gates fly open where he came. Out issues Otho the Queens husband with an army of men out of Naples, and most stoutly bids him battel, but is overthrown; yet was he suffered fairly to depart the kingdome, dismiss'd with this commendation, That never a more valiant Knight fought in defence of a more vitious Lady.

Queen Joan finding it now in vain to bend her fist, fell to bowing of her knees, and having an excellent command of all her passions save her lust, fell down flat before Charles the Conquerour, and submitted her self: *Hitherto*, said she, *I have esteemed thee in place of a sonne, but seeing God will have it so, hereafter I shall acknowledge thee for my Lord.* Charles knew well that Necessity, her Secretary, endited her speech for her, which came little from her heart; yet, to shew that he had as plentifull an Exchequer of good language, promis'd her fairly for the present: But mercy it self would be asham'd to pity so notorious a malefactour. After some moneths imprisonment she was carried to the place where her husband was murder'd, and there accordingly hang'd, and cast out of the window into the garden, whose corps at last was buried in the Nunnery of S. Clare.

CHAP. 3.

## Chap. 3.
## *The Witch.*

BEfore we come to describe her, we must premise and prove certain propositions, whose truth may otherwise be doubted of.

1. *Formerly there were Witches.* Otherwise Gods * Law had fought against a shadow, *Thou shalt not suffer a Witch to live*: yea we reade how King Saul, who had formerly scoured Witches out of all Israel, afterwards drank a draught of that puddle himself.

   * *Exod. 18.22.*

2. *There are Witches for the present, though those Night-birds flie not so frequently in flocks since the light of the Gospel.* Some ancient arts and mysteries are said to be lost; but sure the devil will not wholly let down any of his gainfull trades. There be many Witches at this day in Lapland, who sell winds to Mariners for money (and must they not needs go whom the devil drives?) though we are not bound to believe the old story of Ericus King of Swedeland, who had a * cap, and as he turned it the wind he wish'd for would blow on that side.

   * *Therefore called,* Ventosus pileus, *Olaus mag. de Gent. septent. lib. 3. cap. 14.*

3. *It is very hard to prove a Witch.* Infernall contracts are made without witnesses. She that in presence of others will compact with the devil deserves to be hang'd for her folly as well as impiety.

4. *Many are unjustly accused for Witches.* Sometimes out of ignorance of naturall, & misapplying of supernaturall causes; sometimes out of their neighbours mere malice, and the suspicion is increas'd, if the party accused be notoriously ill-favoured; whereas deformity alone is no more argument to make her a Witch, then handsomnesse had been evidence

to prove her an Harlot; sometimes out of their own causlesse confession. Being brought before a Magistrate they acknowledge themselves to be Witches, being themselves rather bewitch'd with fear, or deluded with phancy. But the self-accusing of some is as little to be credited, as the self-praising of others, if alone without other evidence.

5 *Witches are commonly of the feminine sex.* Ever since Satan tempted our grandmother Eve, he knows that that sex is most licorish to tast, and most carelesse to swallow his baits. *Nescio quid habet muliebre nomen semper cum sacris*: if they light well, they are inferiour to few men in piety, if ill, superiour to all in superstition.

<small>* Fulgentius in Sermon.</small>

6 *They are commonly distinguished into white and black Witches.* White, I dare not say good Witches ( *for woe be to him that calleth evil good* ) heal those that are hurt, and help them to lost goods. But better it is to lap ones pottage like a dog, then to eat it mannerly with a spoon of the devils giving: Black Witches hurt, and do mischief. But in deeds of darknesse there is no difference of colours: The white and the black are both guilty alike in compounding with the devil. And now we come to see by vvhat degrees people arrive at this height of profanenesse.

**Maxime I** *At the first she is onely ignorant, and very malicious.* She hath usually a bad face, and a worse tongue, given to railing and cursing, as if constantly bred on mount Ebal, yet speaking perchance worse then she means, though meaning worse then she should. And as the harmlesse wapping of a curs'd curre may stir up a fierce mastiffe to the vvorrying of sheep; so on her cursing the devil may take occasion by Gods permission to do mischief, vvithout her knovvledge, and perchance against her will.

<small>*Multi dum vitare student quæ vitanda non sunt, fugâ vanâ superstitionis superstitiosi fiunt, Cardan. de Subtil. p. 924. lib. 8.</small>

Some have been made * *Witches* by endeavouring to defend *themselves*

themselves against *witchcraft*: for fearing some suspected Witch should hurt them, they fence themselves with the devils shield against the devils sword, put on his *whole armour*, beginning to use spells and charms to safeguard themselves. The art is quickly learnt to which nothing but credulity and practice is required; and they often fall from defending themselves to offending of others, especially the devil not being dainty of his company where he finds welcome; and being invited once he haunts ever after.

*She begins at first with doing tricks rather strange then hurtfull*: yea some of them are pretty and pleasing. But it is dangerous to gather floures that grow on the banks of the pit of hell, for fear of falling in; yea they which play with the devils rattles, will be brought by degrees to wield his sword, and from making of sport they come to doing of mischief.

*At last she indents downright with the devil.* He is to find her some toies for a time, and to have her soul in exchange. At the first (to give the devil his due) he observes the agreement to keep up his credit, else none would trade with him, though at last he either deceives her with an equivocation, or at some other small hole this Serpent winds out himself, and breaks the covenants. And where shall she poore wretch sue the forfeited band? in heaven she neither can nor dare appear; on earth she is hang'd if the contract be proved; in hell her adversary is judge, and it is wofull to appeal from the devil to the devil. But for a while let us behold her in her supposed felicity.

*She taketh her free progresse from one place to another.* Sometimes the devil doth locally transport her: but he will not be her constant hackney, to carry such luggage about, but oftentimes to save portage deludes her brains in her sleep, so that they brag of long journeys, whose heads never travell'd from their bolsters. These with Drake sail about the vvorld, but it is on an ocean of their own phancies, and in a ship of the same: They boast of brave banquets they have been at, but they would be very lean should they eat no other meat: Others will perswade, if any list to believe, that by a Witch-bridle they can make a fair of horses of an acre of besome-weed. Oh silly souls! Oh subtle Satan that deceived them.

6. *With strange figures and words she summons the devils to attend her*: using a language which God never made at the confusion of Tongues; and an interpreter must be fetch'd from hell to expound it. With these, or Scripture abused, the devil is ready at her service. Who would suppose that roaring lion could so finely act the spaniel? one would think he were too old *to suck*, and yet he will do that also for advantage.

7. *Sometimes she enjoyns him to do more for her then he is able*; as to wound those whom Gods providence doth arm, or to break through the tents of blessed Angels, to hurt one of Gods Saints. Here Satan is put to his shifts, and his wit must help him where his power fails; he either exculeth it, or seemingly performs it, lengthning his own arm by the dimnesse of her eye, and presenting the seeming bark of that tree which he cannot bring.

8. *She lives commonly but very poore.* Methinks she should bewitch to her self a golden mine, at least good meat, and whole clothes: But 'tis as rare to see one of her profession as an hangman in an whole suit. Is the possession of the devils favour here no better? Lord, what is the reversion of it hereafter?

9. *When arraigned for her life the devil leaves her to the Law to shift for her self.* He hath worn out all his shoes in her former service, and will not now go barefoot to help her; and the circle of the halter is found to be too strong for all her Spirits. Yea *Zoroastes himself, the first inventer of Magick (though he laught at his birth) led a miserable life, and dyed a wofull death in banishment

* *Plinius, lib. 3. cap. 1.*

ment. We will give a double example of a Witch: first of a reall one, out of the Scripture, because it shall be above all exception; and then of one deeply suspected, out of our own Chronicles.

## Chap. 4.
### The Witch of\* Endor.

\* 1. *Sam.* 28.

HEr proper name we neither find, nor need curiously enquire: without it she is describ'd enough for our knowledge, too much for her shame.

King Saul had banish'd all Witches and Sorcerers out of Israel; but no besom can sweep so clean as to leave no crumme of dust behind it: This Witch of Endor still keeps her self safe in the land. God hath *his remnant* where Saints are cruelly persecuted; Satan also his remnant, where offenders are severely prosecuted, and (if there were no more) the whole *species* of Witches is preserved in this *individuum*, till more be provided.

It happened now that King Saul, being ready to fight with the Philistines, was in great distresse, because God answered him not concerning the successe of the battel. With the silent, he will be silent: Saul gave no reall answer in his obedience to Gods commands, God will give no vocall answer to Sauls requests.

Mens minds are naturally ambitious to know things to come: Saul is restlesse to know the issue of the fight. Alas, what needed he to set his teeth on edge with the sourenesse of that bad tidings, who soon after was to have his belly full thereof.

He said to his servants, *Seek me out* (no wonder she was such a jewell to be sought for) *one with a familiar Spirit*: which was accordingly perform'd, and Saul came to her in a disguise. Formerly Samuel told him

Bbb         that

that his *disobedience was as witchcraft*; now Saul falls from the like to the same, and tradeth with Witches indeed (the receiver is as bad as the thief) and at his request she raiseth up Samuel to come unto him.

What, true Samuel? It is above Satans power to degrade a Saint from glory, though for a moment; since his own fall thence, he could fetch none from heaven. Or was it onely the true body of Samuel? no; the pretious ashes of the Saints (the pawn for the return of their souls) are lock'd up safe in the cabinet of their graves, and the devil hath no key unto it. Or lastly was it his seeming body? he that could not counterfeit the least and worst of * worms, could he dissemble the shape of one of the best and greatest of men?

* Exod. 8. 18.

Yet this is most probable, seeing Satan could change himself into an Angel of light, and God gives him more power at some times then at other. However, we will not be too peremptory herein, and build standing structures of bold assertions on so uncertain a foundation: rather with the Rechabites we will live in tents of conjectures, which on better reason we may easily alter and remove.

The devils speech looks backward and forward, relates and foretells: the Historicall part thereof is easie, recounting Gods speciall favours to Saul, and his ingratitude to God, and the matter thereof very pious. *Not every one that saith Lord, Lord* (whether to him or of him) *shall enter into the kingdome of heaven:* for Satan here useth the Lords name six times in foure verses. The Propheticall part of his speech is harder, how he could foretell *to morrow shalt thou and thy sonnes be with me:* what, with me true Samuel in heaven? that was too good a place (will some say) for Saul: or with me true Satan in hell? that was too bad a place for Jonathan. What then? with me pretended Samuel in ᾅδῃ, in the state of the dead.

But

But how came the Witch or Satan by this knowledge? surely that uggly monster never look'd his face in that beautifull glasse of the Trinity, which (as some will have it) represents things to the blessed Angels. No doubt then he gathered it by experimentall collection, who, having kept an exact Ephemerides of all actions for more then five thousand years together, can thereby make a more then probable guesse of future contingents; the rather because accidents in this world are not so much new as renewed. Besides, he saw it in the naturall causes, in the strength of the Philistines, and weaknesse of the Israelitish army, and in Davids ripenesse to succeed Saul in the Throne. Perchance as vulturs are said to smell the earthlinesse of a dying corps; so this bird of prey resented a worse then earthly savour in the soul of Saul, an evidence of his death at hand. Or else we may say the devil knew it by particular revelation; for God to use the devil for his own turn might impart it unto him, to advance wicked mens repute of Satans power, that they who would be deceived should be deceived to believe that Satan knows more then he does.

The dismall news so frighted Saul, that he fell along on the earth, and yet at last is perswaded to arise and eat meat, she killing and dressing a fat calf for him.

Witches generally are so poore they can scarce feed themselves: see here one able to feast a King. *That which goeth into the mouth defileth not*: better eat meat of her dressing, then take counsell of her giving; and her hands might be clean, whose soul meddled with unclean spirits. Saul must eat somewhat, that he might be strengthned to live to be kill'd, as afterwards it came to passe. And here the mention of this Witch in Scripture vanisheth away, & we will follow her no farther. If afterward she escaped the justice of man, Gods judgement, without her repentance, hath long since overtaken her.

## Chap. 5.

### The life of JOAN of Arc.

JOan of Arc was born in a village called Domrenny upon the Marches of Bar, near to Vaucoleurs. Her parents, James of Arc and Isabell, were very poore people, and brought her up to keep sheep: where for a while we will leave her, and come to behold the miserable estate of the kingdome of France wherein she lived.

In her time Charles the seventh was the distressed French King, having onely two entire Provinces left him, Gascoigne and Languedoc, and his enemies were about them, and in all the rest, which were possessed by the English, under their young King Henrie the sixth, and his aged Generalls the Duke of Bedford, and the Earls of Salisbury and Suffolk. Besides they had besieged the city of Orleance, and brought it to that passe that the highest hopes of those therein was to yield on good terms.

Matters standing in this wofull case, three French * Noblemen projected with themselves to make a cordiall for the consumption of the spirits of their King and Countreymen; but this seemed a great difficulty to perform, the French people being so much dejected: and when mens hearts are once down, it is hard to fasten any pullies to them to draw them up. However they resolved to pitch upon some project out of the ordinary road of accidents, to elevate the peoples phancies thereby, knowing that mens phancies easily slip off from smooth and common things, but are quickly catch'd & longest kept in such plots as have odde angles, and strange unusuall corners in them.

Hereupon they concluded to set up the foresaid Joan of Arc, to make her pretend that she had a revelation

* *Gyrard Seigneur du Haillizan in Charles the seventh.*

JOAN of Arc the victorious Leader of the French Armyes, She was condemned by the English for a Witch, & burnt at Rohan July the 6th 1461. being about 22. yeares of Age.

Page 372.  W. Marshall sculp:

lation from heaven, to be the leader of an army, to drive all the English out of France: and she being an handsome, witty, and bold maid (about twentie years of age) was both apprehensive of the plot, and very active to prosecute it. But other Authours will not admit of any such complotting, but make her moved thereunto either of her own, or by some Spirits instigation.

By the mediation of a Lord she is brought to the presence of King Charles, whom she instantly knew, though never seen before, and at that time of set purpose much disguised. This very thing some heighten to a miracle, though others make it fall much beneath a wonder, as being no more then a Scholars ready saying of that lesson, which he hath formerly learned without book. To the King she boldly delivers her message, how that this was the time wherein the sinnes of the English, and the sufferings of the French, were come to the height, and she appointed by the God of heaven to be the French leader to conquer the English. If this opportunity were let slip, let them thank heavens bounty for the tender, and their own folly for the refusall; and who would pity their eternall slavery, who thrust their own liberty from themselves.

He must be deaf indeed who heares not that spoken which he desires. Charles triumphs at this news: Both his armes were to few too embrace the motion. The Fame of her flies through France, and all talk of her, whom the Divines esteem as Deborah, the Souldiers as Semiramis. People found out a nest of miracles in her education, that so lyon-like a spirit should be bred amongst sheep like David.

Ever after she went in mans clothes, being armed cap-a-pe, and mounted on a brave Steed: and which was a wonder, when she was on horseback, none was more bold and daring; when* alighted, none more tame and meek; so that one could scarce see her for

* *Gerson. lib. de mirab. victoria cujusdam puellæ, paulò post initium.*

for her self, she was so chang'd and alter'd as if her spirits dismounted with her body. No sword would please her, but one taken out of the * Church of S. Katharin in Fierebois in Tourain. Her first service was in twice victualling of Orleance, whilest the English made no resistance, as if they had eyes onely to gaze, and no arms to fight.

* *Polidor.Virg. in Hen. sixth, pag. 471.*

Hence she sent a menacing * letter to the Earl of Suffolk, the English Generall, commanding him in Gods and her own name to yield up the keyes of all good cities to her, the Virgin sent by God to restore them to the French. The letter was received with scorn; and the trumpeter that brought it commanded to be burnt, against the Law of Nations, saith a French * Authour, but erroneously: for his coming was not warranted by the authority of any lawfull Prince, but from a private maid, how highly soever self-pretended, who had neither estate to keep, nor commission to send a trumpeter.

* *See the copy thereof in Speeds King Hen. sixth, pag. 654.*

* *Du Serres in his French Hist. translat. by Grimston, p. 326.*

Now the minds of the French were all afloat with this the conceit of their new Generall, which miraculously raised their Spirits. Phancie is the castle commanding the city; and if once mens heads be possest with strange imaginations, the whole body will follow, and be infinitely transported therewithall. Under her conduct they first drive away the English from Orleance: nor was she a whit daunted, when shot through her arm with an arrow; but taking the arrow in one hand, and her sword in another, *This is a * favour*, said she; *let us go on, they cannot escape the hand of God*: and she never left off, till she had beaten the English from the city. And hence this virago (call her now John or Joan) marched on into other countreys, which instantly revolted to the French crown. The example of the first place was the reason of all the rest to submit. The English in many skirmishes were worsted and defeated with few numbers. But what shall we say? when

* *Idem. p. 317.*

# Chap. 5.   *The life of* JOAN *of Arc.*   375

when God intends a Nation shall be beaten, he ties their hands behind them.

The French followed their blow, losing no time, lest the height of their Spirits should be remitted: (mens Imaginations when once on foot must ever be kept going, like those that go on stilts in fenny countreys, lest standing still they be in danger of falling) and so keeping the conceit of their souldiers at the height; in one twelvemoneth they recovered the greatest part of that the English did possesse.

But successe did afterwards fail this She-Generall: for seeking to surprise S. Honories ditch near the city of S. Denis, she was not onely wounded her self, but also lost a Troup of her best and most resolute souldiers; and not long after, nigh the city of Compeigne, being too farre engaged in fight, was taken prisoner by the bastard of Vendosme, who sold her to the Duke of Bedford, and by him she was kept a prisoner a twelvemoneth in Rohan.

It was much disputed amongst the Statists what should be done with her: Some held that no punishment was to be inflicted on her, because

*Nullum memorabile nomen*

*Fœminea in pœna.*

Cruelty to a woman,

Brings honour unto no man.

Besides, putting her to death would render all English men guilty which should hereafter be taken prisoners by the French. Her former valour deserved praise, her present misery deserved pity; captivity being no ill action but ill successe: let them rather allow her an honourable pension, and so make her valiant deeds their own by rewarding them. However, she ought not to be put to death: for if the English would punish her, they could not more disgrace her then with life, to let her live though in a poore mean way, and then she would be the best confutation of her own

glorious

glorious prophesies; let them make her the Laundresse to the English, who was the Leader to the French army.

Against these arguments necessity of State was urged, a reason above all reason; it being in vain to dispute whether that may be done which must be done. For the French superstition of her could not be reformed except the idole was destroyed; and it would spoil the French puppet-playes in this nature for ever after, by making her an example. Besides she was no prisoner of warre, but a prisoner of Justice, deserving death for her witchcraft and whoredomes; whereupon she was burnt at Rohan the sixth of July 1461, not without the aspersion of * cruelty on our Nation.

> * Sententia post homines natos durissima, Pol.Vir. pag. 477.

Learned * men are in a great doubt what to think of her. Some make her a Saint, and inspired by Gods Spirit, whereby she discovered strange secrets and foretold things to come. She had ever an old * woman which went with her, and tutoured her; and 'tis suspicious, seeing this clock could not go without that rusty wheel, that these things might be done by confederacie, though some more uncharitable conceive them to be done by Satan himself.

> * Gersonin the book which he wrote of her, after long discussing the point leaves it uncertain, but is rather charitably inclined.
> * Serres, pag. 325.

Two customes she had which can by no way be defended. One was her constant going in mans clothes, flatly against Scripture: yea mark all the miracles in Gods Word, wherein though mens estates be often chang'd (poore to rich, bond to free, sick to sound, yea dead to living) yet we reade of no old Æson made young, no woman Iphis turn'd to a man, or man Tiresias to a woman; but as for their age or sex, where nature places them, there they stand, and miracle it self will not remove them. Utterly unlawfull therefore was this Joans behaviour, as an occasion to lust; and our English Writers say that when she was to be condemned she confess'd her self to be with * child to prolong her life; but being reprived seven moneths for the triall

> Pol. Virgil. ut prius.

triall thereof, it was found false. But grant her honest: though she did not burn herself, yet she might kindle others, and provoke them to wantonnesse.

Besides, she shaved her hair in the fashion of a *Fri-er, against Gods expresse word, it being also a Solecisme in nature, all women being born votaries, and the veil of their long hair minds them of their obedience they naturally owe to man: yea, without this comely ornament of hair, their most glorious beauty appears as deformed, as the sunne would be prodigious without beams. Herein she had a smack of Monkery, which makes all the rest the more suspicious, as being sent to maintain as well the Friers as the French Crown. And if we survey all the pretended miracles of that age, we shall find what tune soever they sung, still they had something in the close in the favour of Friers, though brought in as by the by, yet perchance chiefly intended, so that the whole sentence was made for the parenthesis.

*Gerson.*

We will close the different opinions which severall Authours have of her with this Epitaph,

> *Here lies Joan of Arc, the which*
> *Some count saint, and some count witch;*
> *Some count man, and something more;*
> *Some count maid, and some a whore:*
> *Her life's in question, wrong, or right;*
> *Her death's in doubt, by laws, or might.*
> *Oh innocence take heed of it,*
> *How thou too near to guilt dost sit.*
> *( Mean time France a wonder saw,*
> *A woman rule 'gainst Salique Law. )*
> *But, Reader, be content to stay*
> *Thy censure, till the Judgement-day:*
> *Then shalt thou know, and not before,*
> *Whether Saint, Witch, Man, Maid, or Whore.*

Some conceive that the English conquests, being come to the verticall point, would have decayed of themselves,

themselves, had this woman never been set up, which now reaps the honour hereof as her action: Though thus a very child may seem to turn the waves of the sea with his breath, if casually blowing on them at that very instant when the tide is to turn of it self. Sure after her death the French went on victoriously, and wonne all from the English, partly by their valour, but more by our dissensions; for then began the cruell warres betwixt the Houses of York and Lancaster, till the Red rose might become White, by losing so much bloud, and the White rose Red by shedding it.

## Chap. 6.

### The *Atheist*.

THe word *Atheist* is of a very large extent: every Polytheist is in effect an Atheist, for he that multiplies a Deitie, annihilates it; and he that divides it, destroyes it.

But amongst the heathen we may observe that whosoever sought to withdraw people from their idolatry, was presently indited and arraign'd of Atheisme. If any Philosopher saw God through their Gods, this dust was cast in his eyes, for being more quick-sighted then others, that presently he was condemn'd for an Atheist; and thus Socrates the Pagan Martyr was put to death * ὡς Ἄθεος. At this day three sorts of Atheists are extant in the world:

* *Justin. Martyr secund. Apolog. pro Christian. pag. 56.*

1 In life and conversation. Psal. 10. 4. *God is not in all his thoughts*; not that he thinks there is no God, but thinks not there is a God, never minding or heeding him in the whole course of his life and actions.

2 In will and desire. Such could wish there were no God, or devil, as thieves would have no judge nor jaylour; *Quod metuunt periisse expetunt.*

3 In judgement and opinion. Of the former two sorts of Atheists, there are more in the world then are generally thought; of this latter, more are thought to be, then there are, a contemplative Atheist being very rare, such as were *Diagoras, Protagoras, Lucian, and Theodorus, who though carrying God in his name was an Atheist in his opinion. Come we to see by what degrees a man may climbe up to this height of Profanenesse. And we will suppose him to be one living in wealth and prosperity, which more disposeth men to Atheisme then adversity: For affliction mindeth men of a Deity, as those which are pinched will cry, *O Lord*: but much outward happinesse abused occasioneth men, as wise Agur observeth, *to deny God, and say, who is the Lord.*

* *August. tom. 7. lib. 3. contra Petilianum, c. 1. David cùm dicit,* Stultus dixit in corde, *&c. videtur Diagoram predixisse.*

*First he quarrels at the diversities of religions in the world:* complaining how great Clerks dissent in their judgements, which makes him scepticall in all opinions: Whereas such differences should not make men carelesse to have any, but carefull to have the best religion.

Maxime 1

*He loveth to maintain Paradoxes, and to shut his eyes against the beams of a known truth;* not onely for discourse, which might be permitted: for as no cloth can be woven except the woof and the warp be cast crosse one to another, so discourse will not be maintained without some opposition for the time. But our encliningatheist goes further, engaging his affections in disputes, even in such matters where the supposing them wounds piety, but the positive maintaining them stabs it to the heart.

2

*He scoffs and makes sport at sacred things.* This by degrees abates the reverence of religion, and ulcers mens hearts with profanenesse. The Popish Proverb well understood hath a truth in it, *Never dog bark'd against the Crucifix, but he ran mad.*

3

**4**    *Hence he proceeds to take exception at Gods Word.* He keeps a register of many difficult places of Scripture, not that he desires satisfaction therein, but delights to puzzle Divines therewith, and counts it a great conquest when he hath posed them. Unnecessary questions out of the Bible are his most necessary study; & he is more curious to know where Lazarus his soul was the foure dayes he lay in the grave, then carefull to provide for his own soul when he shall be dead. Thus is it just with God that they who will not feed on the plain meat of his Word, should be choked with the bones thereof. But his principall delight is to sound the alarum, and to set severall places of Scripture to fight one against another, betwixt which there is a seeming, and he would make a reall, contradiction.

**5**    *Afterwards he grows so impudent as to deny the Scripture it self.* As Sampson being fastned by a web to a pin, carried away both web and pin; so if any urge our Atheist with arguments from Scripture, and tie him to the Authority of Gods Word, he denies both reason and Gods Word, to which the reason is fastened.

**6**    *Hence he proceeds to deny God himself.* First in his Administration; then in his Essence. What else could be expected but that he should bite at last, who had snarl'd so long? First he denies Gods ordering of sublunarie matters; *Tush doth the Lord see, or is there knowledge in the most Highest?* making him a maimed Deity, without an eye of Providence or an arm of Power, and at most restraining him onely to matters above the clouds. But he that dares to confine the King of heaven, will soon after endeavour to depose him, and fall at last flatly to deny him.

**7**    *He furnisheth himself with an armoury of arguments to fight against his own conscience*: Some taken from

    1. The impunity and outward happinesse of wicked men: as the heathen \* Poet, whose verses for me shall passe unenglished.

*Esse*

> *Esse Deos credamne ? fidem jurata fefellit,*  
> *Et facies illi, quæ fuit ante, manet.*

<small>* Ovid. lib. 3. Amor. Eleg. 3.</small>

And no wonder if an Atheist breaks his neck thereat, whereat the foot of David himself did almost *slip, when he saw the prosperity of the wicked; whom God onely reprives for punishment hereafter.

<small>* Psal. 73. 2, 3.</small>

2. From the afflictions of the godly, whilest indeed God onely tries their faith and patience. As Absalom complain'd of his Father Davids government, that none were deputed to redresse peoples grievances; so he objects that none righteth the wrongs of Gods people, and thinks (proud dust) the world would be better steered if he were the Pilot thereof.

3. From the delaying of the day of Judgement, with those mockers 2. Peter 3. Whose objections the Apostle fully answereth. And in regard of his own particular the Atheist hath as little cause to rejoyce at the deferring of the day of Judgement, as the Thief hath reason to be glad, that the Assizes be put off, who is to be tryed, and may be executed before, at the Quarter-sessions: So death may take our Atheist off before the day of Judgement come.

With these and other arguments he struggles with his own conscience, and long in vain seeks to conquer it, even fearing that Deity he flouts at, and dreading that God whom he denies. And as that famous Athenian souldier *Cynegirus catching hold of one of the enemies ships held it first with his right hand, and when that was cut off, with his left, and when both were cut off, yet still kept it with his teeth; so the conscience of our Atheist, though he bruise it, and beat it, and maim it never so much, still keeps him by the teeth, still feeding and gnawing upon him, torturing and tormenting him with thoughts of a Deity, which the other desires to suppresse.

<small>* Justin. lib. 2.</small>

8

*At last he himself is utterly overthrown by conquering his own conscience.* God in justice takes from him the light which he thrust from himself, and delivers him up to a seared conscience, and a reprobate mind, whereby hell takes possession of him. The Apostle saith, Acts 17. 27. That a man may feel God in his works: But now our Atheist hath a dead palsey, is past all sense, and cannot perceive God who is everywhere presented unto him. It is most strange, yet most true, which is reported, that the armes of the Duke of Rohan in France, which are *fusills* or *lozenges*, are to be seen in the wood or stones throughout all his countrey, so that break a stone in the middle, or lop a bough of a tree, and one shall behold the grain thereof (by some secret cause in Nature)* diamonded or streaked in the fashion of a lozenge: yea the very same in effect is observed in England: for the resemblances of starres, the armes of the worshipfull family of the Shugburies in Warwickshire, are found in the * stones within their own mannour of Shugbury. But what shall we say? The armes of the God of heaven, namely Power, Wisdome, and Goodnesse, are to be seen in every creature in the world, even from worms to men, and yet our Atheist will not acknowledge them, but ascribes them either to Chance (but could a blind painter limme such curious pictures) or else to Nature, which is a mere slight of the devil to conceal God from men, by calling him after another name; for what is *natura naturans* but God himself?

* *Because of these naturall forms in wood and stone, it seems that from thence the Dukes assum'd their armes.*
* *Cambd. Brit. in Warwickshire.*

9

*His death commonly is most miserable*: either burnt, as Diagoras, or eaten up with lice, as * Pherecydes, or devoured by dogs as Lucian, or thunder-shot and turn'd to ashes, as Olimpius. However descending impenitent into hell, there he is Atheist no longer, but hath as much religion as the devil, *to confesse God and tremble*:

*Paul. Diacon. lib. 15.*

    *Nullus in inferno est Atheos, ante fuit.*
    On earth were Atheists many,
    In hell there is not any.

All speak truth, when they are on the rack; but it is a wofull thing to be hells Convert. And there we leave the Atheist, having dwelt the longer on his Character, because that speech of worthy Mr. * Greenham deserves to be heeded, *That Atheisme in England is more to be feared then Popery.*

* *In his grave Counsell, p. 3.*

To give an instance of a speculative Atheist, is both hard and dangerous: hard; for we cannot see mens speculations otherwise then as they cloth themselves visible in their actions, some Atheisticall speeches being not sufficient evidence to convict the speaker an Atheist. Dangerous; for what satisfaction can I make to their memories, if I challenge any of so foul a crime wrongfully? We may more safely insist on an Atheist in life and conversation; and such a one was he whom we come to describe.

## Chap. 7.
## The life of Cesar Borgia.

Cesar Borgia was base-son to Rhoderick Borgia, otherwise called Pope Alexander the sixth. This Alexander was the * first of the Popes who openly owned his bastards; & whereas his Predecessours (counting fig-leaves better then nothing to cover their nakednesse) disguised them under the names of Nephews and God-sonnes, he was such a savage in his lust as nakedly to acknowledge his base children, and especially this Cesar Borgia, being like his Father in the swarthinesse of the complexion of his soul.

* *Guicciard. History of Italy lib. 1. pag. 10.*

His Father first made him a Cardinall, that thereby his shoulders might be enabled to bear as much Church preferment as he could load upon him. But Borgia's active spirit disliked the profession, and was *ashamed of the Gospel*, which had more cause to be ashamed of him; wherefore he quickly got a dispensation to uncardinall himself.

The next hindrance that troubled his high designes was, that his elder brother, the Duke of Candia, stood betwixt him and preferment. It is reported also that these two brothers justled together in their * incest with their own sister Lucretia, one as famous for her whoredomes, as her namesake had * formerly been for her chastity. The throne and the bed cannot severally abide partners, much lesse both meeting together as here they did. Wherefore Cesar Borgia took order that his brother was kill'd one night as he rode alone in the city of Rome, and his body cast into Tyber; and now he himself stood without competitour in his fathers and sisters affection.

*Idem lib. 3. pag. 179.*

*Liv. lib. 1.*

His father was infinitely ambitious to advance him, as intending not onely to create him a Duke, but also to create a Dukedome for him, which seemed very difficult if not impossible; for he could neither lengthen the land, nor lessen the sea in Italie, and petty Princes therein were already crouded so thick, there was not any room for any more. However the Pope by fomenting the discords betwixt the French and Spanish about the kingdome of Naples, and by embroyling all the Italian States in civill dissensions, out of their breaches pick'd forth a large Principality for his sonne, managed in this manner.

There is a fair and fruitfull Province in Italie, called Romania, parcelled into severall States, all holding as feodaries from the Pope, but by small pensions, and those seldome paid. They were bound also not to serve in armes against the Church, which old tie they little regarded, and lesse observed, as conceiving time had fretted it asunder; souldiers generally more weighing his gold that entertaineth them, then the cause or enemy against whom they fight. Pope Alexander set his sonne Borgia to reduce that countrey to the Churches jurisdiction, but indeed to subject it to his own absolute hereditary Dominion. This in short time

# Chap. 7. *The life of* Cesar Borgia. 385

time he * effected, partly by the assistance of the French King, whose pensioner he was (and by a French title made Duke Ualentinois) and partly by the effectuall aid of the Ursines, a potent Family in Italie.

*\* Guicciard. lib. 4. pag. 237.*

But afterward the Ursines too late were sensible. of their errour herein, and grew suspicious of his greatnesse. For they in helping him to conquer so many petty States, gathered the severall twigs, bound them into a rod, and put it into his hands to beat them therewith. Whereupon they began by degrees to withdraw their help, which Borgia perceived, and having by flattery and fair promises got the principall of their Family into his hands, he put them* all to the sword. For he was perfect in the devilish art of dealing an ill turn, doing it so suddenly his enemies should not heare of him before, and so soundly, that he should never heare of them afterwards, either striking alwayes surely, or not at all.

*\* Machiavill in his Prince, cap. 7.*

And now he thought to cast away his crutches, and stand on his own legs, rendring himself absolute, without being beholden to the French King or any other: Having wholly conquer'd Romania, he cast his eyes on Hetruria, and therein either wan to submission or compliance most of the cities, an earnest of his future finall conquest, had not the unexpected death of his father Pope Alexander prevented him.

This Alexander with his sonne Cesar Borgia intended to poyson some rich Cardinalls, to which purpose a flagon of poysoned wine was prepared: But through the * errour of a servant, not privy to the project, the Pope himself and Borgia his sonne drank thereof, which cost the former his life, and the other a long languishing sicknesse.

*\* Guicciard. l. 6. pag. 307.*

This Cesar Borgia once bragg'd to Machiavill, that he had so cunningly contrived his plots, as to warrant himself against all events. If his father should die first, he had made himself master of such a way, that by the

D d d                    strength

strength of his party in the city of Rome, and conclave of Cardinalls, he could chuse what Pope he pleased, so from him to get assurance of this province of Romania to make it hereditary to himself. And if (which was improbable) Nature should crosse her hands, so that he should die before his father, yet even then he had chalked out such a course as would ensure his conquest to his posterity: so that with this politick dilemma he thought himself able to dispute against heaven it self.

But (what he afterwards complained of) he never expected that at the same time, wherein his father should die, he himself should also lie desperately sick, disenabled to prosecute his designes, till one unexpected counterblast of Fortune ruffled yea blew away all his projects so curiously plaited. Thus three aces chance often not to rub; and Politicians think themselves to have stopp'd every small cranny, when they have left a whole doore open for divine providence to undo all which they have done.

The Cardinalls proceed to the choice of a new Pope, whilest Borgia lay sick abed, much bemoaning himself; for all others (had they the command of all April showrs) could not bestow on drop of pity upon him. Pius the third was first chosen Pope, answering his name, being a devout man (such black swans seldome swim in Tyber) but the chair of Pestilence choked him within twenty six dayes, and in his room Julius was chosen, or rather his greatnesse chose himself, a sworn enemy to Cesar Borgia, who still lay under the Physicians hands, and had no power to oppose the election, or to strengthen his new-got Dukedome of Romania: the state of his body was to be preferred before the body of his state, and he lay striving to keep life, not to make a Pope. Yea the operation of this poyson made him vomit up the Dukedome of Romania which he had swallowed before, and whilest

# Chap. 7    *The life of* Cesar Borgia.    387

whilest he lay sick the States and cities therein recovered their own liberties formerly enjoyed.

Indeed this disease made Borgia lose his nails, that he could never after scratch to do any mischief; and being banished Italie, he fled into Navarre, where he was obscurely kill'd in a tumultuous insurrection.

He was a man master in the art of dissembling, never looking the same way he rowed; extremely lustfull, never sparing to tread hen and chickens. At the taking of Capua, where he assisted the French, he reserved * fourty of the fairest Ladies to be abused by his own wantonnesse. And the prodigality of his lust had long before his death made him bankrupt of all the moysture in his body, if his Physicians had not dayly repaired the decayes therein. He exactly knew the operations of all hot and cold poysons, which would surprise nature on a sudden, and which would weary it out with a long siege. He could contract a hundred toads into one drop, and cunningly infuse the same into any pleasant liquour, as the Italians have poysoning at their fingers ends. By a fig ( *which restored Hezekiahs* * *life* ) he took away the lives of many. In a word, if he was not a practicall Atheist, I know not who was.

If any desire to know more of his badnesse, let them reade Machiavills Prince, where Borgia is brought in as an * instance of all vilany. And though he deserves to be hiss'd out of Christendome, who will open his mouth in the defence of Machiavills precepts, yet some have dared to defend his person; so that he in his Book shews not what Princes should be, but what then they were, intending that work, not for a glasse for future Kings to dresse themselves by, but onely therein to present the monstrous face of the Politicians of that Age. Sure he who is a devil in this book, is a Saint * in all the rest; and those that knew him, * witnesse him to be of honest life and manners: so that

* *Idem, lib.* 5. *pag.* 250.

* 2. *Kings* 20. 7.

* *Nunquam verebor in exemplum Valentinum subjicere, Machiavel Prince, cap.* 13. *pag.* 73.

* *His notes on Livy, but especially his Florentine History favours of Religion.*
* *Boissardus part.* 3. *Iconum virorum illustrium.*

D d d 2         that

that which hath sharpned the pens of many against him, is his giving so many cleanly wipes to the foul noses of the Pope and Italian Prelacy.

## Chap. 8.

### The Hypocrite.

BY *Hypocrite* we understand such a one as doth (Isaiah 32. 6.) *practise hypocrisie*, make a trade or work of dissembling: For otherwise, * *Hypocriseorum macula carere, aut paucorum est aut nullorum.* The best of Gods children have a smack of hypocrisie.

* *Hieronym. lib. 2. contra Pelag. & August in eadem verba, Serm. 59. de Tempore*
**Maxime** 1.

*An Hypocrite is himself both the archer and the mark, in all actions shooting at his own praise or profit.* And therefore he doth all things that they may be seen: What with others is held a principall point in Law, is his main Maxime in Divinity, To have good witnesse. Even fasting it self is meat and drink to him, whilest others behold it.

2. *In the outside of religion he out-shines a sincere Christian.* Guilt cups glitter more then those of massie gold, which are seldome burnish'd. Yea, well may the Hypocrite afford gaudy facing, who cares not for any lining; brave it in the shop, that hath nothing in the ware-house. Nor is it a wonder if in outward service he out-strips Gods servants, who out-doeth Gods command by will-worship, giving God more then he requires, though not what most he requires, I mean, his heart.

3. *His vizard is commonly pluckt off in this world.* Sincerity is an entire thing in it self: Hypocrisie consists of severall pieces cunningy closed together; and sometimes the Hypocrite is smote(as Ahab with an arrow,1.Kings 22. 34.) betwixt the joynts of his armour, and so is mortally wounded in his reputation. Now by these shrewd signes a dissembler is often discovered: First,
heavie

heavie censuring of others for light faults: secondly, boasting of his own goodnesse: thirdly, the unequall beating of his pulse in matters of pietie, hard, strong and quick, in publick actions; weak, soft and dull, in private matters: fourthly, shrinking in persecution; for painted faces cannot abide to come nigh the fire.

*Yet sometimes he goes to the grave neither detected nor suspected.* If Masters in their art, and living in peaceable times wherein pietie and prosperity do not fall out, but agree well together. Maud, mother to King Henry the second, being besieged in * Winchester castle, counterfeited herself to be dead, and so was carried out in a coffin whereby she escaped. Another time being besieged at * Oxford in a cold winter, with wearing white apparell she got away in the snow undiscovered. Thus some Hypocrites by dissembling mortification that they are dead to the world, and by professing a snow-like purity in their conversations, escape all their life time undiscerned by mortall eyes.

* *Cambd. Brit. in Hantshire.*

* *Matth. Paris in Anno Dom. 1141.*

*By long dissembling piety he deceives himself at last:* Yea, he may grow so infatuated as to conceive himself no dissembler but a sincere Saint. A scholar was so possessed with his lively personating of King Richard the third, in a Colledge-Comedy, that ever after he was transported with a royall humour in his large expences, which brought him to beggery, though he had great preferment. Thus the Hypocrite by long acting the part of piety, at last believes himself really to be such an one, whom at first he did but counterfeit.

*God here knows, and hereafter will make Hypocrites known to the whole world.* Ottocar King of Bohemia refused to do homage to Rodulphus the first, Emperour, till at last, chastised with warre, he was content to do him homage privately in a tent; which tent was so contrived by the* Emperours servants, that by drawing one cord, it was all taken away, and so Ottocar presented on his knees doing his homage, to the view of three Armies

* *Pantaleon in vita Rodulph. Imperat lib. de Illustrib. Germ. part.2.285.*

in presence. Thus God at last shall uncase the closest dissembler to the sight of men angels and devils, having removed all veils and pretences of piety: no goat in a sheepskin shall steal on his right hand at the last day of judgement.

## Chap. 9.
### The life of Jehu.

Jehu the sonne of Jehosaphat, the sonne of Nimshi, was one of an active spirit, and therefore employed to confound the house of Ahab; for God, when he means to shave clear, chooses a razour with a sharp edge, and never sendeth a slug on a message that requireth haste.

A sonne of the Prophets sent by Elisha privately anointed him King at Ramoth Gilead, whereupon he was proclaimed King by the consent of the army. Surely God sent also an invisible messenger to the souls of his fellow-captains, and anointed their hearts with the oyl of Subjection, as he did Jehu's head with the oyl of Sovereignty.

Secrecie and celerity are the two wheels of great actions. Jehu had both: he marched to Jezreel faster then Fame could flie, whose wings he had clipt by stopping all intelligence, that so at once he might be seen and felt of his enemies. In the way meeting with Jehoram and Ahaziah, he conjoyned them in their deaths who consorted together in idolatrie. The corps of Jehoram he orders to be cast into Nabaoths vineyard, a garden of herbs royally dung'd, and watered with bloud.

Next he revengeth Gods Prophets on cruell Jezabell, whose wicked carcase was devoured by dogs to a small reversion, as if a head that plotted, & hands that practis'd so much mischief, & feet so swift to shed bloud were not meat good enough for dogs to eat. Then by a letter he
commands

mands the heads of Ahabs seventy sonnes (their Guardians turning their executioners) whose heads being laid on two heaps at the gate of Jezreel served for two soft pillows for Jehu to sleep sweetly upon, having all those corrivalls to the Crown taken away.

The Priests of Baal follow after. With a pretty wile he fetches them all into the temple of their Idole, where having ended their sacrifice, they themselves were sacrificed. However I dare not acquit Jehu herein. In Holy Fraud I like the Christian but not the sirname thereof, and wonder how any can marry these two together in the same action, seeing surely the parties were never agreed. This I dare say, Be it unjust in Jehu, it was just with God, that the worshippers of a false God should be deceived with a feigned worship.

Hitherto I like Jehu as well as Josiah; his zeal blazed as much: But having now got the Crown, he discovers himself a dissembling Hypocrite. It was an ill signe when he said to Jonadab the sonne of Rechab, *Come with me, and see my zeal for the Lord.* Bad inviting guests to feed their eyes on our goodnesse. But Hypocrites rather then they will lose a drop of praise will lick it up with their own tongue.

Before, he had dissembled with Baal, now he counterfeits with God. *He took no heed to walk in the way of the Lord God of Israel with all his heart:* formerly his sword had two edges, one cut for Gods glory, the other for his own preferment. He that before drove so furiously, whilest his private ends whipt on his horses, now will not go a footpace in Gods commandments, *He departed not from the golden calves in Dan and Bethel.*

I know what Flesh will object, that this State-sinne Jehu must commit to maintain his kingdome: for the lions of gold did support the throne of Solomon, but the calves of gold the throne of Jeroboam and his Successours. Should he suffer his Subjects to go up to Jerusalem

*Exod. 34.23.* salem *thrice a yeare* ( as the Law * of Moses commanded)this would un-King him in effect, as leaving him no able Subjects to command. And as one in the heathen Poet complains,

*Tres sumus imbelles numero, sine viribus uxor,*
*Laertesque senex, Telemachusque puer.*

Three weaklings we, a wife for warre too mild,
Laertes old, Telemachus a child.

So thrice a yeare should Jehu onely be King over such an impotent company of old men, women, and children. Besides, it was to be feared that the ten Tribes going to Jerusalem to worship, where they fetch'd their God, would also have their King.

But Faith will answer, that God that built Jehu's throne without hands, could support it without buttresses, or being beholden to idolatry: And therefore herein Jehu, who would needs piece out Gods providence with his own carnall policie, was like a foolish greedy gamester, who having all the game in his own hand steals a needlesse card to assure himself of winning the stake, and thereby loses all. For this deep diver was drown'd in his own policie, and Hazael King of Syria was raised up by God to trouble and molest them. Yet God rewarded him with a lease of the Kingdome of foure successive lives, who had he been sincere would have assured him of a Crown here and hereafter.

CHAP. 10.

## Chap. 10.

## The Heretick.

IT is very difficult accurately to define him. Amongst the Heathen *Atheist* was, and amongst Christians *Heretick* is the disgracefull word of course, always cast upon those who dissent from the predominant current of the time. Thus those who in matters of opinion varied from the * Popes copie the least hair-stroke, are condemned for Hereticks. Yea, Virgilius Bishop of Saltzburg was branded with that censure for maintaining that there were * Antipodes opposite to the then known world. It may be, as Alexander, hearing the Philosophers dispute of more worlds, wept that he had conquered no part of them; so it grieved the Pope that these Antipodes were not subject to his jurisdiction, which much incensed his Holinesse against that strange opinion. We will branch the description of an Heretick into these three parts.

* Hìc videtur quòd omnis qui non obedit statutis Romanæ sedis sit Hæreticus, *Glossa in 6. nulli dist.* 19. *in verbo* Prostratus.
* *Joh. Avent. lib.* 3. *Annial. Boior*

First, he is one that formerly hath been of the true Church: *They went out from us, but they were not of us.* These afterwards prove more offensive to the Church then very Pagans; as the English-Irish, descended anciently of English Parentage (be it spoken with the more shame to them, and sorrow to us) turning wild become worse enemies to our Nation then the Native Irish themselves.

*1.John 2.19.

2. Maintaining a Fundamentall errour. Every scratch in the hand is not a stab to the heart; nor doth every false opinion make a Heretick.

3. With obstinacy. Which is the dead flesh, making the green wound of an errour fester into the old soare of an Heresie.

It matters not much *what manner of person he hath.* If beautifull, perchance the more attractive of feminine followers:

*Maxime* 1.

lowers: If deformed, so that his body is as odde as his opinions, he is the more properly entitled to the reputation of *crooked Saint.*

2. *His naturall parts are quick and able.* Yet he that shall ride on a winged horse to tell him thereof, shall but come too late to bring him stale news of what he knew too well before.

3. *Learning is necessary in him if he trades in a criticall errour:* but if he onely broches dregs, and deals in some dull sottish opinion, a trovell will serve as well as a pencill to daub on such thick course colours. Yea in some Heresies deep studying is so uselesse, that the first thing they learn, is to inveigh against all learning.

4. *However some smattering in the originall tongues will do well.* On occasion he will let flie whole vollies of Greek and Hebrew words, whereby he not onely amazeth his ignorant Auditours, but also in conferences daunteth many of his opposers, who (though in all other learning farre his superiours) may perchance be conscious of want of skill in those languages, whilest the Heretick hereby gains credit to his cause and person.

5. *His behaviour is seemingly very pious and devout.* How foul soever the postern and backdoore be, the gate opening to the street is swept and garnished, and his outside adorned with pretended austerity.

6. *He is extremely proud and discontented with the times,* quarrelling that many beneath him in piety are above him in place. This pride hath caused many men which otherwise might have been *shining lights* prove smoaking firebrands in the Church.

7. *Having first hammered the heresie in himself, he then falls to seducing of others:* so hard it is for one to have the itch and not to scratch. Yea Babylon her self will alledge, that *for Sions sake she will not hold her peace.* The necessity of propogating the truth is errours plea to divulge her falshoods. Men, as naturally they desire to know, so they desire what they know should be known.

*If*

# Chap. 10. *The Heretick.* 395

8. *If challenged to a private dispute, his impudence bears him out.* He counts it the onely errour to confesse he hath erred. His face is of brasse, which may be said either ever or never to blush. In disputing his *Modus* is *sine modo*; and as if all figures (even in Logick) were magicall, he neglects all forms of reasoning, counting that the onely Syllogisme which is his conclusion.

9. *He slights any Synod if condemning his opinions*; esteeming the decisions thereof no more then the forfeits in a barbers shop, where a Gentlemans pleasure is all the obligation to pay, and none are bound except they will bind themselves.

10. *Sometimes he comes to be put to death for his obstinacy.* Indeed some charitable Divines have counted it inconsistent with the lenity of the Gospel, which is to expect and endeavour the amendment of all, to put any to death for their false opinions; and we reade of S. Paul (though the Papists paint him always with a sword) that he onely came *with a rod*. However the * mildest Authours allow that the Magistrate may inflict capitall punishment on Hereticks, in cases of

*Gerards Common places de Magistrat. Polit. p. 1047.

1. Sedition against the State wherein he lives. And indeed such is the sympathy betwixt Church and Commonwealth that there are few Heresies, except they be purely speculative (and so I may say have heads without hands or any practicall influence) but in time the violent maintainers of them may make a dangerous impression in the State.
2. Blasphemy against God, and those points of religion which are awfully to be believed.

For either of these our Heretick sometimes willingly undergoes death, and then in the Calendar of his own conceit he canonizeth himself for a Saint, yea a Martyr.

E e e 2     Chap. 11.

## Chap. II.

### The rigid Donatists.

*Anno Domini 331.*

THe Donatists were so called from a double Donatus, whereof the one planted the sect, the other water'd it, & the devil by Gods permission gave the increase. The elder Donatus being one of tolerable parts, and intolerable pride, rais'd a Schisme in Carthage against good Cecilian the Bishop there, whom he loaded unjustly with many crimes, which he was not able to prove; and vexed with this disgrace he thought to right his credit by wronging religion, and so began the * heresie of Donatists.

*\* Augustin. ad Quod vult Deum.*

His most dominative tenet was, that the Church was perished from the face of the earth, the reliques thereof onely remaining in his party. I instance the rather on this Heresie, because the reviving thereof is the new disease of our times. One * Vibius in Rome was so like unto Pompey, *ut permutato statu Pompeius in illo, & ille in Pompeio salutari possit*: Thus the Anabaptists of our dayes, and such as are Anabaptistically inclin'd, in all particulars resemble the old Donatists, abating onely that difference which is necessarily required to make them alike.

*\* Valer. Max. lib. 9. cap. 15.*

The epithet of *rigid* I therefore do adde, to seperate the Donatists from themselves, who seperated themselves from all other Christians. For there were two principall sides of them: first, the Rogatists, from Rogatus their teacher, to whom S. Augustine beareth witnesse that *they had zeal but not according to knowledge*. These were pious people for their lives, hating bloudy practices, though erroneous in their doctrine. The learned * Fathers of that age count them part of the true Church, and their brethren, though they themselves disclaim'd any such brotherhood with other Christians.

*\* Ipsum Fraternitatis nomen utcunque Donatistis fastidiosum, est tamen orthodoxis erga ipsos Donatistas necessarium, Optat. lib. 3. init.*

Christians. Oh the sacred violence of such worthy mens charity in plucking those to them which thrust themselves away! But there was another sort of Jesuited Donatists, as I may say, whom they called *Circumcellions*, though as little reason can be given of their * name as of their opinions, whom we principally intend at this time.

Their number in short time grew not onely to be considerable but terrible: their tenet was plausible and winning; and that Faith is easily wrought which teacheth men to believe well of themselves. From Numidia, where they began, they overspread Africa, Spain, France, Italie and Rome it self. We find not any in Brittain, where * Pelagianisme mightily reigned: either because God in his goodnesse would not have one countrey at the same time visited with a double plague, or else because this infection was to come to this Iland in after-ages, furbished up under a new name.

Their greatest increase was under Julian the Emperour. This Apostate next to no religion loved the worst religion best, and was a profess'd friend to all foes of goodnesse. The Donatists, being punished under former Christian Emperours, repaired to him for succour, not caring whether it was an Olive or a Bramble they fled to, so be it afforded them shelter. They extoll'd him for such a godly man (flattery and false doctrine go ever together) *with whom alone* * *justice did remain*, and he restored them their good Churches again, & armed them with many priviledges against Christians. Hereupon they raised a cruell persecution, killing many men in the very Churches, murthering women and infants, defiling virgins, or ravishing them rather, for consent onely defiles. God keep us from standing in the way where blind zeal is to passe, for it will trample down all before it, and mercy shall as soon be found at the hands of prevailing cowards. What the

* S. *August*. in *Psal*. 132. *quia circum cel as vagantur, count them so called*; which is rather his *Allusion* then the true *Etymologie*.

* Sr H. Spelman *Councells*, pag. 446.

* *Quòd apud eum solum justitia locum habeiet*, Aug. contra literas Petil. lib. 2. cap. 97.

Anabaptists

Anabaptists did in Germany, we know; what they would do here, had they power, God knows. The best security we have they will do no harm is because they cannot.

We come to set down some of their principall opinions: I say, Principall; for at last they did enterfere with all Hereticks, Arians, Macedonians, &c. ignorant zeal is too blind to go right, and too active to stand still: yea all errours are of kinne, at the farthest but cousens once removed; and when men have once left the truth, their onely quiet home, they will take up their lodging under any opinion which hath the least shadow of probability. We will also set down some of their reasons, and how they torture Scripture with violent interpretations to wrest from it a confession on their side, yet all in vain.

### First Position.

That the true Church was perished from the face of the earth, the remnants thereof being onely *in parte Donati*, in that * part of Africa where Donatus and his followers were. The Anabaptists in like manner stifle Gods Church by crowding it into their corner, confining the monarchy of Christ in the Gospel unto their own toparchy, and having a quarrell to the words in the Creed, *Catholique Church*.

*\* August. lib 2. contra Crescon. cap. 37.*

### The Donatists Reasons.

It is said, Canticles. 1. 7. *Tell me, O thou whom my soul loveth, where thou feedest, where thou makest thy flocks to rest in the South.* By this the Donatists are meant: Africa wherein they lived was in the South.

### Confutation.

An argument drawn from an * allegorie is weak, except all the obscurities therein be first explained. Besides, Africa Cesariensis (where the Donatists were) was much more West then South from Judea. But Gods Church cannot be contracted to the Chapell of Donatus, to which God himself (the truest surveyour) alloweth

*\* Quis non impudentissimè nitatur aliquid in allegoria positum pro se interpretari, nisi habeat & manifesta testimonia quorum lumine illustrentur obscura, Aug. Tom. 2. Epist. 48. ad Vincent.*

# Chap. 11. *The rigid Donatists.* 399

alloweth larger bounds, Psalm. 2. 8. *Ask of me, and I will give thee the Heathen for thine inheritance, and the uttermost parts of the earth for thy possession.* Now the restrainers of the Church to a small place (as much as in them lies) falsifie Gods promise and shorten Christs portion. Many other *places speak the large extent of the Gospel, Gen. 22. 17. Gen. 28. 14. Psal. 72. 8. &c.

*Optat. Milev. lib. 2. & Aug. contra liter. Petil. cap. 6, 7, 8.*

### Second Position.

That their Church consisted of an holy company, pure and undefiled indeed. Thus also the Anabaptists brag of their holinesse, as if nothing else were required to make men pure but a conceit that they are so. Sure had they no other fault but want of charity, their hands could not be clean who throw so much dirt on other mens faces.

### Reasons.

It is said, Ephes. 5. 27. *That Christ might present to himself a glorious Church, without spot, or wrinkle, or any such thing, but that it should be holy and without blemish*: which the Donatists appropriate to themselves.

### Confutation.

This glorious presentation of the Church is * performed in the world to come. Here it consisteth of sinners (who had rather confesse their wrinkles then paint them) and had need to pray dayly, *And forgive us our trespasses.*

* *Aug. ut prius adVincentium, & epist. 50. ad Bonifac.*

### Third Position.

That mixt Communions were infectious, and the pious promiscuously receiving with the profane are polluted thereby. Heare the Anabaptizing sing the same note, *By*profane and ignorant persons coming to the Lords table, others also that communicate with them are guilty of the same profanation.*

* *Protestation protested, p. 14.*

### Reasons.

Because severall places of Scripture commend, yea command, a separation from them. Jerem. 15. 19. *Take forth the pretious from the vile.* 2. Cor. 6. 17. *Be ye separate,*

*parate and touch no unclean thing.* 2. Theſſ. 3. 6. *Withdraw your ſelves from every brother that walketh diſorderly.* 1. Cor. 5. 7. *Purge out therefore the old leven,* &c.

### Confutation.

In theſe and the like places two things are enjoyned: firſt, a ſeparation from intimate familiarity with profane perſons; ſecondly, a ſeparation from their vices and wickedneſſe, by deteſting and diſclaiming them: but neither civill State-ſociety, nor publick Church-communion is hereby prohibited. By *purging out the old leven,* Church-cenſures are meant, to excommunicate the openly profane. But that mixt Communions pollute not, appears, becauſe S. Paul ſaith, 1. Cor. 11. 28. *But let a man examine himſelf, and ſo let him eat of that bread,* &c. but enjoyns not men to examine others; which was neceſſary if bad Communicants did defile. It neither makes the cheere or welcome the worſe to ſit next to him at Gods table who wants a wedding-garment, for he that touches his perſon, but diſclaims his practices, is as farre from him, as the Eaſt from the Weſt, yea as heaven from hell. In bodily diſeaſes one may be infected without his knowledge, againſt his will: not ſo in ſpirituall contagions, where * *acceditur ad vitium corruptionis vitio conſenſionis,* and none can be infected againſt their consent.

<small>*Auguſt. contr. Don. poſt Coll. Lib.*</small>

### Fourth Poſition.

That the godly were bound to ſever from the ſociety of the wicked, and not to keep any communion with them. Thus the moſt rigid of modern Factours for the Independent congregations would draw their files out of the army of our Nationall Church, and ſet up a congregation wherein Chriſt ſhall reigne in Beautie and Puritie. But they may flie ſo far from myſticall Babylon as to run to literall Babel, I mean bring all to confuſion, and founder the Commonwealth: For they that ſtride ſo wide at once will go farre with few paces.

*Reaſon.*

### Reason.

Because it is written, 2 Cor. 6. 14. *What* communion *hath light with darknesse?* and in other places, to the same effect.

<sup>margin:</sup> * *Aug. lib. 2. contra Petill. cap. 39.*

### Confutation.

The answer is the same with the former: But the tares shall grow with the corn. And in the visible militant Church and kingdome of grace, that wicked men shall be unseparablie mingled with the godly, besides our Saviours testimonie, Matt. 13. 30. these reasons do approve: first, because Hypocrites can never be severed, but by him that can search the heart; secondly, because if men should make the separation, weak Christians would be counted no Christians, and those who have a grain of grace under a load of imperfections would be counted reprobates; thirdly, because Gods vessells of honour from all eternitie, not as yet appearing, but wallowing in sinne, would be made castawayes; fourthly, because God by the mixture of the wicked with the godly will try the watchfulnesse and patience of his servants; fifthly, because thereby he will bestow many favours on the wicked, to clear his justice, and render them the more inexcusable: lastly, because the mixture of the wicked, grieving the godly, will make them the more heartily pray for the day of judgement. The desire of future glory makes the godly to cry, *Come Lord Jesus*; but the feeling of present pain (whereof they are most sensible) causeth the ingemination, *Come Lord Jesus, come quickly*. In a word as it is wholsome for a flock of sheep for some goats to feed amongst them, their bad sent being good Physick for the sheep to keep them from the *Shakings*; so much profit redounds to the godly by the necessary mixture of the wicked amongst them, making the pious to stick the faster to God and goodnesse.

### Fifth Position.

That * the efficacie of the Sacrament depends on the

<sup>margin:</sup> * *Aug. lib. 1. contra liter. Petil. cap. 1.*

piety of the Minister; so that in effect his piety washeth the water in baptisme, and sanctifieth it, whereas the profanenesse of a bad man administring it doth unsacrament baptisme it self, making a nullity thereof. Herein the Anabaptists joyn hands with them, as 'tis generally known by their re-baptizing: Yea* some tending that way have maintained, that Sacraments received from ignorant and unpreaching Ministers are of no validity.

*J.Peny p.46. and 49.*

### Reason.

It is written, Matth. 7. 18. *A good tree cannot bring forth evil fruit, neither can a corrupt tree bring forth good fruit.*

### Confutation.

This is true of mens personall, but not of their ministeriall acts: that Minister that can adde the word * of institution to the element, makes a sufficient Sacrament: And Sacraments, like to shelmeats, may be eaten after fowl hands, without any harm. *Cum* obsint indigne tractantibus, profint tamen digne sumentibus.* Yet God make all Ministers pious, painfull, and able: we, if beholding the present age, may justly bemoan their want, who remembring the former age, must as justly admire their plenty.

*Aug. tract. 80. in Johan.*

*Idem contra Parmen. lib.2. cap. 10.*

### Sixth Position.

That all learning and * eloquence was to be condemn'd. Late Sectarists go farther: Greenwood and Barrow * moved Queen Elizabeth to abolish both Universities,

*Idem. lib. 1. contra Gresco. cap. 30.*
*Dr Soame writing against them, lib. 2. pag. 4.*

*Which we believe and wish may then be done,*
*When all blear eyes have quite put out the sunne.*

### Reason.

Because learning hath been the cause of many Heresies, and discords in the Church.

### Confutation.

Not learning but the conceit thereof in those that wanted it, and the abuse thereof in such as had it, caused Hereticks.

### Seventh Position.

That Magistrates have no power to compell people to serve God by outward punishment: which is also the distill'd position of our Anabaptists, thus blinding the Ministers, and binding the Magistrate, what work do they make?

### Reason.

Because it is a breach of the * liberty of the creature: The King of heaven gave not men freewill, for the Kings of the earth to take it away from them.

* *August. lib. 3. cont. Crescon. cap. 51.*

### Confutation.

God gave men freewill to use it well; if they abuse it, God gave Magistrates power to punish them, else they *bear the sword in vain*. They may command people to serve God, who herein have no cause to complain; better *to be compell'd to a feast*, Luke 14. 23. then to runne to a fray. But these men who would not have Magistrates compell them, *quære* whether if they had power they would not compell Magistrates.

The Donatists also did mightily boast of miracles and visions: they made nothing to step into the third heaven, and have familiar * dialogues with God himself: they used also to cite their revelations as arguments for their opinions; we will trust the coppy of such their visions to be true, when we see the originall produc'd: herein the Anabaptists come not behind them. Strange was the Donatists ambition of Martyrdome; they used to force such as they met to wound them mortally, or violently to stab and kill them; and on purpose to fall down from * steep mountains, which one day may wish the mountains to fall on them. For Martyrs are to die willingly but not wilfully; and though to die be a debt due to nature, yet he that payes it before the time, may be called upon for repayment to die the second death.

* *Donatus oravit, respondet ei Deus de cœlo, Aug. in Johann. tract. 3. prope finem.*

* *Theodoretus in fabulis Hæret.*

Once many Donatists met a noble * Gentleman, and gave him a sword into his hand, commanding him

* *Centuriator. cent. 4 c. 5 p. 211. ex Theodoreto.*

to kill them, or threatning to kill him. Yet he refus'd to do it, unlesse first they would suffer him to bind them all; for fear, said he, that when I have kill'd one or two of you, the rest alter their minds and fall upon me. Having fast bound them all, he soundly whipt them, and so let them alone. Herein he shewed more wit then they wanted, and more charity then wit, denying them their desires, and giving them their deserts, seeking to make true Saints by marring of false Martyrs.

These Donatists were opposed by the learned writings of private Fathers, Optatus Milevitanus, and S. Augustine ( no Heresie could bud out, but presently his pruning-hook was at it ) and by whole Councells, one at Carthage, another at Arles. But the Donatists, whilest blessing themselves, cared not for the Churches Anathema's, being so farre from fearing her excommunications, that they prevented them in first excommunicating themselves by separation; and they count it a kindnesse to be shut out, who would willingly be gone. Besides, they called at * Carthage an Anti-councell of their own faction, consisting of two hundred seventy Bishops, to confirm their opinions. Let Truth never challenge Errour at the weapon of number alone, without other arguments; for some Orthodox Councells have had fewer suffrages in them, then this Donatisticall conventicle; and we may see small Pocket-Bibles, and a great Folio-Alchoran.

But that which put the period to this Heresie (for after the six hundredth yeare of Christ the Donatist appears not, *I looked after his place and he was not to be found*) was partly their own dissensions, for they * crumbled into severall divisions amongst themselves: Besides the honest Rogatists ( of whom before ) they had severall sects, some more, some lesse strict, called from their severall masters, Cresconians, * Petilians, Ticonians, Parmenians, Maximians, &c. which much differed amongst

* *Aug. Epist. ad Vincentium.*

* *In minutula frustula, Idem.*
* *Petilian went not so farre as the rest, Aug. lib. 3. de correct. Donati c. 17. 19. Vid Aug. de schism. Maxim. brevi. collat. 3 diei.*

amongst themselves. Thus is it given to all Heresies to break out into under-factions, still going further in their tenets; and such as take themselves to be twice-refined will count all others to be but drosse, till there be as many Heresies as Hereticks, like the Ammonites, so scattered by Saul, 1. Sam. 11. 11. *that there remained not two of them which were together.*

But chiefly they were suppressed by the civill Magistrate (Moses will do more with a frown then Aaron with a blow, I mean with Church-censures) for * Honorius the godly Emperour (with his arm above a thousand miles long) easily reach'd them in Europe, Asia, and Africa, and by punishments mixt with the Churches instructions converted and reclaimed very many.

*He caused the Patent of priviledge which Julian granted the Donatists, publicis locis affigendum in ludibrium: vide Baron. in Anno. 362. num. 264.*

In such a case teaching without punishment had done little good, and punishment without teaching would have done much harm; both mingled together, by Gods blessing, caused the conversion of many, and finall suppression of that Heresie.

The same God of his goodnesse grant that by the same means such as revive this Heresie nowadayes may have their eyes opened and their mouthes stopp'd, their pride lesse and their knowledge more, that those may be stayed which are going, and those brought back which are gone into their dangerous opinions. For if the angels in heaven rejoyce at the conversion of a sinner, none but devils and men devilishly minded will be sorrowfull thereat.

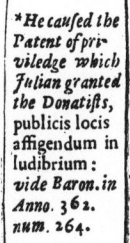

## Chap. 12.

### The Lyer

IS one that makes a trade to tell falshoods with intent to deceive. He is either open or secret. A secret Lyer or Equivocatour is such a one as by mentall reservations and other tricks deceives him to whom he speaks, being lawfully called to deliver all the truth. And sure speech being but a coppy of the heart, it cannot be avouched for a true coppy, that hath lesse in it then the originall. Hence it often comes to passe,

*When Jesuites unto us answer* Nay,
*They do not English speak, t'is Greek they say.*

Such an Equivocatour we leave, more needing a Book then Character to describe him. The open Lyer is first, either Mischievous, condemn'd by all; secondly, Officious, unlawfull also, because doing ill for good to come of it; thirdly, Jesting, when in sport and merriment. And though some count a Jesting lie to be like the dirt of oysters, which (they say) never stains, yet is it a sinne in earnest. What Policie is it for one to wound himself to tickle others, and to stab his own soul to make the standers by sport? We come to describe the Lyer.

*Maxime 1.* *At first he telles a lie with some shame and reluctancy.* For then if he cuts off but a lap of Truths garment his heart smites him; but in processe of time he conquers his Conscience, and from quenching it there ariseth a smoak which soots and fouls his soul, so that afterwards he lyes without any regret.

2. *Having made one lye he is fain to make more to maintain it.* For an untruth wanting a firm foundation needs many buttresses. The honour and happinesse of the * Israelites is the misery and mischief of lyes, *Not one amongst them shall be barren,*but miraculously procreative to beget others.

\* *Deut. 7. 14.*

He

Chap. 12.  *The Lyer.*  407

*He hath a good memory which he badly abuseth.* Memory in a Lyer is no more then needs. For first lies are hard to be remembred, because many, whereas truth is but one: secondly, because a lie cursorily told takes little footing and settled fastnesse in the tellers memory, but prints it self deeper in the hearers, who take the greater notice because of the improbability and deformity thereof; and one will remember the sight of a monster longer then the sight of an handsome body. Hence comes it to passe that when the Lyer hath forgotten himself, his Auditours put him in mind of the lye, and take him therein.

*Sometimes though his memory cannot help him from being arrested for lying, his wit rescues him*: which needs a long reach to bring all ends presently and probably together, gluing the splinters of his tales so cunningly that the cracks cannot be perceived. Thus a reliquemonger bragg'd he could shew a feather of the dove at Chrifts baptisme; but being to shew it to the people, a wag had stollen away the feather and put a coal in the room of it. *Well,* quoth he to the Spectatours, *I cannot be so good as my word for the present; but here is one of the coals* that broil'd S. Laurence, and that's worth the seeing.*

\* *Chamnitius in exam. cont. Trident. part. 4. p. 12.*

*Being challenged for telling a lye no man is more furiously angry.* Then he draws his sword and threatens, because he thinks that an offer of revenge, to shew himself moved at the accusation, doth in some sort discharge him of the imputation; as if the condemning of the sinne in appearance acquitted him in effect: or else because he that is call'd a Lyer to his face, is also call'd a Coward in the same breath if he swallows it; and the party charged doth conceive that if he vindicates his valour, his truth will be given him into the bargain.

*At last he believes his own lies to be true.* He hath told them over and over so often, that prescription makes a right, and he verily believes that at the firſt he gathered the ſtory out of ſome authenticall Authour, which onely grew in his own brain.

7 *No man elſe believes him when he ſpeaks the truth.* How much gold ſoever he hath in his cheſt, his word is but braſſe, and paſſeth for nothing: yea he is dumb in effect, for it is all one whether one cannot ſpeak, or cannot be believed.

To conclude: Some of the weſt Indians to expiate their ſinne of lying uſe to let themſelves bloud in their tongues, and to offer the bloud to their idols: A good cure for the ſquinancie, but no ſatisfaction for lying. Gods word hath taught us better, *What profit is there in my bloud?* The true repentance of the party waſh'd in the bloud of Chriſt can onely obtain pardon for this ſinne.

## Chap. 13.

### *The common Barreter.*

A Barreter is an horſeleach that onely ſucks the corrupted bloud of the Law. He trades onely in tricks and quirks: His highway is in by-paths, and he loveth a cavill better then an argument, an evaſion then an anſwer. There be two kinds of them: either ſuch as fight themſelves, or are trumpeters in a battel to ſet on others. The former is a profeſt dueller in the Law that will challenge any, and in all ſuite-combats be either principall or ſecond.

Maxime 1 *References & compoſitions he hates as bad as an hangman hates a pardon.* Had he been a Scholar, he would have maintained all paradoxes; if a Chirurgion, he would never have cured a wound but alwayes kept it raw; if a Souldier, he would have been excellent at a ſiege, nothing but *ejectio firma* would out him.

2 *He is half ſtarv'd in the lent of a long vacation for want of imployment;*

### Chap. 13. *The common Barretour.*

*imployment*; save onely that then he brews work to broach in Term-time. I find one so much delighted in Law-sport, that when *Lewis the King of France offered to ease him of a number of suits, he earnestly besought his Highnesse to leave him some twenty or thirty behind, wherewith he might merrily passe away the time.

*He hath this property of an honest man, that his word is as good as his band*; for he will pick the lock of the strongest conveiance, or creep out at the lattice of a word. Wherefore he counts to enter common with others as good as his own severall; for he will so vex his partners, that they had rather forgoe their right, then undergoe a suit with him. As for the trumpeter Barretour,

*He falls in with all his neighbours that fall out, and spurres them on to go to law.* A Gentleman, who in a duell was rather scratcht then wounded, sent for a Chirurgion, who having opened the wound, charged his man with all speed to fetch such a salve from such a place in his study. *Why* (said the Gentleman) *is the hurt so dangerous?* Oh yes (answered the Chirurgion) *if he returns not in post-hast the wound will cure it self, and so I shall lose my fee.* Thus the Barretour posts to the houses of his neighbours, lest the sparks of their small discords should go out before he brings them fuell, and so he be broken by their making up. Surely he loves not to have the bells rung in a peal, but he likes it rather when they are jangled backward, himself having kindled the fire of dissension amongst his neighbours.

*He lives till his clothes have as many rents as himself hath made dissensions.* I wonder any should be of this trade, when none ever thrived on't, paying dear rates for their counsells: for bringing many crack'd titles, they are fain to fill up their gaping chinks with the more gold.

But I have done with this wrangling companion, half afraid to meddle with him any longer lest

Ggg        he

*Stephens Apol. for Herodotus.*

3

4

5

he should commence a suit against me for describing him.

The Reader may easily perceive how this Book of the Profane State would swell to a great proportion, should we therein character all the kinds of vicious persons which stand in opposition to those which are good. But this pains may well be spared, seeing that *rectum est index sui & obliqui*; and the lustre of the good formerly described will sufficiently discover the enormity of those which are otherwise. We will therefore instance in three principall offenders, and so conclude.

## Chap. 14.
### The Degenerous Gentleman.

Some will chalenge this title of incongruity, as if those two words were so dissonant, that a whole sentence cannot hold them; for sure where the Gentleman is the root, Degenerous cannot be the fruit. But if any quarrell with my words, Valerius Maximus shall be my champion, who styleth such, * *Nobilia Portenta*. By *Gentleman* we understand one whom the Heralds (except they will deny their best Records) must allow of ancient parentage. Such a one, when a child, being kept the devils Nazarite, that no razor of correction must come upon his head in his fathers family, see what he proves in the processe of time, brought to extreme poverty. Herein we intend no invective glance on those pious Gentlemen, whose states are consumed through Gods secret judgement, and none of the owners visible default; onely we meddle with such as by carelesnesse and riot cause their own ruine.

* *Valer. Max. lib. 3 cap. 5.*

Maxime 1. *He goes to school to learn in jest and play in earnest.* Now this Gentleman, now that Gentlewoman begges him a playday, and now the book must be thrown away, that he may see the buck hunted. He comes to school late,

# Chap. 14. *The Degenerous Gentleman.*

late, departs soon, and the whole yeare with him (like the fortnight when Christmas day falls on a tuesday) is all Holidayes and half-Holidayes. And as the Poets feigne of Thetis, that she drench'd Achilles her sonne in the Stygian waters, that he might not be wounded with any weapon; so cockering mothers inchant their sonnes to make them rod-free, which they do by making some golden circles in the hand of the Schoolmaster: thus these two conjoyning together make the indentures to bind the youth to eternall ignorance; yet perchance he may get some almes of learning, here a snap, there a piece of knowledge, but nothing to purpose.

*His fathers Servingmen (which he counts no mean preferment) admit him into their society.* Going to a drinking match they carry him with them to enter him, and applaud his hopefulnesse, finding him vicious beyond his age. The Butler makes him free (having first pai'd his fees accustomed) of his own fathers cellar, and guesseth the profoundnesse of his young masters capacity by the depth of the whole-ones he fetcheth off.

*Coming to the University, his chief study is to study nothing.* What is Learning but a cloakbag of books, cumbersome for a Gentleman to carry? and the Muses fit to make wives for Farmers sonnes: perchance his own Tutour, for the promise of the next living (which notwithstanding his promise he afterwards sells to another) contributes to his undoing, letting him live as he list: yea, perhaps his own mother (whilest his father diets him for his health with a moderate allowance) makes him surfet underhand by sending him money. Thus whilest some complain that the University infected him, he infected the Universitie, from which he suck'd no milk but poysoned her nipples.

*At the Innes of Court under pretence to learn Law, he learns to be lawlesse;* not knowing by his study so much as what an Execution means, till he learns it by his own dear experience. Here he grows acquainted with the *Roaring Boyes*, I am afraid so called by a wofull Prolepsis, Here, for Hereafter. What formerly was counted the chief credit of an Oratour, these esteem the honour of a Swearer, *Pronunciation*, to mouth an oath with a gracelesse grace. These (as David saith) *cloath themselves with curses as with a garment*, and therefore desire to be in the latest fashion both in their cloaths and curses: These infuse all their skill into their young novice, who shortly proves such a proficient, that he exceeds his Masters in all kinds of vicious courses.

5. *Through the mediation of a Scrivener he grows acquainted with some great Usurer.* Nor is this youngster so ravenous, as the other is ready to feed him with money, sometimes with a courteous violence forcing on him more then he desires, provided the security be good, except the Usurer be so valiant as to hazard the losing of a small hook to catch a great fish, and will adventure to trust him, if his estate in hope be overmeasure, though he himself be under age. Now the greater part of the money he takes up is not for his own spending, but to pay the shot of other mens riot.

6. *After his fathers death he flies out more then ever before.* Formerly he took care for means for his spending, now he takes care for spending for his means. His wealth is so deep a gulf, no riot can ever sound the bottome of it. To make his guests drunk is the onely seal of their welcome. His very meanest servant may be master of the cellar, and those who deserve no beere may command the best wine: such dancing by day, such masking by night, such roaring, such revelling, able to awake the sleeping ashes of his Great-great-grandfather, and to fright all blessing from his house.

7. *Mean time the old soare of his London-debts corrupts and festers.* He is carelesse to take out the dead flesh, or to discharge either principall or interest. Such small leaks are not worth the stopping or searching for till they be

greater;

## Chap. 14. *The Degenerous Gentleman.*

greater; he should undervalue himself to pay a summe before it grew considerable for a man of his estate. Nor can he be more carelesse to pay, then the Usurer is willing to continue the debt, knowing that his bands, like infants, battle best with sleeping.

8. *Vacation is his vocation, and he scorns to follow any profession;* and will not be confin'd to any laudable employment. But they who count a calling a prison, shall at last make a prison their calling. He instills also his lazie principles into his children, being of the same opinion with the Neapolitane Gentry, who stand so on the * puntoes of their honour, that they preferre robbery before industry, and will rather suffer their daughter to make merchandise of her chastity, then marry the richest merchant.

*\* Sr William Segar in his Honours milit. and civill.*

9. *Drinking is one of the principall Liberall Sciences he professeth.* A most ungentile quality, fit to be banished to rogues and rags. It was anciently counted a Dutch vice, and swarmed most in that countrey. I remember a sad accident which hapned to Fliolmus King of Gothland, who whilest a Lord of misrule ruled in his Court, and both he and his servants were drunk, in mere merriment, meaning no harm, they took the King and put him in * jest into a great vessel of beere, and drowned him in earnest. But * one tells us that this ancient and habited vice is amongst the Dutch of late years much decreased: which if it be not, would it were. Sure our Mariners observe that as the sea grows dayly shallower and shallower on the shoars of Holland and Zeland, so the channell of late waxeth deeper on the coasts of Kent and Essex. I pray God if drunkennesse ebbes in Dutchland, it doth not flow in England, and gain not in the Iland what it loseth in the Continent. Yea some plead, when overwhelm'd with liquour, that their thirst is but quenched: as well may they say, that in Noahs floud the dust was but sufficiently allayed.

*\* Olaus mag. Hist. septent. p. 531.*
*\* Versteg. restitut. of decas'd intellig. p. 53.*

Ggg 3    *Gaming*

**10**

*Liv. lib. 27.*

Gaming *is* another art he studies much: an enticing witch, that hath caused the ruine of many. *Hanniball said of Marcellus, that *nec bonam nec malam fortunam ferre potest*, he could be quiet neither conquerour nor conquered; thus such is the itch of play, that Gamesters neither winning nor losing can rest contented. One propounded this question, Whether men in ships on sea were to be accounted among the living or the dead, because there were but few inches betwixt them and drowning. The same scruple may be made of great Gamesters, though their estates be never so great, whether they are to be esteemed poore or rich, there being but a few casts at dice betwixt a Gentleman (in great game) and a begger. Our Gallant games deeply, and makes no doubt in conscience to adventure Advousands, Patronages, and Church-livings in gaming. He might call to mind Sr Miles Pateridge, who (as the Souldiers cast lots for Christ his coat) plaid at dice for *Jesus bells with King Henry the eighth, & wonne them of him. Thus he brought the bells to ring in his pocket, but the ropes afterwards catch'd about his neck, and for some offenses he was hang'd in the dayes of King Edward the sixth.

*These were foure bells the greatest in London hanging in a fair Tower in Pauls Churchyard, Stowes Survey of London, pag. 357.*

**11**

Then first he sells the outworks of his State, some stragling mannour. Nor is he sensible of this sale, which makes his means more entire, as counting the gathering of such scattering rents rather burdensome then profitable. This he sells at half the value, so that the feathers will buy the goose, and the wood will pay for the ground: with this money if he stops the hole to one Creditour, by his prodigality he presently opens a wider gappe to another.

**12**

By this time the long dormant Usurer ramps for the payment of his money. The Principall, the grandmother, and the Use, the daughter, and the Use upon use, the grandchild, and perchance a generation farther, hath swell'd the debt to an incredible summe, for the satisfying

whereof

whereof our Gallant sells the moity of his estate.

13    *Having sold half his land he abates nothing of his expenses*: but thinks five hundred pounds a yeare will be enough to maintain that for which a thousand pound was too little. He will not stoop till he falls, nor lessen his kennell of dogs, till with Acteon he be eaten up with his own hounds.

14    *Being about to sink he catcheth at every rush to save himself.* Perchance sometimes he snatcheth at the thistle of a project, which first pricks his hands, and then breaks. Herein it may be he adventured on a matter wherein he had no skill himself (hoping by letting the Commonwealth bloud to fill up his own veins again) and therefore trades with his partners brains, as his partner with his purse, till both miscarry together: or else it may be he catcheth hold on the heel of another man, who is in as dangerous a case as himself, and they embracing each other in mutuall bands hasten their drowning together. His last mannour he sells twice, to a countrey-Gentleman, and a London-usurer, though the last, as having the first title, prevails to possesse it: Usurers herein being like unto Foxes; they seldome take pains to digge any holes themselves, but earth in that which the foolish Badger made for them, and dwell in the mannours and fair houses which others have built and provided.

15    *Having lost his own legs, he relyes on the staff of his kinred;* first visiting them as an intermitting ague, but afterwards turns a quotidian, wearing their thresholds as bare as his own coat. At last he is as welcome as a storm; he that is abroad shelters himself from it, and he that is at home shuts the doore. If he intrudes himself, yet some with their jeering tongues give him many a gird, but his brazen impudence feels nothing; and let him be arm'd on free-cost with the pot and the pipe, he will give them leave to shoot their flouts at him till they be weary. Sometimes he sadly paceth over the ground he

he sold, and is on fire with anger with himself for his folly, but presently quencheth it at the next ale-house.

16. *Having undone himself, he sets up the trade to undoe others.* If he can but scrue himself into the acquaintance of a rich heir, he rejoyceth as much at the prize as the Hollanders when they had intercepted the Plate-Fleet. He tutours this young Gamester in vice, leading him a more compendious way to his ruine then possibly he could find out of himself. And doth not the guide deserve good wages for his direction?

17. *Perhaps he behaves himself so basely that he is degraded*; the sad and solemn Ceremonies whereof we may meet with in old Presidents: but of them all, in my apprehension, none should make deeper impression in an ingenuous soul then this one, That at the solemn degradation of a Knight for high misdemeanour, the *King and twelve Knights more did put on mourning garments, as an embleme of sorrow for this injury to honour, that a man Gentile by birth and bloud, or honoured by a Princes favour, should so farre forget not onely himself but his Order, as to deserve so severe punishment.

*Markams Decads of Honour, pag. 76.

18. *His death is as miserable, as his life hath been vicious.* An Hospitall is the height he hopes to be advanced to: But commonly he dies not in so charitable a prison, but sings his last note in a cage. Nor is it impossible, but that wanting land of his own he may incroch on the Kings high-way, and there, taking himself to be Lord of the soyl, seise on Travellers as Strayes due unto him, and so the hangman give him a wreath more then he had in his Armes before. If he dyes at liberty in his pilgrimage betwixt the houses of his acquaintance, perhaps some well-disposed Gentleman may pay for his buriall, and truly mourn at the funerall of an ancient Family. His children, if any, must seek their fortunes the farther off, because their father found his too soon,

before

Chap. 14.   *The Degenerous Gentleman.*   417

before he had wisdome to manage them. Within two generations his name is quite forgotten that ever any such was in the place, except some Herald in his visitation passe by, and chance to spell his broken Arms in a Church-window. And then how weak a thing is Gentry, then which (if it wants virtue) brittle glasse is the more lasting monument?

 We forbear to give an instance of a degenerous Gentleman; would to God the world gave no examples of them. If any please to look into the forenamed * Valerius Maximus, he shall there find the base son of Scipio Africanus, the conquerour of Hanniball and Africk, so ill imitating his father, that for his viciousnes he received many disgracefull repulses from the people of Rome, the fragrant smell of his Fathers memory making him to stink the more in their nostrils; yea they forced him to pluck off from his finger a signet-ring, whereon the face of his Father was engraven, as counting him unworthy to wear his picture who would not resemble his virtue.

* *Loco prius citato.*

Hhh    Chap. 15.

## Chap. 15.

### The Traytour.

<sup>*</sup> *He is either against the Soveraigne Person alone, or against the State wherein he lives. We deal onely in describing the former, because to character the other, exact skil in the Municipal Laws of that State is required, wherein he is charged of treason.*

**Maxime 1.** A Traitour* works by fraud as a Rebell does by force, and in this respect is more dangerous, because there's lesse stock required to set him up: Rebellion must be managed with many swords, Treason to his Princes person may be with one knife. Generally their successe is as bad as their cause, being either detected before, defeated in, or punished after their part acted; detected before, either by wilfulnesse or weaknesse of those which are privie to it.

A plotter of Treason puts his head into the halter, and the halter into his hand to whom he first imparts it. He oftentimes reveals it, and by making a foot-stool of his friends head, climbs up the higher into the Princes favour.

**2.** Some mens souls are not strong enough, but that a weighty secret will work a hole through them. These rather out of folly then falseneſſe, unawares let fall words, which are taken up by the judicious eares of such who can spell Treason by putting together distracted syllables, and by piecing of broken sentences. Others have their hearts swoln so great with hope of what they shall get, that their bodyes are too little to hold them, and so betray themselves by threatnings and blustring language. Others have cut their throats with their own hands, their own writings, the best records, being produced against them. And here we must know, That

**3.** Strong presumptions sometimes serve for proofs in point of Treason: For it being a deed of darknesse, it is madnesse to look that the Sunne should shine at midnight, and to expect evident proof. Should

Princes delay till they did plainly see Treason, they might chance to feel it first. If this *semiplena probatio* lights on a party suspected before, the partie himself is the other part of the proof, and makes it complete. And here the Rack, though Fame-like it be

*Tam ficti pravique tenax, quam nuncia veri,*

is often used; and the wooden horse hath told strange secrets. But grant it passe undiscovered in the plotting, it is commonly prevented in the practising,

*By the Majestie, Innocency, or Valour of the Prince, or his attendants.* Some have been dazeled with the divine beams shining in a Princes face, so that coming to command his life, they could not be masters of their own senses. Innocency hath protected others, and made their enemies relent; and pitie (though a stranger to him for many years before) hath visited a Traitours heart in that very instant. If these fail, a Kings valour hath defended him; it being most true of a King, what Plinie reports of a *lion, in hunting if he be wounded and not killed, he will be sure to eye and kill him that wounded him.

*Some by flourishing aforehand, have never stricken a blow:* but by warning have armed those to whom they threatned. Thus madde Somervile, coming to kill Queen Elizabeth, by the way (belike to trie whether his sword would cut) quarrelled with and wounded one or two, and therefore was apprehended before he came to the Court.

*The palsie of guiltinesse hath made the stoutest Traitours hands to shake, sometimes to misse their mark.* Their conscience sleeping before, is then awakened with this crying sinne. The way seems but short to a Traveller when he views it from the top of an hill, who finds it very long when he comes into the plain:

* *Nat. hist. lib. 8. cap. 16.*

plain: so Treason surveyed in the heat of bloud, and from the height of passion, seems easie to be effected; which reviewed in cold bloud on even terms, is full of dangers and difficulties. If it speed in the acting, generally it's revenged afterwards: For,

7 *A King though killed is not killed, so long as he hath sonne or subject surviving.* Many who have thought they have discharged the debt, have been broken afterwards with the arrearages. As for journey-men-Traytours who work for others, their wages are ever paid them with an halter; and where one gaineth a garland of bayes, hundreds have had a wreath of hemp.

CHAP. 16.

## Chap. 16.

### The Pazzians conspiracie.

IN the city of * Florence, being then a Popular State, the honourable familie de-Medices managed all chief affairs, so beloved of the people for their bounty, that the honour they had was not extorted by their greatnesse, but seemed due to their goodnesse. These Miceans depressed the Pazzians, another familie in that State, as big set, though not so high grown, as the Medicei themselves, loading them with injuries, and debarring them not onely from Offices in the city, but their own right. The Pazzians, though highly wrong'd, counterfeited much patience, and, which was a wonder, though malice boyled hot in their hearts, yet no scumme ran over in their mouthes.

At last, meeting together, they concluded, that seeing the Legall way was stopp'd with violence, the violent way was become Legall, whereby they must right themselves; and they determined to invite Julian and Laurence Medices, the Governours of the State, to dinner, with Cardinall Raphael Riarius, and there to murther them. The matter was counted easie, because these two brethren were but one in effect, their heads in a manner standing on the same shoulders, because they alwayes went together, and were never asunder. Fifty were privy to this plot; each had his office assigned him. Baptista Monteseccius was to kill Laurence, Francis Pazzius and Bernardus Bandinius were to set on Julian, whilest the Archbishop of Pisa, one of their allies, was with a band of men to seise on the Senate-house. Cardinall Raphaels company rather then assistance

*Anno 1478. April 26. The summe hereof is taken out of Machiavels Florent: Hist lib. 8. pag. 407. & sequent.*

was required, being neither to hunt, nor kill, but onely to start the game, and by his presence to bring the two brothers to the dinner All appointed the next morning to meet at Masse, in the chief Church of S. Reparata.

Here meeting together, all the designe was dash'd: for here they remembred that Julian de Medices never used to * dine. This they knew before, but considered not till now, as if formerly the vapours arising out of their ambitious hearts had clouded their understanding. Some advised to referre it to another time, which others thought dangerous, conceiving they had sprung so many leaks of suspition, it was impossible to stop them, and feared, there being so many privie to the plot, that if they suffered them to consult with their pillows, their pillows would advise them to make much of their heads; wherefore not daring to stay the seasonable ripening of their designe, they were forced in heat of passion to parch it up presently, and they resolved to take the matter at the first bound, and to commit the murther (they intended at dinner) here in the Church, taking it for granted, the two Mediceans would come to Masse, according to their dayly custome.

But changing their stage, they were fain also to alter their Actours. Monteseccius would not be employed in the businesse, to stain a sacred place with bloud; and the breaking of this string put their plot quite out of tune. And though Anthony Volateran and Stephen a Priest were substituted in his room, yet these two made not one fit person; so great is the difference betwixt a choice and a shift. When the Host was elevated, they were to assault them; and the Sacrament

* *Machiav. disput. de Repub. lib. 3. cap. 6. pag. 397.*

ment was a signe to them, not of Chrifts death paſt, but of a murther they were to commit.

But here again they were at a loſſe. Treaſon, like Pope Adrian, may be choak'd with a flie, and marr'd with the leaſt unexpected caſualtie. Though Laurence was at Church, Julian was abſent. And yet by beating about, they recover'd this again: for Francis Pazzius and Bernard Bandinius going home to his houſe, with complements and courteous diſcourſe brought him to the Church. Then Bandinius with a dagger ſtabb'd him to the heart, ſo that he fell down dead, and Francis Pazzius inſulting over his corps (now no object of valour but cruelty) gave it many wounds, till blinded with revenge, he ſtrook a deep gaſh into his own thigh.

But what was over-meaſure in them, in over-acting their parts, was wanting in Anthony and Stephen, who were to kill Laurence in the Quire. *You* \* *Traitour*, ſaid Anthony; and with that Laurence ſtarting back avoided the ſtrength of the blow, and was wounded onely to honour, not danger, and ſo recovered a ſtrong chapell. Thus Malice, which vents it ſelf in threatning, warns men to ſhun it, and like hollow ſinging bullets, flies but halfway to the mark. With as bad ſucceſſe did the Archbiſhop of Piſa ſeiſe on the Senate-houſe, being conquered by the Lords therein aſſembled, and, with many of his Complices, hung out of a window.

The Pazzians now betake themſelves to their laſt refuge which their deſperate courſes had left them. James the chief of their family with one hundred more repair to the market-place, and there crie, *Liberty, Liberty*. A few followed them at firſt,

\* *Machiav. diſp. de Repub. lib. 3. cap. 6. pag. 399.*

but

but the snow-ball by rolling did rather melt then gather, and those, who before had seen the foul face of their treason naked, would not be allured to love it now masked with the pretences of the publick good ; and at last, the whole strength of the State subdued them.

Every tree about the city bare the fruit of mens heads, and limbes : many were put to death with torment, more with shame, and onely one Renatus Pazzius with pity, who loved his conscience better then his kinred, that he would not be active in the conspiracy; and yet his kinred better then his conscience, that he would not reveal it ; Treason being like some kind of strong poyson, which though never taken inwardly by cordiall consenting unto it, yet kill's by being held in ones hand, and concealing it.

CHAP. 17.

## Chap. 17.

## The Tyrant.

A Tyrant * is one whose lust is his law, making his subjects his slaves. Yet that is but a tottering Kingdome which is founded on trembling people, which fear and hate their Sovereigne.

*He is twofold,
1. *In Titulo,* (properly an Usurper.
2. *In Exercitio,* whom we onely describe.
Maxime 1.

*He gets all places of advantage into his own hands:* yea he would disarm his subjects of all sythes and pruning hooks, but for fear of a generall rebellion of weeds and thistles in the land.

*He takes the Laws at the first, rather by undermining then assault*: And therefore to do unjustly with the more justice, he counterfeits a legalitie in all his proceedings, and will not butcher a man without a Statute for it.

2

*Afterwards he rageth freely in innocent bloud.* Is any man vertuous? then he is a Traytour, and let him die for it, who durst presume to be good when his Prince is bad. Is he beloved? he is a rebell, hath proclaimed himself King, and reignes already in peoples affections, it must cost him his life. Is he of kinne to the Crown, though so farre off that his alliance is scarce to be derived? all the veins of his body must be dreined, and emptyed to find there and fetch thence that dangerous drop of royall bloud. And thus having taken the prime men away, the rest are easily subdued. In all these particulars Machiavell is his onely Confessour, who in his Prince seems to him to resolve all these cases of conscience to be very lawfull.

3

*Worst men are his greatest favourites.* He keeps a constant kennel of bloud-hounds to accuse whom he pleaseth. These will depose more then any can suppose, not sticking to swear that they heard fishes speak,

4

speak, and saw through a mil-stone at mid-night: these fear not to forswear, but fear they shall not forswear enough, to cleave the pinne and do the deed. The lesse credit they have, the more they are believed, and their very accusation is held a proof.

5 *He leaves nothing that his poore subjects can call their own but their miseries.* And as in the West-Indies thousands of kine are killed for their tallow alone, and their flesh cast away: so many men are murdered merely for their wealth, that other men may make mummey of the fat of their estates.

6 *He counts men in miserie the most melodious instruments:* Especially if they be well tuned and play'd upon by cunning Musicians, who are artificiall in tormenting them, the more the merrier, and if he hath a set, and full consort of such tortur'd miserable souls, he danceth most cheerfully at the pleasant dittie of their dying grones. He loves not to be prodigall of mens lives, but thriftily improves the objects of his cruelty, spending them by degrees, and epicurizing on their pain: So that as Philoxenus wished a cranes throat, he could desire asses eares, the longer to entertain their hydeous and miserable roaring. Thus Nature had not racks enough for men (the Colick, Gout, Stone, &c.) but Art must adde to them, and devils in flesh antedate hell here in inventing torments; which when inflicted on malefactours, extort pitie som mercifull beholders, (and make them give what is not due) but when used by Tyrants on innocent people, such tender hearts as stand by suffer what they see, and by the proxie of sympathy feel what they behold.

7 *He seeks to suppresse all memorialls and writings of his actions:* And as wicked Tereus after he had ravished Philomela cut out her tongue; so when Tyrants have

have wronged and abused the times they live in, they endeavour to make them speechlesse to tell no tales to posterity. Herein their folly is more to be admired then their malice, for learning can never be dreined dry: though it may be dambd up for one Age, yet it will break over; and Historians pens, being long kept fasting, will afterwards feed more greedily on the memories of Tyrants, and describe them to the full. Yea, I believe their ink hath made some Tyrants blacker then they were in their true complexion.

*At last he is haunted with the terrours of his own conscience.* If any two do but whisper together (whatsoever the Propositions be) he conceives their discourse concludes against him. Company and solitarinesse are equally dreadfull unto him, being never safe; and he wants a Guard to guard him from his Guard, and so proceeds *in infinitum.* \* The Scouts of Charles Duke of Burgundy brought him news that the French army was hard by, being nothing else but a field full of high thistles, whose tops they mistook for so many spears: On lesser ground this Tyrant conceives greater fears. Thus in vain doth he seek to fence himself from without, whose foe is within him.

7

\* *Comineus Comment. lib.* 1. *juxta finem*

*He is glad to patch up a bad nights sleep, out of pieces of slumber.* They seldome sleep soundly, who have bloud for their bolster. His phansie presents him with strange masques, wherein onely Fiends and Furies are actours. The fright awakes him, and he is no sooner glad that it was a dream, but fears it is propheticall.

8

*In vain he courts the friendship of forrein Princes.* They defie his amity, and will not joyn their clean hands with his bloudy ones. Sometimes to ingratiate himself he doth some good acts, but virtue becomes him worse then vice, for all know he counter-

9

counterfeits it for his own ends.

10. *Having lived in other mens bloud, he dies commonly in his own.* He had his will all his life, but seldome makes his Testament at his death, being suddenly taken away either by a private hand, or a publick insurrection. It is observed of the camell that it lies quietly down till it hath its full load, and then riseth up. But this *Vulgus* is a kind of beast, which riseth up soonest when it is overladen; immoderate cruelty causing it to rebell. Yet *Ferio* is a fitter motto then *Ferio* for Christians in their carriage towards lawfull Authoritie, though unlawfully used.

We will give a double example of a Tyrant: the one an absolute Sovereigne, the other a Substitute or Vice-roy under an absolute Prince.

CHAP. 18.

## Chap. 18.
## The life of ANDRONICUS.

ANdronicus Comnenus,* descended of the Grecian Emperiall bloud, was a Prince most vicious in his life, and perfidious in his dealing, and for his severall offenses, after long banishment, was at length by Emmanuel the Grecian Emperour, his kinsman, confined to a private city in Paphlagonia.

*The summe of this chapter is taken out of Nicetas Choniates his Annalls lib. 1. & 2. of Andronic. Comnenus.*

Here Andronicus hugg'd himself in his privacie, though all that time he did but levell, and take aim, intending at last to shoot at the Empire, though for a while he lay very still, and with the Hedgehog seemingly dead, he rounded himself up in his own prickles without any motion.

Leave we him there, and come to behold the face of the Grecian Empire, which presents us with all the Symptomes of a dying State. Emmanuell being dead Alexius his sonne succeeds him, a Minor of twelve years of age, wanting wit to guide himself, and his friends care to govern him. Xena the Mother-Empresse wholly given to her pleasures, with her minion Alexius Protosebastus, who ruled all in the State. The Nobility factious, snatching what they could get, and counting violent possession the best and onely title. The people of Constantinople valiant onely to make mutinies on every occasion, in confused multitudes, without any Martiall discipline; as who could expect that a rolling snow-ball should have any curious fashion?

Andronicus, hearing of these misdemeanours, found that opportunity courted him to procure the Empire for himself. Wherefore he remonstrates to the whole world the great grief he conceived at these disorders: For though patience had made him past feeling of any private

private injuries offered to himself, yet he must be stark dead indeed, if he were not moved with these generall miseries of the Empire. He being a Prince of the bloud could not without grief behold how Xena the Empresse, and Protosebastus had conspired to abuse the tender age of young Alexius, so to draw all dominion to themselves; and who kowing that their strength consisted in the young Emperours weaknesse, intended so to breed him, that in point of judgement he should never be of age, and onely *able in pleasures*. Whereupon Andronicus resolved to free his young kinsman, and the Empire from this thraldome. Treason is so uggly in her self, that every one that sees it will cast stones at it, which makes her seldome appear but with a borrowed face, for the good of the Commonwealth; but especially when ambition hath caught hold on pretended religion, how fast will it climbe?

Andronicus with an army of Paphlagonians marched to Constantinople, in which city he had a great party on his side, Maria Cesarissa, half sister to the Emperour, with her husband, and many other good Patriots, which bemoaned the distempers in the State, applying themselves to Andronicus for help, counting a bad physician better then none at all. Besides, there were in the city many turbulent spirits, desirous of alterations, as profitable unto them, counting themselves the petty-Landlords of the times, to whom rich fines and herriots would accrue upon every exchange, and all those took part with Andronicus.

Many more did Andronicus winne to his party by his cunning behaviour, for he could speak both eloquently and religiously. He would ordinarily talk Scripture-language (often fouly misapplyed) as if his memory were a Concordance of the whole Bible, but especially of S. Pauls Epistles, which he had by heart. Besides, no man had better command of rain and
sunshine

sunshine in his face, to smile and weep at pleasure: his tears flowed at will, which caught the affections of many, though others, better acquainted with his tricks, no more pitied his weeping, then they bemoaned the moist dropping of stone walls against rainy weather.

Small resistance was made against him, onely some seemed to fight against him in complement, so that with ease he made himself master of Constantinople, and not long after he caused Xena the Empresse to be choked, the eyes of whose Favourite Protosebastus he had formerly bored out.

The next care of Andronicus was to cut off all those steps by which he had ascended to this height, left leaving those stairs still standing, others also might climbe up the same way. All those friends who had assisted him in this his designe, he rewarded with death: yea though at first his cruelty might seem to shoot at a mark, in taking of some prime men, for whose death some reason might be rendred, his malice afterwards shot at rovers, as if he had a quarrell at mankind, killing all he came near. When any party accused recriminated the accuser, the sword of Andronicus cut on both sides; the accuser and accused were sent the same way, and what cup one began, the other was made to pledge. Those Sycophants which ingratiated themselves with him, escaped no better then others, it being equally dangerous to please and displease him. Men met every where with his cruelty, but no where with the reasons thereof. But who can expect other reasons of Tyrants actions, but that they are Tyrants actions?

But his dealing with young Alexius the Emperour (whose death was methodically contrived with some politick pauses) deserves observation. At first entrance into the city, Andronicus observed his awfull distance towards the Emperour, teaching others that the minority of Princes ought not to lessen their Subjects reverence unto them. Afterwards, he emboldned himself to make his nearer approches, chalenging in young Alexius that interest which carefull tutours claim in those whose protection they tender. Hence he proceeded to set a guard about him, not to defend but watch him, and to guard him from his friends; who, though allowed to follow his sports in hunting, was indeed made sport of himself, and the hunter kept in a net. Then Andronicus was forced by his friends importunity (whom he himself had secretly importun'd) to be elected joynt-Emperour with Alexius, and with much unwillingnesse this great dissembler (who could have taught Tiberius craft, and Nero cruelty) was driven up the Emperiall throne. Next day in all publick Edicts the name of Andronicus was set before Alexius, it seeming preposterous that a child should be preferred before so sage and grave a man.

Hitherto the life of Alexius was profitable to Andronicus, but now his death would be more behooffull. Wherefore Andronicus counting it cumbersome now any longer to wear a cloke in the sunshine and heat of his happinesse, abandoned all uselesse dissembling, and appear'd like himself. The next news we heare of Alexius, is that his neck is broken with a bowstring by command from Andronicus; his body was spurn'd and abus'd, a hole bored in his ear with a spit, his head cut off, and shamefully dealt with, his body cast into the sea, with many more cruell outrages, as much against policie as piety, and not onely needlesse, but scandalous to Andronicus. Thus Tyrants, having once given the rains to their cruelty, are not able to stop themselves.

But this innocent bloud cryed to God for revenge, and obtained it. Next yeare Isaacius Angelus was chosen Emperour by the people, and Andronicus chased

chased out of the city and pursued after. Andronicus got into a ship, and had conveyed himself away, had not the winds and the waves (as if knowing him though disguis'd) refused to be accessary to his escape, and beaten him back again, till he was taken by his pursuers. Being carried into the presence of Isaacius the new Emperour, he there was beaten, spurn'd, kick'd on, and had an arm cut off, and an eye bored out. But all this was mercy, in respect of what he next day suffered by the rascall multitude, being carried on a scabb'd Camell thorow Constantinople, happy he that could do most unhappinesse unto him: all sorts of people sought to mischief him, throwing that upon him, in comparison whereof that which runneth in the channell may be counted rosewater. Thus orphanes thought to revenge the death of their fathers, widows of their husbands: one ran him thorow with a spit, another threw scalding water in his face. At last he could hardly die, being hang'd up by the feet betwixt two pillars after a thousand abuses offer'd unto him.

It may seem miraculous how his body could make room for all their blows, or that he so old a man could find so many lives for their cruelty, were it not that passing with some speed thorow the city, few had their full blows at him; and they were somewhat mannerly in their revenge, in that they would not take all to themselves, but leave some to others. And indeed after long throwing of dirt upon him, their darts became his shield, being so covered over with the filth, that the mire kept him from the mire.

All which time he brake not out into any impatience, but still cryed, *Lord have mercy upon me*, and, *Why break you a bruised reed?* and bore all with an invincible quietnesse of mind. Surely God measured unto him a time of repentance by a large houreglasse; and haply (it were tyranny to think otherwise of the worst Tyrant) the tempest of the peoples fury might drive his

soul

soul to the best * shelter, the mercy of the God of heaven. It is a good signe when one hath his hell in this world, and true repentance is never too late. As for those that hold repentance on the death-bed unprofitable, by this their tenet they would make heaven very empty, and yet never a whit the more room therein for the maintainers of so uncharitable an opinion.

Andronicus reigned two years, having a beautifull aspect, and majestick stature, almost ten foot high, of a strong constitution, advantaged by the temperatenesse of his diet. In all his life time he took but one antidote, and never purged but once, and then the Physick found no obnoxious humour to work upon, so healthfull was his temper. His death happened *Anno Dom.* 1183.

*† See how charitably Drexelius is opinion'd of him in his book de Æternitate, Consider. 5. Sect. 3.*

CHAP. 19.

Chap. 19.   *The life of Duke* D'Alva.   435

FERDINAND Alvarez de Toledo Duke of Alva, Viceroy of the Netherlands under Philip the 2d. He dyed in Portugall Anno Dm̄ 1582. in the 75. yeare of his Age.
W.M. sculp:

## CHAP. 19.
### *The life of Duke* D'Alva.

FErdinand Alvarez de Toledo, Duke of Alva, one bred abroad in the world in severall warres (whom Charles the fifth more employed, then affected, using his churlish nature to hew knotty service) was by Philip the second, King of Spain, appointed Governour of the Netherlands.

At his first arrivall there, the loyalty of the Netherlanders to the King of Spain was rather out of joint, then

then broken off, as not being weary of his government but their own grievances. The wound was rather painfull then deadly, onely the skirts of their lungs were tainted, sending out discontented not rebellious breath, much regretting that their Priviledges, Civil and Ecclesiasticall, were infringed, and they grinded with exactions against their Laws and Liberties.

But now Duke D'Alva coming amongst them, he intended to cancell all their charters with his sword, and to reduce them to absolute obedience. And whereas every city was fenced not onely with severall walls, but different locall liberties, and municipall immunities, he meant to lay all their priviledges levell, and casting them into a flat to stretch a line of absolute command over them. He accounted them a Nation rather stubborn then valiant, and that not from stoutnesse of nature, but want of correction, through the long indulgence of their late Governours. He secretly accused Margaret Dutchesse of Parma, the last Governesse, for too much gentlenesse towards them, as if she meant to cure a gangren'd arm with a lenitive plaister, & affirmed that a Ladies hands were too soft to pluck up such thistles by the root. Wherefore the said Dutchesse, soon after D'Alva's arrivall (counting it lesse shame to set, then to be outshin'd) petitioned to resigne her regencie, and return'd into Italie.

*Ann.Dom. 1568.*
*\* Famianus Stra. de Bello Belgico, p.430.*

To welcome the Duke at his entrance, he was entertain'd with prodigies and monstrous * births, which hapned in sundry places; as if Nature on set purpose mistook her mark, and made her hand to swerve, that she might shoot a warning-piece to these countreys, and give them a watch-word of the future calamities they were to expect. The Duke, nothing moved hereat, proceeds to effect his project, and first sets up the *Counsell of troubles*, consisting of twelve, the Duke being the President. And this Counsell was to order all things in an arbitrary way, without any appeal from

from them. Of these twelve some were strangers, such as should not sympathize with the miseries of the countrey; others were upstarts, men of no bloud, and therefore most bloudy; who being themselves grown up in a day, cared not how many they cut down in an houre. And now rather to give some colour, then any virtue to this new composition of counsellours, foure Dutch Lords were mingled with them, that the native Nobility might not seem wholly neglected. Castles were built in every city to bridle the inhabitants, and Garisons put into them. New Bishops Seas erected in severall cities, and the Inquisition brought into the countrey. This Inquisition, first invented against the Moores, as a trappe to catch vermine, was afterwards used as a snare to catch sheep, yea they made it heresie for to be rich. And though all these proceedings were contrary to the solemn oath King Philip had taken, yet the Pope ( who onely keeps an *Oath-office*, and takes power to dispence with mens consciences) granted him a faculty to set him free from his promise.

Sure as some adventurous Physicians, when they are posed with a mungrell disease, drive it on set purpose into a fever, that so knowing the kind of the maladie they may the better apply the cure: So Duke D'Alva was minded by his cruell usage to force their discontents into open rebellion, hoping the better to come to quench the fire when it blazed out, then when it smok'd and smother'd.

And now to frighten the rest, with a subtle train he seiseth on the Earls of Egmond and Horn. These counted themselves armed with innocencie and desert, having performed most excellent service for the King of Spain. But when subjects deserts are above their Princes requitall, oftentimes they study not so much to pay their debts, as to make away their creditours. All these victories could not excuse them, nor the laurel wreaths on their heads keep their necks from the ax, and the rather, because their eyes must first be closed

closed up, which would never have patiently beheld the enslaving of their countrey. The French Embassadour was at their execution, and wrote to his Master Charles the ninth, King of France, concerning the Earl of Egmond, * *That he saw that head struck off in the Market-place of Brussels, whose valour had twice made France to shake.*

> * Fam. Strad. de bell. Belgico, pag. 449.

This Counsell of troubles having once tasted Noble bloud, drank their belly-fulls afterwards. Then descending to inferiour persons by apprehensions, executions, confiscations, and banishments, they raged on mens lives and states. Such as upon the vain hope of pardon returned to their houses, were apprehended, and executed by fire, water, gibbets, and the sword, and other kinds of deaths and torments: yea the bodyes of the dead (on whom the earth as their common mother bestowed a grave for a childs portion) were cast out of their * tombes by the Dukes command, whose cruelty outstunk the noysomnesse of their carcases.

> * Grimst. Hist. of the Netherlands, pag. 413.

And left the maintaining of Garisons might be burdensome to the King his Master, he laid heavy impositions on the people: the Duke affirming that these countreys were fat enough to be stewed in their own liquour, & that the Souldiers here might be maintained by the profits arising hence; yea he boasted that he had found the mines of Peru in the Low-countreys, though the digging of them out never quitted the cost. He demanded the hundredth peny of all their moveable and immoveable goods, and besides that, the tenth peny of their moveable goods that should be bought and sold, with the twentieth peny of their immoveable goods; without any mention of any time, how long those taxes and exactions should continue.

The States protested against the injustice hereof, alledging that all trading would be press'd to death under the weight of this taxation: weaving of stuffs (their staple trade) would soon decay, and their shuttles

tles would be very flow, having so heavy a clog hanging on them; yea hereby the same commodity must pay a new tole at every passage into a new trade. This would dishearten all industry, and make lazinesse and painfulnesse both of a rate, when beggery was the reward of both, by reason of this heavy imposition, which made men pay dear for the sweat of their own brows. And yet the weight did not grieve them so much, as the hand which laid it on, being impos'd by a forein power against their ancient priviledge. Hereupon many Netherlanders, finding their own countrey too hot, because of intolerable taxes, sought out a more temperate climate, and fled over into England.

As for such as stayed behind, their hearts being brimfull before with discontents, now ran over. 'Tis plain these warres had their originall, not out of the Church, but the State-house. Liberty was true doctrine to Papist and Protestant, Jew and Christian. It is probable that in Noahs Ark the wolf agreed with the lambe, and that all creatures drowned their antipathy, whilest all were in danger of drowning. Thus all severall religions made up one Commonwealth to oppose the Spaniard: and they thought it high time for the Cow to find her horns, when others not content to milk her, went about to cut off her bag.

It was a rare happinesse that so many should meet in one chief, William of Nassaw, Prince of Orange, whom they chose their Governour. Yea he met their affections more then half way in his loving behaviour; so that Alva's cruelty did not drive more from him, then Nassaw's courtesie invited to him. His popular nature was of such receipt, that he had room to lodge all comers. In peoples eyes his light shined bright, yet dazled none, all having free accesse unto him: every one was as well pleased as if he had been Prince himself, because he might be so familiar with the Prince. He was wont to content those, who reproved

proved his too much humanity, with this saying,* *That man is cheap bought, who costs but a salutation.*

*Barcl. Icon. Anim. cap. 5

I report the Reader to the Belgian Histories, where he may see the changes of warre betwixt these two sides. We will onely observe that Duke D'Alva's covetousnesse was above his policy in fencing the rich inland and neglecting the barren maritime places. He onely look'd on the broad gates of the countrey whereby it openeth to the continent of Germany and France, whilest in the mean time almost half the Netherlands ran out at the postern doore towards the sea. Nassaw's side then wounded Achilles in the heel indeed, and touch'd the Spaniard to the quick, when on Palm-sunday ( as if the day promised victory ) at Brill they took the first livery and seasin of the land, and got soon after most cities towards the sea. Had Alva herein prevented him, probably he had made those Provinces as low in subjection as situation.

Now at last he began to be sensible of his errour, and grew weary of his command, desiring to hold that staff no longer, which he perceived he had taken by the wrong end. He saw that going about to bridle the Netherlanders with building of castles in many places, they had gotten the bit into their own teeth: He saw that warre was not quickly to be hunted out of that countrey, where it had taken covert in a wood of cities: He saw the cost of some one cities siege would pave the streets thereof with silver, each city, fort, and sconce being a Gordian knot, which would make Alexanders sword turn edge before he could cut thorow it, so that this warre and the world were likely to end together, these Netherlands being like the head-block in the chimney, where the fire of warre is alwayes kept in ( though out every where else ) never quite quench'd though rak'd up sometimes in the ashes of a truce. Besides, he saw that the subdued part of the Netherlands obeyed more for fear then love, and
their

their loyalty did rather lie in the Spanish Garisons, then their own hearts, and that in their sighes they breathed many a prosperous gale to Nassaw's party: Lastly, he saw that forrein Princes, having the Spaniards greatnesse in suspicion, desired he might long be digesting this break-fast, lest he should make his dinner on them, both France and England counting the Low-countreys their outworks to defend their walls: wherefore he petitioned the King of Spain his Master to call him home from this unprofitable service.

Then was he called home, and lived some years after in Spain, being well respected of the King, and employed by him in conquering Portugall, contrary to the expectation of most, who look'd that the Kings displeasure would fall heavy on him, for causing by his cruelty the defection of so many countreys; yet the King favourably reflected on him, perchance to frustrate on purpose the hopes of many, and to shew that Kings affections will not tread in the beaten path of vulgar expectation: or seeing that the Dukes life and state could amount to poore satisfaction for his own losses, he thought it more Princely to remit the whole, then to be revenged but in part: or lastly, because he would not measure his servants loyalty by the successe, and lay the unexpected rubs in the allie to the bowlers fault, who took good aim though missing the mark. This led many to believe that Alva onely acted the Kings will, and not willed his acts, following the instructions he received, and rather going beyond then against his Commission.

However most barbarous was his cruelty. He bragg'd as he sate at dinner (and was it not a good grace after meat) that he had caused eighteen thousand to be executed by the ordinary minister of justice within the space of six years, besides an infinite more murthered by other tyrannous means. Yea some men he killed many times, giving order to the executioners to pronounce each syllable of torment long upon them, that the thred of their life might not be cut off but unravell'd, as counting it no pain for men to die, except they dyed with pain; witnesse Anthony Utenhow, whom he caused to be tied to a stake with a chain in *Brussells, compassing him about with a great fire, but not touching him, turning him round about like a poore beast, who was forced to live in that great torment and extremity, roasting before the fire so long, untill the Halberdiers themselves, having compassion on him, thrust him through, contrary to the will both of the Duke and the Spanish Priests.

*Grimst. Hist. of the Netherlands, pag. 411.

When the city of Harlem surrendred themselves unto him on condition to have their lives, he suffered some of the Souldiers and Burgers thereof to be starved to death, saying that *though he promised to give them their lives, he did not promise to find them meat.* The Netherlanders used to fright their children with telling them, Duke D'Alva was coming; and no wonder if children were scared with him, of whom their fathers were afraid.

He was one of a lean body and visage, as if his eager soul, biting for anger at the clog of his body, desired to fret a passage through it. He had this humour, that he neglected the good counsel of others, especially if given him before he ask'd it, and had rather stumble then beware of a block of another mans telling.

But as his life was a miroir of cruelty, so was his death of Gods patience. It was admirable, that his tragicall acts should have a comicall end; that he that sent so many to the grave, should go to his own, & die in peace. But Gods justice on offenders goes not alwayes in the same path, nor the same pace: And he is not pardoned for the fault, who is for a while reprived from the punishment; yea sometimes the guest in the inne goes quietly to bed, before the reckoning for his supper is brought to him to discharge.

*FINIS.*